THE GLAMOUR BOYS

THE GLAMOUR BOYS

The Secret Story of the Rebels
who Fought for Britain to
Defeat Hitler

Chris Bryant

BLOOMSBURY PUBLISHING
LONDON · OXFORD · NEW YORK · NEW DELHI · SYDNEY

BLOOMSBURY PUBLISHING
Bloomsbury Publishing Plc
50 Bedford Square, London, WC1B 3DP, UK

BLOOMSBURY, BLOOMSBURY PUBLISHING and the Diana logo are
trademarks of Bloomsbury Publishing Plc

First published in Great Britain 2020

A catalogue record for this book is available from the British Library

ISBN: HB: 978-1-5266-0171-1; TPB: 978-1-5266-3055-1; EBOOK: 978-1-5266-0175-9

2 4 6 8 10 9 7 5 3 1

Typeset by Newgen KnowledgeWorks Pvt. Ltd., Chennai, India
Printed and bound in Great Britain by CPI Group (UK) Ltd, Croydon CR0 4YY

To find out more about our authors and books visit www.bloomsbury.com and
sign up for our newsletters

JCƆB

There are men who shine in the public eye, whose names are a household word; and there are others of whom the general public knows little or nothing, and who have yet equally the quality of greatness.

Lord Salisbury's obituary of Paul Emrys-Evans (1894–1967), The Times, *3 November 1967*

Contents

List of Principal Characters

Rob Bernays (1902–45), Liberal National MP for Bristol
North 1931–45, parliamentary secretary to the Ministries
of Health 1937–9 and Transport 1939–40. Married Nancy
Britton in 1942.

Bob Boothby (1900–86), Conservative MP for Aberdeen and
Kincardine East 1924–50 and then East Aberdeenshire
until 1958, parliamentary private secretary to Winston
Churchill 1926–9. Twice married, but had affairs with
men and women.

Ronnie Cartland (1907–40), Conservative MP for
Birmingham King's Norton 1935–40, served in 53rd Anti-
Tank Regiment (Worcestershire Yeomanry) of the Royal
Artillery from 1937. Unmarried.

Victor Cazalet (1896–1943), captain in Queen's Own West
Kent Yeomanry, awarded MC for gallantry in 1917, MP for
Chippenham 1924–43, parliamentary private secretary to
the Board of Trade 1924–6 and Dominions Office 1931–2,
commanded an anti-aircraft battery and was appointed
liaison officer with the free Poles in the war. Unmarried.

Harry Crookshank (1893–1961), seriously injured as
captain in the Grenadier Guards in the First World War,
Conservative MP for Gainsborough 1924–56, under-
secretary in the Home Department 1934–5, Secretary for
Mines 1935–9, Financial Secretary to the Treasury 1939–
43. Unmarried.

Jack Macnamara (1905–44), Conservative MP for
Chelmsford 1935–45, served in the Territorial and regular
armies, rising to Colonel of the 1st Battalion London
Irish Rifles in the Second World War. Commanded the
RAF Regiment and joined staff of Land Forces Adriatic.
Unmarried.

Harold Nicolson (1886–1968), National Labour MP
for Leicester West 1935–45, diplomat and author,
chargé d'affaires in Tehran 1925–7 and Berlin 1927–8,
parliamentary secretary at the Ministry of Information
1940–1. Married to Vita Sackville-West, although both
had homosexual affairs.

Philip Sassoon (1888–1939), Conservative MP for Hythe
1912–39, private secretary to Field Marshal Douglas Haig
1915–18, parliamentary private secretary to David Lloyd
George in 1920, Under-Secretary for Air 1924–9 and
1931–7, First Commissioner of Works 1937–9. Unmarried.

Jim (J. P. L.) Thomas (1903–60), MP for Hereford 1931–55,
parliamentary private secretary to Anthony Eden as
foreign secretary. Unmarried.

Ronnie Tree (1897–1976), Conservative MP for Harborough
1933-1945. Twice married but had affairs with women
and men.

Preface
The Hidden Story

If you look carefully behind the Speaker's chair in the House of Commons, just underneath the press gallery, there is a row of twenty-three shields, each of them about five inches high. Some have letters surrounded by laurels painted in gold on a blue background. The third from the left has 'R B' for Robert Bernays and one in the middle has 'J R J M' for John Robert Jermain Macnamara. Others have ornate crests. Ronald Cartland's (sixth from the left) has three bushels and a golden griffin, and immediately next to it Victor Cazalet's sports a castle, a boar and two fleurs-de-lys. Each shield commemorates an MP who lost his life in active service in the Second World War, but you will probably never have heard of them. Cartland's name may ring a bell, because of his novelist sister Barbara, but you will almost certainly not know that at least four of the men were queer or nearly queer – that is to say, gay, bisexual or somewhere in-between – and that they had shown as much courage personally and politically before the war as they did during it, defying convention and the party managers in Parliament, the whips, with remarkable sangfroid. Most families, biographers and historians deliberately excised any hint of their sexuality from such accounts of their lives as do exist – and virtually wiped them from the history books. Even recent historians have seen these men's shared sexuality as an irrelevance. This, then, is their true unexpurgated story – a story of unsung bravery at a defining moment in Britain's history.

They visited Germany in the early 1930s because Berlin was the most sexually liberal city in the world and men could have sex with one another there with impunity, unlike in Britain. They knew plenty of queer Germans, including several leading Nazis, and as young, mostly Conservative Members of Parliament they supported a rapprochement with Germany. However, they saw danger when Hitler won power, as the Nazis arrested their queer and Jewish friends, sent them to concentration camps and murdered them. So they were among the very first to warn Britain about Hitler and the most vocal in demanding that Britain oppose him, not appease him. They were attacked as warmongers, their phones were tapped, and they were threatened with deselection and exposure, but they repeatedly demanded that Britain rearm so as to challenge Nazism. The very fact that they were different from the rest of society made it easier for them to differ from the rest of the public. They were already outsiders, and were accustomed to the opprobrium of others. The architect of Britain's policy of appeasement, the prime minister, Neville Chamberlain, hated them and branded them and their close associates as 'the Glamour Boys', but time and again they spoke out and bravely voted against their own government. When war came, they insisted on doing their bit in the heat of battle, with no thought for their own safety. Two of them led units that were safe havens for other queer officers and men.

Their sexuality was an essential aspect of their bravery, because they had been schooled in courage by a society that hated homosexuality. Every era in history has had its share of men who love men. They have faced prejudice, violence, imprisonment and even execution. But throughout this period the law in Britain was extraordinarily strict. Thousands of men were ostracised, humiliated, blackmailed and imprisoned for the slightest misdemeanour and on the flimsiest evidence. They were referred to in derogatory code as 'flamboyant', 'colourful', 'unconventional', 'bohemian', 'artistic', 'versatile' or even 'musical'. They were forced to live in the shadows, always looking over their shoulder before they took another man's hand or entered one of the secretive queer bars that managed to survive. Lies and half-truths became a way of life. They invented a secret code of their own, whereby other homosexuals were 'so' or 'TBH' (to be had). Some tried to be celibate, others led a double life in a marriage of convenience, which often left pain and anguish in its wake. Many hated themselves as much as they feared detection. The lucky ones could hide behind a wall of privilege in a coterie of like-minded souls, just so long as they chose their company carefully and never made their true nature explicit. Just a few dared the world to condemn them, and shared a life, a home and a bed with another man. That took considerable courage and frequent acts of subterfuge, but it also made them outsiders.

They learned to dissemble. They recruited obliging female friends who were in the know to accompany them to parties. So as not to embarrass anyone, they masked their lovers' gender behind invented female names. They switched 'he' to 'she' and 'his' to 'hers' with ease. They made their excuses early at polite parties so they could seek more enticing company at less salubrious late-night haunts. They ruffled the sheets in the second bedroom, so nobody knew they had slept together. They pretended to be master and servant. It was not all miserable, of course. Plenty of bars, clubs and restaurants welcomed a queer clientele. If you were bold and grand enough, you could always find a guardsman in St James's Park or a porter behind the Theatre Royal. If you had two shillings and sixpence for the entrance fee you could get a rub from a gentleman in the Turkish baths, and if your funds couldn't stretch that far you could scout out a stranger in a public toilet. The risk of arrest and exposure even added a frisson to these stolen moments of gratification.

For obvious reasons, there are very few remaining records of these men's private lives. In many cases their families destroyed what little was left of their personal correspondence. I have had to dig deep into the archives and read between the lines to assemble their untold story. I have tried never to go beyond what I can state with certainty, but my working assumption has been that they had more sex than we know about. They would not have used the modern term 'gay', so I have avoided it except in its historic meaning of light-hearted or brightly coloured. They would almost certainly have denied that they were 'homosexual', although the term was in use and I use it where appropriate. They might have preferred now-obsolete terms like 'invert', 'uranist' or 'urning', but 'queer' was regularly used in a pejorative sense during this period, so I have decided to own it and used it in a non-pejorative sense to include all men who had same-sexual feelings or lived outside the heterosexual norms of the day.

This hidden story matters because homosexual men have been portrayed for centuries as hedonistic, effeminate, limp-wristed and flighty. It was assumed that they would be physically and morally weak, that they would run away from danger and undermine morale. Many queer men overcompensated by choosing supposedly manly pursuits like boxing or bodybuilding. Often they condemned in others what they refused to accept in themselves. Some, like the MP Bob Boothby, who always denied any hint of homosexuality, even perpetuated the stereotype. 'Homosexuals', he wrote, 'do not believe in a future. They are, therefore, not good at sustained fortitude over long periods of time. But they are reckless; and on the spur of the moment, they can be immensely brave.'[1] Yet the queer Glamour Boys were the ultimate exemplars of sustained fortitude. They swam against the tide in their private and their political lives; they faced down overwhelming political opinion and showed the courage of their convictions by enlisting. Without them we would never have gone to war with Hitler, Churchill would never have become prime minister and Nazism would never have been defeated.

This is not a simple story. Although four of them were killed in action, these men were not always heroic. They were often deeply conflicted. They were never part of a gay rights movement and they would have been amazed at the freedoms enjoyed today. If anything, they reckoned that men like them simply had to make the best of a bad lot. They would probably have hated to be identified as homosexual, queer or gay. And yet I hope they would have been as proud of this book as we should be of them, because, as one of them put it in 1943, 'This is part and parcel of the battle we are fighting – the battle for justice, liberty and toleration.'[2]

Introduction
Cocktails and Laughter

At the opening night of *On with the Dance* in March 1925, Alice Delysia's ballsy rendition of Noël Coward's song 'Poor Little Rich Girl' brought the audience to its feet. It was full of his trademark bittersweetness. It both celebrated the quintessential flapper girl of the 'Roaring Twenties' and saw through her. 'Cocktails and laughter, but what comes after?' ran the refrain.

It certainly felt like a time for cocktails and laughter. Moving pictures, telephones and automobiles were making the Western world jangle with opportunity. Jazz was spicing up the music scene with new syncopated rhythms and risqué lyrics. Black American blues singers like Bessie Smith and Ma Rainey topped the charts. There were other changes, too. Women over the age of thirty could vote. For the first time the Matrimonial Causes Act 1923 meant that *either* a husband's *or* a wife's adultery could be grounds for divorce, not just a wife's. The rich and edgy American-born Nancy Astor had been an MP since 1919 and in 1924 the former shop girl Margaret Bondfield had been a minister in a short-lived minority Labour government, which was led by Ramsay MacDonald, the illegitimate son of a farm labourer and a housemaid, something that would have been unthinkable in 1914. Lloyd George's budget of 1909 had dealt a blow to the entitled landed aristocracy, who offloaded Titians, tiaras and acres and pulled down crumbling surplus stately homes to pay death duties, but they still maintained retinues of servants at their London mansions and country piles, and their sons and daughters danced the Charleston, mixed cocktails named Sidecars, Bees' Knees and Mary Pickfords, and learned how to fly.

That was only half the story in Britain, though. 'What comes after?' was the question everybody had been asking ever since Armistice Day in 1918. Yes, Britain was still an empire. George V was king and emperor. If you included Britain's colonies, protectorates and mandates, the Empire coloured half the world pink. Australia, New Zealand, Canada, the whole of the Indian subcontinent, large swathes of Africa from Capetown to Cairo, even Palestine – they were all under nominal British rule. The nation was bruised, though. Roughly a million of her empire's subjects had been killed in the 'Great War' and another 2 million who had been wounded were a constant reminder. Many men – including leading politicians – were mentally scarred by what they had seen, felt and smelt in the trenches – the rats, the gas, the blood-drenched mud, the blown-out dugouts and the widespread incompetence. Women had lost husbands, fiancés, lovers, brothers and sons. Some families had lost every man. People were still angry with Germany, but nobody wanted another war. Many began to think that the Treaty of Versailles had been too vengeful and that Germany should be given a chance to get up off her knees, especially as unemployment and inflation ripped through the German economy.

Britain's finances were equally parlous. She owed America $4.4 billion, her annual debt repayments amounted to 44 per cent of all government expenditure and the total debt stood at 172 per cent of UK GDP. Working men and women were growing impatient, too. The recruiting officers had promised a land fit for heroes, but soldiers and nurses had returned to a shrunken economy, high unemployment, slave wages, miserly dole payments, sweatshops and slum housing. The Poor Law was still on the statute books and every town still had its workhouse. The nation's industrial heartlands in South Wales, the North East, the North West and Clydeside, which had been dominated by shipbuilding, coal, and iron and steel, were in sharp decline and politicians produced endless reports about the 'Depressed' or 'Special Areas'.

The political pendulum swung this way and that. The general election of 1918 had delivered the Liberal Prime Minister David Lloyd George and his coalition partners a massive majority, but the Conservative Party (or, to give it its full title, the Conservative and Unionist Party) dismantled that coalition and formed its own government in 1922, following which there were three general elections in two years. First the Conservatives won a majority in November 1922, as the Liberal Party split in two, thereby allowing Labour to make gains. When the Conservatives opted for an unnecessary election under their new leader Stanley Baldwin in December 1923, the electorate delivered a hung parliament, in which the Conservatives had the most seats, but Labour could outnumber them with Liberal support. So Ramsay MacDonald formed a fragile minority government, which fractured following a vote of no confidence in October 1924. The subsequent election was dominated by the leaking of the faked 'Zinoviev letter', which purported to prove that the Labour Party was in league with communist Russia – and the complete collapse of the Liberal vote. The result was a comfortable Conservative victory under the mild-mannered Baldwin, but his parliamentary majority of 209 could not protect him from economic gales and talk of social unrest. The nation had achieved minimal growth in 1924, but this was scotched by the decision of the new Chancellor, Winston Churchill, to return the pound to the gold standard, rendering British exports even less competitive. Soon, organised Labour was itching for a fight as the dole queues lengthened and people lined up at soup kitchens.

It was an anxious, questioning, turbulent time and it was hardly surprising that many saw cocktails and laughter as a perfect antidote. The poor struggled on while the bright young things of the leisured class danced and drank and strained at the leash of sexual convention.

There was no such loosening of the corsets for homosexual men, however, who experienced a sharp escalation in moral panic. It was not strictly speaking a criminal offence to *be* homosexual. Nobody, after all, recognised that anyone could be inherently homosexual. The almost universal view, however, was that same-sex acts of whatever kind were unnatural, a deliberate perversion of what God intended (and most people believed in God). Any infraction or deviation should therefore be severely punished – and no distinction was drawn between sex between two consenting adult men and paedophilia. Some brave souls had questioned this revulsion at consensual homosexuality. The poet and anthologist Edward Carpenter had lived with his much younger working-class partner George Merrill since 1898 and had praised what he called 'Uranian' love in his 1908 book *The Intermediate Sex*, claiming that 'Eros is a great leveller'.[1] The sexologist Havelock Ellis had published the first medical treatise on homosexuality in 1897, the same year that the poet George Ives created the secret Order of Chaeronea, named after the Sacred Band of Thebes, the elite force of 150 same-sex couples who had died in battle in 338 BC. In 1914 Ives had founded the British Society for Sex Psychology along with Carpenter, writer Laurence Housman and the German Jewish sexologist Magnus Hirschfeld, hoping to drag society round to a more rational, less judgemental understanding of human sexuality.

Yet the ghost of Oscar Wilde was everywhere. His double trial, humiliation, imprisonment, ostracism and exile were stories everybody knew. The thrice-married Irish-British-American journalist and novelist Frank Harris wrote that after his friend Oscar's conviction in 1895 'every train to Dover, every steamer to Calais thronged with members of the aristocratic and leisured classes, who seemed to prefer Paris, or even Nice out of season, to a city like London, where the police might act with such unexpected vigour'.[2] Although Harris's controversial autobiography was very explicit about his own numerous affairs, he did not expressly state that the ex-minister, the recently ennobled millionaire who was 'celebrated for his exquisite taste in art' and the famous general, all of whom had suddenly moved to the Continent, were guilty of Wilde's crime – he merely called them 'aesthetes' – but the imputation was clear. Fearing prosecution, hundreds of wealthy men made their homes abroad. Oscar Wilde died in 1900 but his trial cast a long shadow. Two decades later the bestselling author William Somerset Maugham ('Willie') was forced to set up residence at the Villa La Mauresque at Cap Ferrat with his American lover Gerald Haxton because Gerald had been arrested with another man in a hotel during the war and, although acquitted, was thereafter refused entry to the UK. Willie was a regular at Mayfair dinner parties, but it was only in France that the couple could entertain their coterie of queer friends in safety.[3]

The law was strict, but some bars and venues managed to get away with hosting a mixed or queer clientele. The Cave of the Golden Calf only survived for a couple of years before the Second World War in a basement in a cul-de-sac off Regent Street, but others had sprung up: the Long Bar in the Trocadero, the Criterion, Chez Victor and the Fitzroy Tavern. You had to be careful: you could never be certain if the man asking you for a light was an undercover policeman, but London was not entirely without possibilities.

Things were different on the Continent. Whatever the Catholic Church said, the framework of French law, the Napoleonic Code, was silent on homosexuality, and the literary salons of Paris had a large number of prominent queer writers, who wrote about homosexuality and were privately open about their own preferences, even if they tried to avoid being publicly identified as queer. These included André Gide, who discovered his sexuality in the sand dunes of Tangiers; Marcel Proust, who wrote about same-sex attraction but tried desperately to avoid being labelled as queer; Jean Cocteau, who made little secret of his love of what he called 'the strong sex, which I find legitimate to call the fair sex';[4] and Jean Genet, who left his foster mother's house at night in full make-up. As if to prove the difference

5

between the two countries, the restaurateur Marcel Boulestin, who brought French cuisine to Britain in the 1920s, published a successful novel on a homosexual theme, *Les Fréquentations de Maurice*, in France in 1911, but nobody dared print it in England.*

The Weimar Republic, which constituted the German Reich from 1919, was even more liberal and saw an extraordinary flowering of homosexual liberation. In theory, Paragraph 175 of its penal code proscribed homosexuality across the whole country, but the Social Democrat government in the regional Free State of Prussia, led by Otto Braun, declared that the Prussian authorities would urge the Reich to reform Paragraph 175 and in the meantime would not enforce it in their territory (which covered 60 per cent of Germany and included Berlin). This allowed Magnus Hirschfeld, who had been campaigning for reform for decades (his early work proved that three out of every hundred homosexual men committed suicide), to open his Institute for the Science of Sexuality (and accompanying Museum of Sex) in Berlin, not far from the Reichstag. Not everyone agreed with this relaxation of the law. Hirschfeld was badly beaten up in 1920. But dozens of bars, clubs, restaurants and Turkish baths started to cater for a queer clientele. As Christopher Isherwood, who briefly lived at the Institute, revealed in his autobiographical novels *Mr Norris Changes Trains* and *Goodbye to Berlin* (which were later the basis of the 1972 musical *Cabaret*), by the middle of the 1920s Berlin was the most sexually liberated city in the world. British men who could afford it, including many of the men in this book, made regular pilgrimages to Berlin, largely so as to enjoy sex with impunity. Many also committed themselves to ending Germany's pariah status. They actively campaigned for an end to the harsh clauses of the Versailles Treaty and for a rapprochement between Germany and Britain.

* E. M. Forster (1879–1970) wrote *Maurice*, about a love affair between two men, in 1913–14 and revised it several times, but sadly never dared publish it in his lifetime. It first appeared in 1971.

Some barely quibbled at Hitler's initial ascent. They thought the 'new Germany' was thrilling and full of energy. She should be given the benefit of the doubt. But the men this book is about were among the earliest critics of Nazism in Britain. Bob Boothby and Rob Bernays were warning about Hitler's territorial ambitions as early as 1932. For some it was the treatment of the Jews that turned them into ardent campaigners for rearmament. Others like Philip Sassoon and Harold Nicolson were revolted by the assassinations of homosexuals in the Night of the Long Knives in 1934, or by the imprisonment of homosexual friends thereafter. For Jack Macnamara it was a chance visit to the concentration camp at Dachau in 1936 that changed his mind. For Victor Cazalet it was rich Jews in Austria begging him to take them back to Britain after the Nazi annexation of Austria in the *Anschluss*, even if it meant working as a gardener. Each had a personal reason to want Britain to oppose Hitler with all her might, but their shared determination made them braver than they might have been alone.

After all, this was not a popular stance in Britain. Sympathy for the Jews was in short supply thanks to endemic anti-Semitism. Right-wing organisations proliferated, spreading deliberately false anti-Semitic rumours. According to the entirely fictitious *Protocols of the Elders of Zion*, which acquired an extraordinary currency at this time, the Jews had long planned global domination. It was said they were in cahoots with the communists, that they wanted to make money out of a new war and they were renowned for crafty manipulation behind the scenes. Anti-Semitic tropes about their unexplained wealth, their miserliness, their desire for global domination and their 'hidden hand' proliferated. There was little British sympathy, either, for the many homosexuals Hitler despatched. He was, in the words of *The Times*, simply 'clearing up'.[5]

There was another reason for political reluctance to rearm. Before the First World War, the British Army was so tiny that Otto von Bismarck had joked as German Chancellor that the German police could arrest it. Unlike other countries, Britain had only reluctantly introduced conscription and millions had volunteered. Propaganda had helped win the war in 1918. Public morale mattered for once – and the electorate had nearly tripled in 1918 with the inclusion of all men over twenty-one and women over thirty. It was difficult to gauge public opinion, though. Stanley Baldwin wrote to his fellow Conservative Austen Chamberlain just before the 1924 general election that he was confident, though not boastful, of a comfortable victory. But in truth no politician in the 1920s or 1930s had a secure way of knowing what the wider public felt. There were no opinion polls on voting intentions or individual subjects. Politicians relied on the opinions of the small set of people they met every day, attendances at rallies, their postbag and their own gut instincts. As Baldwin admitted, it was 'impossible to prophesy with this unwieldy electorate'.[6]

In addition, the National Government, which was formed in 1931 following the collapse of the Labour Government and consisted of Conservative, National Labour and Liberal National MPs, enjoyed a vast majority over the Labour Party Opposition. This meant Parliament was an echo chamber where MPs confirmed their own prejudices, while most of the press was affiliated to one party or another and subject to the political whims of their proprietors. There was one weathervane – parliamentary by-elections. Baldwin certainly felt that the East Fulham by-election in 1933, which saw a National Government majority of 14,521 converted into a Labour victory by 4,840, sent out a clear statement from 'this pacific democracy' that rearmament was unthinkable. He was contemplating holding an early general election, but, 'I cannot think', he said, 'of anything that would have made the loss of the election more certain.'[7] You could also read the results of the League of Nations Union's Peace Ballot announced in June 1935 in several ways. There was a three to one majority in favour of using military measures, if necessary, to tackle an aggressor nation. But of the 11.6 million people who took part, 90 per cent supported disarmament, the prohibition of private arms manufacture and the abolition of national military and naval aircraft. Against this background, it is unsurprising that

Neville Chamberlain and the vast majority of Conservative MPs *believed* that the public supported disarmament, appeasement and the avoidance of war. Whether they were right or not is merely a matter for speculation.

Given the British revulsion against homosexuality and apparent fear of and opposition to another war, it is extraordinary that a group of queer men should play a prominent role in urging Britain to oppose Hitler and Mussolini. They were taking a double risk, challenging their government and society. Yet from 1934 onwards, as Hitler ratcheted up attacks on homosexuals and Jews, a number of queer and nearly queer politicians, most of them Conservatives and all of them sitting on the National Government benches, allied themselves with Anthony Eden and Winston Churchill and pushed for their government to rearm against Hitler. The new prime minister in 1937, Neville Chamberlain, who disliked being contradicted at the best of times, loathed everything about them. He launched a secret campaign to discredit them and labelled them the 'Glamour Boys', a term he and his secretive master of the dark arts, Sir Joseph Ball, craftily coined as a term of abuse because it insinuated something sexually untoward about the informal grouping of anti-appeasement MPs that coalesced in 1938 and 1939. 'Glamour', after all, denoted something bewitching, misleading, ephemeral and fundamentally feminine or effeminate. It was not the only term Chamberlain and his allies used. They also called them 'the boys' brigade', 'the glory boys', 'rebels', 'malcontents' and 'insurgents'. But the term 'Glamour Boys' was insidiously successful because although not all the opponents of appeasement were queer (and not all queer MPs opposed appeasement), the number of government rebels who were queer is striking. Of course, Chamberlain and Ball were careful never to make a direct allegation. Nor was there ever a definitive list of the Glamour Boys, although one of Chamberlain's most ardent supporters, the married but queer MP Henry 'Chips' Channon, named seventeen 'insurgents' in March 1938.[8]

Who were they? Some of the leading figures in the list were, so far as we are aware, entirely heterosexual. There was Winston Churchill, then in his fifties and preaching rearmament and enhanced air power in his wilderness years. Equally consistent was Leo Amery (1873–1955), a noted skier and mountaineer, who was happily married with two sons and served as First Lord of the Admiralty and Secretary of State for the Colonies in the 1920s and repeatedly argued for strengthening the British Army. Another of Churchill's close allies was his son-in-law Duncan Sandys (1908–87). Others in the list were Edward Spears (1886–1974), the socially awkward Francophile brigadier-general who had led the British military mission in Paris at the end of the First World War and was married to the American novelist Mary Borden; Derrick Gunston (1891–1985), who was awarded the Military Cross for his service in the Irish Guards in the war; Paul Emrys-Evans (1894–1967); Leonard Ropner (1895–1977), who started his working life in the family shipping firm but joined the Royal Artillery during the war and was also awarded the MC; and Godfrey Nicholson (1901–91), the affable son of a family of gin distillers, who was too young to serve in the First World War and was father to four children. Channon's list was not definitive. On other occasions he reckoned the group numbered as many as forty and he omitted Foreign Secretary Anthony Eden (1897–1977), Eden's deputy at the Foreign Office, 'Bobbety' Viscount Cranborne (1893–1972), his parliamentary private secretary (PPS) Jim Thomas (1903–60), and Cranborne's PPS Mark Patrick (1893–1942), all of whom resigned over Chamberlain's handling of foreign affairs in February 1938. Others regularly appeared in the same rebellious lobby, including Lord Wolmer (1887–1971), Duff Cooper (1890–1954), Robert Bower (1894–1975), Harold Macmillan (1894–1986), Anthony Crossley (1894–1939), Richard Law (1901–80), Hubert Duggan (1904–43) and Dudley Joel (1904–41). None of these, so far as I am aware, was anything other than heterosexual.

However, seven out of Channon's seventeen were homosexual, bisexual or somewhere in-between: Harold Nicolson, Victor

Cazalet, Ronnie Tree, Bob Boothby, Brendan Bracken (1901–58), Jack Macnamara and Ronnie Cartland. In addition, the government ministers Philip Sassoon, Harry Crookshank and Rob Bernays were critical of the policy of appeasement and were also on a similar scale; and it is highly likely that both Jim Thomas and Hamilton Kerr (1903–74) shared their same-sex preference.

In other words, however you construct the list of Glamour Boys, the majority were heterosexual. Yet the derogatory label only stuck because roughly a quarter of them were queer, and at several key moments these were the most outspoken of the whole group. That is why I have focused especially on the queer Glamour Boys. In a sense they put the glamour into the Glamour Boys and thereby gave their powerful political opponents a stick with which to beat the whole of the group. It is remarkable that this never stopped Eden and Churchill from associating with them, but they were the closest-knit group within the wider alliance and without them the wider group would never have succeeded.

'Cocktails and laughter, but what comes after?' was the theme of many a homosexual man's life in this period. Pleasure, not pride, came before a fall. And yet a few brave men managed to find a way through that complex world of subterfuge and denial. The eldest was Harold Nicolson, who was thirty-nine in 1925. Philip Sassoon and Victor Cazalet had already seen war at close quarters. But Bob Boothby and Rob Bernays were still in their twenties and Jack Macnamara and Ronnie Cartland were not yet old enough to vote. They had everything to learn.

PART ONE

To End All Wars

I

Empire Orphan

In February 1926 a lithe, muscled, twenty-year-old soldier called Jack Macnamara, whose freckles, pale blue eyes and fair hair betrayed his Irish ancestry as readily as his surname, disembarked in the exotic and cosmopolitan French Protectorate of Tunisia. Jack had spent Christmas with his mother and stepfather, who were wintering in Italy, and had decided to take a holiday in Africa before returning to England to take up a commission in the regular army. With him was 49-year-old Lieutenant Colonel Godfrey M. Giles, who was the commanding officer of the 3rd City of London Regiment (Royal Fusiliers), the Territorial Army unit to which Jack already belonged and which afforded plenty of time for the colonel's expensive hobby of collecting Bugatti sports cars. Quite why Jack was travelling alone with his unmarried commanding officer is unclear. It is possible they were lovers. But when Godfrey was unexpectedly called back to England, Jack was left to his own devices and decided to hire an Arab guide and some horses so as to camp out at an oasis in the mountains fifteen miles above the coastal city of Gabès.

This is when things started to go wrong. One night Jack found himself alone with a local Arab policeman in his tent. It is unclear who made the first move, but a misunderstanding led to a tussle and Jack threw the man out, claiming that he had made 'improper' advances. The embarrassed and aggrieved policeman then followed Jack for several days, invited him to dinner and tried to get him drunk in the hope that he would incriminate himself by saying something against the French, all 'in a spirit of revenge'.[1] Jack was young and naïve and fell into the trap. He started holding forth on local politics, speaking admiringly of the rebel leader in Morocco, Abd-el-Krim, and denouncing the French commander in Syria, General Sarrail.[2] The policeman's ruse worked. The French government was paranoid about the rising tide of Tunisian nationalism and had just issued a new decree outlawing seditious talk, so Jack was suddenly put under house arrest for a day and then thrown in a filthy, verminous, overcrowded cell along with a gang of thirty criminals awaiting trial for murder and theft. There he languished without trial for fifteen days. His pencil diary recorded that on many days he was not allowed to wash and that a standard punishment for any minor infraction was denial of food. The few scraps he was allowed to pay for from the local hotel rarely got to him untouched. When he finally appeared before a court, the judge laughed at his complaints, telling him that at least God Almighty had given him lice to play with to pass the time. He did, however, release Jack back into house arrest at the Hotel Regina in Gabès, pending trial in Sousse, 175 miles up the coast.

At this point Jack struck lucky, as he met Arthur Lett-Haines, known as 'Lett', a British sculptor and artist, who was on his second marriage but was the longstanding lover of another artist, Cedric Morris. Lett and Cedric had settled in Paris in 1920 and travelled extensively in North Africa, taking advantage of the fact that although buggery and homosexual acts were banned in Britain, they were not proscribed by the Napoleonic Code. Several of their paintings, such as Cedric's *Dancing Sailor* and Lett's *Rough Trade*, were unambiguously homoerotic, and the couple had a wide circle of queer artistic and literary friends, including the art critic Raymond 'Tray' Mortimer and his boyfriend the architect Paul Hyslop,[3] and the actor John Gielgud and his lover John Perry. Nor were Lett and Cedric frightened of entering the fray on behalf of sexual outcasts, as that same year Cedric was so infuriated when a woman was barred entry to the USA on the grounds of 'moral turpitude' because she was travelling with the co-respondent in her recent divorce that he painted a satirical work entitled *The Entry of Moral Turpitude into New York Harbour.*

Lett fell for Jack the moment he met him. Over three decades later, the lesbian artist Maggi Hambling, who was later taught by Lett and Cedric, found Lett rather frightening when she first took a couple of her paintings round to the 'artists' house', which was 'notorious for every sin under the sun', in 1960 because he was so tall and sophisticated, but she grew to know him as a 'truly generous teacher who gave himself to every student'.[4] Maggi added that although Lett and Cedric stayed together until they died, a multiplicity of lovers passed through their beds – of both sexes in Lett's case – and since Lett and Cedric were going through a rough patch at this time, Jack was probably one.

Aware that the situation with Jack's stepfather was 'a little delicate',[5] Lett took up Jack's case with parental vigour. He advised Jack to be more discreet in future, but immediately wrote to *The Times* claiming that Jack had been forced to 'free himself with some violence' from an 'improper assault' by a native policeman, and referred to an '*agent-provocateur*' coming to Jack's tent 'disguised as an Arab'.[6] He wrote to the British vice-consul in Sousse claiming that Jack was the innocent party, as the whole thing had arisen from his 'resentment of indecent proposals made by the policeman'.[7] Lett also drafted in support from a wealthy retired major who was in town, Eustace Richardson-Cox, promising his 'absolute discretion'.[8] He in turn contacted the British consul general, a Mr McLeod, and proclaimed himself 'convinced of the lad's absolute innocence'.[9] Meanwhile Jack made up a story for his mother Natalie, writing to her that he had been arrested 'as a spy in the pay of the British Government'.[10] When she forwarded this letter to the Foreign Office, the government pounced on this alternative version of events. Clearly it was far more acceptable for a British officer to be accused of spying than of homosexuality. So the consul general suggested that the charge of 'using seditious and violent language against the French authorities to the natives ... [was] not without foundation'.[11] And when the Labour MP Colonel Josiah Wedgwood asked Foreign Secretary Austen Chamberlain a question about the conduct of the Tunisian judge who had supposedly 'recommended this unfortunate prisoner to lead a chaste life', Chamberlain replied that he hoped he might be permitted 'to observe discretion when an Englishman is in trouble'.[12] The rumours continued. The French monthly bulletin *L'Afrique française* intimated that it would be better for this 'imprudent youngster' if one didn't look too closely at what he had been up to.[13] But Britain stuck to the official version of events.

As for Jack, he must have been very frightened. He spoke no Arabic and another British official reckoned that there was 'no saying what the French may do with him'. At one round of the legal proceedings a large crowd continually shouted him down until he was forced to give up making any defence at all. He was denied an interpreter, but lawyers were engaged and on 21 March the Sousse court sentenced Jack to two months' imprisonment, a 3,000-franc fine and a five-year ban from France. Meanwhile, Lett's interventions had borne fruit. There was just enough of a commotion back in England for ministers to take note, but not so much as to cause a major diplomatic row, so ministers announced that the 'hearing was full and impartial'[14] and the Tunisian authorities quietly allowed Jack to slip back to England escorted by Lett and two rather obvious French secret service officers via Marseille before increasing his sentence to six months. When he reached his regimental headquarters, Colonel Giles put him under the strictest orders 'to make no statement whatever to the press'.[15]

In truth, this was a homosexual encounter that had gone wrong and Jack went through precisely what many thousands of homosexual men experienced when they misread the signs of a glance, a hug or an emotional conversation with another man. If they were lucky the other party stalked off with a scowl, but there was always the danger that the offer of a kiss would be met with a fist or a boot. Thousands of men were beaten to a pulp and left for dead in similar situations. Worst of all, the other man might report you to the police. Privately, the government reckoned that 'the young man brought his troubles on his own head by his behaviour'.[16] But in public they stood by the official version.

★

Who was this 'young man'? Jack was a typical product of the British Empire. His Dublin-born father, John Radley Macnamara, was a doctor working for the Assam Tea Company in north-east India when he married Natalie Jermain, the second daughter of a retired captain in the Royal Navy, in the compound chapel in Nazira in November 1904. Jack was born there the following October and was, in his own words, 'virtually weaned as an Indian', as he learned Hindustani and Assamese from his bearer and his early years included escaping the clutches of a leopard, playing with a snake on top of the family piano, being half-poisoned by a vindictive family servant and learning to fear the native bogeymen, the badmashes, the puglas and the head-hunting Naga tribe. Like many a child of the British Raj, though, he was to be, in his own words, 'an Empire orphan from the age of three',[17] as his parents brought him home to be educated in England in 1908. Dr Macnamara returned to Nazira almost immediately, leaving Natalie and the infant Jack with Captain Jermain and his family at his imposing villa in Lower Walmer in Kent, just yards from Deal Castle.

The house was grand – it had formerly been the home of the Countess Stanhope – but it was a harsh, lonely childhood. Jack felt bereft when his mother returned to Assam, as he was 'passed round a forest of long-skirted women for inspection',[18] and he was not to see his father again until he was ten. Despite an impressive naval beard, his grandfather was an unsympathetic figure who dominated the household at Walmer. There was an inspection parade every morning (hands, hair and general appearance), which was followed by a lecture in the captain's study and prayers in the hall. Jack loved swimming in the sea, but this was banned on Sundays. It was a very female household, with unmarried aunts, a couple of female cousins and four female servants, so Jack's only male companion, to whom he became close, was the youngest of his mother's three brothers, Philip, but even he was more than ten years older than Jack.

When Jack's mother returned to England for a few months in 1911 she planted Jack on a friend of hers, a Mrs May, the widow of another retired admiral, who ran a school for young children of the Raj with her daughters at Alverstoke, near Gosport. This was to prove one of the most fortuitous decisions of Jack's young life, as the May girls took to their Empire orphan and stayed in touch with him long after he left their classroom. It was through them that Jack also first met a trendy young curate called John 'Herbert' Sharp, who started courting the fourth of the May sisters, Elsie, in 1914. Herbert was sixteen years older than Jack and barely knew him while he was courting, but Jack tasted his first champagne at their wedding in April 1915 and Herbert was to become a 'life-long friend'.[19]

As for Jack's more formal education, this started at the age of nine, when he was sent to board at Cheam, the oldest preparatory school in the country, whose pupils included Winston Churchill's father, Randolph, and the ostentatiously eccentric composer and novelist Gerald Tyrwhitt, the 14th Baron Berners. This was the bosom of the establishment, but whatever the school's scholastic merits, Jack excused the fact that the headmaster 'hit us and beat us and bruised us black and blue all over' on the grounds that 'we needed it all if anything was to be driven into our heads'.[20] Then in 1919 came Haileybury College in Hertfordshire, which had been founded in 1806 as the East India College to train administrators for British India. Here too there were regular beatings by his Neville House prefects and a 'great deal' of bullying. Jack's fellow students included the artist Rex Whistler, but at this stage Jack was more interested in matters military than academic or artistic. In 1913, when he was still just eight, he had dreaded the very thought that Britain might shy away from its moral duty to Belgium and he had cheered when the Empire declared war. He gloried in his family's record in the Royal Navy, too. His grandfather was an admiral, all three of his uncles signed up in the First World War and he was devastated but proud when his uncle Philip, who was temporarily drafted as a Royal Marine, was killed at Gallipoli in 1915. Jack's adoptive home at Alverstoke was equally patriotic, as it was 'filled with khaki' throughout the war, so it is hardly surprising that Jack knew from an early age that he liked a uniform and recalled as a very young boy running to greet 'a soldier friend in a gorgeous red coat, or, more often, a marine in blue'. The services, and especially the Senior Service, the Royal Navy, seemed a natural choice for him, but when he was told that his eyesight was not good enough, he reflected that 'soldiers were no longer looked down on [but] accorded full equality of rights with sailors',[21] so on his arrival at Haileybury, which had given the Empire a string of generals and a couple of field marshals, and lost scores of men in the war, he joined the Army Officers' Training Corps, wishing that 'the whole school wore uniform always and was run as a barracks'.[22]

By the time Jack left Haileybury in March 1922 it had imbued in him a deep sense of Empire patriotism and military pride. He wavered in his ambitions, though. For a while he toyed with following his father into medicine and registered for medical college, but that ambition evaporated before he took up his place. Instead he went to work for a civil engineering company in the City and took rooms at 4 Grosvenor Street in Stepney in the heart of the East End. The army still beckoned, though, and on 11 January 1924 he joined the Territorial Army's 3rd City of London Regiment (Royal Fusiliers) as a second lieutenant.[23] Based at the Harrow Road near Paddington, the regiment had been formed in 1861 as a volunteer force associated with the railways, but it had taken part in the Boer War and had been drafted into the regular army in the First World War in the scarlet coat and blue facings of the Fusiliers, winning battle honours at Neuve Chapelle, Somme, Arras and Gallipoli. After the war it was reconstituted as part of the Territorial Army and served as a reserve force in India. With many wealthy and aristocratic volunteers, it was a welcoming home for the ambitious and adventurous young man.

Then came a family tragedy. Jack barely knew his father. His parents had made another visit to England in 1920 with Jack's younger brother Brian, who had been born in 1915, but they were such strangers to him that Jack struggled to recognise them when they berthed at Southampton. Dr Macnamara returned to India the following February and although Jack's mother stayed an extra year, the next he saw of either parent was in May 1924 when Natalie returned alone on the *Nyanza*, expecting her husband to join her later in the year. It was not to be. Jack's father sailed on the *Mantola* that November, but he collapsed and died while it was docked in Marseille, where he was cremated with the briefest of ceremonies. Jack had barely spent six months in the same country as his father since the age of three – and his parents had spent long periods apart, which may explain why, less than six months after her first husband's death, Natalie married Henry Stewart Orpen, a relative of the successful Irish artist Sir William Orpen. Jack increasingly felt like an orphan and let it be known that he did not approve of his mother's remarriage.

Several things were now clear about Second Lieutenant Macnamara. He believed in the Empire. He objected to women 'usurping' men's jobs, dressing in men's clothes, smoking, drinking, and 'daub[ing] her face, her finger-nails, her toe-nails, her lips with brilliant woad'.[24] He had a strong sense of public service. He was conservative – and Conservative and Unionist. Yet he was far from conventional. He was not scared of conflict, he was brave and he despised the slogan 'Safety first', which the Conservative leader Stanley Baldwin adopted in the 1924 general election because, because as Jack put it, 'with "Safety first" came the yes-men, for the "yes" is so often safer than "definitely no!"'[25] He also had a genuine concern for those less fortunate than himself. He continued to live in the East End, expressly so as 'to study the workers' problems'[26] and he combined his love of boxing and bodybuilding with helping in a local gym for unemployed young men.

Jack also knew from an early age that he was different from the rest because he was sexually attracted to men and that this was not just a phase he was going through. The all-male environment of Haileybury had offered him plenty of opportunities to explore his sexuality, as several Haileybury pupils of the period admitted that 'masses of sex' was on offer.[27] All one had to do was pass another boy a note asking if he wanted to 'go for a walk' on the heath. If he agreed, then he was clearly up for it. This brought every young lad up against a harsh reality. The rules were clear. Any boy caught with another would be expelled, and most headmasters believed that 'self-indulgence, long pursued, tends ultimately, if carried far enough, to early death or self-destruction'.[28] No wonder the poet John Betjeman, who attended Haileybury's sister school Marlborough, never dared touch anyone, as he thought he 'would have gone to gaol – and hell'.[29] The paradox was that many claimed that British public schools were 'the most sexual places in the world',[30] but England was so uniformly religious that guilt about personal sin weighed heavily on the hearts of many young men who thought or feared that they were 'perverts', 'inverts' or 'homosexuals'. School taught them about classical Greece and even strayed into idealised discussions about male love, but it also drummed into them that buggery and masturbation were evil and would lead to underdeveloped muscles, sunken eyes, a sallow complexion and moist skin.

Many liked to claim that homosexual schoolboy encounters had no lasting effect on their adult sexuality. Marietta Tree, for instance, claimed that her husband Ronnie, who was one of the Glamour Boys, was like many ex-public-school boys. 'Most moved on to heterosexual love and marriage,' she wrote, before adding with more than a hint of disapproval, 'but many never lost the romantic glow of Greek love instilled in them as adolescents.'[31] A few of Jack's contemporaries, though, continued to have adult sexual relations with men long after leaving school, including Rex Whistler and the famous explorer Stewart Perowne. As for Jack, he had known from an early age that his preference was for men – and had fretted about what that might entail. When he was just eight, he worried about the loneliness that seemed to be the fate of unmarried men. Edward Lear's nonsense poem about two old bachelors who lived in a house – 'one caught a muffin, the other caught a mouse' – particularly vexed him and prompted him to declare that their fate was so awful 'that

I decided I must never be a bachelor'.[32] When everyone teased him for such precocious concerns he boldly asked his nurse Lucy to marry him – and when, years later, people asked why he was still unmarried at the age of thirty-three, he told the story of his 'engagement' to Lucy, a tale that appeared in the *Chelmsford Chronicle* under the headline 'Never be a bachelor'.[33] His closest friends, who knew the whole truth, must have smiled.

Jack's trip to Tunisia almost certainly had a sexual element to it, but the *News of the World* sprang to his defence on his return to London, claiming that it was able to set at rest 'various rumours as to what had happened to the young fellow' and asserting that as there was no suggestion that he has been guilty of anything 'detrimental to his honour, he has not jeopardised his chances of gaining a commission in the Regular Army'.[34] Jack must have breathed an enormous sigh of relief when he read that. An officer's 'honour' was everything. If it were tarnished, his career would be over. And in England at that time there was no charge that could be more damaging than that of homosexuality, as successive generations of British politicians had drawn up the most stringent set of anti-homosexuality laws imaginable.

The list of offences was comprehensive. The 'abominable crime of Buggery' attracted a penalty of penal servitude for life, or at least ten years, and *attempting* buggery attracted between three and seven years' penal servitude or imprisonment with hard labour. The far more common charge, though, was of 'gross indecency', an offence that had been introduced thanks to a late-night amendment to the Criminal Law Amendment Bill of 1885. 'Gross indecency' attracted a maximum sentence of two years with hard labour and was an all-embracing offence, as it stipulated that 'any male person who, in public or private, commits, or is a party to the commission of, or procures, or attempts to procure the commission by any male person of, any act of gross indecency with another male person, shall be guilty of a misdemeanour'.[35] What constituted 'gross indecency' was left to the imagination and the courts. It included any form of contact between two men, whether overtly sexual or merely affectionate. It caught men who had not touched each other, but had merely attempted to meet up, for instance by sending one another letters seeking an assignation. Worst of all, by specifying that the misdemeanour was committed whether 'in public or private', the new clause also allowed a dramatic incursion into men's private lives. No place would be safe from the tentacles of the law, not even a gentleman's bedroom.

That was not all. Back in 1824 Parliament had sought to tackle the perceived threat of lawlessness from the number of men returning homeless at the end of the Napoleonic Wars with a Vagrancy Act that declared a long list of categories of people as 'rogues and vagabonds', including fortune tellers, beggars, prostitutes and anyone 'wilfully openly, lewdly, and obscenely exposing his person in any street, road, or public highway, or in the view thereof, or in any place of public resort, with intent to insult any female'.[36] The maximum sentence for such 'rogues and vagabonds' was up to three months' hard labour in a house of correction, and for repeat offenders or those who resisted arrest, who were deemed 'incorrigible rogues', it was a year with the additional option of whipping. A new Vagrancy Act in 1898 then extended the list of potential offenders to anyone who 'persistently solicits or importunes for immoral purposes',[37] another imprecise phrase that was seized upon by the police to refer to men seeking sex with men. It was an offence that required so little evidence that eager police constables were able to bring hundreds of successful prosecutions in the first decade of the new century and the courts regularly added whipping to men's prison sentences. One man, for instance, was given twelve months' hard labour and twelve strokes with a birch rod in London in July 1904.

A few brave souls condemned the use of the rod. The pacifist MP and owner of the *Yorkshire Observer*, Sir William Byles, took the home secretary, Reginald McKenna, to task when two men were sentenced to nine months' hard labour and fifteen strokes for importuning in May 1912. McKenna, though, defended flogging for such offences and the two men's appeal was rebuffed in stinging terms by the Court of Criminal Appeal, which pronounced that: 'If ever there was a case for corporal punishment it is for that particular class of offence of which these applicants have been guilty – soliciting men for immoral purposes.' The court went even further, declaring that in another case of the same kind it might be necessary 'to consider whether such sentences should not be increased'.[38] By the end of the year a new Criminal Law Amendment Act had doubled the sentence for importuning to six months for a first offence and two years with hard labour for 'incorrigible rogues'.

As an army officer Jack did not just have these civilian offences to contend with. They were mirrored in the Army Discipline and Regulations Act 1881, which included a parallel series of catch-all offences, which prohibited 'disgraceful conduct of a cruel, indecent or unnatural kind', including any sexual conduct between men. A senior officer could summarily dismiss a man at the slightest hint of homosexuality – and none dared to challenge such a ruling for fear of the inevitable court martial. Moreover, a separate section stipulated that an officer who 'behaves in a scandalous way unbecoming the conduct of an officer and a gentleman' should be cashiered (i.e. dismissed and dishonoured). This was more frequently used in cases of fraud, but many queer officers feared a court martial for 'conduct unbecoming'.[39]

Arrests, prosecutions and convictions had come thick and fast. Some, like that of Oscar Wilde, attracted reams of press coverage, but hundreds of arrests passed with little more than a couple of column inches in the local newspapers. Often neither the trial nor the sentence was reported, as the arrest was humiliation enough, conviction was almost certain and the prisoner served his term conjuring up the demons of ostracism and self-loathing in a lonely cell in a harsh prison where other prisoners treated him as a pariah and drew no distinction between those whose offence had been with a consenting adult or with a child. Moral panic meant that the number of prosecutions rose inexorably. In

London alone there were 132 such cases in 1922, 144 in 1927, 162 in 1932 and 251 in 1937.

Jack was fully aware of the dangers of zealous policemen who started to enforce the law with ever-increasing severity just as he left school. It was a dangerous time, as virtually anything could now constitute an offence. As the poet George Ives, who had courageously campaigned for penal reform for decades, pointed out, an alleged smile, wink or look could lead to an arrest and young men were at the mercy of 'any two detectives hunting in couples', who enjoyed 'a degree of unchecked authority which places the liberty of citizens entirely in their hands'.[40] Jack would have heard the many stories that were doing the rounds, but a few instances will suffice to show how little evidence was necessary for a conviction. When two plain-clothes detectives had watched a young man entering three separate urinals in Covent Garden in 1913, for instance, the police never suggested that he had touched or spoken to anyone or that anyone had been offended, yet the church-going judge, Lord Alverstone, stated that the fact that the defendant had 'artificially reddened lips', that he 'wriggled his body' and was found with a powder puff with pink powder on it in his pocket was 'not unimportant in connection with an offence of this kind' and that it was not necessary that evidence be given that 'some person was annoyed or had made a complaint'.[41] In other words, there was no need to prove that anyone had been solicited in order to convict someone for soliciting.

It was not just camp men and rent boys who were arrested. Men from all sorts of walks of life had their names plastered across the press throughout 1926. Just before Jack returned from Africa, a watchmaker and a bricklayer's labourer were sent down for gross indecency for six months in York. Two sailors were charged with gross indecency in Portsmouth in June, as were two miners in separate cases in Nottingham and Wigan, and a labourer in Belper. In September charges were pressed against a teacher in Lydney, a German seaman in Aberdeen and a stoker in Portsmouth – and in November a 61-year-old vicar was sentenced to six months' imprisonment on eight cases of gross indecency, even though the judge recognised that 'the time might come when such cases would be treated medically'.[42]

The police were determined to tackle what they saw as a scourge. When they caught wind of the Eccentric Club at the Adelphi Rooms, near Jack's regiment in the Edgware Road, they sent undercover officers to investigate and brought charges that December against two men for running a disorderly house. The officers claimed in court that they had seen 250 or so male members dancing together, hugging closely, cuddling and 'behaving suggestively', and that another fifty men had been dressed as women in thick make-up.[43] The two men pleaded guilty at the Old Bailey the following January and their lawyer Sir Henry Curtis-Bennett tried his best for them, but the court sentenced them to twelve and twenty-one months with hard labour. In passing judgement, the Recorder referred to the two men as 'pests of society' and pronounced 'this case should also be a lesson to people who attend promiscuous dances'.[44]

All this might have been enough to put the fear of God into Jack. More than one man sobbed 'This means complete ruin' to the police when they were arrested, and many took what they felt was the only honourable way out by taking their own lives. When allegations were made in 1902 against Major-General Sir Hector MacDonald, a war hero from the Nile Expedition and the Boer War, he shot his brains out in a hotel in Paris on his way back to Ceylon to face a court of inquiry.[45]

This, then, was the world that Jack grew up into, a world where a wink or a tender glance could get you arrested. It was a world of clandestine liaisons and constant fear. Men scoured the press to see if their friends or acquaintances had been arrested. They were made to feel ashamed of themselves, to deny their real nature and to hide their feelings. Often this led them into hideous contortions. The novelist Hugh Walpole, for instance, admitted to Virginia Woolf that he 'only loved men who did not love men' and tried to kill himself over an affair with the Danish-American Wagnerian *Heldentenor* Lauritz Melchior, who was married but queer. As Virginia noted in staccato fashion in her diary, 'Jumped into a river; stuck in mud; seized a carving knife; saw himself in the glass; all became absurd; reconciliation.'[46] One of Jack's friends, Micky Burn, felt even more conflicted. 'It shamed me,' he wrote, 'to be relieved that physically I did not look like the general view of one of those. I did not make up or step out in drag. I was not a limp wristed teapot.'[47] So too architectural historian and diarist James Lees-Milne declared that he hated 'queens', even though his wedding party consisted of himself, his bride and four homosexual men, three of whom were his former lovers. 'Their mannerisms, their social contacts, their sharp little jokes are the same the world over,' he wrote. 'How is it they do not recognise that they are artificial, shallow, slick, sophisticated, absurd?'[48] Likewise Harold Nicolson's son Ben privately acknowledged that his 'domesticity, love of children [and] love of normality' conflicted with his homosexuality, but he was full of remorse the morning after he drunkenly poured out his own 'secret sorrow' to a friend at the Fitzroy Tavern one night in 1939.[49] It is easy to deride such evident self-loathing. Psychiatrists would call it 'projection'. But palpable, visceral fear forced queer men to accentuate their masculinity, condemn effeminacy in others and deny their identity. Terrified that the search for a partner would lead them to ruin, they were all too often condemned to loneliness.

Just occasionally they fought back. Micky Burn successfully went to the police twice to complain about blackmailers. Likewise, in December 1926 a Doncaster solicitor pressed charges against two undercover police officers who had followed him into a public lavatory in Bradford and threatened to arrest him for 'indecency' unless he paid them £1 each. The two officers were sentenced to four years' penal servitude, but it took considerable courage for the solicitor to storm into the police station and demand justice. Likewise, a Bromsgrove School housemaster called Francis Champain appealed when he was convicted in a much-publicised case for importuning a police officer in the urinals at the Adelphi Arches in August 1926, even though he had been cautioned for a similar offence in 1922. His lawyer – Curtis-Bennett again – argued that because Champain was a gentleman of the highest possible character and an impressive cricketer and rugby player, it was inconceivable that he was guilty. Amazingly, the appeal court quashed the verdict and awarded him costs.

Jack would have applauded Champain's sangfroid, but his own experience in Tunisia had given him a very nasty fright. He had come remarkably close to ruin and it was only his friends' quick-wittedness that had managed to get the real story covered up. He was not a man to let fear conquer him and he knew that his attraction to men was not something he could ignore, but he knew too that he would have to be careful if he wanted to avoid the sharp claws of the British criminal justice system.

2

Bright Young Things

A crisis had been brewing in the coal industry since the First World War. Prices had fallen, miners' wages had been slashed already and now mine owners wanted another cut. But the Miners' Federation of Great Britain demanded 'not a penny off the pay and not a minute on the day'. When negotiations with the government collapsed a few weeks after Jack's return to England, the Trades Union Congress called a general strike in sympathy with the miners, to start on 3 May 1926. The next nine days acted as a rallying cry for the left, as 1.7 million workers went out, but it was a call to arms for young Conservatives, too; many of them rushed to volunteer as special police constables. Jack was among the first to sign up at the police station in Paddington, where he was issued with a truncheon, a warrant card and a police armband or brassard, with which he sallied forth into several pitched battles. On at least one occasion he was knocked unconscious, but he knew no fear and he was utterly convinced that right was on his side. The Red Flag 'jarred the soul', he said; and Britain was 'near to civil war'.[1]

Another young Conservative who volunteered in the strike was very different from Jack. Tall, slim and dark-haired, Ronnie Cartland was no Empire orphan, although he too had lost his father when he was young. Nor was he handy with his fists, although he was a good shot. His parents, Bertie and Mary, had been wealthy, as Bertie's father, James Cartland, had made a fortune as a brass founder and financier in the Midlands and had become a magistrate and prominent member of the Conservative Party. Likewise, Mary – who was always known as Polly because she was tiny and chattered away like a parrot – had brought a significant dowry with her. So they had started married life with a grand Georgian home, Bowbrook House in Peopleton in Worcestershire, staffed with eight servants and surrounded by an estate, which they thought had been given to them by James. Here their first child, Barbara, was born in 1901. But then in October 1903 came the first of several family tragedies: James Cartland's company collapsed, and when an attempt to cut family living costs and shore the business up failed, James went out into a field near his Edgbaston home and shot himself in the head. For a while Bertie and Polly managed to keep going at Bowbrook, but soon the bailiffs moved in, seizing furniture, silver and jewellery. Bowbrook belonged to the defunct firm, not the family, and had to be sold to satisfy the creditors, so Bertie and Polly were forced to let the servants go before moving to a less imposing home, a two-storey farmhouse in nearby Pershore known as Amerie Court, where their son Ronnie ('a big baby, bright yellow with jaundice'²) was born on 3 January 1907, followed by Tony in 1912. It was no hovel. Formerly the home farm for Pershore Abbey, it was one of the three oldest farmhouses in the village; parts of it dated back to the sixteenth century, its fine stuccoed exterior included an impressive porch with a beautiful cornice and arched doorway, and it had a tennis court, stables and four acres of garden. Yet it was a definite step down in the world. Bertie and Polly continued to hunt and attend balls, but they thought they were poor and for the first time in his life Bertie was paying rent and had to earn a living. This was not easy for a man whose only work thus far had been a commission as a captain in the Territorial Army. But then he caught the political bug at a series of Conservative and Unionist Party meetings, at which he met the handsome young Conservative candidate for South Worcestershire, Commander Bolton Eyres-Monsell of Dumbleton Hall. Bertie became secretary of the local Tory-supporting membership mobilisation organisation, the Primrose

League, and campaigned for the commander's election – and became his secretary on £150 a year when he won the seat. Polly later claimed that this was the making of Bertie. Gone was the arrogant gentleman of leisure and in his place was a diligent, well-organised and rather sensitive public servant.

Then came a second family blow – albeit one shared by many thousands of other families. Bertie was thirty-eight when the war came, but he promptly rejoined the 1st Worcestershire Regiment and was soon made major and second in command. Nearly a fifth of officers were killed in the war, but despite long periods at the front, Bertie managed to get to May 1918 with little more than a severe bout of dysentery. At 5 a.m. on the first day of the battle of the Aisne, 27 May 1918, he and his men were in the support or 'travel' trench behind the front line between Pontavert and Berry-au-Bac when the Germans made their last concerted efforts to break through. The assault started with a mass barrage from 3,000 guns, and soon Bertie and his men were under attack on all sides: front, flank and rear. He dashed out of the dugout to give orders to some of his men. In the ensuing confusion his regimental sergeant major thought he saw Bertie being led away wounded, but a captain reported that a sudden barrage of shellfire killed him outright. Barbara later wrote with considerable pride, 'There was no surrender – all fought to the last. Bertram Cartland was killed in the trenches with his men.'[3] It was a story that stuck with Ronnie, who was just eleven and about to have his tonsils out when Polly received the news of her husband's death. Ronnie wrote in a touching letter to his mother, 'I feel so awfully proud of him and in a way it's lovely to remember him so young and cheery.'[4]

Bertie's death was not only a personal tragedy, it was also a financial one for the family, which was forced to fend for itself. Amerie Court had to go, and Polly, who was immensely resourceful, set up in business running a successful knitwear shop in Mayfair. Barbara proved just as entrepreneurial, as she started writing – first a racy high society novel with a fair amount of sexual innuendo, *Jig-Saw* (1923), then a column for the *Daily Express*, followed by risqué plays (one of which, *Blood Money*, was initially banned by the Lord Chamberlain) and 723 other titles before her death in 2000. As for young Ronnie, the family's travails made him extremely close to both Barbara and his mother. He loathed being parted from his mother in 1914 when he started boarding at Parkfield, a preparatory school in Haywards Heath, and wrote to her, 'I am so *very, very, very* depressed and I cry every evening and nearly every morning.' Yet he urged her, 'because I am depressed *you* won't get depressed, will you? Darling, *don't.*' When it came to chosing a public school, Ronnie secured a free place at Charterhouse in Surrey, thanks to a scholarship for the sons of former pupil war casualties and started in Lockites House in Oration (autumn) term 1920. This was a far older establishment than Haileybury, as it had been founded on the site of an old Carthusian monastery in London in 1611 and had moved to a more rural site near Godalming in 1872, but it was just as sexually charged. The writer Robert Graves, who attended the school a decade before Ronnie, claimed that its two chief interests were games and romantic friendships, and drew a distinction between 'amorousness', which he described as 'a sentimental falling in love with younger boys', and 'tarting', whereby 'boys of the same age, who were not in love, coldly used each other as convenient sex instruments'.[5] Graves was ambivalent about what he called 'homosexuality and pseudo-homosexuality' and got into trouble when he refused to abandon a crush on a handsome aristocratic younger boy, but it was clear that whatever your eventual sexual disposition in life, you had to learn to navigate the complex boundaries between sexual intimacy and sentimental crushes if you wanted to prosper.

Here too Ronnie missed his mother. 'Oh darling, it's beastly without you,' he wrote to her, adding, 'Why can't you always be with me?'[6] He was no great academic, so he was placed in the 'Modern' rather than the 'Classical' part of the school, which was designed to prepare boys for the armed forces or for a family firm rather than Oxford or Cambridge. He regularly came in the bottom half of the class, too, only ever excelling at English and history and coming last in maths. His form master in his first year repeatedly punished him for minor misdemeanours – 'Latin verbs not known', 'idle and frivolous' and 'imposition [punishment] not done' – but he knuckled down and became a monitor in 1924. In Oration term 1925 he was made head monitor of Lockites, although, as his own note in the house term-report records, he was out of action for the first four weeks of term as he had 'been the victim of a shooting accident in the holidays'.[7] There was an irony in this, as Ronnie won competitions at Bisley clay-pigeon-shooting ground and was captain of shooting. Yet while he was shooting partridge on a summer holiday with his mother and brother Tony at Dumbleton House, another young boy's gun went off just a yard away from him and Ronnie received the entire charge in his leg. He was carried back to the house on a gate and from there to a hospital in Cheltenham. A surgeon had to remove a large chunk of bone along with several hundred pellets, which left him in hospital for weeks and on crutches for the rest of the term. The accident depressed him and yet again he turned to his mother, writing that he was a perfect fool because he so hated leaving her.

Ronnie's one other great interest at Charterhouse was the debating society, at which he regularly adopted the maverick stance that would become such a noted part of his adult career. Despite his Conservative upbringing, he wrote to his mother in 1924 that he had been talking to some of the men working on the road nearby and that they had convinced him 'that Socialism is the right policy' and a few months later he supported the motion 'this House deplores the temporary defeat of the Labour Government', pointing out that 'Socialism was not Communism'.[8] His housemaster, Mr Wilson, was not impressed. 'If he can curb his revolutionary tendencies I expect him to do well,' he wrote in Ronnie's end-of-term report.[9] But Ronnie was not to be dissuaded from stirring things up and he apparently brought the house down in two further speeches in which he opposed prohibition and told his fellow pupils they were not fit for a manure heap. As the school magazine, the *Carthusian*, reported, 'He said we were soaked in a rotten tradition, the result of which was the late war ... We were stagnating, were liars and uneducated. He concluded by an attack on marriage.'[10] Evidently he was quite prepared to take on all comers. As later events would prove, he never feared saying what he believed, even if it lost him friends.

Thanks to his modest educational success and the poor state of family finances, university was out of the question, so Polly and Barbara tried to call in favours from old family friends, including the retired director of the Hong Kong trading company Jardine Matheson and Co., William Jardine Gresson, who told a fellow director that Ronnie was 'rather above ordinary intelligence'. That led to a recommendation that Ronnie should be considered 'before outsiders' as 'the youngster is evidently from a good family'[11] but when no job materialised, Polly secured an introduction to Sir Harold Snagge from her socialite friend the Countess of Rothes, which did lead to an offer from another trading house, Edward Boustead & Co. of Singapore, for whom Ronnie started work as a cashier after leaving Charterhouse at Christmas in 1925. The expectation was that he would undergo three years' training before moving to Singapore, but politics began to get in the way the moment he started work the following March, as he came home from his first visit to the House of Commons brimming with excitement and an ambition to be an MP.

Then came the general strike of 1926 – and another accident. A friend called Geoffrey Pritchett gave Ronnie a lift on his motorbike and as they were crossing Westminster Bridge a car swerved so close to them that Ronnie instinctively drew in his long legs. His foot got caught in the spokes and his heel was sheared off. Doctors sewed it back on, but he walked with a limp for the rest of his life. It did bring a piece of good luck, though, as he was sent to recuperate at the Priory, the house of his wealthy, unmarried great-uncle Major Howard Cartland. There he met and impressed the affable Irish MP for Birmingham Moseley,

Patrick Hannon, whom he heard speak at a public meeting in Paddington that September. A week later Ronnie joined the Young Conservatives, and through Hannon he met another MP, Sir Henry Page Croft, who offered him a job working for the Empire Industries Association, based in Birmingham, starting in January. Ronnie resigned from Boustead, packed his bags and went to live with his great-uncle again, but the job proved to be less engaging than he had hoped, and he found himself irritably kicking his heels. He wrote to Polly, 'I am too hatefully depressed – but I think it's only lack of work at the moment and being away from you.'[12] Finally, another chance meeting led to another job offer. He had met the director of education at Conservative Central Office, Colonel H. F. Williams, on a London bus and in March he accepted a post as his personal secretary and assistant director of the department, based in London.

So, on 4 April 1927 Ronnie turned up for work at Palace Chambers in Westminster, the home of the Conservative Party. It was a big change. Politics fascinated him. He wanted to change the world. He hoped to be an MP one day. And the work was absorbing. But London was new to him and full of opportunity. He knew his way round country life: he was a good shot, he liked riding with the hounds and he regularly attended hunt balls. His mother knew all the great Worcestershire families, too, especially the Eyres-Monsells, who continued to be generous with invites to Dumbleton House. But Ronnie now found himself on the fringes of a select social circle, largely courtesy of his sister Barbara. Lively, generous, flirtatious and 'admitted to be one of the prettiest girls and best dancers in London',[13] she was already a successful gossip columnist and novelist, but just weeks after Ronnie started work at Palace Chambers, she married Captain Alexander 'Sachie' McCorquodale in a grand society wedding at St Margaret's, Westminster. The marriage proved to be unhappy, but it was certainly advantageous, as her father-in-law owned a profitable printing firm, a house in Belgrave Square, the magnificent Cound Hall in Shropshire and a shooting lodge in Orkney – all of which was due to come to Sachie as the sole son and heir. Barbara knew how to work the scene, too. She posed for *The Sketch*, a high-society magazine, reading proofs of a new book at her new home off Park Lane and in a swimsuit on board her husband's yacht *Njala* off Orkney. She opened a hat shop in Albermarle Street called Barbara, she organised 'Empire balls', a Hallowe'en 'pageant of the superstitions' at the Dorchester, a Christmas pageant at the Kit-Cat Club and a charity performance of a musical for the Middlesex Hospital with a cast consisting almost entirely of aristocrats. Invitations flowed to and fro for dinners, fancy-dress parties, champagne suppers, coming-out balls and country-house weekends, as Barbara joined the ranks of London's society hostesses alongside the likes of Nancy Astor, Sibyl Colefax and Emerald Cunard.

Her early books also strayed a long way from the moral conventions of the day. Yes, her heroines tended to find true love with improbably strapping heroes. But they were highly sexed women with a sense of their own destiny and Barbara clearly enjoyed writing paragraphs like the following from *For What?*, published in 1930:

> His nature had been pent up for so many years. He had repressed and subdued his feelings with the sternness of Scottish reserve; but, like a volcano, they had erupted into an overwhelming passion and with a force that he could not control. He wanted Diana, and he meant to have her.

Barbara was no prude. She wrote wry and naughty copy for *Bystander* under the pseudonyms 'Miss Hamilton' or 'Caviare', she turned out gossipy pieces for *Tatler* as 'Miss Scot' and passed on titbits of society news as 'Miss Tudor' in the *Daily Mail*. The copy she filed was invariably bubbly and enthusiastic with no hint of the prim coyness that was so common at the time. Her advice to young women in her book of modern morals, *Touch the Stars: A Clue to Happiness*, was remarkable:

Remember that you are not a miserable sinner ... Nor were you born in original sin; the sex instinct is one of the most beautiful things in the world. It is sent to inspire us, and to help us understand Nature and the workings of the Divine. It is the nearest approach we get to the beauty, the intensity and the power of Life.[14]

The West End was scattered with venues that promoted such ambivalence, if you could afford it. Most famous of all was Oscar Wilde's favourite, the Café Royal on Regent Street, with its ostentatious woodwork and bare-breasted caryatids supporting the painted ceiling. Here the 'conversation was easy, lewd and loud'[15] as Cedric Morris and Lett, along with other artists, writers and 'aesthetes' dined, caroused and bitched with like-minded MPs and peers − and flirted with one another over glasses of absinthe. A few paces away stood the most sumptuous place to dine, dance or hold a reception, the Hotel Splendide in Piccadilly. Gennaro's Rendezvous in nearby Dean Street was famous for its beautiful waiters, 'who were carefully selected by the flamboyant old proprietor during holidays back in his native Italy',[16] in Wardour Street there was its French counterpart Chez Victor, and in Bury Street there was Quaglino's, where Barbara once found a real pearl in her oyster. On the Fitzrovia side of Oxford Street there was the favourite restaurant of the wealthy queer MP Sir Philip Sassoon, the Tour Eiffel at 1 Percy Street, where Rudolph Stulik, the former chef to Lord Kitchener (who in addition to being war secretary in the First World War and the face behind the 'Your Country Needs You' recruitment posters was widely rumoured to be homosexual), welcomed artists, writers and politicians and covered the walls in paintings proffered in exchange for free meals. The smartest of all was Boulestin, the creation of the French writer, interior designer and restaurateur Marcel Boulestin, which was financed and decorated by Cedric and Lett's wealthy textile designer and manufacturer friend Allan Walton. From the moment it opened its doors in Leicester Square in 1925,[17] it was reckoned to be the most expensive eatery in London, yet Marcel only managed to keep it afloat by writing books about French cookery (one of which was illustrated by Cedric) and appearing on the BBC's first cookery programmes. He wrote the scandalous homosexual novel, *Les Fréquentations de Maurice*, and counted Oscar Wilde's lover Lord Alfred Douglas as a friend and Cecil Beaton as a regular customer. Most importantly, from 1923 until his death in 1943 Marcel's constant companion and literary collaborator was Arthur 'Robin' Adair; and the two men offered an especially warm reception to those in the know.

If you wanted more than just dinner, there was the voluminous Kit-Cat Club in the basement of the Capitol Cinema on the Haymarket, which was the first venue in London designed specifically as a dance club. Here polite society delighted in risqué performances. Sophie Tucker, 'the last of the red hot Mammas', would slink round the tables and sit on men's laps, Ella Retford sang her camp signature song, 'All the Nice Girls Love a Sailor', and the French singer Alice Delysia, who regularly attracted the attention of the Lord Chamberlain for her revealing outfits, launched into Coward's 'Poor Little Rich Girl'.* When the cabaret was over, hundreds of single young men in evening dress took to the floor with the crop-haired androgynous flappers.

For later-night entertainment there was the Blue Lantern in Ham Yard, where the red-headed actress Tallulah Bankhead, who was described as a 'symbol of sexual liberation for young women',[18] sipped cocktails and composer Hugh Wade played old wartime tunes on the piano, accompanied by drums and a saxophone, while 'painted and twittering young men' crowded the dance floor. Jocelyn Brooke, who began his autobiography with the words 'at the age of six I was, like most normally constituted children, a polymorphous pervert', pointed out the Blue Lantern anomaly that the young men's dancing partners, 'though technically of the female sex (for the Lantern was rather

---

* She was reported to have told Coward, when he tried to give the song to another actress, 'You are a *sheet* and a *boogair.*'

fussy about such conventions), appeared for the most part to be a good deal more virile than their cavaliers'.[19] Next door to the Blue Lantern was the 'chronically Bohemian'[20] Hambone, where the lesbian writer Radclyffe Hall, the impecunious but aristocratic antiquarian Eddie Gathorne-Hardy, his housemate the 'aesthetic bugger'[21] Brian Howard and the writer Evelyn Waugh were members.

Nowhere was more enticingly ambivalent, though, than the Gargoyle Club, which David Tennant, one of the sons of Lord Glenconner, opened in Dean Street in 1925. With its large dance floor and roof garden (accessed by a rickety lift), the Gargoyle gave off an air of 'mystery suffused with a tender eroticism'[22] and became an instant success, hosting all-in wrestling sessions and fencing exhibitions in front of a smart crowd dressed in white tie and tails, who danced the night away. It boasted in its advertising that it had peers and 'modern Painters' on its distinguished list of members, and that 'from roof garden to ground floor of the club there is colour and design to please conservative and advanced taste'.[23] Its clientele included a large number of queer men, not least Tennant's brother Stephen, who was a lover of the much older Siegfried Sassoon until he suddenly broke off the relationship in 1933, leaving Sassoon distraught.

This was the London Ronnie came to in 1927. It was a city where select circles of very wealthy people guaranteed a relatively safe haven for queer men, if they were extremely discreet. Knowing repartee was allowed. When Somerset Maugham left one of Lady Emerald Cunard's dinner parties early, claiming, 'I have to keep my youth,' she swiftly replied, 'Then why didn't you bring him with you?'[24] That left many men who had queer friends outside that hallowed circle of discretion with a nagging fear that those 'two worlds might collide'.[25] But the rule was clear: keep them guessing and never make the implicit explicit.

At first Ronnie took a small bachelor flat at 2 Pont Street, near Belgrave Square, and he rapidly made so many new friends that he reckoned he could lunch and dine out practically every day of his life – if he had the money. It was at Dumbleton Hall that he first met the six-foot Welshman Jim Thomas,* who had just left Oxford with an aegrotat (an unclassified pass degree, due to illness) degree in French, but it was as work colleagues that they came to be close. Barbara later described Jim as 'good-looking, charming and intensely loyal'[26] and others reckoned that with his love of gossip and his gift as a raconteur he 'had a genius for friendship'.[27] There was something of the gentle patrician about him, as his father was a Justice of the Peace, his maternal grandfather was a commander in the Royal Navy and the family home in Llandeilo was a rambling manor house. He also had a large house of his own at 16 Great College Street near Westminster, where he enjoyed entertaining and hosting occasional lodgers like the lanky bisexual Alan Lennox-Boyd before Alan's marriage in 1938. Jim shared Ronnie's ambition to become an MP, so the two became instant friends, regularly visiting the theatre and music hall together and staying together with friends near the Malvern Hills. Jim also told everyone he would never marry and was more amused than embarrassed when Stanley Baldwin let out that a young MP had received three proposals of marriage following a sympathetic speech on maternal mortality. The press soon worked out that Jim was the MP in question. He commented drily, 'I have not *yet* replied to them,' in a way that suggested he never would.[28]

It was another bachelor work colleague, though, Antony Bulwer-Lytton, who, as eldest son and heir to the Earl of Lytton, was known by his courtesy title as Viscount Knebworth, who was to become Ronnie's closest friend. Just four years older than Ronnie, Antony had everything in life. His father was wealthy and well-connected. The architect Sir Edwin Lutyens was an uncle, Oscar Wilde dedicated *Lady Windermere's Fan* to his grandfather, his great-grandfather was one of the Victorians' favourite writers, and the poet Byron was a distant forebear. Ronnie might have envied

* James Purdon Lewes Thomas, not to be confused with the Labour and latterly National Labour MP James Henry Thomas.

Antony's easy and conventional career pattern of Eton, Oxford and the City, but Antony was a man of complex, wavering and often exhilarating passions. When his father became Governor of Bengal and took the rest of the family to India, he confessed a real sense of depression. 'All my boy friends,' he wrote, 'dont [*sic*] quite fill the gap. They're wonderful when one is gay; they're splendid people to have fun with, and they'd do anything for you when you're down and out, but when you're just depressed you dont really want sympathy or help.'[29] He suffered considerable mood swings, claiming that he was 'always drunk, not constantly, but always' with the sun, with excitement, with happiness, with an idea. Sometimes depression itself intoxicated him and he admitted that, 'A little dissipation I also like at intervals. It is my nature.'[30] His older friend, the writer A. A. Milne, claimed that he had 'never heard a more glorious laugh in man or boy; it overfilled him', but Antony agonised that there was something of Dr Jekyll and Mr Hyde about him, as he wrote to his mother about his mixed feelings about relations with women: 'I come here [Oxford], where I get no female society and only my men friends, and then all I want to do is to dash off to London and fall in love with an actress!' He was deeply conflicted. 'I have met so few girls who I really think anything of,' he wrote. 'I sometimes get attracted to them, because they're pretty, but the attraction is always accompanied by a feeling of deep humiliation at caring about anything which is so worthless – which in my heart of hearts I feel infinitely superior to.'[31]

Knebworth loved the fast life and enjoyed his fair share of bright young things high jinks. He was also a keen competitive boxer, who boxed for Oxford, won several welterweight championships, trained at the gym four evenings a week and published a well-illustrated guide to the sport. Considered one of the best skiers in Europe, he made regular appearances on the slopes at Mürren in Switzerland, including one occasion when he competed in a race hosted by Lady Denman in drag as 'Martha Mainwaring', much to the amusement of the *Daily Mirror*.

By the time Ronnie arrived at Palace Chambers, Knebworth had fixed his eyes on a political career, hence his working in the education department at Conservative Central Office. He and Ronnie hit it off immediately and became inseparable, dining out together (largely at Antony's expense), turning up late to Barbara's parties, dancing together as the 'gladdest people there'[32] and then returning to Antony's Mayfair home, where they argued about politics late into the night. They had much in common. When Antony stood for the Conservatives in the Labour stronghold of Shoreditch in the 1929 general election, Ronnie spent every day of the campaign by his side. Ronnie held Antony's coat when he defeated a local police constable in a boxing match as part of the electoral contest – and cheered 'Good Old Nebby' along with the rest of the crowd.[33] Although they were both committed Conservatives, they distrusted the tribal nature of partisan politics, too, as Antony reckoned that the Shoreditch Labour Party people were much nicer than their Conservative counterparts.

They shared something else. Barbara Cartland destroyed her brother's papers not long before she died, but even from what she quoted from his diaries it is possible to detect his ambiguous and ambivalent feelings about sex. Ronnie was overtly religious and some of his letters come across as pious, yet in 1926 he told his diary that *The Constant Nymph* was the best play he had seen that year. Based on a best-selling novel by Margaret Kennedy, this opened in September 1926 at the New Theatre with Noël Coward and Edna Best in the leads. Coward was already famed for his sexually explicit play *Vortex* and the caustic comedy *Hay Fever*, but *The Constant Nymph* portrayed the tragic story of Tessa Sanger, who falls in love with her father's composer friend Lewis Dodd, with whom she elopes after he has married a respectable socialite who had little interest in his music. The message was clear. Yes, marriage could be sensible, respectable and safe, but a relationship based on free love, spontaneity and art was infinitely preferable – whatever society might say. Ronnie thought it magnificent. It appealed to the daring, extravagant side of his personality, which he could not always keep in check.

This same ambivalence afflicted Knebworth, who entered into a long correspondence with Stanley Baldwin's fiercely independent second son, Windham, known as 'Willow', about the supposedly pernicious 'tendency in modern thought' exemplified by Coward and the young wealthy American socialite Chips Channon, both of whom were closeted homosexuals. Like every loyal Conservative, Antony enjoyed Coward's patriotic extravaganza *Cavalcade*, which premiered just before the general election in 1931, but when he went with his sister Davina to Coward's 1932 satirical revue *Words and Music*, which includes the songs 'Mad Dogs and Englishmen' and 'Mad About the Boy' (which Coward conceived of as possibly being sung by a man), he questioned whether Coward was a good influence on society or 'even a great artist'. One can only speculate on what his sister Davina meant when she said as they left the theatre, 'But he's on your side.'[34] Or what Antony meant when he wrote to Willow: 'We don't have to kill [the dragon]. Well, in my vain way, I have been at it a long time. I have felt its fiery breath, and the awful deadening weight of its body, and the slimy cold sickly feel of its skin. It has had me down, as I say, many times.'[35] It is difficult to tell whether this was an abhorrence of anything sexual or a specific rejection of Coward and Channon's breezy private nonchalance about homosexuality, but it is clear that Antony felt he was wrestling with dark forces.

Antony was not the only young unmarried aristocrat in Ronnie's life. His other closest friend, George Lionel Seymour Dawson-Damer, Viscount Carlow, was the son and heir of the 6th Earl of Portarlington. He too so loathed convention that he left the Grenadier Guards after a couple of years and joined the Auxiliary Air Force, prompting his mother to have a nervous breakdown with the shame, because she thought airmen 'were thought of as such fast-living, irresponsible young men'.[36] Carlow's son, the 7th Earl, says that 'Ronnie and my father were always each other's "number one friends"'.[37] Although he claimed that his father actively disliked the social whirl and was teetotal, Carlow regularly appeared with Ronnie at society occasions listed in the *Court Circular*, and *Bystander* told its readers that it had spotted the two of them at Quaglino's restaurant, sipping 'a geranium-coloured liquid', a cocktail of orange juice, water and grenadine apparently invented by Carlow.[38]

Bystander's unnamed source was Barbara, who delighted in including naughty in-jokes in her column. At one point she told the world that Barbara McCorquodale (i.e. she herself) had been warmly congratulated at a party on completing the first long-distance glider-tow in Britain. She repeatedly teased her brother's close friends, too. She included Knebworth in a whole page article devoted to portraits of six young eligible men headlined as 'Bachelors All'.[39] A few months later she wrote that 'in spite of tactical advance and heavy barrage, a great number of eligible bachelors are still at large', and noted that, 'Lord Carlow still prefers aeroplanes to matrimony [and] Lord Knebworth is politically-minded.'[40] She larded them with praise. She thought Knebworth 'the cleverest man in Mayfair' and Carlow 'the most difficult to meet'.[41] She listed Knebworth's 'attractiveness' as one of the few things in life she would never want to alter and predicted a great political and social future for him before adding, 'Note: I think him very attractive.'[42] Ronnie would have smiled when he read that. He probably agreed.

Ronnie loved the daredevil in Carlow and often stayed the night with him at his family house in Chesham Place in Belgravia, so it seemed the most natural thing in the world that when Carlow eventually married Peggy Cambie from Toronto in 1937, Ronnie was his best man. True to his unruly nature, Carlow insisted that the wedding should be as unconventional as possible. The guest list was limited to barely sixty people and no photographs were allowed – although *The Times* reported that Peggy wore 'a gown of oyster-tinted satin, with a swathed neckline, and the corsage and bell sleeves embroidered with the satin in a lattice design. Her veil of tulle was weighted at the foot with an inset of old family lace, and held in place by a wreath of miniature arum lilies and green leaves.'[43] A few weeks later Barbara complained anonymously in *Bystander*, 'Lord Carlow never gets in a photograph; even at his wedding he avoided it.'[44] As for Ronnie, when I asked the 7th Earl of Portarlington whether I could ask him an indelicate question, he replied: 'You're going to ask whether my father was homosexual. I certainly don't know that he was – after all, he died when I was just seven – but I can tell you this: his best man, his best friend Ronnie, well, he certainly was.'[45]

One other bachelor became particularly close to Ronnie, the eclectic philosopher, sculptor, teacher, Arabist, journalist and author Rom Landau, who made a strong impression on him when they met at a dinner party in 1928. Ronnie wrote to Polly that they spent an evening together dining at Chez Taghoni, catching a terrible play and going on to the Nightlight and Chez Victor, another French bar/restaurant in Soho that was popular with actors, artists and queer men. 'Mr. Landau,' he wrote, 'said I am one of the few young Englishmen he has met whom he considers really interesting – wants to meet again.'[46] Nothing came of that first encounter, but Ronnie and Carlow bumped into Landau at *Parsifal* at Covent Garden the following year, and Ronnie immediately reignited the friendship. Born in Poland and educated in Germany, Rom travelled extensively in North Africa and the Middle East and espoused a quixotic blend of Christianity, psychiatry, spiritualism and mysticism. His bestselling book *God is My Adventure* (1935) was a series of pen portraits of 'modern mystics, masters and teachers', which he admitted might be construed as 'sacrilegious'.[47] His belief in the 'creative power of a self-conscious Creator' attracted Ronnie, as did his injunction that 'the road to truth and thus to God is shortest when we search for Him within ourselves'.[48] Ronnie also agreed with his critical assessment of the new 'Aryan Gods' of Nazi Germany, as he thought most people would find the 'arbitrary and fantastic deductions' of the self-appointed 'cultural leader of the Nazi Party' Alfred Rosenberg (who was head of the Nazi Party's Foreign Policy Office) to be 'perversions' and 'too childish for serious consideration'.[49] But Rom had another attraction. He was handsome, in an intense, moustachioed way;

he had learned to be very relaxed about homosexuality on his regular visits to Morocco; and after the Second World War he would become a passionate advocate of homosexual law reform. Even in the thirties, though, he asked quite openly whether people's 'sex instinct' had to be regulated according to the conventions in which they had been brought up. Ronnie liked having such a sexually liberal father confessor.

These early years in London were exciting, but Ronnie was living way beyond his means and was constantly asking his family for help. The job at Conservative Central Office was never secure or well paid, and he was socialising with friends who had considerable private incomes. He was enjoying life, though, and was at least half in love with his bachelor friends. Quite often he would spend his whole day in the sole company of other men, at work in Palace Chambers, reading in the Travellers Club, sipping cocktails at Quaglino's, dining at Boulestin, taking in a late-night drink at Chez Victor or the Hambone and going home to his bachelor's apartment. It was a social coterie that blurred boundaries. Neither social nor sexual distinctions seemed to matter too much, as respectable scions of the nobility rubbed shoulders with louche libertines. Ronnie was too earnest for some of their antics and plenty of people condemned such ostentatious hedonism, including a Labour MP who demanded that the recently appointed Commission for Lunacy enquire into 'this exhibition of smart set imbecility'.[50] Yet Ronnie appreciated that his milieu was discreetly relaxed about homosexuality. Even the prime minister's wife, Lucy Baldwin, could joke that the Earl Winterton was in danger of 'becoming another Nancy' and greet Bob Boothby with the words, 'Still a fairy?' when he had just returned from Aix-les-Bains.[51] There were frustrations in this world of deliberate ambiguity. You could jest about fairies and nancies, you could camp it up, but you absolutely had to maintain the fiction that this was all just a joke, because homosexuality was, at best, tolerated in select society and there was always the threat of exposure. In certain circles you could let your guard down a bit, but you knew full well the dangers of a misplaced sign of affection and it took immense courage to open your heart to another man in private, let alone cause anyone else to suspect anything untoward. It was frustrating – a life half lived – but you had to keep yourself to yourself, hence the desperate and often futile attempts to repress same-sexual feelings. Sometimes these found a tortuous expression in highly charged bromances, but as often as not these relationships remained sexually unfulfilled. No wonder so many men ended their days in sterile, loveless marriages or enforced loneliness. That must have been Ronnie's hidden fear. He was sociable and he was in with the 'in crowd', but he was never fully part of it. At times that left him feeling maudlin, but more often he sought a role where he could be himself – and his heart was fixed on being an MP.

3

Berlin – the Perverts' Paradise

On the evening of Sunday 23 October 1927 Harold Nicolson settled into his luxurious Pullman carriage at Liverpool Street station on the boat train to Harwich. He was forty-one and although his hair, which he washed with an expensive shampoo from Floris, was slightly receding, he looked younger than his age. He had small, gentle, sleepy eyes and a fashionably clipped moustache. In his pocket was an effusive letter from his wife, Vita, and in his suitcase was a smart new set of clothes he had bought for the posting he was about to take up as chargé d'affaires at the British Embassy in Berlin. Harold had a habit of worrying. After eighteen years in the diplomatic service, his career had hit the buffers when he was sacked for publicly criticising his superior in Tehran, and although he had already published half-a-dozen well-received books, he feared it might all end in failure. He had adored Tehran, the city where he was born in 1886 as the third son of the British chargé Arthur Nicolson, and he hated the very idea of Berlin. He had been demoted and he thought the city was downright ugly. But it did have one undoubted attraction. It was, in the words of the artist Wyndham Lewis, 'the Perverts' Paradise'[1] – and despite his marriage, Harold was predominantly homosexual.

True, Paragraph 175 of the German Reich's Criminal Code still prohibited homosexuality, but Berlin enjoyed a carnival of emancipation, as its Social Democratic Prussian government instructed the police to turn a blind eye and give homosexual venues official licences, enabling more than 130 bars, cafés, nightclubs and Turkish baths to cater for virtually every sexual taste – and every pocket. There was the Salomé, painted gold and inferno-red with 'crimson plush inches thick, and vast golden mirrors';[2] the Karls-Lounge, where the staff dressed as sailors; the Café Olala, where Salvation Army uniforms were preferred; the Silhouette, with its intimate private boxes for male transvestites; and the Mikado for females dressed as men. There was the Eldorado, where, under the watchful eye of its owner and impresario, Ludwig Konjetschni, transvestite hostesses served pink champagne and elaborate cocktails while bisexual and lesbian singers like Marlene Dietrich and Claire Waldoff performed sexually explicit songs, and where the clientele was as louche, debauched or artistic (depending on your outlook) as the staff. In one corner would be a gaggle of men wearing make-up, immaculately fashionable frocks, coquettish hats and strings of pearls. In another, 'monocled, Eton-cropped girls in dinner jackets play-acted the high jinks of Sodom and Gomorrah'.[3] Thanks to the telephones on every table at the Rhezi, if you fancied someone on the other side of the room you could dial their number and arrange to meet.

The Salomé and the Eldorado were expensive, but for those who preferred something less pretentious, there was Noster's Restaurant zur Hütte in the rough, working-class district of Hallesches Tor. Noster's, which was known as the 'Cosy Corner' by many British visitors, hardly reeked of decadence. If anything, it was plain and homely, with a vast old-fashioned iron stove and photographs of toned boxers and cyclists pinned up above the bar. Here, unemployed working-class young men sat around waiting for a pick-up with their shirts unbuttoned to the navel and their sleeves rolled up to the armpits, 'partly because of the great heat of the stove, partly because they knew it excited their clients'.[4] As the Jewish Austrian novelist Stefan Zweig put it, 'in the dimly-lit bars one might see government officials and men of the world of finance tenderly courting drunken sailors without any shame'.[5] Some, in the words of the British eccentric Gerald Hamilton, 'hoped to meet their destiny at such places'.[6] Others just wanted to lose themselves in the pleasure of uninhibited sexual freedom.

Berlin shone out as a beacon of permissiveness. It was a place for young men to experiment, discover and embrace their homosexuality and maybe even find the love of their life. As two of Harold's friends, the young writer Christopher Isherwood and the schoolmaster and poet Wystan Auden put it, the city was 'a bugger's daydream' and 'Berlin meant boys'.[7] And, as Harold rapidly discovered, it attracted large numbers of wealthy foreigners who came to enjoy a sexual freedom that was denied them at home.

Harold was no stranger to such liberty. He and Vita Sackville-West, the daughter of Lord and Lady Sackville, had married in October 1913. Two sons, Ben and Nigel, had followed in 1914 and 1917. But by the time Harold took up residence at No. 24 Brücken Allee, their marriage had become extremely elastic, as both of them enjoyed several homosexual affairs. They were quite open with one another about their liaisons. Harold enjoyed one-off sexual encounters, brief liaisons and longer affairs with many clever and wealthy young men, including Emerald Cunard's nephew Victor, Tray Mortimer, Edward Molyneux, James Pope-Hennessy, James Lees-Milne and many others. He was very unapologetic with Vita. When he met the lascivious and aristocratic French painter Jean de Gaigneron, who introduced him to Marcel Proust and Jean Cocteau while he was in Paris in 1921 researching a biography of the homosexual poet Paul Verlaine,* he asked Vita to arrange for de Gaigneron 'to sleep at Hill Street with me (!!)' on the implausible grounds that he was 'a nice friend' and he knew 'all the clevers'.[8] On another occasion he confessed that he might have caught a sexually transmitted disease from another man when he and Vita were staying at Knebworth House along with the socialite Osbert Sitwell and Winston Churchill's longstanding private secretary, the high-pitched, immaculate and monocled patron of the

---

* He made no mention of Verlaine's sexuality in the book.

arts Eddie Marsh, both of whom were homosexual. Without a murmur of apology, Harold wrote to Vita about his impending medical tests, 'I haven't the courage to face it all.'[9]

Vita also had several passionate affairs, most notably with an old school friend, Violet Keppel, with whom she eloped to France on several occasions, leaving the children with her mother and Harold in distress. This relationship continued even after Violet's marriage in 1919 to Denys Trefusis, who improbably signed up to a dubiously legal pre-marriage agreement that he would never require her to have sex with him. Another of Vita's conquests, Pat Dansey, referred to her with some bitterness as 'a romantic young man who treats his women badly', and even her son Nigel reckoned that 'her only problem was to free herself of one love affair in order to begin the next'.[10] She admitted as much to Harold. 'Wild oats are all very well,' she wrote, 'but not when they grow as high as a jungle.'[11]

At times things got very catty. Vita complained that Harold was too fast as a lover and one of Harold's bachelor friends, Oswald Dickinson, gossiped about the most intimate aspects of their marriage. Yet Lady Sackville believed that Vita was absolutely devoted to Harold but not in the least bit jealous of him. The couple both told her that Vita 'willingly allows him to relieve himself with anyone if such is his want or his fancy'.[12] This latitude enabled their relationship to survive many bouts of turbulence and their lengthy correspondence shows the couple had a deep and enduring affection for one another. They supported each other's literary endeavours, they gave each other space and they created a beautiful home in Sissinghurst, which eventually rivalled Vita's own childhood home, Knole Park. The only rule was that nothing should ever become a public scandal. Vita's mother wrote, 'It is nobody's business to know our private lives ... the less said about it the better. Silence is wiser.'[13] But they were so adept at keeping up appearances that in 1929 they even got away with broadcasting a BBC *Discussion on Marriage*.

Such permissiveness was not always plain sailing. The need for secrecy meant both Harold and Vita were susceptible to bouts of self-loathing and double standards. Harold could be judgemental about others. On his first visit to the Eldorado he failed to spot that a bunch of hearty old men in plus fours were women and wrote snootily to Vita, 'I was rather shocked and disgusted; these people danced together.'[14] Vita's reply showed that she was having none of it, though. She knew her husband was protesting too much. 'Please get compromised,' she replied, 'and then you'll be removed from Berlin.'[15] Likewise, when Vita's homosexual cousin Eddy Sackville-West came to stay with him in Berlin for the first time, Harold fretted that Eddy was so flamboyant that 'what remains of my reputation will be gone for ever'.[16] Vita could be just as rude. She complained that she had seen Eddy 'mincing in black velvet' at Knole. As she put it, rather unconvincingly, 'I don't object to homosexuality but I do hate decadence. And it is a nasty fungoid growth on Knole of all places.'[17] On another occasion she complained that Victor Cunard was little more than 'a nice, easy, pleasant, ineffectual little thing' and added, 'What contempt one has, *au fond*, for the Victors, Eddie Marshes and Ozzies [Dickinson] of this world.'[18]

So, too, Harold maintained that 'the idea of a gentleman of birth and education sleeping with a guardsman is repugnant to me'.[19] Yet during his posting in Tehran he had complained to Tray Mortimer that Turkish baths only existed there 'in a degraded and highly dangerous form'[20] and that he was feeling 'rather restless in the sex way', as there was nowhere safe to 'rest his head'.[21] Likewise, when Vita visited Harold briefly in Berlin — she did not accompany him on his diplomatic postings — she reported to another lover, the novelist Virginia Woolf, that she had been to 'the sodomites' ball', at which a lot of them were dressed as women, although she fancied she was 'the only genuine article in the room'. She summed up, 'There are certainly very queer things to be seen in Berlin, and I think [Harold] will enjoy himself.'[22]

Harold claimed that he felt homesick, but he hosted a string of queer friends — many of them lovers. Noël Coward turned up in February 1928, followed by the equally successful young

Welshman Ivor Davies, who had struck up a close friendship with Eddie Marsh and had taken part of his mother's maiden name for his stage name, Novello. Coward claimed that 'the two most beautiful things in the world are Ivor's profile and my mind'[23] and Harold wrote gushing letters about Ivor to Vita, though he declared himself sceptical when Ivor claimed Marsh had never attempted even to stroke his hair. The truth was that sex was definitely in the air. When Gladwyn Jebb, who had worked with Harold in the embassy in Tehran, stayed, Harold thought him 'a little too heterosexual even for me'[24] and was amused when Ivor made an unsuccessful pass at him. But when the Countess of Drogheda appeared with her eighteen-year-old son Garrett Moore, who had been the page at Harold and Vita's wedding, Harold was besotted with his 'amazing beauty', telling Vita 'you can't imagine the charm and beauty of that young man', whom he declared 10 per cent more attractive even than the chisel-jawed soldier, fencer and artist, Ian Campbell-Gray.[25]

Living up to his billing, Eddy Sackville-West wrote to his friend Molly that he had had a 'very wild' time with Harold over Christmas and New Year at the end of 1927 and gave his friend, the novelist and academic E. M. Forster, more intimate details, claiming that he was dragged about at night from one homosexual bar to another and that the behaviour was so open that 'there are even large dance halls for inverts'. He spent a pleasurable night with a twenty-year-old Lithuanian peasant, who was covered with mother-of-pearl buttons and was so passionately interested in revolvers that he insisted on taking one to bed and slowly loading its six chambers. Despite this, Eddy said he was not frightened by this 'very beautiful creature [who] was very friendly & charming'.[26] New Year's Eve at the *Ball der Jugend* (Vita's 'sodomites ball') was equally riotous. 'At midnight lights went on & off, paper streamers became like a wild entanglement, the champagne was filled with falling confetti. I was kissed indiscriminately … the night passed like a dream.'[27] On another occasion Eddy went dancing at the Silhouette with a wealthy, good-looking man from one of the best families in Cologne. Harold commented that when they danced together 'the powder from Eddy's cheek came off white on the man's strong black arm'.[28] Eddy also admitted that smart, chic, Embassy Club nightlife depressed him, as he liked it all 'rather squalid and furtive'[29] – and Berlin offered plenty of that.

Harold's other guests during his two-year stay read like a catalogue of Britain's wealthy homosexuals: Lord Berners was an early visitor, as was the poet Edward James, whose marriage to an Austrian dancer collapsed in 1934 under the weight of his homosexuality. In May the impecunious literary critic Cyril Connolly made the first of several visits, returning in August with Tray Mortimer and later with David Herbert, the second son of the Earl of Pembroke, who was briefly Coward's housemate and was cruelly nicknamed the 'Queen of Tangier' by Ian Fleming. Soon other Etonians followed Connolly. The first thing Henry 'Chips' Channon did when he arrived at the Hotel Adlon with his friend Viscount Gage was demand that Harold take them round the cabarets, though Harold objected that he didn't like 'other people's vices'.[30] Another friend, the handsome 28-year-old Conservative MP Bob Boothby, was so enamoured of the city, which he too described as 'Paradise',[31] that he provided 'addresses and letters of introduction' to two fellow Oxford students, Maurice Bowra and John Sparrow, who arrived in September 1928. The nature of their visit was made plain by Bowra's letter to Sparrow in which he asked whether they should take two rooms or one, as two 'might be better if we were to introduce guests late at night. But perhaps one takes them elsewhere.'[32] Bowra was to become a very regular visitor to Berlin. In 1929 he and Sparrow met up with Nicolson and Boothby and another Tory, Duff Cooper, who had just lost his seat in Parliament. Bowra complained that Harold and Duff had shown too many 'ties with respectability', but he declared the whole visit 'a *succès fou*' and resolved to return for the New Year.[33] On another visit with Duff Cooper in August 1930 the two of them met up with another friend, Adrian Bishop, who was far more openly homosexual and proved 'most generous in the matter of boy friends'.[34]

Such openness was extraordinary for its time, but Berlin offered liberation to many men who had been forced to hide their true nature back in England. They threw themselves into the maelstrom of sexual opportunity with abandon. Harold Nicolson had to maintain a degree of respectability as a British diplomat, but he and his friends exploited their moment of freedom to the full, in the knowledge that eventually they would have to return home to England.

Early Nazis relished this freedom, too, including a five-foot, five-inches tall, bull-necked 42-year-old German with a scar where half his nose had been shot off in the Great War, who took up almost nightly residence at the Eldorado not long after Nicolson returned to England. Although the man had been away from Germany for two years, his name, Ernst Röhm, was well known to the staff, as he had been a regular before he accepted a job training soldiers for the Bolivian army in 1928.

He had returned home at the express insistence of his friend, Adolf Hitler, who had just won ninety-five additional seats in the federal elections, making the National Socialist People's Party (the NSDAP) the second-largest party in the Reichstag for the first time. The two men had first met in Munich in 1919. Never shy of violence, Röhm had played a key role in the brutal but unsuccessful Beer Hall Putsch in 1923, when Hitler and his henchmen had violently attempted to seize control of Munich, and although they had fallen out in 1925, Röhm had contemptuously refused to answer questions the following year from a Reichstag Committee about his role in the 'Feme'* murder of the waitress Maria Sandmeyer back in 1920. For both offences he proudly spent time in Stadelheim prison. Aware of Röhm's capacity for violence and his ability to inspire devoted loyalty from his men, Hitler now wanted to put him in charge

---

* *Feme*: an ultra-right-wing paramilitary group set up in 1920s Germany to punish 'traitors', based on the *Feme* – or *Vehmegerichte* (vigilante courts) – of Westphalia in the Middle Ages.

of the paramilitary wing of the Nazi party, his *Sturmabteilung*, the Nazis' brown-shirted SA or Stormtroopers, a role Röhm had always coveted.

Many would have been surprised to see Röhm at the Eldorado, though. The Nazi Party, after all, publicly abhorred homosexuality. They saw it as a stain on German morality and a threat to the Aryan race, and they opposed any attempt to reform Paragraph 175. When the first German film to show same-sex relationships in a positive light, *Anders als die Andern* (*Different from the Others*), was released in 1919, the Nazis violently forced cinemas that showed it to close, and the following year they beat its author, Magnus Hirschfeld, so ferociously that he was initially pronounced dead by the police. Likewise they protested against the Hamburg production of Ferdinand Bruckner's play *Der Verbrecher* (*The Criminal*) in 1928, because it featured a homosexual blackmail victim. They linked homosexuality to Judaism, too. The official Nazi magazine *Völkischer Beobachter* (*National Observer*) claimed in 1929 that one of the many 'evil instincts' that characterised Jews was that they were 'forever trying to propagandise sexual relationships between siblings, men and animals, and men and men'. Consequently, it was the Nazis' declared intention that these 'perverted crimes' should be punished by banishment or hanging.[35]

Yet as he awaited trial in jail in Stadelheim, Röhm had come to realise that, as he himself put it in 1929, he was 'same-sex oriented'.[36] More than that, he resentfully refused to hide his true nature. 'The struggle against the cant, deceit and hypocrisy of today's society,' he argued in his 1928 autobiography, 'must take its starting point from the innate nature of the drives that are placed in men from the cradle.'[37] In his case these 'innate drives' included a compelling desire for sex with other men. He confessed as much when another arch-nationalist, a secretive homosexual psychologist called Karl-Günther Heimsoth, wrote to him to ask whether that phrase in his autobiography meant what he thought and hoped it did, namely that Röhm was himself a '175-er'. Röhm's swift response was, 'You have understood me completely!'[38] Röhm also told Heimsoth that the bathhouse, where many men went for sex, was 'the peak of all human happiness ... [as] the type and manner of intercourse there pleased me exceptionally'.[39] He was even happy to take the German-born but British-educated journalist Sefton Delmer on a tour of nightspots. Delmer, who was heterosexual, wrote that he 'did not relish the prospect of a tête-à-tête night-out with the sex-hungry little major', but he was eager for a story and they dined at Peltzer's before going to the Eldorado, where 'the much powdered and painted hostesses were all boys dressed up as girls with wigs and falsies and low-cut evening dresses'. Delmer was surprised when one of the waitresses, 'a huge creature with a very prominent Adam's apple', sat down with them uninvited and started chatting about a rather wild party she and Röhm had attended together a few days earlier. Delmer told Röhm he was shocked by the waitress's lack of discretion in talking about a former client, but Röhm unexpectedly took offence. 'I am not his client,' he said, 'I am his commanding officer. He is one of my Stormtroopers!'[40]

Röhm was supremely self-confident. One casual pick-up, whom he met in the Marien-Kasino and took back to his hotel in 1925, had the audacity to steal Röhm's suitcase, presuming that Röhm would fear exposure if he went to the police. He could not have been more mistaken. Röhm immediately reported the theft and even when the thief was caught and claimed that Röhm had tried to force him to perform illegal sex acts, Röhm nonchalantly stood his ground. That Hitler chose to appoint Röhm to such a senior command was remarkable, as he knew about this and other blackmail attempts. But Röhm could rely on a personal bond of comradeship. He alone of the senior Nazis was allowed to contradict the leader and even use the familiar term *du* to him.

The phenomenal leeway Hitler gave to Röhm meant that within weeks of taking over command of the SA Röhm was able to gather around himself an extraordinary group of homosexual Nazis. There was the man who claimed to have 'perverted' him,

Gerhard Rossbach, who had set up his own mercenary *Freikorps* unit after the First World War. He had also participated in the Beer Hall Putsch and openly admitted in 1928 that he had murdered 'a number' of labourers and left-wing sympathisers, claiming that he had done so in the greater interest of the nation.[41] Rossbach's successor as leader of the *Freikorps* unit was another putschist from Bavaria called Edmund Heines, who had won the Iron Cross in the war at the age of seventeen and brought the unit into full membership of the SA. A tall, broad-shouldered but lithe man with a square jaw and a winsome smile, Heines was an equally ardent Nazi and homosexual, whom Röhm defended when he too was convicted of a *Feme* murder and was sentenced to fifteen years' fortress imprisonment in 1928. Heines was utterly unapologetic about his vigilante violence. He even referred to himself as a '*Feme* judge' at a rally, but such was the turmoil in German politics that he was soon granted an amnesty along with several other SA murderers. He was elected to the Reichstag in September 1930 and four months later Röhm appointed him as his SA deputy. Others were promoted, too. Karl Ernst had been such a pretty nineteen-year-old when he joined the SA in 1923 that he got a job on the door at the Eldorado and soon came to Röhm's attention. He had helped run the SA in Munich, but when another leading SA officer, Walter Stennes, mounted two rebellions against the leadership in Berlin in the autumn and spring of 1930–31, Röhm appointed Ernst head of the local SA troop in Berlin in his place. In 1932 Ernst was elected to the Reichstag, as were Peter von Heydebreck and Hans Hayn, two more of Röhm's loyal homosexual SA *Gruppenführers*.

The open swagger of permissive Berlin did not please everyone. It shocked Oswald Mosley when he and his wife visited Harold Nicolson in Berlin in October 1928. Mosley was then a Labour MP, and wrote that they 'had never seen anything like that night in our lives. In several of the many resorts to which we were taken, the sexes had simply exchanged clothes, make-up and the habits of Nature in the crudest form. Scenes of decadence and depravity suggested a nation sunk so deep that it could never rise again.'[42] There were those in the Nazi Party who agreed. Alfred Conn wrote that Bruckner's play *The Criminal* represented everything the Nazis opposed 'as part of our fight against shame and filth'.[43] The view was echoed in 1932, when Wyndham Lewis derided what he called Berlin's 'night-circuses … flagellation-bars, and sad wells of super-masculine loneliness' in his 1932 book *Hitler*.[44] Lewis claimed to welcome 'the fact that the Nazi is not a sex moralist at all',[45] yet, like Mosley, he reckoned that 'sooner or later [the Nazi] would desire to be at the head, or in the midst, of his *Sturmabteilung* – to roll this nigger-dance luxury-spot up like a verminous carpet, and drop it into the [river] Spree'.[46] The irony would become horribly evident over time. But well into the early 1930s, leading SA officers were happy to be seen in the Eldorado, in the Turkish baths and the other homosexual bars of Berlin. Berlin, after all, remained the perverts' paradise.

4

A Luscious Freedom

Jack Macnamara, meanwhile, had set sail on the troopship *Neuralia* on 22 February 1927 to join his new unit, the 1st Battalion of the Royal Fusiliers, in India. If he had been expecting life in the regular army in India to be as easy-going as his childhood in Nazira, he was to be sorely disappointed. The journey out was hideous, as the troop accommodation was so crowded that there was not enough room for men to sling their hammocks and the toilets couldn't cope with demand. Seasickness took hold as they crossed the Bay of Biscay and vomit poured in stinking cascades everywhere. It was not just that the conditions for the soldiers would have made any self-respecting leader blush with shame. Jack was incensed by the fact that the ninety first-class passengers, senior officers and their wives had half the ship to themselves, while the 1,200 third-class passengers were cooped up in hot, noisy and airless cabins. Languishing in third class, he complained that he had never known class distinction 'so unnecessarily exaggerated'.[1] Things did not improve when he finally joined the regiment in Ambala in the northern state of Haryana on the border with Punjab, as he found that his accommodation was 'a mud-and-plaster erection with a canvas ceiling between which and the thatched roof scuttled rats and snakes who lived in a state of constant warfare'.[2] Military life was expensive and he had to meet all his costs from his own pocket, including his uniform, which differed inexplicably from the made-for-India rig he had been issued in Britain. He disliked the hierarchical attitudes, which allowed an officer to spar with a soldier but not box with him, and he resented the intense snobbery of the clubhouse set. There were moments of light relief. He trained as a boxing referee; he decided polo was the best game in the world; he travelled extensively throughout the country; and he visited some of the Indian princes (including the nearby Maharajah of Chhatarpur who, although married, was a lonely homosexual man of 'a certain femininity of gesture and a taste for regal finery').[3] He thoroughly enjoyed a 400-mile march from Ambala to Jhansi and relished the challenge of defending the Khyber Pass and policing riots in Peshawar. He liked the Indian people and was especially grateful to his resourceful bearer, Juggernaut, who wept on the station platform when they parted. But he never really felt well in India. A severe bout of blood poisoning put him in hospital for weeks and although he was promoted to lieutenant in January 1930, he felt miserable, lonely and depressed, and reckoned that 'the private soldier did not look forward to a very gay existence in the Jewel of his Empire'.[4] He consoled himself that 'life is not worth living unless one risks it',[5] but suffering from severe insomnia, he was keen to write the India trip off to experience as soon as possible.

Somehow or other back in England the May sisters, who thought of themselves as his surrogate parents, caught wind of his travails and decided that their brother-in-law Herbert Sharp should go and bring him home. This was a strange request. Born in 1888, Herbert was sixteen years older than Jack and barely knew him. He was the eldest son of a merchant from Dundee who had made a substantial fortune out of spinning jute, which had paid for a handsome eighteenth-century mansion, Balmuir House, on the outskirts of Dundee and the crenellated baronial-style Dalnaghar Castle in Glenshee. His father had died in 1916 and had left his son a very wealthy man, so Herbert could certainly afford the trip. Moreover his ecclesiastical career had taken an odd direction, which left him free to travel. The curacy at Farnborough was followed by a conventional spell at St James's Church in Edinburgh, but in 1921 he launched himself into that strange backwater of Anglicanism, the Diocese of Gibraltar, which provides a form of chaplaincy for Anglicans across Europe. First, he was chaplain in Naples, where his youngest daughter Katherine, who recorded her vivid memories of her father in 1997, was born in 1925. The following year the family moved to Diano Marina and in 1928 he became chaplain to the Bishop of Gibraltar, Nugent Hicks, whose episcopal throne was in Gibraltar but whose residence was in Westminster. When Herbert's sisters begged Herbert to go and rescue Jack, Herbert had already purchased the beautiful eighteenth-century Box House near Stroud, and the family was about to move back to Britain. So Herbert left his wife Elsie behind and set off to find Jack.

It is difficult to know exactly what happened at this stage. Jack's army records show that he was granted nine months' sick leave in March 1930 and ships' records show him arriving in England on 1 April. Those are the hard facts. But Herbert's daughter Katherine later recorded that Herbert's return journey with Jack marked a turning point in Herbert's life. While at Rugby he had fallen in with a 'homosexual group' surrounding Rupert Brooke, but it was only now, as he sailed back with Jack, that Herbert discovered his own latent homosexuality. Jack only ever published one sentence about Herbert, when he included the following in his memoirs: 'A temporary relief from the war came when one of the [May] daughters got married to a parson, who has remained a lifelong friend of mine ever since.'[6] Yet the truth was far tenderer than this throwaway line suggests. Jack, who had scarcely known his father's love, felt comfortable with an older, wealthier man; he unlocked something in his older companion and the two men formed a deep and lasting bond. Herbert dressed as a conventional parson, with a three-inch clerical collar, but his full lips, high cheekbones and dreamy eyes betrayed an adventurous spirit. In later photographs he looks chubby, but as a young curate he was tall and handsome, fashionably dressed in loose-fitting Oxford bags. His wealth meant that he could afford to take risks and he was attracted to the risk-taker in Jack. It was a long journey from Bombay via Suez, Port Said, Marseille and Gibraltar, but the luxurious Anchor Line steamship *Tuscania* provided a romantic setting for what Katherine called Herbert's 'male menopause'. By the time they finally berthed at Liverpool in April they were the most intimate of friends. Whether or not the two men shared a bed is immaterial. Back in England their friendship blossomed and for the rest of their lives they remained as close as two men can be.

If they were lovers, they were certainly not monogamous. One of the first things Jack did on returning to England was get back in touch with Lett and Cedric, who had set up house together in a battered farmhouse, known as Pound Farm, in Higham in Suffolk, where they regularly hosted an extensive list of queer friends. Jack often drove up from London and stayed with them for days. Occasionally he helped out by dropping their paintings off with London galleries – and in July he turned up with an extremely handsome, rough-hewn eighteen-year-old called Patrick Kennedy, whom Lett carefully described in his diary on his first appearance as Jack's 'servant'. That camouflage was very soon lifted in private, though, as Patrick rapidly became 'Paddy' and Lett reported the two men dining as equals at Pound Farm with John Gielgud and his lover John Perry, going bathing at the local beach, shooting rabbits for the pot and boxing together in Battersea. By all accounts Paddy was as forthright in his youth as he was later to be as the licensee of the Star Tavern near Berkeley Square. Opinionated, loud-mouthed, fun-loving and daring, he challenged Jack in a way that delighted, engaged and seduced him. It was just the kind of provocative relationship he loved.

None of that stopped Jack and Herbert from cementing their friendship. Jack became a regular feature at the Sharp family home and that summer the two men organised a European trip together (avoiding France, where Jack was still barred entry). Herbert commissioned a private plane for the two of them, Jack got further permission from his regiment to travel on the Continent and on 1 August they posed for photographs at Croydon aerodrome before flying off for a fortnight's holiday.

After Amsterdam and Brussels they were off to sample the delights of Berlin. Herbert did not think to take his wife or children, but stuck beaming photographs of Jack and himself in their bathing trunks in the family album.

On their return Jack bought his first property, Justice Wood Farm near Hadleigh, some five miles from Pound Farm. Cedric had helped him find the property, which set Jack back £500, but Lett teased Jack about it, noting in his diary for 11 October, 'Jack's birthday. Baby Farming at Justice Wood begins.' Jack's sick leave ran out in November, but soon he and Paddy were welcoming guests, including Herbert, at the seventy-six-acre farm. Ostensibly they were master and servant, but most of their friends knew them as partners. By November Lett was describing them in his diary as 'Patrick and Jack McN' and that Christmas the two men joined Cedric and Lett as part of a larger party at the Greyhound Hotel by Corfe Castle in Dorset.

The next two years represented liberation for Jack, as he was posted from September 1930 to the regimental headquarters or 'Depot' at the swanky cavalry barracks on Hounslow Heath. He was still a full member of the British Army and his career advanced as he passed his commissioning exams; he was made a captain in 1931 and completed the small arms course at Hythe early the following year. His military record was exemplary. More importantly, though, this stint at Hounslow afforded him considerable freedom, as the barracks had its own underground station straight into London and whatever the law said, the capital had several venues that were more explicitly queer than anything frequented by Ronnie Cartland, varying from the racy to the seedy, the long-running to the here-today-gone-tomorrow. These were still illegal and dangerous – but they managed to prosper. Piccadilly Circus was the centre of the action. A stone's throw away was the art deco Lyons' Corner House (the 'Lily Pond') on the corner of Coventry Street, where, according to the angry campaigning journal *John Bull*, 'Painted and scented boys congregate every day without molestation of any kind ... sitting with their vanity bags and their high-heeled shoes, calling themselves by endearing names and looking out for patrons.'[7] When the police started to move the 'painted boys' on in 1930, more discreet gentlemen colonised the first-floor restaurant, where they betrayed nothing about their sexuality to the untrained eye, but the sympathetic waitresses encouraged women to sit elsewhere. Immediately opposite was the Trocadero Long Bar, so named because it claimed it had the longest bar in London, running the entire length of the room. This was very much a men-only venue, as the Welsh actor and playwright Emlyn Williams remembered men clustering around little tables 'in the old uniform of bowler, dark suit, rolled umbrella and starched collar'.[8] It sounds staid and respectable, but there was an air of camp naughtiness, as the *Evening Standard* reported that Maurice, the maître d', insisted that the band play his favourite song every night: 'Make Way Boys – Here Comes a Sailor'.[9] According to the theatre historian and publicist Walter MacQueen-Pope, that 'was as nothing to the Long Bar at the Cri', the ornate Criterion Theatre and restaurant across the road, which had an even longer bar and where marble pillars and arches supported 'a sort of mosaic roof'.[10] Its bar was nicknamed the 'Witches Cauldron' or the 'Bargain Basement', which would start every evening as the height of respectability before steadily descending into decadence. Here the band played 'Five Foot Two, Eyes of Blue' whenever a handsome man arrived – and every eye in the house swivelled to watch him descend the great staircase. By ten o'clock the whole place would be full of 'well-behaved male trash'.[11]

In Wardour Street there was another bar, the Rendezvous, which was discreetly run by two men and was 'always full of gay people trying very hard to pretend they weren't gay'.[12] If you wanted something rougher or cruisier, there was the White Room off Shaftesbury Avenue. Not far away were the York Minster, the Marquis of Granby and the Fitzroy Tavern in Charlotte Street, where the landlord, Charlie Allchild, was reputed to have bribed the police to stay away. You would look round to make sure nobody saw you before you entered any of these venues – and once inside, men moodily and nervously watched each other in the hope of a pick-up (and in fear of a constable).

Sometimes eating and drinking in camp surroundings was not enough, though, for a man with a roving eye like Jack. Which is where the Turkish baths came in. They had started as a health fad for Victorian gentlemen and ladies, and in 1930 there were fourteen across London, several of which catered exclusively to men. Two rival companies dominated the market: the Nevill Company, which ran the Edgware Road, Charing Cross and Bishopsgate Turkish baths; and the Savoy, which had the baths at the Elephant and Castle and Jermyn Street. To all intents and purposes these were sex clubs. As film director Derek Jarman put it, 'Anyone who went to them would have been propositioned during the course of an evening [as] they were a well-known hangout: dormitory and steam rooms full of guardsmen cruising.'[13] What with the heat, the steam and the naked men, this was a haven for queer men. The brochure for Jermyn Street virtually said as much, claiming that it 'attracted the enthusiastic patronage of connoisseurs and those "who know"', and declaring that its doors were open day and night offering 'suites – bachelor chambers ... to let at very moderate rentals'.[14]

Fortuitously for Jack, the Edgware Road baths stood just down the Harrow Road, near his old regimental barracks. Here, behind a normal shopfront with a plain red door, lay a world of Moorish delight, which was available all night for a mere two shillings and sixpence. As one attendee put it, 'Everything went on there, fairly discreetly.'[15] Bathers would push back a deep-red curtain to find a private cubicle with a bed, where they would undress and don a towel after stowing their valuables at the reception desk. Other cubicles – some with two beds – were ranged round a galleried second floor where men eyed up new arrivals. The main action was in the hammam in the basement, though, where men shampooed one another on marble slabs, gave each other a 'rub' in one of the increasingly hot rooms or chatted and relaxed on the canvas cushions. It was a welcoming and remarkably open space for queer men who would gossip with old friends and hope to meet new ones, including men from the barracks. One always had to be careful. The staff had to maintain a semblance of order, so sexual relations were reserved to the cubicles and Jack always had the fear of bumping into a fellow officer. But, as many a man rationalised to himself, there was no crime in attending a Turkish bath, and Nevill's was so respectable that it had a clergyman on the board of directors.

The baths were one of the safest places for same-sex encounters because London County Council licensed them and so the writ of the Metropolitan Police did not extend past their doors. Occasional incidents passed off without arrests. Thus the press reported under the headline 'Happenings at Turkish Baths, Stories of Improper Conduct', that two inspectors had twice visited the Savoy Baths and 'on both occasions there were incidents which pointed to a most serious state of affairs [and] incidents of a disgusting nature had taken place'.[16] When the Savoy's licence was opposed in 1930, their lawyer, Henry Curtis-Bennett, argued that it was 'a very large old-established business to which ... a great number of highly reputable gentlemen go continuously'.[17] Consequently, so he argued, it was inconceivable that any kind of indecent conduct should have occurred. They won their case and the licence was reissued on the proviso that there be 'more adequate supervision'. The following year there was another public hearing and this time the licence was revoked, although on appeal the Marlborough Street magistrate decided that he was 'not in the least satisfied ... that anything had happened which would justify him, or ... any other court, in taking the licence away'.[18]

So safe were the baths that they became a rite of initiation for queer men arriving in London. When the bisexual writer Stephen Spender's friend William Plomer moved to London from South Africa in 1929, their mutual friend, an aristocratic Frenchman called René Janin, took him round the baths, and when the American actor Robert Hutton arrived in London after the war he reckoned that 'the next three weeks came as near to killing me as the war ever had ... I slept for a week in a Turkish bath, which meant, virtually, that I did not sleep at all'.[19] When Christopher Isherwood and W. H. Auden took the 24-year-old Benjamin Britten to the Savoy Baths in 1937, Britten recorded that the 'very pleasant sensation' had been 'completely sensuous, but very healthy'. The only trouble was that he couldn't sleep a wink 'in the perpetual restlessness of the surroundings'.[20] The guardsman and MP Harry Crookshank and Harold Nicolson both recorded their attendance at the Turkish baths in their diaries and several of their parliamentary colleagues were happy to refer to a visit to 'the Savoy' on the assumption that the uninitiated would presume they were referring to the hotel, the grill or even the chapel rather than the Jermyn Street baths. Jarman even claimed that the former guards officer and future Prime Minister Harold Macmillan 'was expelled from Eton for an "indiscretion" [and] used to spend nights at the Jermyn Street baths'.[21]

Some had mixed feelings though. Alec Guinness claimed that the Savoy 'revolted' him, but he kept on going back. Likewise, when Harold Nicolson joined Eddie Gathorne-Hardy, Brian Howard and Brian's lover Sandy Baird at the Blue Lantern Club, Harold wrote, 'I cannot say I enjoyed it,' but added wistfully, 'I have lost my gambol faculties.'[22] The prolific author Rupert Croft-Cooke, who would later be best known for the detective novels he wrote under the pseudonym Leo Bruce, was even more vicious about the Criterion in *The Cloven Hoof: A Study of Contemporary London Vices*, which he published in 1932 under the pen name Taylor Croft. He declared himself 'amazed' by the clients' blatancy and the café management's utter disregard for the law. He reckoned he had seen 'nearly 200 perverts', many of them with berets on the back of their heads or wearing coloured roll-neck sweaters, but many others 'painted and rouged [and] one boy actually in women's clothes'. To cap it all, he complained, 'One man took out a lipstick and openly used it.'[23] *

---

* Croft-Cooke published a book on domestic architecture in 1952, which included a photograph of his 'secretary' Joseph Sussainathan, and a year later the two men were arrested for gross indecency and received six and three months respectively. They eventually moved to Tangier. Yet he repeatedly claimed to loathe bars crowded with writers and 'pansies'.

London's many public urinals or 'cottages' also provided much cheaper clandestine opportunities. One anonymous booklet entitled *For Your Convenience* even featured a coded conversation between two men praising unattended men's toilets because they afforded 'excellent rendezvous to people who wish to meet out of doors and yet escape the eye of the Busy'.[24] It also included a helpful map of where to go. Sex here was far more dangerous, as the police regularly patrolled in plain clothes and sought to entrap the uninitiated. Notwithstanding newspapers' ardent demands for a crackdown and the zeal of individual officers, there were moments when law enforcement collapsed into farce. Entrapment was officially frowned upon and constables were keen not to be thought of as too interested in other men's proclivities, so they pretended not to be looking out for 'that sort of thing'. One case gives a flavour of events, though. Two constables, Knight and Halliday, were on duty in plain clothes in Brixton when they mounted surveillance on the urinals in Popes Road, a vast cast-iron construction with a solid body and a filigree panel covering the ventilator in the roof. Much to the evident excitement of the policemen, two men, Charles Pearson and Ralph Byrne, entered the urinal and stayed for a few minutes. At this point the constables climbed a lamp post so as to peer into the urinal through the filigree, but when they tried to get higher so as to get a better view, Halliday nudged Knight and noisily fell off the lamp post, thereby alerting the two men, who rapidly parted. They panicked and attempted to flee the scene, but were both arrested and charged with gross indecency. The police doctor found 'no semen or stains of semen' on them, so the only evidence of any offence was that of the policemen themselves, but the two men were convicted.[25]

Jack had one other source of potential relief, thanks to one of the oldest traditions of the British Army. For decades guardsmen had made themselves available for hire in Hyde Park, Green Park and around Piccadilly Circus, and wealthy men had taken regular advantage of this trade. Some men expressly preferred this social mix. Eddie Gathorne-Hardy, for instance, liked to garnish his parties with guardsmen[26] and Stephen Spender admitted that part of his love for the former guardsman Tony Hyndman lay in their difference of class, as he was in love 'with his background, his soldiering, his working-class home'.[27] The authorities loathed the practice, though. They argued that it sapped men's masculinity, it undermined morale, it disturbed the social order, and it spread venereal diseases. Yet it was commonplace. During the trial of a Welsh guardsman in 1931 the recorder asked Police Inspector Sharpe 'if the Guardsmen lent themselves to this sort of thing?' and was shocked to hear the reply: 'I am afraid they do ... there is an atmosphere of this kind permeating a section of the Guards.'[28] When Captain Preston of the Military Police at Regent's Park Barracks wrote to complain about 'persons suspected to be consorting with soldiers for improper purposes (perverts)', a special conference was called between the adjutant general of the forces, the Director of Public Prosecutions and the assistant commissioner of the Metropolitan Police. They heard that 127 soldiers had been arrested for importuning in the last twelve months, that six guardsmen had been charged and a further fifty men dismissed, and that, as the officer commanding London District, General Charles Corkran, put it, a section of the Guards 'lent themselves to these practices'.[29] Yet again they determined to stamp the practice out. One suggestion was a series of 'considered lectures in the law on the subject'.[30] Another idea was to report any 'premises frequented by soldiers for improper purposes (Perverts) especially private houses and clubs'[31] and to inform MI5. Yet again they failed.

Despite this, Jack found army life at Hounslow remarkably welcoming. Marriage was banned for all bar the most senior officers and actively discouraged for all ranks, so the vast majority of men were single and the officers' mess felt like a gentlemen's club. The extensive barracks housed several cavalry and infantry regiments and was a hive of masculinity. There were gyms, boxing rings and all-male bars. The several hundred men dressed, undressed, slept and did their ablutions together. Manly camaraderie was not that different from queer friendship and the frisson of unexpected attention was always in the air. Jack regularly entertained his friends overnight at the barracks, apparently without anyone blinking an eye. He invited several queer friends, including Lett and Cedric, to the annual regimental All Ranks Party and hosted many others overnight, including the aristocratic pioneering documentary producer Arthur Elton. When Lett stayed at the barracks in June 1931, he and Jack lunched at the Gargoyle, dined at Viani's, caught a show at the Palladium and joined Eddie Gathorne-Hardy at the Blue Lantern. At weekends Jack and Paddy would either go home to Justice Wood Farm or go to Pound Farm, where Lett put together impressive dinners and regaled them with tales of impropriety, while Cedric rolled his eyes and affected boredom. Their fellow dinner companions would include Tray Mortimer with Paul Hyslop, Vita Sackville-West and her flamboyant cousin Eddy. Afterwards, Jack and Paddy would retire to Justice Wood Farm, where they occasionally had Jack's mother and stepfather to stay. There were more foreign trips, too. In November 1931 Jack went to Italy, probably with both Paddy and Herbert, and in 1932 he visited Germany again. At Christmas that year Jack and Paddy again joined Lett and Cedric, this time staying at College Farm in Llangennith on the Gower Peninsula, where there must have been plenty of raised eyebrows when the two queer male couples joined the supper dance in the local parish hall accompanied by just one woman, the painter Eve Disher.

Jack fully exploited the delights of London, but there were risks in attending many of the more overtly queer venues, as the police kept them under surveillance and there was always the danger that the handsome stranger on the other side of the bar was an undercover policeman. The police mounted so many raids that many men felt that nearly all their 'very charming, very sensitive' friends were sent to jail, where they had a really rough time. As one man put it, 'Their jobs, their careers, everything was gone.'[32] In December 1932 two officers – one of them dressed as a woman – pretended to be a couple and eyed up an unsuspecting man in the Mitre on Holland Park Avenue in the hope that he would help them gain entry to an illegal drag ball at the Park House Private Ballroom across the road.[33] The unsuspecting chap breezily told the doorman that they were 'two camp boys, friends of mine'. Once inside, the police officers danced together, talked in the queer lingo of the day about 'queans', 'bitches' and 'trade' and allowed other men to fondle them until the place was raided and sixty men were arrested. Their testimony (and a bright red silk pyjama suit, which was seized) led to the Old Bailey trial of the barman, 'Lady' Austin Salmon, the waiter John Packer and the hostess Kathleen O'Donnell for keeping a disorderly house and conspiracy to corrupt morals, and of thirty-three of the partygoers for a variety of sexual offences. The trial, which received considerable attention, was traumatic. The defendants had to run the gauntlet of angry crowds and were forced to wear numbered cards round their necks in court. There were some lighter moments, as the defendants all burst into laughter when one of them was referred to as the 'duchess', and when another was asked why he wore a pale blue low-back dress, he replied that he was merely impersonating the comic actress Miss Beatrice Lillie 'and he could see no indecency in that'.[34] The Recorder, Sir Ernest Wild, did not see the funny side of it, though. He repeatedly rebuked them and pronounced that they had 'degraded their manhood' by attending 'a horrible club where perverse practices were being actively encouraged'. O'Donnell was acquitted, but Salmon and Packer were given fifteen and twenty months respectively and twenty-five others were sent down for between three and sixteen months. Such was the shock that one paper reported that 'some of the defendants almost collapsed when sentence was passed'.[35]

Despite the dangers, Jack managed to survive his two years of liberty without getting into any more trouble than being arrested in Essex for speeding at over ten miles an hour, but it all came to an end early in 1933. He had been passed unfit in a medical in August 1932 and granted sick leave until 12 November 1932, but almost as soon as he was fit again he was posted to India. The moment he heard the news he started organising a great fancy-dress farewell party in London to be held on Saturday 28 January. He persuaded a friend to lend his mews house in fashionable Fitzrovia for the night and sent out large numbers of handwritten invitations. Lett went to considerable efforts over his costume, and after lunch with Cedric he went to the Fitzroy Tavern for cocktails before getting dressed and turning up at 4 Gower Mews, where he ended up staying the night.[36] It is unclear exactly what kind of fancy dress Jack intended. One party that Lett's sculptor friend John Skeaping attended at that time required guests to turn up naked either from the waist up or the waist down. At another the gorgeous redhead Tallulah Bankhead marched up to Emerald Cunard and ripped her skimpy dress down to her waist, remarking, 'I always wanted to see your tits.' And often the choreographer Frederick Ashton and ballet designer Billy Chappell would turn up in ballet costumes and dance libidinously together. Whatever Jack intended, Lett used just two words to describe his friend's farewell party: 'Grand Camp.'

Jack held a couple more cocktail parties in February – and wrote a will. He and Paddy stayed at Pound Farm overnight on Thursday 23 February and the following Tuesday Jack sailed reluctantly back to India. His days of luscious freedom seemed over.

5

Learning the Hard Way

On Saturday 13 September 1930, three men joined the officers on the top deck of the luxurious steamship, the *Niagara*, as she sailed into Sydney Harbour and dropped anchor in Rose Bay. The tallest of the three – slender and bespectacled – was a 28-year-old journalist called Robert Bernays. Everything about him spoke of middle-class English propriety. His grandfather Leopold had been rector of Stanmore and his father Stewart had followed in his footsteps at Stanmore before taking on the more lucrative rectory at Finchley in 1924. Yet there was always something slightly on edge about Rob. Partly it was just that he had two older brothers, John and Gorton, and a very capable older sister Lucy, so he suffered from the conventional youngest sibling's need to prove himself. But Rob also always felt himself slightly on the sidelines of respectability. He was conscious of his family's Jewish origins – his great-grandfather Adolphus had been a professor of German at King's College London and his great-uncle Isaac was a noted chief rabbi in Hamburg – and he was sensitive to the subtle gradations of English society, which ranked a Church of England rector alongside the aristocracy even though the family was far from affluent and could barely afford the cook and housemaid that were necessary to keep up appearances.

Fortunately Rob was bright, energetic and good with words. He won a scholarship in 1916 to one of the newer public schools, Rossall, near Fleetwood in Lancashire, where he worked hard and prospered, winning cricket and rugby colours, and becoming a monitor in Anchor House and a lance corporal in the Officer Training Corps. In October 1921 he won another scholarship, to read modern history at Worcester College, Oxford, where he rowed in the college eight and threw himself into student politics as a convinced member of the Liberal Party. He organised campaign visits from Oxford to assist Liberal candidates in the 1922 general election in Taunton, Brighton and Skipton;[1] and worked on Frank Gray's successful campaign in Oxford in 1923.[2] He was elected president of the Worcester College Junior Common Room and in the Hilary (spring) term of his final year, 1925, he was elected president of the Oxford Union. Then things started to go awry, as he fell ill during finals and went to recuperate at Blagroves Farm near Taunton, the home of Sir John Hope Simpson, who had recently lost his seat as a Liberal MP. 'I know you will be wondering how I am getting on,' Rob wrote to the junior bursar at Worcester in July. 'I have been down here since Friday and am getting better each day, I have certainly made up my arrears of sleep and though my memory has not yet properly returned I have made no attempt to force it.'[3] It reads like the flimsiest of excuses for not having studied for his exams, but he was summoned for a viva voce by the history department, which awarded him an aegrotat degree.

None of this got in the way of what looked like a promising career. After a brief spell as a schoolmaster in Solihull, he joined an Oxford Union debating team on tour in America and on his return was offered a highly coveted post on the editorial team of the Liberal-supporting *Daily News*. Months later, in September 1927, he was selected to fight Rugby – a seat that the Liberals had previously held – and many saw him as one of the most promising young Liberal candidates. As the Rugby Liberal Association put it, he was 'a young man of fine presence, most agreeable manners and ... in the early twenties'.[4] Thus far everything had been going his way and he stood a chance of winning, but the Labour candidate died just three days before polling at the end of May 1929, so the Rugby contest was delayed by a fortnight, during which Labour won the largest number of seats in the Commons and formed a new government under Ramsay MacDonald. Suddenly the wind changed. On the eve of poll of the subsequent by-election, the press claimed that after a lightning tour of twenty-nine meetings, Rob was escorted 'by a solid phalanx of bright young people'[5] and excitement was at 'fever heat'.[6] All three parties hoped to win. Yet the sitting Tory MP, Captain David Margesson, who listed his sole recreations as 'hunting and shooting',[7] made wild allegations about the evils of socialism, and the new Labour candidate denounced capitalism in similarly apocalyptic terms, thereby squeezing the Liberal vote in a pincer. As Rob confessed a few years later, 'the whole Liberal army was in retreat, not to say rout, and here I was, left behind in the same entrenchment as when the battle began six weeks before'.[8] When the final result came in at 3.15 in the afternoon, Margesson won comfortably and Rob Bernays came last. He was magnanimous in defeat and claimed that although 'individual Liberals may be defeated ... Liberalism is never beaten',[9] but his fortunes did not immediately improve. The following February he broke two ribs when he fell from a horse and in June the *Daily News* was swallowed whole by the *Daily Chronicle*, leaving him unemployed with next to no savings. He did a few reporting jobs, which he hated, including doorstepping the MP Duff Cooper to ask what his newborn son would be called, but with little prospect of serious work he raised a loan and set off on a round-the-world 'Empire tour', hoping to wire some lively and lucrative international copy back to London.

Rob did have one other significant asset, though: his close connection to the man in whose company he now travelled as speechwriter and personal assistant, William Lygon, the 7th Earl Beauchamp, whose support had helped secure him the nomination at Rugby. The earl was now in his late fifties. He had put on a bit of weight – 'robust and well set up'[10] was how one Australian journalist put it, while another reckoned that he was 'stouter than of old'[11] – and his light brown hair was now slightly streaked with grey. Yet he was still a handsome figure, generally reckoned to be one of the best-dressed members of the House of Lords. His blue eyes still sparkled 'with alert vitality' and there was considerable excitement about his arrival, as each stage of his long voyage from England via Vancouver, Suva and Auckland had been reported in the press. Even the New South Wales premier, Thomas Bavin, joined the *Niagara* as part of the official welcoming party, as Beauchamp was one of the Empire's political celebrities. In 1899 the Conservative prime minister, the Marquess of Salisbury, had appointed him Governor of New South Wales, much to his own surprise, as he was just twenty-seven, single and a Liberal. He held this post for two years, and since then he had served in both the royal household and in the Cabinet. He had carried the Sword of State at George V's coronation in 1911, he had witnessed the declaration of war in Buckingham Palace in 1914, and he was still the leader of the Liberals in the House of Lords. He was also the first governor ever to return to Australia.

Beauchamp – or 'Boom' as his friends knew him – also arrived with a reputation. It was thirty years since he had set foot in Australia, but Sydney-siders had long memories. His parties at Government House had been famous, as he recruited the city's most bohemian poets, authors and artists to his salon and entertained them extravagantly. The poet Victor J. Daley described arriving at one such event in an article in the *Australia Star* in 1900: 'Rosy cheeked footmen, clad in liveries of fawn, heavily ornamented with silver and red brocade, with many lanyards of the same hanging in festoons from their broad shoulders, stood in the doorway, and bowed as we passed in.' That was not all. Daley was piloted to a seat by a well-attired 'pretty, young, peach-cheeked gentleman in a Court suit of black velvet, adorned with buttons of cut steel and with a cunning little Court sword hanging at his side'. Daley made the knowing point that Beauchamp deserved 'great credit for his taste in footmen', since the most striking feature of the vice-regal ménage was 'the youthfulness of all its members'.[12] You didn't have to be all that savvy to get Daley's drift. Beauchamp had in the meantime married Lettice, a daughter of the Earl Grosvenor, in a grand society wedding in England in 1902 and the couple now had three sons and four daughters, but the rumour was that he was not *really* the marrying kind, as was intimated when a journalist mischievously asked one of Beauchamp's female friends why his countess had not accompanied him. He was told that although they had originally intended to travel together, he decided to travel solo 'at her express wish' when she took seriously ill. The journalist was very sceptical about the claim that Beauchamp was 'very glum about it', alleging that the noble Earl *might* have been disguising his feelings but he neither looked not acted very glum about it at all. In fact 'he enjoyed himself immensely but never publicly, or privately – so far as I can ascertain – did he mention his wife'.[13] He added, for good effect, that some people regarded Beauchamp as 'a queer chap', a word that could still in 1930 suggest mere eccentricity but more often implied sexual deviancy.

Far from being embarrassed by such comments, Beauchamp relished sailing close to the wind. He pasted a copy of Daley's 1899 article in his commonplace book alongside photographs of semi-naked men from Rheims and classical marble statues of athletes. At one reception in Sydney he proclaimed that 'Bohemia is one of the greatest correctives that philistinism can have'[14] and that he was sick of people being 'good'. When asserting that the glorious new sport of surfing was 'fit for kings' at a Royal Empire Society luncheon, he said that he had never enjoyed himself so much as when he was able 'to see your very beautiful women and girls on the beaches', and added with a wink, 'and also the finely-built men'.[15] A few months later he completed that homoerotic thought in an article for the *Empire Review*. 'The men are splendid athletes,' he wrote, 'like the old Greek statues. Their skins are tanned by sun and wind and I doubt whether anywhere in the world are finer specimens of manhood than in Sydney. The lifesavers are wonderful.'[16] It was a view Rob endorsed, as he compared the well-developed lifeguards at Bondi in their skimpy swimming trunks to the German bodybuilder Eugen Sandow and wrote, 'They told me that Sydney was depressed. I tremble to think what orgiastic scenes there must be when it is prosperous. For me it is the gayest city in the world.' [17]

The lifesavers were not the only reason to visit Sydney, as it was by now one of the fifteen largest cities in the world, and as early as 1895 the paper *Scorpion*, whose subtitle claimed it was 'Stinging, Spicy, Sensational', reckoned that there was a haunt for the 'Oscar Wilde's [*sic*] of Sydney in Bourke Street Surry Hills' and that the 'part of College Street from Boomerang-street to Park-street is a parade for them'.[18] There were two luxurious Turkish baths in Liverpool Street and Oxford Street, which were 'men only' all day Tuesday, Wednesday, Friday and Saturday, and on Monday and Thursday afternoons. There were several bars that deliberately catered for a queer clientele, including the Latin Café run by Madam Helen Pura, Mockbell's, Pelligrini's, Cahill's Coffee Shop and the Academy School of Dancing. This last, also known as 'Black Ada's', allowed a few women to mix among the male customers solely so that if the vice squad appeared, the men could instantly spring apart and the women would take their place. Even the church Beauchamp attended in both 1899 and 1930 – and to which he donated several sets of vestments – the Anglo-Catholic shrine of St James', King Street – was a sanctuary for devout men who preferred the company of men, thanks to its unmarried High Church clergy and their preference for incense, genuflection, gin and lace.

Beauchamp loved this hypocritical world of bluff and double bluff, where people pretended to be shocked, and he took plenty of risks. He had sex with his doctor and several of his male servants, and according to Virginia Woolf, her fellow novelist Hugh Walpole had seen Beauchamp (and even more scandalously Lord Carisbrooke, who was a member of the royal family) having sex with another man at the Elephant and Castle baths. On one occasion Harold Nicolson had to cover for Beauchamp when a shocked dinner guest thought he had overheard the earl say,

'*Je t'adore*,' to his handsome butler, Bradford. 'Nonsense!' Harold affirmed, he had merely said, 'Shut the door.'

None of these stories ever reached the public ear, but he was courting disaster on this trip thanks to his choice of a second companion on the *Niagara*. George Roberts was the nice-looking nineteen-year-old second footman from Beauchamp's great family home at Madresfield near Worcester, but Beauchamp treated him as a partner. They travelled together in first class. They rented a flat at Darling Point – and sent Rob to stay at the Australia Club. They attended balls and receptions together. They were constant companions. Rumours instantly spread that Roberts was his lover – or that Bernays was, or that they both were. This was especially dangerous for Rob Bernays. Australia was a long way from home and distance afforded many men a cloak of anonymity. But Beauchamp was famous and had political enemies, one of whom was the Governor General in Canberra, a former Conservative MP, John Baird, who had held several ministerial posts under Lloyd George, Bonar Law and Baldwin. He had many reasons to dislike Beauchamp, whom he knew from of old, having first sat as MP for Rugby, where Beauchamp prominently campaigned for each of the Liberal candidates in hard-fought contests. Baird was envious, too. He was of landed stock – he had attended Eton and Christ Church College, Oxford and he inherited a Scottish baronetcy – but his title as Baron Stonehaven was only newly branded for him when he became Governor General in 1925, unlike Beauchamp's title, which stretched back to 1806. So when he heard that Beauchamp was intending to bring Roberts with him to visit the new Australian capital and stay at the official residence, Yarralumla, he made it clear to Rob that Roberts would not be welcome.

When Rob recounted these events in 1937, he portrayed himself as a scandalised innocent. He claimed to have known nothing of Roberts until they set sail at Liverpool and to be outraged when George started calling Beauchamp 'Beau' instead of 'm'lord' and when he told his lordship 'you pack your own bloody bags' when they arrived in Australia. Yet Rob's manuscript diary from 1930, which has never been published, shows this was not the whole truth. When he first met George in Liverpool he noted that, 'He seems friendly but very shy.'[19] He laughed with George when Beauchamp fussed about his appearance, and when George said his master could not compete with Tallulah Bankhead for high camp behind Boom's back. Rob spent hours with George in his cabin listening to tales of how Beauchamp used to come to find him in the kitchen back at Madresfield, and one evening he listened to George's 'love affairs with sympathetic ears till bed-time'.[20]

According to the diary, Beauchamp was also open with Rob about the relationship when they were alone on a train from Quebec to Montreal, as he apologised for his valet taking his meals with them but said that, 'He may go with women otherwise!'[21] Rob even had to go into battle for Beauchamp when they joined the *Niagara*, as an officious ship's purser insisted that no valet could dine in the first-class saloon. Beauchamp had a letter from the owner of the shipping line granting George an exemption from the usual rules, but he sent Rob 'tremblingly' to persuade the purser that since George had a first-class ticket, he could have a first-class dinner. When Rob returned in triumph, he was exasperated that Beauchamp only said that he hoped he had not upset the purser. 'We must be very courteous to him now,' he said, as he 'could make it very uncomfortable for us'.[22] All of which goes to show that in truth, Rob might have been embarrassed, but he was perfectly au fait with what was going on. He gave a rather different version of events to Harold Nicolson in 1937, though, as he told him that a very tense conversation ensued when Rob told Beauchamp that he could not take George to Canberra. Beauchamp angrily barked, 'Why not?' Rob was deliberately evasive. 'Well,' he said, 'people are talking about it,' without specifying what 'it' was. Beauchamp was not going to let him off that easily, though. 'Talking about what?' he asked peremptorily. 'Well, about you and George,' Rob replied, maintaining his air of deliberate ambiguity. 'Why?' was Beauchamp's defiant response, which finally forced Rob to pour out the whole story.

The silence only ended when Beauchamp muttered, 'Incredible, simply incredible,' and asked, 'And you believed this thing?' as if to suggest it was all a pack of lies.[23]

It is difficult to explain the difference between Rob's two accounts. Memory can play tricks. And perhaps Rob was uncertain how Harold Nicolson would react to such a story, as they were only beginning to get to know each other. But Rob was young, cautious and proper in 1930. He was self-conscious, too. When a poisonous Conservative diplomat said to him after dinner at Cliveden a few years later, 'Don't you agree with me, no man can really be a gentleman unless he's been to Eton?' he caustically replied, 'No, I don't, seeing that I was educated at Solihull Grammer [sic] School.'[24] He had none of the self-assurance that an old title, a vast house and a solid inheritance had given Beauchamp. He was at the start of his career and Lord Stonehaven had put him in a very difficult position. The threat was abundantly clear. If Rob were to acknowledge the Governor General's insinuation of sexual impropriety he would effectively implicate himself. That could lead to all sorts of unnerving questions. As for Beauchamp, he was frightened too, and he was uncertain how much he could trust his young speechwriter. The two men clammed up and it is hardly surprising that they both resorted to evasion and half-truths. Frustrated and nervous, Rob decided that he had had enough and the two men agreed to part.

Rob's fears were understandable. Plenty of queer men married to produce an heir, avoid loneliness and provide cover for their real preferences. Sometimes this was a perfect arrangement, if both partners entered the affair with their eyes wide open – Aimee Lett-Haines, for instance, never complained about her time with Lett. Yet it often caused deep distress to all involved. When, after several homosexual affairs, Siegfried Sassoon announced his engagement in 1933, for instance, Christabel McLaren wrote to congratulate him, gently suggesting, 'I think, perhaps, you haven't always been very happy – now you will be.' But his homosexual friend Bob Gathorne-Hardy (Eddie's younger brother) was less convinced. 'It would be humbug not to say that I was startled and incredulous at the great news,' he wrote, 'but when I thought it over I realised that you had been clever & sensible, doing what was just needed to make you contented. I've always known that what you ought to do was to live with someone devoted to you and whom you were truly fond of.' It was hardly a ringing endorsement of the arrangement, as he added in a postscript, 'One thing I must ask. Please don't now add one startling change to another and become a Tory.' It was not just frustrated wives who could get hurt. One oblique note to Sassoon simply read: 'Congratulations. From an old bachelor friend J. R. N.' And a letter from 'Les' at the Gunnery School at West Lulworth offered Siegfried belated congratulations on his engagement, but added, 'It certainly took me by surprise,' and ended with the words 'Much Love', which would have been enough to convict both men of gross indecency if it had fallen into the wrong hands.[25]

Living a lie was dangerous. Like Jack Macnamara, Beauchamp had tried to pass his companion off as his servant, but he had been found out. He had presumed that none of his social equals would call him out and that the rest of society would show him due deference, but he was wrong. Even his marriage to Lettice and their seven children had failed to obscure his sexuality from view. The episode instilled in Rob an anxiety that he would always struggle to shed. He had enjoyed his time with Beauchamp and George, what with the luxury on board the *Niagara* and the buff blond bodies on Bondi. He was tempted. But at heart he was a very proper Englishman with a low threshold for shame, and it felt as if he had come horribly close to an exposure that could ruin his reputation for ever. He learned in the most abrupt fashion possible that same-sex feelings were dangerous and had to be denied.

By chance, Rob enjoyed a sudden reversal of fortunes when he left Beauchamp in Australia and continued on his 'Empire tour', as he fortuitously arrived in India just as the Indian delegates arrived in London for the first Round Table Conference on the country's future. With the campaign for self-rule in full spate and tens of thousands of Indians under arrest, the *News Chronicle* was suddenly eager for Rob's account of the Indian reaction to the proceedings in London, so he wired copy back to London on an almost daily basis. So impressed was the paper that Rob stayed for five months, and when he returned to England in the spring of 1931 he was put on a permanent contract on double what he had earned previously. He swiftly published a popular account of his stay, *Naked Fakir*, which provided the first British study of Gandhi.

Then came the sudden implosion of the Labour government. The prime minister, Ramsay MacDonald, had been looking ill and worn. When Harold Nicolson and Vita had visited him at Chequers in late 1930 he said he was getting no more than two hours' sleep a night and when he embarrassingly forgot the new prime minister of Canada's name on introducing him to Vita, he wailed, 'My brain is going, my brain is going.' The trouble was, he explained, 'The moment I disentangle my foot from one strand of barbed wire it becomes entangled in another.'[26] He was not exaggerating. The country was living through one of its most turbulent periods. In the 1929 general election Labour had won twenty-seven more seats than the Conservatives but had failed to gain a majority in the House of Commons. Labour's manifesto had been bold, but MacDonald's government was precarious from the outset. Just five months after he entered Downing Street, the US stock market collapsed, on 24 October 1929. British exports rapidly halved in value and unemployment doubled to 2.5 million (nearly 20 per cent). Labour MPs found themselves caught between the manifest despair of their constituents and the howls of the great and the good, who demanded a retrenchment of the welfare state. Sir Oswald Mosley, then a Labour MP and the chancellor of the Duchy of Lancaster, was infuriated by Labour apathy and drew up a yet more radical programme based on corporatism and mass nationalisation. When the Cabinet and Labour Conference rejected this, he and his wife Cynthia (also a Labour MP) left to form the New Party, which edged towards fascism.

The simmering rows came to the boil in the summer of 1931, when the Chancellor, Philip Snowden, proposed a 20 per cent cut in unemployment benefit, which his Cabinet colleague Arthur Henderson and the trades unions refused to support. When the measure was only carried by eleven votes to nine in the Cabinet, MacDonald tendered his and the Labour government's resignation on 24 August. In the normal course of things this should have led to the Conservatives being asked to form a minority government or to new elections, but MacDonald formed a new 'National Government' with the Conservatives, who were led by the former prime minister, Stanley Baldwin. The Labour Party felt betrayed as MacDonald formed a new Cabinet with four Labour ministers, who were promptly expelled from the official Labour Party, four Conservatives and two Liberals. Since the main phalanx of the new government's support consisted of 260 Conservative MPs, the temptation to deliver a knockout blow to Labour was intense, and Baldwin soon persuaded MacDonald to call a general election in which the National Government parties would not stand against each other. MacDonald sought what he called a 'doctor's mandate' to restore the nation's economic health, but in truth the election was a prescription for a very bitter two-way contest between Labour Party candidates and those supporting the National Government (i.e. National Labour, Liberal National or Conservative candidates).

Rob felt hopeful for himself in the midst of this national crisis. He knew all the leading Liberals, *Naked Fakir* had been a success and he was witty and personable. A Scottish friend, Jean Campbell, Lady Stratheden, wrote of him that there has never been anyone 'who could make out of the dreariest material … such side-splitting, ridiculous, heavenly fun'.[27] Archie James, who shared a room with him on a visit to Italy in 1945, agreed. 'His dry humour was the life and soul of the party,' he wrote.[28] Yet Rob could also be shy and diffident. His account of his first experience of surfing in Honolulu betrays the anxiety of a bookish young man hanging back when it comes to sport lest he appear inadequate or effete. He had gone with experienced surfers who were all in the water by the time he had changed, so he entered the sea alone and was swept off his board 'into a maelstrom, punched by an unseen giant six times in the ribs, and carried out at a hundred miles an hour to the open sea'. His friends did not return for hours and then told him off for being foolish. He tried to make a joke out of it, but his response made him seem even less manly: 'I tried to tell them that as a boy I had been regarded as very promising at croquet.' In a second attempt he felt a sudden grip on his legs. 'In a flash I knew it was a shark', he wrote. Terrified, he swam back to shore as fast as he could and it was only when he collapsed on the beach that he realised that a large piece of seaweed had fastened itself round his legs.[29] He also suffered from a pronounced stutter. His parents had sent him to 'stammering curers' in his youth, but they had come up with little more than breathing exercises and he resented the fact that these 'old rogues' said that he could not have been doing the exercises properly. 'The assumption, presumably,' he caustically pointed out, 'was that one liked stammering.'[30]

Rob had another anxiety. The Beauchamp saga was far from over, as Beauchamp's brother-in-law Bendor Grosvenor, the 2nd Duke of Westminster, had caught wind of what had happened in Australia and had dug up some additional dirt, which he presented to the king. The story that George V replied, 'Why, I thought people like that always shot themselves,' may be apocryphal, but Westminster's vendetta gathered force. Westminster persuaded Beauchamp's wife Lettice to move out of Madresfield to his own estate in Cheshire, which she confusingly explained to a friend was because 'Benny tells me it's because [Boom's] a bugler'.[31] Matters remained very hush-hush while the Lord Chancellor, Lord Sankey, gathered further evidence for the king, but when the Conservative Party leader Stanley Baldwin and his wife stayed at Madresfield to attend the enthronement of a new Bishop of Worcester, Westminster and his other sister Lady Shaftesbury wrote to complain to Baldwin in the strongest possible terms – little knowing that both the bishop's diplomat son Stewart Perowne and the Baldwins' son Oliver (who was a Labour MP) were also homosexual. Lettice then sued for divorce in the most coruscating terms, claiming that Beauchamp had committed gross indecency with several of his male servants, including George Roberts, 'masturbating them with his mouth and hands and compelling them to masturbate him and lying upon them and masturbating between their legs'.[32] Then, just as Rob returned to England, the king sent three Knights of the Garter and privy councillors to Madresfield to issue Beauchamp with an ultimatum: leave the country immediately or face arrest, humiliation and imprisonment with hard labour. Within forty-eight hours he followed the well-frequented path into homosexual exile. For years he wandered. He bought a house in Sydney, rented the *piano nobile* of the Palazzo Morosini on the Grand Canal in Venice, stayed with Lord Berners in Rome and welcomed the actor Ernest Thesiger (who had several affairs with men and women) to an apartment in Paris. He was not alone. An elegant valet called Robert Byron and a secretary called David Smyth were in regular attendance and Vita Sackville-West met him in Algeria with 'a sulky, embarrassed and bored young man called George',[33] who was probably George Roberts.

This was precisely what Rob Bernays feared. Beauchamp's fate taught Rob a horrible lesson – that if you sailed too close to the wind you risked being hounded out of society. He did not sever all links with Beauchamp, though. In 1933 he wrote to his sister Lucy that he had heard that 'poor B associates with nobody except the beachboys at Bondi and that [his son] Hugh has gone the same way'. He ambiguously added, 'All Sydney is shocked to its heman depths as well it might be.'[34] Rob visited Beauchamp in Paris a few years later, too, when he was pleased to find the earl more reconciled to his lot, 'though he is still vainly hoping that with the change of monarchs he will be allowed to return'.[35] Rob suspected Beauchamp's hopes would prove fruitless, but he did not reckon with Sir Samuel Hoare, who was appointed home secretary in 1937. Hoare was married to Beauchamp's younger sister Maud and although they had a loving marriage, he was rumoured not only to be the nattiest dresser in Parliament, but celibately homosexual. Hoare quietly lifted the warrant and allowed Boom to return home, but by then Beauchamp was suffering from cancer, and a year later he died in a suite in the Waldorf Astoria in New York.

Beauchamp's exile started just days before another of Rob's friends was faced with an identical dilemma, as the police also came knocking at one of the grandest houses in the land, Cliveden, the home of Nancy Astor and her husband Waldorf, the Viscount Astor. Nancy's exceptionally good-looking son by her first marriage, Bobbie Gould Shaw, had served in the Guards Machine Gun Regiment in the war but had found it difficult to find a clear purpose in life thereafter. He flirted with plenty of society girls, but in 1929 he was caught in an act 'unbecoming an officer and a gentleman' with another soldier and was, like Beauchamp, given an ultimatum – resign his commission or face a court martial. He chose the former, so a cock-and-bull story was invented about his being found drunk on duty. Two years later, though, he was apprehended for importuning a guardsman. This led to a tougher ultimatum – flee the country or face arrest. This time, on the advice of Philip Kerr, the unmarried Marquess of Lothian, who was about to travel to Russia with the Astors, Bobbie decided to face the music. On 16 July 1931 he settled up with his landlady and servants, he resigned from his clubs, sent his car and clothes to Cliveden and gave his spaniel to his cousin. The following day he pleaded guilty at Marlborough Street and was sentenced to six months in prison. Nancy was terrified of the adverse publicity, but her husband owned the *Observer*, his brother, who was also an MP, controlled *The Times*, and she was able to prevail on Beaverbrook to keep her name out of his titles. 'Nothing matters very much about me,' she wrote, 'but I felt I should like to spare the other children. I know you appreciate that. For the first time in years I am really fond of my son – Bobbie.'[36] The only public notice of Bobbie's conviction was in the official *London Gazette*, which noted on 21 August that 'Lt. R. G. Shaw ... having been convicted by the

Civil Power, is removed from the Army, his Majesty having no further occasion for his services.' Everyone knew, though. The Irish playwright George Bernard Shaw wrote to Nancy that 'the natural affections of many men … take that perverse turn; and in many countries adults are held to be entitled to their satisfaction in spite of the prejudices and bigoted normality of Virginians and Irishmen like our two selves. Bobbie can claim that he has to suffer by a convention of British law, not by Nature's law.'[37] A few years later when Rob Bernays had become a regular at Cliveden and he and Nancy went to the Gary Cooper film *The Lives of a Bengal Lancer*, she told him that if only Bobbie had had the chance of 'that sort of life, with pig-sticking and frontier warfare, the disaster would never have happened'.[38] It was a long time before she came to terms with Bobbie's sexuality, but she did eventually refer to his lover Frank as 'the prettiest of all my children's girlfriends; the rest of them are just over-painted hussies'.[39]

Yet again the message was rammed home to Rob – same-sex longings could only bring trouble and loneliness. It stayed with him the rest of his life.

6

The Bachelor MPs

In 1931, Rob's biggest problem, politically at least, was that he was a Liberal and his party had few prospects of adding to its fifty-nine seats, as it was split into three.* On the night the Labour government imploded, though, he was staying with Lloyd George and two weeks before the election was called he was selected as the Liberal candidate in Bristol North, a seat that the Liberals had won consistently, apart from in 1923 and 1929, when the Methodist lay preacher and temperance campaigner Walter Ayles had won it for Labour in three-way contests. Rob knew he would have to engage in some nimble footwork if he wanted to win, so he sought out the Conservative candidate, Major P. H. Jephson, and somehow persuaded him to defy his party executive and refuse to stand, thereby making it a straight Liberal fight with Labour. Rob was remarkably nonchalant about the fact that he had no connection with Bristol – he even claimed that carpetbagger MPs were vital because 'a man is a member for the nation first, and his constituency a long way afterwards'[1] – but above all he made it clear that he supported the 'full programme of Mr Ramsay MacDonald and the National Government'.[2] With nowhere else to go, Conservative voters delivered him a hefty majority of more than 13,000 votes and within weeks he had taken a lease on a smart, maroon-carpeted

---

* Herbert Samuel led the official Liberal Party, John Simon led the Liberal National Party and David Lloyd George led his own splinter group of Independent Liberals.

'bachelor apartment' at Albany Chambers, 86 Petty France, not far from Parliament.

His immediate impression of the new Parliament was that 'the Conservatives are everywhere. They flood over all the benches on the Opposition side below the gangway.'[3] He was right. The election delivered an astounding result: 235 Labour MPs, including the leader and deputy leader, were swept away. Just twelve National Labour MPs sat on the government benches, where 470 Conservatives, thirty-five Liberal National MPs and thirty-three Liberals swamped them. In all, the National Government could count on 554 out of 615 seats.[4] Nicolson, who was a friend of the Mosleys and was excited by what he saw as the New Party's vigour, stood as its candidate in one of the two Combined Universities seats and came a very distant fifth out of five, blamed 'a panic swing towards the Tories' and concluded that 'the whole thing is so absurd and sensational that there is little to be said about it'.[5] He had a point. MacDonald had received the largest electoral mandate in British history, but it did the nation few favours. His near-pacifism was admired and shared by many, but it blinded him to dangers overseas. He had few true allies within his own government and such was the Conservatives' preponderance that there was always a danger of peer pressure crowding out independent thought. Yet this Parliament was elected at a key moment in European history. Benito Mussolini had already turned Italy into a fascist one-party police state with himself as its self-appointed dictator and was beginning to flex his muscles in Africa. In Germany the Nazi Party was on the rise. With such events unfolding across the Channel, Nicolson was right to find it 'most disquieting that at this crisis of our history we should have a purely one-party House of Commons'.[6] As one of Nicolson's friends, Victor Cazalet, the Conservative MP for Chippenham and parliamentary private secretary to the National Labour MP and Dominions Secretary J. H. Thomas, had predicted at the start of the election, 'We shall obviously be 80 to 90% of the New Nat. Gov. If so, we can do anything we like.'[7]

But there was another phenomenon. The Conservative group had a large contingent of bachelors – roughly 200 out of the 470 – quite out of proportion to the wider population. More men have married than have not in every era, and the twentieth century saw a steady increase in the popularity of marriage. So just under 30 per cent of adult men were single in 1921, but by 1931 that figure had fallen to 27 per cent, and in 1951 it was just under 20 per cent. Among Conservative MPs the figure stood at 42.5 per cent. The statistics mask many realities, as 'unmarried' and 'never married' are not the same, but so many men *were* married that it felt noticeably out of the ordinary not to marry.

Consequently, many bachelor MPs felt they had to give an excuse for remaining 'unmarried'. When a newspaper caught wind of a 'Bachelor MPs' dinner' at the Commons in 1926 and asked attendees why they were still unmarried, one said he had just been unlucky, while another replied, 'People I have liked have never liked me, and people who have liked me I have never liked.'[8] Interestingly, he carefully avoided mentioning the gender of the 'people' he might have liked.

Victor Cazalet was another of the 'bachelor MPs' at the dinner. Born in 1896 of a wealthy aristocratic family with roots in Languedoc and St Petersburg, homes in Mayfair and Cimiez, and a large twenty-servant country house at Fairlawne in Kent, he had been a star pupil at Eton – in his final year elected president of the Eton Society or 'Pop', which acted as school prefects – and when he left in 1915 he signed up to the West Kent Yeomanry before being transferred as a captain to the Household Cavalry. He hated the army. 'Everything goes against everything I like,' he wrote in his journal. 'It is like being a little school-boy again. No common sense is allowed, no words to superiors: that's where it really *is* worst.'[9] Yet he served with distinction on the front line, most notably at the battle of Poelcappelle in October 1917, when he led the defence of Requette Farm against overwhelming odds with 'no ammunition, no food and no relief'.[10] His fellow officers thought he was the hero of the hour and Second Lieutenant

Nevile Butler, one of just two out of fifteen officers to survive (there were 420 casualties out of 550 men), wrote to Victor's mother that he expected Victor to pick up a Distinguished Service Order (DSO). So it was a surprise when a senior officer who had played no part in the day's events was awarded the DSO and Victor had to put up with the Military Cross. Victor claimed not to care and made his mother write to congratulate the unnamed officer, but the episode clearly rankled. After the war he was appointed to General Sir Henry Wilson's staff of the Supreme War Council (as little more than 'a super-telephone operator')[11] for the initial negotiations of the Versailles Peace Treaty, and spent the best part of a year in Siberia liaising with the White Russian forces as they attempted to hold out against the Russian Revolution. Here he learned Russian, saw men in horrific conditions that reminded him of the trenches, honed his hatred of communism and developed a general distrust of easy solutions to intractable problems like post-imperial Russia. After studying as a relatively mature student at Christ Church College in Oxford and enduring a spell as a civil servant, he stood unsuccessfully for the Conservatives in Chippenham in 1923 but managed to overturn the Liberal majority the following year, entering Parliament alongside Bob Boothby, Harry Crookshank and Duff Cooper. Soon he was described as 'a new force in Parliament'[12] and was made parliamentary private secretary to the President of the Board of Trade.

Cazalet was an impressive all-rounder. He was an astute businessman, a director of the Dorchester Hotel and the Hudson Bay Company, and chairman in 1937 of the witty satirical magazine *Night and Day*, which was edited by Graham Greene. He loved classical music and was an accomplished singer and pianist. He was a serious sportsman, too. Having represented Oxford against Cambridge in three sports, he was a triple Half Blue at Oxford, he won the all-England amateur squash championship four times and captained the England squash team. His wealth – much of it acquired by his grandfather and father in Russia prior to the revolution in 1917 – meant that politics sometimes seemed more of a hobby than a vocation, but it also allowed him to travel extensively, crossing the Atlantic most years and regularly spending several months at a stretch abroad. His Huguenot ancestry and his grandfather Edward's revulsion at the Tsarist pogroms in Russia in the 1870s gave him a sympathy with refugees, especially the Jews. His first visits to Poland in 1922 and the Middle East in 1924 made him an unusually knowledgeable and passionate advocate for Polish independence and a Jewish homeland. He formed strong friendships with international figures like the World Zionist Organization leader Chaim Weizmann. Not all his constituents approved of these extended absences, but the Conservative-supporting *Wiltshire Gazette* was impressed that Victor managed to play matches, hold constituency meetings and deal with his correspondence, telling its readers in 1926 that, 'those who have been in correspondence with Captain Cazalet during these days will know that they have received return-of-post replies to their letters, so one begins to wonder whether he ever gets to bed'.[13] So too when he travelled the length of Africa in 1932, visiting the Cape, Nairobi, Darfur, Serengeti, Khartoum, Aswan, Luxor and Cairo, he had to face down criticism with a dollop of pomposity. 'If there was ever a time,' he said, 'when a Member of Parliament was at liberty to see the Empire and gain experience, it was now when the Government had no fewer than 500 supporters.'[14]

His answer about his status as a bachelor was the least convincing of all. 'A good mother and a good sister,' he said, 'are worth two good wives, and are far less expensive.'[15] His devoted sister Thelma, who was elected MP for Islington East in 1931, also adopted this affected jollity when she wrote in 1967 that she was indignant about the insinuations 'whispered' about her brother. 'The reason,' she insisted, 'why Victor never married is that he dreaded becoming too engrossed with one person, and too fond of his own children to bring them up properly. He valued independence too much to risk being the slave of his own character and losing the essential element of universality in his humanity.'[16] Thelma's indignation was overblown. Victor had become a Christian Scientist at Eton when a bout of pneumonia was 'miraculously' cured and he had dedicated himself, like another lifelong bachelor, his close friend Philip Kerr, the Marquess of Lothian, to the faddish religion, which preached abstinence from alcohol, tobacco and all forms of extramarital sex. That did not prevent the diminutive 'Teenie' from being an entertaining host, nor from mixing with a large circle of homosexuals, including the writers Hugh Walpole and Willie Somerset Maugham, the author of the successful play *Journey's End*, R. C. Sherriff (whose autobiography rejoiced under the title *No Leading Lady*), and the ubiquitous Eddie Marsh and Noël Coward. Victor could come across as priggish. When Lady Cunard seated him at lunch next to the Irishman George Moore, who had written several successful novels that dealt with prostitution and lesbianism, he declared that he was disappointed that 'sex questions interest him – to me they are taboo'.[17] But this is difficult to square with the other Victor: the man who declared his schoolfriend and travel companion Eddy Sackville-West 'delightful and stimulating'; the man who claimed, after visiting Berlin, that he loved Harold Nicolson 'a bit'; the man who hired Tray Mortimer's lover Paul Hyslop to redesign a home for him in Kent, Great Swifts, at which he held lavish parties for his theatrical friends; the man who invited the married but homosexual Cole Porter back to his rooms to sing to him alone; the man who struck up an enduring friendship with the homosexual German tennis champion Gottfried von Cramm; and the man whose closest friend in Parliament was another Etonian and lifelong bachelor, the American-born sportsman, artist and writer Sir Hamilton Kerr. The gossip columns picked up on this. When Victor reminded everyone that he was a bachelor in a speech in 1930, *Bystander* cattily added, 'as a matter of fact, his double-breasted beige waistcoat told one that'.[18] And when there was a World Conference in London in 1933 the 'Un-Parliamentary Asides' column by 'Big Ben' recommended that the delegates should be boarded out at weekends in some of the smaller country houses of England.

'Besides,' it asked, 'wouldn't Captain Victor Cazalet ... have thrilled to entertain some great man from overseas?'[19]

The truth was the parliament Rob Bernays joined in 1931 provided a surprisingly welcome home to a large number of queer or nearly queer bachelors, in part because the Commons was, as Churchill told Rob, 'a masculine assembly and the whole spirit and comradeship of it and the jokes too are essentially appertaining to men'.[20] There were just fifteen female MPs, so men could easily spend their whole day with other men in a world that was not homosexual but was certainly homosocial.

A few had been MPs for some time. The 'fabulously rich'[21] baronet, Sir Philip Sassoon, for instance, was first elected as Conservative MP for Hythe in 1912. He had been military secretary to Earl Haig in the war and parliamentary private secretary to Lloyd George in 1920 before serving as Under-Secretary for Air in Baldwin's government from 1924 to 1929, a post to which MacDonald now reappointed him. Sassoon's inherited wealth – he was part of the extended Rothschild family – enabled him to entertain in extravagant style at his sprawling London mansion on Park Lane, his quintessentially English country house at Trent Park and the elaborate fantasia he built and rebuilt overlooking the Romney Marshes at Port Lympne. He was also a liberal patron of the arts who amassed a significant collection of British paintings by Gainsborough, Zoffany and Reynolds and commissioned friends to decorate his homes. The 'Tent Room' at Lympne was painted by Jack Macnamara's schoolmate Rex Whistler as a trompe l'oeil with whimsical references to their mutual friend Lord Berners and their favourite Soho restaurant, the Eiffel Tower, while the dining room was given a homoerotic frieze of naked, muscled Egyptians by the portraitist Glyn Philpot (which had to be covered up when Queen Mary came to visit).[22]

Trent Park and Lympne were ideal spots for him to indulge another of his passions, flying. He invested heavily in his own planes and was for several years the commanding officer of 601, a voluntary squadron of the RAF, which was known as the 'millionaire's mob' because it included so many danger-seeking wealthy young men. It is said that it took him a long time to learn how to fly, but he threw himself into it. On one occasion he insisted that his instructor fly directly over Blenheim Palace, as a friend was thinking of buying it, and often he would fly friends from Lympne to another country house for lunch. He was so enamoured of the new Percival Petrel monoplane that he commissioned one with an interior lined in expensive blood-red leather. When he crashed a plane into a hedge at Cranwell, where the air force training college was, he summoned up another, and when two airmen made a quick dash to Dubrovnik and one landed Sassoon's Moth on a cow and the other crashed into the back of the Moth, Sassoon laughed and paid for the repairs. Once he had mastered flying he made several daring long-haul flights, including a tour of Mediterranean and Middle Eastern RAF stations in his Blackburn Iris biplane flying boat, and wrote a history of the 'Third Route' to India, which was published in 1929. This brought him into contact with another sexually ambiguous figure, T. E. Lawrence, who was effectively in self-imposed exile, masquerading as 'Aircraftman Shaw'. They became friends and Sassoon persuaded Lawrence to join the British Seaplanes racing team for the 1929 Schneider Trophy. Lawrence was a notoriously complex human being and as there is no unambiguous evidence that he ever engaged in physical affection with anyone, many have concluded that he was asexual, yet he wrote to George Bernard Shaw's wife Charlotte that he had 'seen lots of man-and-man loves: very lovely and fortunate some of them were'[23] and ironically enough he congratulated the many-layered Sassoon on *The Third Route*, saying, 'Your book feels easy, as if you had written it easily. Curious since fortune made you complicated!'[24] That last word seems like code.

There was another advantage to having an aerodrome on the lawn, as Sassoon fitted out a bachelor's wing for airmen at Lympne and insisted on one-on-one dinners for all applicants to the 601 Squadron. Often there would be dozens of officers lounging around the pool or picking guests up from the station.

All the leading politicians of the day made it repeatedly to one or other of his homes. Lloyd George came with his mistress and then wife, Frances Stevenson, who thought him clever and most amusing 'but one of the worst gossips I have ever come across'.[25] Churchill, whose house at Chartwell was largely the work of Sassoon's architect Philip Tilden (another aviator), was a regular. The guest list at Christmas and Easter read like a *Who's Who* of queer society, and when Victor Cazalet visited Lympne for the bank holiday in July 1933 he commented that it was 'very agreeable' dipping in the pool with Noël Coward and Lord Berners as it was '<u>boiling hot</u>'.[26]

For the best part of a decade, one of Sassoon's most frequent guests was Bob Boothby. Born the son of a successful Edinburgh banker in 1900, Bob had attended Eton and Oxford before becoming a City stockbroker and standing for Orkney in 1923. He was unsuccessful there, but in the general election a year later he was elected as Conservative MP for Aberdeen and Kincardine East. The two colleagues rapidly became such close friends that Sassoon rented or lent him a recently restored fifteenth-century farmhouse at Lympne known as the French House. Bob later declared that the decade he spent at Lympne was 'one of sheer enjoyment [and] of endless gaiety and entertainment' and confessed that he owed Sassoon 'far more enjoyment than to anyone else'.[27] They were a formidable pair. As a young man Bob was indubitably handsome, with a babyish round face, a come-hither frown and a sexually charged attitude. He boldly declared in his 1987 autobiography that homosexuality 'is more prevalent than most people want to believe' and claimed that when he attended Magdalen College immediately after the First World War, 'Oxford was, basically, a homosexual society.' Yet throughout his life he was keen to assert that he had no vested interest, as he had 'detected the danger, and sheered away from it'.[28] According to him, he expressly resolved that if he ever went into public life, he would completely stop talking about homosexuality, 'and instead do something practical to remove the fear and misery in which many of our most gifted citizens were then compelled to live'.[29] This seems categorical enough, and it is true that he married – twice – and engaged in several adulterous affairs, including a thirty-year romance with Dorothy Cavendish, the wife of his colleague Harold Macmillan. Yet the facts point to a more complex sexual identity. Many of his closest friends were homosexual, including Maurice Bowra, Somerset Maugham and fellow MP Tom Driberg, and he kept a letter from Nicolson with details of a harbour in Greece where pretty young sailors hung about drinking and smoking. His amorous affairs were much talked about, too. At one point in September 1932 Brendan Bracken (another bachelor) put about a rumour that Bob had got engaged, which led Robert Bruce Lockhart[30] to spend half the morning trying to ascertain whether it was true. In the end Bob himself denied it and Bruce Lockhart concluded it was all 'a degrading performance'.[31] Almost the moment he proposed to Diana Cavendish in 1935, he realised he had made a terrible mistake and told several of his friends as much. The marriage lasted barely two years, but, tellingly, it prompted a sudden falling out with Philip Sassoon.

Moreover, the most notorious episode of Bob's later life – his relationship in the 1960s with the boxer/burglar Leslie Holt and through him with the East End gangster Ronnie Kray – proved that Bob was perfectly capable of a barefaced lie. He sued the *Sunday Mirror* for libel when it claimed that the police were investigating the two men – and won £40,000 – but according to recently released MI5 papers Holt stated that Bob and Kray attended 'several homosexual parties together' and were '"hunters" of young men'.[32] Another supposedly reliable MI5 source added that Holt's relationship with Bob was no 'fly-by-night affair', as he had given him expensive cars and taken him to the opera (which the MI5 officer reckoned was 'rather bold'). MI5's clear conclusions were that 'Boothby is a kinky fellow and likes to meet odd people', and that both Bob and Ronnie were 'queers'.[33]

Philip and Bob's closest friend during these early years was yet another devotee of amateur aviation, Noël Coward. He too publicly denied his homosexuality until his dying day, but he lived with his partner Jack Wilson at another nearby farmhouse called Goldenhurst near Aldington, and on alternate weekends he would welcome Bob's political friends and take his theatrical friends over to the French House. Coward liked to shock and on one occasion impressed Bob's secretary by sending him an ambiguous telegram, 'Meet me in dreamland tonight at ten o'clock.'[34] How was she to know that Dreamland was the funfair in Margate?

One other bachelor MP, Harry Crookshank, was a 'Colleger' at Eton with Harold Macmillan and came from a similarly wealthy background. He saw fierce action as a captain in the Grenadier Guards – a severe shrapnel injury left him wearing a truss for the rest of his life – and spent five years as a diplomat before being elected MP for Gainsborough in 1924. He lived for many years with his mother Emma and sister Betty at 51 Pont Street in Knightsbridge, where the Stygian gloom was described by Macmillan's brother-in-law: 'As you entered through the heavily leaded glass door the catacomb-like gloom was relieved only by one small weak electric bulb, like the light on the tabernacle "dimly burning".'[35] Although Harry kept another house at 4 Lyall Mews in Belgravia, where his longstanding valet Bertie Page lived with his wife Alice and her brother David Gresham, who was Harry's chauffeur, Harry was the soul of discretion while his mother was alive. His life was filled with dinners at Pratt's, meetings of the freemasons, sherry with the Bishop of Lincoln after morning prayer at the Cathedral and trips to the Cavendish Hotel in Eastbourne with his mother, his sister, the MP Richard Law and half the household staff. His sole vice seems to have been the Turkish baths. Soon after his mother died, though, he set up house with a merchant seaman called Desmond Kilvington, who had been a regular companion on the campaign trail for years. It was only when he secured Kilvington the selection as Conservative candidate in Grimsby – and the Conservative Association started to object to Kilvington's alcoholism – that Crookshank's homosexuality became more widely known.

By contrast, doubts were expressed from the beginning about Paul Latham, who was elected as MP for Scarborough in a by-election in May 1931, aged twenty-six. Soon after the election he inherited a baronetcy and a considerable fortune from his father, who was the joint managing director of the fabric manufacturer Courtaulds, for many years, which allowed him to buy the best grouse moor in Yorkshire at Danby Lodge, a grand London house with a new dining-room for twenty-eight and Herstmonceux Castle ('one of the most beautiful show places in England').[36] Latham's frequent appearances in the society press, which showed him sipping champagne with a string of glamorous young women at the Gargoyle, did not fool anyone. Nor did his marriage in 1933 to the 'society beauty' Lady Patricia Moore, the daughter of the Earl and Countess of Drogheda (and younger sister of the young man Harold Nicolson had so admired in Berlin). Latham hired a train for 200 constituents to attend the ceremony at St Margaret's, Westminster, but the *Bystander* commented that 'the engagement of Sir Paul Latham and Lady Patricia Moore was certainly a surprise to me. Sir Paul never seemed the marrying type.'[37] As if this was not clear enough, *Bystander* carried the couple's stiff engagement photograph on the same page as one of Eddie Marsh embracing Ivor Novello at the first night of *When Ladies Meet* under a joint banner headline: 'The Bystander holds up the Mirror to the Gay World'.[38] People were right to be sceptical − at the time of the wedding Latham was halfway through a decade-long relationship with Eddy Sackville-West.

The House of Commons that Rob Bernays joined in late 1931 had plenty of queer members. Many were independently wealthy. They had been to the best schools, they belonged to the smartest clubs, they dined at the swankiest restaurants and the grandest society hostesses invited them to the most resplendent parties, at which they quaffed the best champagne. They hung out together with actors, writers and artists and created a safe haven for themselves. Above all they knew discretion was not just the better part of valour − it was a social prerequisite. The rules of the game were clear. As one book advised in 1927 'don't be too meticulous in the matter of your own clothes' and 'don't let your enthusiasm for particular male friends make you conspicuous'.[39]

Rob had learned that lesson the hard way with Beauchamp, but Parliament was to give him a new chance to build deep, affectionate friendships with other men. He still fretted about loneliness. He looked on the widowed but queer MP Malcolm Bullock and thought him a 'rather sad figure, living alone in this lovely house'. For a while Rob tentatively courted Katharine 'K' Tennant, the imposing much younger Scottish half-sister of Margot Asquith, who was a formidable huntswoman, farmer and Conservative Party activist. That soon petered out, although they remained close friends when she married another MP, Rob's friend Walter Elliot, and Rob would often visit K and Walter at their Borders home, Harwood. Rob was a strange mix of principle and ambition. He hated being short of money, he was worried that he might lose his seat and he constantly courted wealthy Conservatives. But the life of an MP brought that dilemma to a head. On the one hand he knew that society expected any ambitious young MP to have a charming wife on his arm, but at the same time Parliament introduced him to a circle of men with whom he formed a far deeper bond than he had ever thought possible. It was a dilemma he would wrestle with for the rest of his life.

PART TWO

The Turning Point

7

Germany Changes

For a moment on 10 November 1931 the lights were dimmed in the House of Lords for the State Opening of the new Parliament. The robes and jewels of the peers and their wives were cast in darkness and a single lamp threw a soft light on the empty throne. Then Big Ben gave out a muffled peal, the lights came up, the gathering rose with a rustle of ermine and satin, the Prince of Wales took his place and the king and queen processed in, holding hands. George V started 'His Majesty's Gracious Speech' with a bold assertion: 'My relations with foreign Powers continue to be friendly,' he said, before committing the government to promoting peace and goodwill, the League of Nations and the upcoming Disarmament Conference.[1] The MPs gathered at the bar of the House, including Rob Bernays, Bob Boothby, Victor and Thelma Cazalet, Philip Sassoon, Harry Crookshank, Paul Latham and Viscount Knebworth, all nodded their approval. In the subsequent debate in the Commons that afternoon, Abraham Flint, the National Labour MP for Ilkeston, was equally optimistic. He had just defeated the Labour candidate by two votes (after four recounts), so he felt in a perfect position to state that: 'Just as we, being one nation, can sink our differences, forget our quarrels, and unite together for the common good, surely it is possible for humanity itself to cease from war and to remember that we are all sprung from the same stock.'[2] It was to be one of few references to international affairs that day, as most MPs were more exercised by domestic issues, but it embodied the predominant view in Britain. The 'Great War' had been a hideous mistake. Former enmities had to be put aside and Britain must do all in its power to seek common ground with other nations. Above all, Germany should be allowed to flourish. As the Labour leader George Lansbury said of the Versailles Treaty, 'a peace was made which was no peace'.[3]

Although many had clamoured for retribution in 1918, this was a pervasive and strongly held view by 1931. The strained patriotism of poets Rupert Brooke and Siegfried Sassoon was well known, but two plays on the subject – both also by queer men – had caught the public imagination. The writer J. R. Ackerley, who attended Rossall a few years before Rob Bernays, translated his wartime experience into *Prisoners of War* and managed to slip both its homoeroticism and its scepticism about the war past the censor in 1925; and Victor Cazalet's friend R. C. (or 'Bob' to Victor) Sherriff's poignant elegy to wasted youth, *Journey's End*, enjoyed a two-and-a-half-year run from 1928 and was made into a successful film by the tall, red-headed homosexual James Whale in 1930. With no female characters, it played on the overlap between male camaraderie in the face of danger and same-sex yearnings, and its characters and claustrophobic setting became such a standard reference that when Rob Bernays was crossing to Australia, a group of bright young things dressed up as the characters in the play.

The logical conclusion was that Britain should normalise relations with Germany, even if that meant amending the Treaty of Versailles. Many had argued from the outset that its terms were overly punitive. In addition to financial reparations and major territorial concessions, Versailles required Germany to dissolve its central command, the General Staff, slash the army and navy, abolish conscription and demolish all their fortifications in a fifty-kilometre strip east of the Rhine. To cap it all, they were banned from having submarines or an air force, and they had to guarantee the territorial integrity of Czechoslovakia. It was a harsh settlement and many argued that Britain had sided too readily with France. Yes, it was irritating that successive German governments unilaterally disregarded their international obligations, but there was considerable pressure to improve relations with Germany. Britain was struggling economically. Industrialists wanted to re-establish commercial relations with one of the largest markets in Europe. Britain's military and financial resources were overstretched defending and containing the Empire. Some thought that the only way of preventing another war was mutual disarmament, and many British politicians were keen to establish friendlier relations with Germany because they held the view, as one newspaper put it, that 'no nation in the world comes nearer to ourselves in character and sentiment than the Germans'.[4] This was mirrored by the first British ambassador to Berlin after the war, Viscount d'Abernon, who wrote in his diary in 1925 that it was time 'to abandon the view that Germans are such congenital liars that there is no practical advantage in obtaining from them any engagement or declaration'. He added, 'Personally I regard the Germans as more reliable and more bound to written engagements than many other nations.'[5]

This was also the view of most, but not all, Conservative MPs. Bob Boothby had long been fascinated by Germany and in 1928 he was one of a group of politicians, along with Malcolm Bullock and Harold Nicolson, who founded the Anglo-German Association with the express intention of improving relations. This was about as Establishment-minded a body as could be imagined. Its president was Rufus Isaacs, the Marquess of Reading, who had risen to be the first Jewish Lord Chief Justice of England and Viceroy of India, and its members included several senior men who had fought the Germans in the war, including the former First Sea Lord, Admiral John (now Earl) Jellicoe, and General Sir Ian Hamilton, who had commanded the Mediterranean Expeditionary Force at Gallipoli and was now Scottish president of the British Legion.[6] The association attracted plenty of parliamentary support. When the German Chancellor, Heinrich Brüning, visited London in June 1931, he was received at Buckingham Palace and at Chequers as the first German minister since 1914, and the association welcomed him at a celebratory lunch. 'At the present time,' he boasted, 'our two countries for the last year have been moving steadily closer to each other.'[7] The association helped push the pace of rapprochement throughout 1931. The Royal Navy visited the German naval base at Kiel, the British Council promoted British writers in Germany, the International Friendship League brought German students over to learn English and sing German songs, and a new Anglo-German Club was formed with d'Abernon as its president, and Harold Nicolson, Buck De La Warr and the Master of Semphill as directors. Soon the club had a new periodical, a smart clubhouse with a dining room, ballroom, *Bierstube* and bedrooms 'fitted with every possible requirement' near the German Embassy at 6 Carlton Gardens, where there were regular dinners and cultural evenings for German and British diplomats and businessmen.

It was against this background that Bob travelled to Germany to give a couple of lectures in Hamburg and Berlin just a month after the State Opening of Parliament. This time he was shocked by the economic situation facing the country. Hamburg was full of workmen with no jobs, the River Elbe was full of ships with no crews, and he detected a mood of 'gradually increasing desperation, which finds political expression in "Hitlerism"'.[8] Things had certainly changed in recent months. Hitler's phalanx of 107 deputies was still outnumbered in the 1930–2 Reichstag by Brüning's Social Democrats (SPD) on 143 and the Communists on seventy-seven, but with the Centre Party and the German National People's Party (the DNVP) securing sixty-eight and forty-one seats respectively and largely swinging to the right, the arithmetic left Brüning in a state of constant uncertainty. Hitler had deliberately exploited this throughout the year with a sustained campaign of violence. Ernst Röhm's SA ruthlessly stirred up brutality on the streets. They sought out socialists, communists and Jews to beat up, and created a climate of chaos that they hoped would eventually make the nation clamour for the firm grip of authoritarian rule, which they alone, in their smart new uniforms from Hugo Boss, could provide. By the end of 1931 more than 8,000 people had been injured or killed, and forty-seven SA men and eighty communists had been killed.

By a quirk of fate Bob was granted a whole hour with Hitler at his temporary headquarters in the Esplanade Hotel at the very moment that a letter was delivered to Brüning from Hitler breaking off negotiations about a coalition government. It was a strange meeting. Hitler subjected Bob to a long harangue about the injustices of Versailles, but Bob thought Hitler's youth, passion and 'abundant vitality' should not be underestimated. Hitler told him that his rise to power was now inevitable – and would come 'in a measurable space of time' – yet in a moment of naïveté Bob wrote that 'if Hitler wins it is highly improbable that he himself will accept office'.[9] Bob's visit was not all hard work. For the best part of a year he had been engaged in a barely concealed affair with Dorothy, the highly sexed wife of his friend Harold Macmillan, who had returned to the Commons in the 1931 election. Yet Bob later wrote that 'homosexuality was rampant' among Germany's young men and 'as I was very good-looking in my twenties, I was chased all over the place, and rather enjoyed it'.[10] So, not surprisingly, he stayed on after his lectures for the New Year's Eve ball that Vita had so despised. He expressed surprise that many of the women were actually men, but admitted that he enjoyed the evening so much that he would never forget it. In bed that night he pondered whether such a party was symptomatic of the decadence of a great nation, 'and decided, rightly, that it was not'.[11] Even with Hitler on the rise, one could enjoy a queer night out in Berlin.

There was a reason for this, as the higher echelons of the NSDAP still retained several openly homosexual members. Ernst Röhm had proved himself a successful political organiser. He grew the SA from 60,000 to 427,000 members within eighteen months and developed a vast infrastructure, with SA-only rooms in hotels, new homes for SA men, special training camps and a string of 'Brown Houses' – barracks – with gyms, libraries, dining halls and dormitories, all fostering an intense sense of male camaraderie. He had a direct line to Hitler and he seemed to embody the ethos of the Nazi Party, with its combination of grievance, discipline, revolution and violently rough-hewn masculinity. Röhm was under constant attack, though, from both the SPD and his NSDAP colleagues, who united in trying to expose his weakest flank, his sexuality. Quite early in his time as chief of staff there was a major rebellion within the SA ranks in Berlin. It was rumoured that Röhm was in a three-way relationship with an old friend and ally from the *Frontbann*, the front organisation that had been set up to carry on the work of the SA when it was banned after the Munich Putsch, Paul von Röhrbein, who was now in his forties, and the head of the Berlin SA, Karl Ernst. Then came an attack from the left. On 2 June the SPD newspaper *Münchener Post* launched a broadside at his dodgy finances and three weeks later they published an article entitled 'Homosexuality in the Brown House. Sexual Life in the Third Reich'. Within days Röhm's enemies within the NSDAP leapt on the bandwagon, when a large crowd of supporters of the recently sacked SA leader in Berlin, Walter Stennes, gathered outside the Halenseer Hütte, where Ernst and Röhrbein were dining, and started chanting 'queer pigs'. Ernst had to summon SA reinforcements to get them out alive. Ernst's good looks, incidentally, masked a vicious streak. That September, on the night of the Jewish New Year, he led a thousand of his SA members in a riot through the Kurfürstendamm, attacking Jews as they left synagogue and shouting 'Die, Jew!' and 'Kill the Jews.' Ernst was convicted of public-order offences that December and sentenced to six months in prison, but in February the sentence was lifted and in the three elections of July 1932, March 1933 and November 1933 he was elected to the Reichstag.

Meanwhile the *Münchener Post* continued its campaign. Some how they caught wind of Röhm's incriminating autobiographical letters to the psychologist Heimsoth, which were seized by the police and landed in the lap of a one-time Nazi member who became an SPD deputy, Dr Helmuth Klotz. Klotz felt he could not pass up an opportunity to expose the Nazis' hypocrisy, so in March 1932, just before the new elections, he published the full text of Röhm's correspondence and distributed 300,000 copies. It made no difference to the election result, but it dramatically increased the mutual antagonism between the main parties. Not long after the election Edmund Heines, who was by now a Reichstag deputy, head of police in Breslau and head of the SA for all Silesia, came across Klotz in the restaurant at the Reichstag and he and three other Nazi deputies beat him up. When the SPD president of the Reichstag, Paul Löbe, demanded that the four Nazi deputies be suspended, they refused to cooperate and by the time they were eventually sentenced to three months in prison, Hitler's ascendancy was so assured that the sentence was never implemented.

Despite this violence, Röhm and Heines fascinated several queer British men. The wealthy British painter Sir Francis Rose, who included Jean Cocteau and Christopher Wood among his lovers,* became Röhm's intimate, confidant and lover. Rose claimed in his fanciful memoirs that their relationship was entirely platonic, as there was nothing effeminate about the SA chief of staff. 'He abided by the old Potsdam tradition,' so Rose argued, 'that soldiers scented themselves, sent each other flowers for certain occasions, clicked heels, fought duels, and managed to look like carved wooden puppets with the help of steel corsets and tight uniforms.'[12] Yet Rose was not unique in seeking out these queer Stormtroopers. When a journalist for the *Charleston Daily Mail* met Heines in the Reichstag in September 1932 and was invited to Breslau to see his SA men in action, he portrayed Heines in adulatory terms, as 'the beau ideal of a soldier'. Noting that he was physically impressive – tall and heavyset, but also lithe and dynamic, handsome, with a devil-may-care smile – he commended Heines above all for having 'the rare quality of being able to fraternize and at the same time to maintain discipline'. He added, 'Heines typifies what war-and-peace-weary Germany seeks – youth, vitality, burning nationalism, discipline and leadership.'[13]

---

* Wood painted Rose in *Nude in a Bedroom*.

Nine months after Bob's meeting with Hitler, Rob Bernays had a similar experience. Rob had struggled to find his voice in Parliament, both literally and metaphorically. His maiden speech had been a bit of a disaster, as he stuttered terribly over the word 'Bombay' and Winston Churchill, whose imperialist policy on India Rob was attacking, deliberately threw him off his stride by sitting in front of him and muttering throughout. Moreover, with the Liberals sharply divided, Rob was worried about his seat, so he had continued working as a journalist, and in September 1932 he set off for Germany intending to garner impressions of the new Nazi party for the News Chronicle. With him was his oldest and closest friend from university days, Frank Milton, who was a wealthy bachelor, a successful lawyer, and a fellow Liberal who had come third in Islington South in 1929. He was also Jewish, although he had dropped his original surname, Lowenstein, in 1924. They, too, arrived at a climactic moment. Bob had been proved wrong about Hitler's personal ambitions, as Hitler had stood in the presidential elections on 10 April 1932. He lost in the final round to Paul von Hindenburg, but there was a sense that he was still on the rise, as he got 36.8 per cent of the vote, and at the end of May Hindenburg replaced Brüning with Franz von Papen of the Centre Party as the new Chancellor, with Hitler's support. Papen dissolved the Reichstag, ordered new federal elections for July, initiated a crackdown on Paragraph 175 'immorality' and introduced expedited trials and the death sentence for politically inspired murder. Yet again SA violence destabilised the government when five drunken, uniformed SA men in the Silesian village of Potempa seized a communist labourer called Konrad Pietrzuch in front of his mother, beat him, tortured him, castrated him, shot him twice, stabbed him twenty-nine times and left him to drown in his own blood before attacking his brother. A special court convened in Beuthen quickly convicted the 'Potempa Five' and under Papen's new law they should have been executed, but the local Nazi paper threatened that if the court dared to pass a single death sentence 'a storm will be raised throughout

Germany and the results will be incalculable'.[14] When the verdict was announced, Heines stood up in court in his SA uniform and bellowed, 'The German people will in future pass other verdicts.'[15] Moments later he commandeered the balcony of a local café, from which he repeated his call to arms to a band of Nazi followers, who started shouting 'Heil Hitler' and went on the rampage, smashing the windows of Jewish-owned shops and socialist and Catholic newspapers. Heines was soon backed up by Röhm, who visited the five in prison, and by Hitler and Hermann Göring, the new President of the Reichstag, who sent messages of support, claiming the five were national heroes. Papen capitulated, initially commuting their sentence to life imprisonment and later freeing them. Days later, Hitler, whose party had won an additional 123 seats in the July elections and had become the largest party, asked Hindenburg to make him Chancellor. Hindenburg refused and Papen prepared for the first meeting of the Reichstag by securing Hindenburg's support for yet another dissolution.

Rob Bernays and Frank Milton were present for that key meeting of the Reichstag on 12 September 1932. Göring had just been elected presiding officer. Papen tried to catch Göring's eye, but Göring refused to acknowledge him, even though he frantically waved the papers granting the dissolution. In Rob's words, Göring 'pushed aside the decree when it was presented to him, with the palm of his hand. It was a significant gesture. It was really the new Germany rejecting once and for all ... the Government of the old governing class.'[16] It was a decisive moment. Instead of dissolving the Reichstag, Göring allowed a vote on a motion tabled by the Communists, which declared no confidence in Papen's government. This was carried with Nazi support by 513 votes to thirty-two. Rob added an ominous note, suggesting that the Communists should have been more reluctant to vote with the NSDAP that afternoon 'for they were next to meet in the concentration camps, with the Nazis as guards'.[17]

Like Bob Boothby, Rob had not just come to see German politics. In a convoluted section of *Special Correspondent*, the book he published in 1934, he stated that he had wanted to examine the nightlife in Berlin, which, so he had heard, was 'the centre of obscure and unsavoury abnormalities', and when his unnamed guide told him that this was 'an abomination' and that when Hitler came to power he would burn the whole district down, Rob insisted that they immediately go on a tour of the queer bars, cafés and clubs. Clearly Rob was fascinated – and his guide knew exactly where to take him – as they went to a place 'as to the nature of which there was absolutely no doubt. Middle-aged men were dancing with boys not out of their teens, and young men with powdered faces and swaying hips sidled up and down in women's evening dress.'[18] Rob's prim phrases mask his true fears, as he added, 'I imagine that such a place could be paralleled in London, but at least it would be down some dingy back stairs, and the proprietor would be in constant terror of raids by the police.'[19] In other words, it was the fear of arrest that really inspired his distaste. No wonder he put up a scandalised front. He had seen what Beauchamp had been put through. And besides, so he confessed in his customary self-deprecatory way, 'My very presence can reduce the brightest party to the deepest gloom.'[20]

Even at this early stage, when much of Britain was still ambivalent about Hitler, Rob understood the attraction of Nazism and saw its dangers. In other circumstances, he commented, one might think Hitler no more than 'a hard-working scout master out for the day', but put him on a political platform and he became something else. 'The moment he began to speak,' Rob wrote, 'he was transformed from a vulgar, self-advertising politician to an orator, a prophet with a flaming mission to his people.'[21] On his return home Rob was absolutely clear. 'In Germany to-day,' so he told a meeting in Bristol, 'there are all the elements of a resurgent militarism.'[22]

He was to be proved right. Even though the NSDAP lost a handful of seats in a new round of elections in November 1932, Hitler skilfully played Papen off against the defence minister, General Kurt von Schleicher, who ousted Papen as Chancellor in December. With the former allies Papen and Schleicher at each other's throats, it was only too easy to take the final step. On 30 January 1933 Hindenburg made Hitler Chancellor, with Papen as his deputy. This prompted a new round of visits from British politicians. Within days, Bob Boothby persuaded Philip Sassoon to travel with him to Berlin. As air minister, Philip would soon be sitting round the table at the Disarmament Conference with the new German government, so he should see things for himself. No records of this visit exist, as the two men, who were both already convinced of the need for Britain to rearm, deliberately circumvented the Foreign Office, and it is likely that Philip flew them in one of his own planes. But when Bob mentioned that a German friend thought that Hermann Göring was '*au fond* a good apple', Philip rang him up and arranged a meeting for the next day. Göring was as eager an aviator as Philip, but given his profound anti-Semitism it is unlikely they got on and Philip seems to have been far more interested in Bob, as he wrote to him on their return to England, 'This is to confirm (1) that you are a good apple, (2) that I am crackers about you, (3) that I am so glad that after all my shilly-shallying, beating about the bush and blowing hot and cold, I should come to the decision not to let you down! It was all grand, tip-top and top-hole, and must be repeated.'[23] Whether Philip had blown hot and cold about Germany or about Bob we do not know.

Philip and Bob thought themselves lucky to get half an hour with Göring, but when Rob Bernays returned to Germany with Frank Milton that June, Rob reckoned they 'struck oil'.[24] This time he billed himself as a 'National' rather than a 'National Liberal' MP and they were granted a whole day with Edmund Heines. Rob's account of the meeting is extraordinary. On the one hand he acknowledged that Heines 'had, so far as the atrocities were concerned, the most evil and extraordinary reputation in all Germany'.[25] Yet his pen-portrait of Heines has more than a hint of homoeroticism about it. Rob said Heines 'appeared a charming fellow − young, about thirty-five years of age, fair hair, blue eyes, smiling, boyish'. He waxed lyrical about his strong, broad shoulders, his crippling handshake and his smart Nazi uniform. He thought Heines was such 'a fine figure of a man' that he reminded him of an English staff officer, or the captain of a rugby fifteen who has just been made head boy. He even praised him for being so gloriously self-confident, 'so naively exultant in his new sense of power'. Rob barely commented on what Heines actually said, but he noted other details, especially the young, good-looking aide-de-camp, with long, drooping eyelashes and a gold wrist watch, who 'kept fingering his Master's uniform – pulling down a sleeve or putting a badge straight'.[26]

Heines offered to take Rob to Breslau concentration camp, which Heines had set up in an old fertiliser factory within a fortnight of Hitler becoming Chancellor to provide 'protective custody' to 200 or so Silesian Jews and political prisoners from the Communist and Social Democrat parties. The camp barely lasted five months before it was closed down and its inmates were transferred to another at Osnabrück, but Heines was unabashed about it. He even boasted to Rob when one prisoner walked past that he was the 'late Mayor of Breslau'. Rob may have misheard, as there is no evidence of a former mayor being incarcerated there, but several senior politicians were, including the former President of the Reichstag, Paul Löbe, who had excluded Heines from the Reichstag over the incident with Klotz. This was a prison and the inmates were given backbreaking and nugatory tasks. One group was turning a marshy wasteland into municipal baths (which were never completed). Another was watering plants by the barbed wire in the shape of a swastika. When the visitors approached an inmate he would mechanically repeat the line that the work was hard but they were getting used to it and that they were well fed. If there were questions about a prisoner who had never been heard of again, the stock answer was trundled out: 'Shot while trying to escape.' As Rob left he concluded, 'We had seen no actual evidence of cruelty, and yet we had the haunting sensation of nameless evils in that camp. What abominations were hidden behind that barbed wire?'[27]

The visit did not end there. Later that day Heines took Bernays and Milton to the local SA barracks, the Breslau *Braun Haus*, where men lounged about in uniform in the reading room, dining room and large shared dormitory, or exercised in the well-equipped gym. Rob noted that there were photographs of Heines everywhere and confessed that he could well understand his appeal to militant youth. He claimed that he could not exaggerate the feeling of revulsion he felt when meeting some of the Nazi leaders. 'They had homo-sexuality and sadism written all over them,' he wrote.[28] Yet he seemed smitten with Heines, who, he admitted, 'had all the attributes that make for hero-worship'.[29]

A couple of months later Victor Cazalet also came to have a look at Nazi Germany. He was feeling rather proud of himself. His political career had stalled, as his spell as parliamentary private secretary to J. H. Thomas had ended after less than a year in 1932, but he had just played in the men's singles competition at Wimbledon. The British player Frank Wilde had beaten him in the first round in straight sets,[30] but Victor reckoned just qualifying was 'quite a considerable effort for one in his 38th year' and that 'one would rather be beaten in [the] first round at W. than be in the final of any other tournament'.[31] He had also made the pleasurable acquaintance of the blond-haired German player Gottfried von Cramm. So, with Wimbledon over, Victor mounted a grand tour of his queer friends on the Continent. After a brief stay with Philip Sassoon at Lympne, Philip's parliamentary private secretary, the wealthy MP and bright young thing Loel Guinness flew Victor to Monte Carlo, from where he travelled to Italy to stay with the married but queer peer Lord George Lloyd, his wife Blanche and his new young secretary, Harold Nicolson's occasional lover James Lees-Milne. The next stop was Lake Como, where he partied with Bob Boothby and Dorothy Macmillan before joining a group of single male friends in Munich, including the young diplomat Tony Rumbold and the journalist Micky Burn. Rob would have been shocked by Victor's views. Victor quarrelled with Lord Lloyd about whether Britain should rearm against a resurgent Germany. 'It's crazy,' he wrote. 'I for one am not prepared to pay higher taxation to increase the Navy, when the German fleet lies at the bottom of the sea ... so there.' Victor's opinions in Munich seem even more extraordinary, as he asked to see the concentration camp at Dachau, which had only recently been converted from an old munitions factory by Heinrich Himmler, soon after the Nazi takeover of Bavaria that spring, and was now a forced labour camp holding a variety of political prisoners under 'protective custody'. Just as at Breslau, there had been a string of unexplained deaths at the camp and the brutal team of Commandant Theodor Eicke and Adjutant Michael Lippert had replaced the first commandant. Yet Victor wrote the following in his diary: 'Great fun. I visit (*sic*) the "Concentration Camp". It was not very interesting. Quite well run, no undue misery or discomfort.'[32] Such was Victor's hatred of communism that when Lippert said most prisoners were communist, he added, 'If that is the case, then they can stay there for all I care.' His only real complaint was that the group's guide, Hitler's American-German confidant Ernst 'Putzi' Hanfstaengl, had an 'incredible ... anti Jew complex'. For years, Micky Burn claimed that he couldn't concentrate when he and Victor attended a Mozart concert later that evening, as he kept on thinking about Dachau, but even he later admitted that he had been impressed by Nazism in 1933. His papers also reveal that the group had been told that ex-prisoners who had spread stories abroad about their ill treatment were hauled back to Dachau and placed in solitary confinement for weeks. That was for a first offence. For a repeat offence the prisoner would be stripped and placed face down on a table and given twenty-five strokes with a rubber truncheon. Victor, though, did not let this spoil his summer tour, which he ended with Chips Channon and his wife Honor in Saint Martin in the Caribbean, where they were joined by the 'very agreeable' society photographer Cecil Beaton, who was also queer.[33] When he returned to Lympne, though, Boothby, Churchill and Eden understandably mounted what he called 'furious attacks on me for being pro Nazi'.[34]

It is easy to condemn Victor's naïveté, but the new regime in Germany fascinated many in Britain in 1933, including queer men, because it felt like a place of liberation and dynamic energy. This was certainly true for Jack Macnamara, who set sail for India a month after Hitler became Chancellor but almost immediately wanted to return home. He missed Paddy and Herbert and pined for his London lifestyle. He disliked the hierarchical, judgemental attitudes of the British Army and its hangers-on, and he was weary of India. Above all, though, it felt as if the real action was now on the continent of Europe, with Germany and Italy making the running. This second Indian tour of duty did not last long, as Jack fell ill again and after less than seven months he was on a ship home for a month's leave. As if to confirm his decision to leave India for good, he woke on his last day to find a poisonous snake in his bedroom. His mind was made up. Back in England, he got back in touch with Herbert and with Lett, he took a large new London house, 8 Kensington Court Place, he spent a few days at Pound Farm with Paddy, and resigned his commission the day after his leave expired.

He immediately threw himself into Anglo-German relations. His interest in Germany was nothing new. The tour of Amsterdam, Brussels and Berlin with Herbert in 1930 was just the first of many visits by the two men to Germany, and over the intervening years Jack had taken every opportunity of building relations with the new breed of German politicians and sampling the full range of adult entertainment Germany had to offer. He and Herbert had visited the Eldorado and the Cozy Corner. They probably attended the same Berlin bathhouse as Röhm. They sunbathed by the lake at Wannsee near Berlin. They struck up friendships with Stormtroopers, they attended party rallies and they met all the leading lights of the NSDAP. Far from being scandalised by the Nazis' rise to power, Jack was intrigued by their seemingly virile combination of energy and vision.

As luck would have it, Lett was curating an exhibition of British art at the Anglo–German Club just when Jack arrived in London – and needed help. The exhibition was intended as a companion to one that had been held in Hamburg the previous summer, which had included a couple of works by Cedric. It had also brought Lett into contact with the Club's secretary, the mysterious young anglophile German journalist and photographer Mark Neven du Mont, as well as with Harold Nicolson, who was one of club's directors, and with Lieutenant Colonel G. Cawson, who supported the two exhibitions in the belief that 'art transcends national and political aims and prejudices'.[35] Lett had put out feelers among his friends for potential exhibitors, but several artists, including Jacob Epstein and Frances Hodgkins, had baulked at participating because they objected to the Nazis' 'atrocious cruelty and hardship … to Germany's own cultured classes'.[36] If anything, though, this gave further impetus to the club's desire to strengthen Anglo–German artistic ties, so Jack volunteered to be the honorary co–organiser of the exhibition and persuaded the club to appoint him as one of its directors.

Jack took his new responsibilities seriously. A week after resigning his commission he wrote to the Foreign Office saying he was 'anxious to develop [the club] as much as possible'.[37] He had been invited to Germany to give a couple of talks on Anglo–German relations and he wondered whether the Foreign Office could furnish him with any suitable contacts. The next day he lunched at the club with du Mont and Herbert Sharp, whom Lett now nicknamed 'the Bishop', and hosted a cocktail party at the club for those involved in the exhibition. A few days later Jack and Herbert dined at the Kensington home of the unmarried Irish barrister Maurice Healy with Pierre Landle, another expert on Germany; on 10 November Jack hosted Lett and du Mont to dinner at Kensington Court Place and on 11 November he and Paddy had lunch with Lett before Jack went off to dinner with the Conservative MP Sir Assheton Pownall, who would later be a leading member of the Anglo-German Fellowship. Jack seemed remarkably cavalier at this point about who knew about his relationships with Paddy and with Herbert (who was almost certainly paying for Kensington Court Place), but Lett noted in his diary that when du Mont came to dinner Jack was careful to have Paddy waiting on them rather than sitting with them.

The Foreign Office was wary of Jack's letter. An initial internal note described him as an officer who 'had to leave the army because of some heart trouble'[38] and commented that the Nazis thought of every better-class young Englishman who came to Germany as 'an unconscious agent for Nazi doctrines'.[39] Things then got a little murkier as Ralph Wigram, who had just completed a spell as first secretary at the British Embassy in Paris and was now head of the Central Department in the Foreign Office, wrote two intriguing notes for colleagues. Winston Churchill later praised Wigram as a 'great unsung hero' for gathering secret intelligence information about German rearmament and providing it to him when Baldwin refused to listen, so Wigram's comments are fascinating. In the first, handwritten note, he raised a query: 'I suppose this Mr. Macnamara who "had to leave the army because of some heart trouble" is not the same young man who got into some trouble in Tunis ... I remember the case in Paris and I do not think the part of Mr Macnamara in question was a very creditable one.'[40] Despite the misgivings – the War Office was said to be investigating exactly what this 'heart trouble' was – M. H. Huxley of the Foreign Office News Section met with Jack just before he left for Berlin and wrote to Basil Newton at the Berlin Embassy that Jack was 'by no means the stereotyped young military man'. He had quizzed Jack on his politics and although Jack thought that the fascist movement was more widely spread in Britain than people realised, 'He dislikes Mosley and is not, I gather, in sympathy with Fascism in general.'[41] It is difficult to avoid the impression that the Foreign Office was sizing Jack up for intelligence gathering in Germany.

Clearly they had doubts about him, but if he were genuinely opposed to German fascism then his already impressive contacts with the NSDAP could be extremely useful, especially to those officials, like Wigram and Newton, who were already unhappy with the British government's policy and were trying to collect concrete evidence of Germany's military ambitions.

Jack and Herbert set off for Berlin on 14 November, where the Nazis gave them a magnificent reception. Jack's large audience included former ministers and Nazi-supporting German princes. Joseph Goebbels, Hitler's euphemistically entitled Minister for Public Enlightenment, who ensured Jack's address was broadcast, must have been pleased, as Jack boldly pronounced, 'Give us time to adjust ourselves to the change in Germany and Hitler will be able to do nothing wrong for us.'[42] This was certainly not the official Foreign Office line and not surprisingly Ralph Wigram wrote a second note after Jack's return but before the exhibition, reporting that 'there is reason to believe that the German Government are intending to use the [Anglo-German] Club for propaganda purposes here'.[43]

Jack's speech in Berlin set tongues wagging, but when the German ambassador and the Conservative MP Lord Balniel turned up at the opening of the exhibition on 14 December, Jack and Lett showed them round a fine display featuring many of the greatest British artists of the day, including Cedric Morris, Paul Nash, Augustus John, Edward Burra, Barbara Hepworth and Frank Dobson. After the opening, Jack, Herbert, Lett and another friend, Tom Allan, enjoyed a celebratory dinner at the club with the famous mountaineer and Conservative MP for Chelmsford, Colonel Charles Howard-Bury (pronounced Bewry). The catalogue, which took a pot-shot at 'English prudery', claimed that people knew astonishingly little of what was happening around them because the press recorded 'only what the proprietors of the papers want the readers to believe' and that the exhibition was merely an attempt to 'provide information'.[44] By that criterion it was a success, but the *Yorkshire Post* drily commented that it would be difficult to organise a parallel exhibition, 'for much German art is now *émigré* and scattered over the world'.[45]

Plenty of people in Britain still wanted a rapprochement with Germany and closed their eyes to the truth. Rob Bernays, though, stuck out as the most ardent, frequent and courageous critic of Nazi Germany, not least because of his personal affinity with the Jews. After his visit in 1932 he wrote that, contrary to much British public opinion, he was in 'no doubt that the drive against the Jews is increasing in ferocity'.[46] In 1933 he and Frank Milton were constantly aware of signs saying 'Jews excluded', they heard desperate tales of Jews being forced to leave all their money and possessions behind when they fled, and Rob was shocked by Heines's insistence that Europe was threatened by a very formidable communist peril and his justification of the attack on the Jews on the grounds that 'Jewish money was behind it all'.[47] When one of Hitler's men kept on referring to German Jews as 'aliens' rather than 'naturalised Germans' in a meeting with MPs at the Commons in April, he tore a strip off the Nazi. Later that year he wrote stinging articles for the *News Chronicle* condemning what he had seen; and after another trip in September 1933 he penned an angry essay entitled 'The Nazis and the Jews', which appeared in the *News Chronicle* and the *Contemporary Review*. This time he thought the attacks on political opponents and on Jews had diminished in number but the 'atrocities to-day are more calculated and systematic'.[48] Time and again that year he warned about what he called the 'pre-war spirit of arrogance and the feeling that the Germans were the children of the earth'.[49] In July 1933 he warned that 'Germany is rearming'.[50] In November he claimed that Germany was an 'armed camp', which already had a 'vast half-trained army' and that pacifism had become a crime in Germany, as he had seen a man who had been beaten for refusing to sell tin soldiers in his shop. He told another meeting in Camberley that same month that all the wrangling in Parliament about domestic affairs while this terrible menace overshadowed everything was like 'the sailors of the doomed *Titanic* ... decorating the saloon as the ship was sinking'.[51] As far as he could see, 'If this spirit is allowed to continue, it means war in ten years.'[52]

Given Rob's clarity, it is disturbing to see Macnamara and Cazalet caught up in the enthusiasm of the moment in 1933. They should have been able to spot the dangerous evil at the heart of the Nazi rise to power. Yet Britain seemingly wanted to give Hitler the benefit of the doubt in 1933. It would take a profound personal experience to change the minds of these two men – but that was coming.

8

The Turning Point

In January 1934 the 66-year-old owner of the *Daily Mail*, Lord Rothermere, who had lost two of his sons in the war, penned an editorial entitled 'HURRAH for the Blackshirts', in which he called on the nation to bring a 'crusading spirit' back into politics, to revolt against the inertia and indecision of the 'Old Gang statesmen' now in power and to back Sir Oswald Mosley's British Union of Fascists 'with enthusiasm'.[1] A parallel piece in the *Daily Mirror*, which he also owned, was equally clear. 'Give the Blackshirts a helping hand,' it urged, while its sister, the *Sunday Pictorial* ran a competition to find the nation's prettiest woman fascist. This was a ringing endorsement for fascism from the heart of the establishment – and led to some *Daily Mail* staff coming to work in black shirts – but Mosley was already busy stirring up the crowds. At a rally of nearly 10,000 people in Birmingham he claimed that he received no instructions from Hitler, but many thought that there was no difference between the fascism of Mosley, Mussolini and Hitler, and noted that Mosley's adoring supporters gave him the fascist salute.

The first to condemn the Rothermere article was Stanley Baldwin's son, Oliver, who had lost his seat as a Labour MP in 1931 and was now living with his lover Johnnie Boyle in a farmhouse in Oxfordshire and making his living as a writer. His ferocious rebuke in the *Daily Herald* included the apocalyptic prediction, 'It may be that the Mark of the Beast is the Swastika. If so, we are heading rapidly for the final struggle.'[2] Rob Bernays was not far behind in condemning what he called the 'fascist call for dictatorship'. 'I wish,' he wrote, 'those who sponsor it had seen what I have seen in countries which already possess a dictatorship. The extinction of freedom of speech … imprisonment without trial,' and the maltreatment of opponents without impunity.' He ended with a warning. Young British fascists might think that they had discovered something with all the excitement of war but none of its dangers, but they would soon find that they have achieved both, 'and that the conflict will be more horrible than any upon which he could possibly engage, for it will begin among his own people'.[3] He felt the same when he saw Mosley in action at a British Union of Fascists rally at the Royal Albert Hall. The audience clearly wanted nothing but 'the full-blooded gospel of Dictatorship maintained by violence and fed by appeals to hatred and prejudice'.[4] It chilled his heart.

Thanks to what he had seen in Germany, Rob was on a mission to expose fascism, but he was also ambitious and had worked out early on in the Conservative-dominated Parliament that the only way to succeed was to insinuate himself into the bosom of the Conservative Party, quietly abandoning his Liberal colleagues and joining the government benches in late 1933. He befriended Unionists like Malcolm Bullock, Bob Boothby, Philip Sassoon and Harry Crookshank, he danced with the smart set at the Gargoyle and regularly got himself invited to supper parties and country-house weekends hosted by the most glamorous socialites of the day. It was at one such weekend at the Astors' Buckinghamshire residence, Cliveden, in February 1934 that he met 'Ronnie' Tree (or to give him his full name, Arthur Ronald Lambert Field Tree).

Ronnie was very different from Rob. He was wealthy, as his mother Ethel was the only daughter of Marshall Field, the millionaire founder of the American department store that bore his name and his father Arthur was the son of a Chicago lawyer, judge and failed US Senate candidate (he lost by one vote) who became an American ambassador. His anglophile parents had moved to England, where Ronnie was born in 1897, but had parted by the time Ronnie was four, as Ethel, whom Ronnie said was 'accustomed to do what pleased her from one moment to the next',[5] had a prolonged affair with a Royal Navy officer, David Beatty. Despite the comedown in life brought about by the departure of his mother (and her wealth), Ronnie's career proceeded on a conventional trajectory. After school at Winchester he served as attaché to his great-uncle, who was US ambassador in Rome, and when he met the 'beautiful, charming, elegant' Nancy Field, who was sailing from New York to London with her aunt, Nancy Astor, he married her in London within a year. In 1927 the couple took a ten-year lease on an elegant Georgian house, Kelmarsh Hall, near Market Harborough in Northamptonshire, where Ronnie went fox hunting with the Pytchley and Nancy redecorated the hall.

Ronnie had been scouting around for something more substantial to do when in August 1933 Arthur Stewart, the 7th Earl Castle Stewart, had 'a nervous breakdown'[6] and resigned as Conservative MP for Harborough. Ronnie reckoned that the election of 1931 had been so overwhelmingly National–Conservative that there were few potential candidates left 'with ambitions unassuaged' and that consequently the local committee consisting of 'a dozen somnolent and elderly ladies and gentlemen of the area'[7] selected him as their candidate for lack of anyone better. As a sign of his commitment, Ronnie and Nancy promptly bought nearby Ditchley Park in Oxfordshire, which consisted of a mansion with twenty-four bedrooms, ten bathrooms and seven reception rooms, numerous outbuildings, thirty tenants' cottages, and 3,300 acres of farms, gardens, lawns and woods. The by-election was delayed until November, as Parliament was in recess and Ronnie confessed that speaking did not come 'naturally or easily'[8] to him, but plenty of Conservative colleagues came to campaign for him, including Victor Cazalet and Duff Cooper, and the contest was never really in doubt. Lord Castle Stewart had secured a 19,578 majority in a straight fight with Labour in 1931 and even with the Liberals putting up a candidate this time, Ronnie romped home on 28 November with 19,320 votes. Thus he arrived on the parliamentary scene with a wife, a majority of 6,860 and a country house in which to entertain on a scale that could almost rival that of Sir Philip Sassoon – once it too had been redecorated with the help of Sibyl Colefax.

Ronnie and Rob did have one thing in common, as Ronnie had several sexual relationships with men. Rob was not always easy on a first acquaintance. Sometimes he was too chippy about his Liberal politics. When he met Viscount Knebworth at Cliveden in 1933 Rob described him to his sister Lucy as 'a foolish young Tory MP [who] declares himself against liberty'.[9] But the next day he was smitten. 'There is a nice young Tory here,' he wrote, confessing 'at least I think he is nice because he can actually quote from a speech I made in the House'.[10] When it came to Ronnie Tree, though, Rob had no hesitation. The two men hit it off instantly. Ronnie later described Rob as 'clever, introspective and humble; his beliefs and feelings ran deep'.[11] Rob made these beliefs abundantly clear just weeks after they met. He was keen to visit Germany again, even though he knew that might be dangerous. On his last visit he had been so worried about getting his German friends into trouble that he sat up in his bunk on the overnight Channel ferry deleting their names and addresses from his address book and transcribing them in code into his notebook. Putzi Hanfstaengl had also been downright abusive when Rob had politely asked for a meeting with the Führer, disdainfully barking at him, 'Do you think I am going to get an interview for a sow of a Jew?'[12] But Rob was determined to expose the brutality of Nazism. Frank Milton was not free this time, so when Rob bumped into Ronnie in the smoking room at the Commons he asked whether he would like to accompany him on what would be his fourth visit in three years, during the forthcoming Whitsun recess. Ronnie had not yet been to Germany and he had stated at his adoption meeting that the Conservative Party stood for 'peace and disarmament'[13] but he eagerly agreed and offered to have his Rolls-Royce sent out to Berlin to drive them around.

Jack Macnamara, meanwhile, found that *his* beliefs were put on trial when he was selected as the Conservative candidate for the Upton by-election in West Ham in the East End of London. His selection came as a surprise to many of his friends, including Lett, as he had shown little interest in Conservative politics thus far, but the sitting Conservative MP Alfred Chotzner had served for many years in the Indian Civil Service, so it is possible that he knew Jack from India. It is more likely, however, that someone in Conservative Central Office recommended Jack when Chotzner announced that he would not be standing at the next general election.

That person was almost certainly one of the shadier characters to have graced the Conservative Party, George 'Joseph' Ball. Born in Luton in 1885, Ball had studied law at King's College London before being called to the Bar at Gray's Inn in 1913, but his life's work was to be devoted to intelligence of one kind or another. In 1915 he joined the War Office's directorate of military intelligence – later known as MI5 – where he stayed until at least 1927, earning himself a string of commendations from his superiors, who wrote of him that he was 'an officer of marked ability, capable and willing to assume responsibility' and that he was 'first class'.[14] So well regarded was he that in 1925 MI5 bumped his salary up from £700 to £800 in the hope of retaining his services, but J. C. C. Davidson, the chairman of the Conservative Party, snared him two years later to run the party's publicity department on the exorbitant salary of £1,400. It was an unusual move, from intelligence gathering to press management, and Ball was not a standard-issue recruit to the Conservative Party, being the son of a milliner and a bookstall clerk-turned-'frame inspector', but one can see why Davidson was attracted to Ball, who was a passionate Conservative and Unionist with a deep hatred of socialism, communism and all points in between. Ball also had a keen understanding of the dark arts of political manipulation, a readiness to use all means at his disposal and an ability to keep himself out of the limelight. He played a key part in enabling the faked 'Zinoviev letter' to get into the right hands at the perfect point on the eve of the 1924 general election, and he knew how to lie and how to keep a secret. Davidson admitted as much, writing that although Ball was 'undoubtedly tough and has looked after his own interests' he had 'about as much experience as anyone I know in the seamy side of life and the handling of crooks'.[15] Collin Brooks, whom Ball later employed, put it slightly differently. Ball, he wrote, was 'one of the too-many Grey Cardinals of official Conservatism'.[16] It was one thing running the party press office, which Ball did for a couple of years, but when Ramsay MacDonald launched the first press office at Downing Street in 1929, Davidson and Ball cooked up a new idea – a countervailing Conservative Research Department that would be wholly independent of Conservative Central Office. Housed separately in Old Queen Street, with a separate chairman, Neville Chamberlain, and a discrete budget, it would be charged with 'organising and conducting research into … the growing complexity of the political aspect of modern industrial, imperial and social problems'.[17] The precise genesis of the project is disputed, but with Ball and Chamberlain as director and chairman, in Davidson's words it became 'a little intelligence service of our own, quite separate from the Party organisation'.[18] It was a formidable operation, as Ball secretly infiltrated the Labour Party's printers, Odham's Press, thereby securing very useful advance copies of Labour's print literature, and claimed to have informers at the very heart of the Labour Party. He also coordinated the secret selling of honours to Conservative supporters, and paid off their homosexual intermediary, Maundy Gregory, when Gregory was charged in 1933 with illegally selling honours and agreed to plead guilty, thereby preventing a trial, which could have brought down the government.

Ball had another strength: he knew how to insinuate himself into the affections of senior politicians. Although he was described by some as 'a hard and humourless man',[19] or 'a burly, slightly sinister figure',[20] or again as 'a tubby man with a dark twinkling eye, persistent but elusive',[21] he got on remarkably well with Neville Chamberlain, who was notoriously aloof and almost entirely bereft of personal friends. Very little of Ball's correspondence has survived, as he destroyed nearly all of it not long before his death, but the few existing scraps of notes he wrote to leading politicians show that he knew how to play his superiors. When he was awarded a KBE he wrote to Baldwin in terms that would be enough to turn most men's stomachs, especially considering how easily he knew such awards could be arranged. Such honours, he wrote,

> mean little to statesmen like yourself ... [but] they mean a great deal to those of us who work on a lower plane – more particularly if, as in this instance, they come from one whom one has been proud and honoured to work for years past; and for whom one has so great a regard.[22]

It was oleaginous – but just right for sentimental Baldwin. By contrast he was businesslike with the more austere Chamberlain, but bonded with him over a shared passion – fly-fishing. In the midst of a letter about copying documents for a committee, he would launch into a description of his weekend on the River Test: 'The worst from a fishing point of view that I ever remember, the wind being so furious as to lash the water ... into waves,' although he managed to catch two trout.[23] Even the detail that the trout weighed respectively 1 lb 9 oz and 1 lb 8 oz was designed to appeal to the number-cruncher in Chamberlain, who responded in kind, recounting one October that he had 'a very delightful and interesting day on the Lugg' when he too caught a brace of trout. It was the closest Chamberlain got to a friendship, as the two men turned the new Conservative Research Department into a personal fiefdom.

Whoever effected Jack's introduction to the Conservative Party, in March 1934 he secured the nomination as the Conservative candidate for Upton. Initially this was for the next general election, which had to be held by 1938, but at the end of April Chotzner decided to stand down immediately, prompting a snap two-week campaign and a by-election on

Monday 14 May. The Belfast-based Unionist-supporting newspaper the *Northern Whig* tried to big Jack up, claiming that although he was still a young man, not yet in his thirties, he had already enjoyed 'a life of unusual variety and experience'. In addition to India and Egypt, he claimed to have visited every country in Western Europe and to have 'studied the French method of colonisation in Africa', which may be a sly reference to his arrest in Tunisia. Moreover, again according to the *Northern Whig*, 'Captain John Macnamara … owns and runs a farm in Suffolk.'[24] This was a double exaggeration, as Jack transferred to a reserve regiment, the 18th London (London Irish Rifles), as a mere lieutenant on 5 May 1934[25] and was not made captain until 1 November that year.[26] As for farming, Lett delighted in teasing Jack about his 'baby farming' and there is no evidence that Jack saw Justice Wood Farm as anything more than a country retreat. It was at Kensington Court Place that he hosted lively cocktail and dinner parties, including an especially fine dinner on Christmas Day 1933, which he persuaded Lett to cook, and which was followed (according to Lett) by 'a party afterwards with 3 soldiers'.[27]

Lett recorded one visit by Jack to Justice Wood in March 1934, but that day ended with Jack, Paddy and Lett going to Colchester for a 'pub-soldier crawl', followed by a trip to the cinema to see Conrad Veidt in his rebuttal of anti-Semitism, *The Wandering Jew*, and a fish supper. It is not difficult to guess what a 'pub-soldier crawl' involved, but this was pretty reckless, considering Jack was a declared Conservative candidate. Tongues started wagging, as people asked how Jack could afford to keep a farm in Suffolk plus a large house in London and a manservant, when he had no discernible income and his father had left him a relatively small estate. Many presumed that the ever-present Herbert was paying the bills – and must have questioned why. The gossip reached such a crescendo that one of Lett's friends, Eve, rang Lett to warn him on the eve of the by-election at the end of April. Lett did not disclose the nature of the gossip, but wrote, '*Pericoloso* [dangerous] & depressing. Bad night.'[28]

Despite this, Jack might have thought that he had a good chance, as Chotzner had had a majority of 5,108, and the Independent Labour Party's candidate, Fenner Brockway, would almost certainly drain votes away from Labour's 68-year-old candidate, Ben Gardner. Yet Gardner thought the seat was his for the taking. As *The Times* put it, 'West Ham as a borough may be regarded as Socialist beyond redemption,'[29] as the three neighbouring seats were all Labour, and besides, Gardner had won the seat in 1923 and 1929, only losing to Chotzner in 1931. Jack might also have thought that his interest in Anglo-German relations would stand him in good stead, but the other candidates ran a relentless campaign against what they described as his pro-Hitler views. Even before Jack launched his campaign, the headline in the Labour Party's official newspaper the *Daily Herald* was 'Upton Tory Goes Fascist', as it claimed that he had said that he could find nothing 'in Fascism that was not in the Conservative programme' and that he would like 'to see the Fascists in the Conservative ranks with the blackshirts changed to the uniform of the Territorial Army'.[30] In a curious and then unusual turn of phrase the paper added the words 'QUEER ANTICS BEWILDER THE ELECTORS' to its headline.[31] The barrage continued throughout the campaign. They attacked him for 'plump[ing] for a big Navy, a big Army and an Air Force "as strong as that of any nation within striking distance of this country"'. And on 8 May the paper recycled Jack's comments from Berlin. From then on, whenever Jack entered a hall he was met with a storm of abuse, which was kept up until 'a combination of curiosity and sore throats allowed [him] to put in a word or two here and there'.[32]

Jack retaliated with a denial, a threat to sue the *Daily Herald* and supporting letters from Baldwin, MacDonald and the Secretary of State for Foreign Affairs, Sir John Simon, the last of whom argued that 'Britain has led the way in disarmament'.[33] Duff Cooper, then the financial secretary to the War Office, launched Jack's campaign and Jack got all his friends to campaign for him, including forty-six Conservative MPs, a band of loyal homosexuals (including William Teeling, who had been the Unionist candidate in nearby Silvertown in 1929), some of Lett's friends (but not Lett or Cedric, who both subsequently joined the Labour Party) and the whole of the Sharp family dressed in kilts. But it was to little avail. The large Jewish community in the constituency, who had taken to Chotzner as the son of a notable rabbi, took understandable exception and remained sceptical about Jack's twice-repeated condemnation of the Nazis' treatment of the Jews. In the end Gardner had 11,998 votes to Jack's 8,534 and Brockway's 748. Jack was disappointed but not bitter and had the good sense to disarm any criticism by apologising for his inexperience and blaming himself for the result. His self-deprecation prompted the *Bystander* to opine that 'he was a good candidate'.[34] It was not until 1936 that Jack complained – in a Commons debate on 'Jew-baiting' – that free speech had been denied in his by-election 'by other parties who organised deliberate resistance and deliberate denial of free speech'.[35] Later he pointed to a flaw in his own campaign: 'The papers that support the government ... were, at the time, amusing themselves and their readers by stabbing the government in the back. I was invited to stab too, but, ignoring the whispered temptations, was duly stabbed instead. I lost.'[36] Jack's connections with Germany had undoubtedly lost him the seat.

Ronnie Tree and Rob Bernays set off for Germany the following week. They had a good idea of what they were letting themselves in for. Ronnie had made discreet enquiries at the German Embassy about possible meetings, but he had been sent off with a flea in his ear, as Prince Otto von Bismarck, whom the Trees had often entertained, told him in no uncertain terms: 'If you go to Germany with a Jew, a Liberal and a liar, then I will do nothing whatever to help you, and will in fact see that you meet as few people as possible.'[37] Tree resolved never to have anything to do with Bismarck again, but Rob was shocked, as he told the West London Synagogue Association, when 'his own slight Jewish ancestry' was constantly brought up like this. The Nazis laid it on thick throughout the visit. One morning Ronnie was wakened in his hotel bedroom by a postman clicking his heels and shouting 'Heil Hitler' as he delivered a letter from Hanfstaengl demanding that he come to meet him alone, without Rob. When Ronnie recounted what Hanfstaengl had said about him, Rob was amazed. 'I was a Bolshevik Jew. I ought to be deported.' Rob found the hatred incredible, but noted that it had affected the British Embassy, too, as they received him as if he was 'a bomb that might explode at any moment'.[38] It was all the more incomprehensible because Rob reckoned that he was 'not a Jew by religion – and only remotely by race'.[39] He did have Jewish relatives. His great-grandfather Adolphus was born a Jew in Germany but moved to England, naturalised and converted after marrying in 1818; his great-granduncle, Adolphus's older brother Isaac Bernays, had been the Chief Rabbi in Hamburg; and two of Isaac's granddaughters, Martha and Minna Bernays, were respectively wife and mistress to Sigmund Freud. But he thought that 'even in Germany' he would 'escape the branding-iron'.[40] Yet when Rob and Ronnie visited the *Deutsches Volk, Deutsche Arbeit* (*German People, German Work*) exhibition, which rammed home an ugly message about racial purity with pictures of disfigured Jewish and mixed-race children, it was all too clear where Nazi ideology was heading.

It was not a fruitful visit. On one day trip out of Berlin Ronnie's Rolls-Royce got stuck in a ditch and the two of them passed the time smoking and playing cards while their Nazi aide sought help. The closest either of them got to any NSDAP figure was when Hanfstaengl appeared at their hotel on their last day in Berlin to ask sarcastically if he could do anything to make their trip more pleasant. Yet Ronnie noted that they 'did the rounds of the nightclubs'[41] and the trip served one important function, as they were both confirmed in the view that Germany was definitely preparing for war. Rob later told a group in Warwick that he had been shocked to hear the rector of Frankfurt University tell his students that it was more important to study the parts of a machine gun than read chemistry textbooks. The trip made Ronnie think, too, especially when they visited Trier and saw a host of young German soldiers in a vast encampment like an army on the eve of a medieval battle. Ronnie wrote that his mind was made up there and then. For five years many of his personal friends in Parliament 'either could not, or would not, face the fact of the Nazi menace' but he knew that 'unless Hitler could be shown early on that we would meet force with force, war on his terms was inevitable'.[42]

At the beginning of July 1934, just a month after Rob and Ronnie's return, the news broke in Britain that Hitler had mounted a major putsch against some of his senior associates. There had been rumours of divisions in the Nazi High Command for some time. Members of the SA were said to be calling for a Nazi 'second revolution', which would give meaning to the 'socialist' part of National Socialism and would bring the German Army under SA command; others thought Röhm's SA had grown too big for its oversized boots and that the SA's thuggery undermined the party's reputation and therefore its destiny. Many military officers and Nazi leaders alike had a reason to want rid of Röhm. He was too close to Hitler, he had too many followers of his own, he was too sympathetic to socialism – and above all, his homosexuality was an affront to Nazism.

Röhm's enemies had been planning Operation Kolibri for months, but it was only at the end of June that they persuaded Hitler to act. So on 28 June Hitler told Röhm to summon senior SA officers to meet with him at the Hanselbauer Hotel in Bad Weissee at 11 a.m. two days later. At 4.30 that Sunday morning Hitler flew to Munich with a troop of loyal *Schutzstaffel* or 'SS' officers who at this point constituted his personal guards. There he angrily arraigned the chief of police for having lost control of the city the night before – and tore the epaulettes off his uniform before having him arrested. Then he set off with an armed guard for Bad Weissee, arriving sometime between 6 and 7 a.m. Storming up the stairs of the hotel, Hitler ordered a soldier to knock at Röhm's door before barging in and having him arrested. Elsewhere in the hotel he found Heines in bed with his driver Erich Schiewek. When Heines refused to get dressed, Hitler bellowed that the two men would be taken out and shot – and moments later they were in the back of a truck bound for the Stadelheim Prison in Munich. Other SA officers, who were arrested as they got off the train to attend the Bad Weissee meeting, joined them there, while Hitler addressed an impromptu crowd, declaiming 'the worst treachery in history', which had supposedly been committed by 'undisciplined and disobedient characters and asocial or diseased elements', all of whom would be 'annihilated'.[43] Wider reprisals started across the country at 10 a.m. Papen was arrested in Berlin and many of his staff were murdered. Schleicher was killed at home with his wife. Gustav Ritter von Kahr, who had repressed the Munich Beer Hall Putsch, was hacked to pieces with pickaxes. Even though Karl Ernst's wedding had been a proud Nazi event attended by Röhm and Göring, the SS forced his car off the road on the way to board the ship at Bremerhaven for his honeymoon, flew him back to Berlin and executed him at the Berlin Lichterfelde barracks. Meanwhile Hitler had left a list of those to be executed in Munich. The executions began just after 7.30 p.m., when Heines and August Schneidhuber (both of whom held the highest rank in the SA below Röhm, that of *Obergruppenführer*), and four other officers faced a firing squad in the prison yard. They protested their innocence – and some thought it was all a plot against Hitler. But one after another the six were shot and buried overnight. The killing spree continued the next morning after cursory one-minute 'trials' at the Leibstandarte barracks. In all, at least eighty-five were killed, thirteen of them elected members of the Reichstag. A significant number were homosexual, including Heines; Ernst; Schiewek; Karl-Günther Heimsoth, who was murdered in Berlin; Paul von Röhrbein, who was already detained in Dachau, where he was shot; former SS-*Oberführer* Emil Sembach, who had been expelled from the SS for having an affair with another man and was shot in the mountains above Oels; Karl Zehnter, whose only 'crime' seems to have been that he owned Röhm's favourite restaurant; SA-*StandartenFührer* Gaiseric Scherl; and the two SA-*Gruppenführers* and Reichstag deputies, Peter von Heydebreck and Hans Hayn.

As for Röhm, he was held overnight in Stadelheim and at 6 p.m. on 1 July he was visited by Theodor Eicke, the SS commandant at Dachau, and his adjutant Michael Lippert, who placed a loaded pistol on the table in front of him, together with a copy of the *Völkischer Beobachter*, the Nazi Party magazine, in which his dismissal and arrest were reported. He was told he had ten minutes to do the honourable thing and take his own life. Eicke and Lippert stepped outside his cell as Röhm shouted that if he was to be killed, then Hitler should do the job himself, but when the ten minutes had passed without a shot, they returned. Röhm defiantly offered his chest and Eicke and Lippert shot simultaneously. In one account Röhm shouted, '*Mein Führer, mein Führer!*' as he died.

The putsch was brutally swift, but Hitler knew that it was important that he win the propaganda war afterwards. Hindenburg naïvely praised him for saving Germany from grave danger and on 3 July the Nazi-dominated Reichstag declared that it had all been entirely legal. Hitler initially claimed Röhm's treasonous plot was the reason the purge was necessary, but when he addressed the Reichstag on 13 July he made darker insinuations. Röhm had 'broken all laws of decent conduct'; he had created a sect within the SA 'sharing a common orientation, who formed the kernel of a conspiracy not only against the moral conceptions of a healthy *Volk*, but also against state security'; he had promoted men 'without regard to National Socialist and SA service, **but only because they belonged to the circle of this orientation**'. Just in case anyone missed the accusation at the heart of Hitler's faux-moral hysteria, the *Hamburger Tageblatt*, a Nazi newpaper, printed this last bit in bold.[44] Goebbels made the same point. Röhm and his cronies had led 'a life of unparalleled debauchery' and had come close to tainting the entire leadership of the party 'with their shameful and disgusting sexual aberrations'.[45] Never mind the fact that

Queer men had limited options between the wars. Harold Nicolson (above, with his wife, Vita Sackville-West) married and had two sons despite being predominantly homosexual. The wealthy MP Philip Sassoon (above right) surrounded himself with men but remained solitary. Ivor Novello's film *The Man Without Desire* (left) hinted at the loneliness and enforced chastity many feared.

© F. A. Swaine/Hulton Archive/Getty Images

© Hulton Archive/Getty Images

Many hundreds of men were publicly humiliated and sentenced to imprisonment with hard labour for the all-encompassing offences of 'gross indecency' and 'importuning' (as per the 1885 Labouchere amendment, below). Nancy Astor's son Bobbie Gould Shaw (right, by John Singer Sargent) was given an ultimatum when he was caught with another guardsman: flee the country or face arrest.

PROTECTION OF WOMEN AND GIRLS.   67

11. Any male person who, in public or private, commits, or is a party to the commission of, or procures or attempts to procure the commission by any male person of, any act of gross indecency with another male person, shall be guilty of a misdemeanor, and being convicted thereof shall be liable at the discretion of the Court to be imprisoned for any term not exceeding two years, with or without hard labour.

The word 'glamour' had a subtly offensive connotation in the 1930s, especially when applied to men. It suggested something alluring, bewitching and ultimately effeminate.

Despite the rigours of the law, there were places for men to meet, including the 'Lily Pond' upstairs at the Lyons' Corner House (right); and Christopher Wood's *Exercises* (below) gives a good impression of the all-night Turkish Baths in Jermyn Street where men cruised and entertained one another with impunity.

Cover of the September 1931 issue of *The Island*, a magazine for homosexuals, edited by Martin Radzuweit. Although illegal, homosexuality was generally tolerated in pre-Nazi Germany, particularly in urban areas. Some thirty literary, cultural and political journals for homosexual readers appeared during the Weimar era.

With dozens of queer bars, Berlin was a magnet for wealthy British men. Bob Boothby (above left) claimed, 'As I was very good-looking in my twenties, I was chased all over the place, and rather enjoyed it.' It was not all easy-going. When the first film to deal with the blackmailing of queer men (*Anders als die Andern*, above right, starring Conrad Veidt) opened, the author Magnus Hirschfield was beat to a pulp.

The young soldier Jack Macnamara (above left) described himself as 'an Empire orphan', but he found a friend and lover in the wealthy, older, married clergyman Herbert Sharp (above right). They enjoyed several sexually adventurous trips to Germany (below, on Wannsee Beach), including with Guy Burgess.

Rob Bernays (above), MP for Bristol North, was a regular visitor to Germany and an early critic of Hitler. When he and the rich American MP Ronnie Tree (right) visited Germany in 1934, they 'did the rounds of the night-clubs'. Tree was shocked to be told by Nazis that Bernays was 'a Bolshevik Jew and ought to be deported'. The two men returned to England as firm friends and predicted war unless Hitler was faced down with force.

THE ILLUSTRATED
LONDON NEWS.

SATURDAY, JULY 7, 1934.

Despite the Nazis' public loathing of homosexuality, several early supporters of Hitler were openly homosexual, including the leading Stormtroopers Ernst Röhm and Edmund Heines (above). Their murder in the Night of the Long Knives in 1934 saw the start of a sustained campaign against homosexuals in Germany – and persuaded many in Britain that this was an especially brutal regime (left).

Victor Cazalet (above), MP for Chippenham, was an impressive all-rounder who played in the men's singles at Wimbledon in 1933, where he befriended the married German tennis star Gottfried von Cramm (below, with Adolf Hitler). Gottfried refused to support the Nazis and was imprisoned for having an affair with Manasseh Herbst, who was both Jewish and a man.

Röhm and Heines had been fist in glove with Hitler from the outset. They had to be purged because they were homosexuals. Even *The Times,* which welcomed the fact that 'the Führer has started cleaning up', thought it odd that since 'the offences of Röhm and his associates were admittedly known for years, the "clean up" was not undertaken long ago'.[46] The *Daily Mail* went further. It praised the putsch for its 'exorable severity' and proclaimed that 'Herr Hitler ... has saved his country'.[47] The *Illustrated London News* carried photographs of Röhm, Ernst and Heines, but could only bring itself to say that Heines was found 'in shameful circumstances' and that Ernst was 'formerly a junior employee in a Berlin hotel'.[48] Only the journalist Sefton Delmer, who was based in Berlin, gave the full story to British readers in the *Daily Express* on 6 July 1934, as he published a list of those murdered – for which Hitler had him expelled from Germany.

Others saw things very differently. Bernays was at another 'ultra grand party' at the Astors' when the story broke and reported that the party talked of little else. Everyone was so intrigued that when dinner was served Nancy asked him to listen to the wireless and relay the news to the rest of them during the main course. When he got to Röhm's refusal to commit suicide and Goebbels's statement that 'the events passed off without a hitch', he was horrified that there was a roar of laughter and a chorus of, 'Well that was a hitch – he refused to commit suicide.' According to Bernays, one of the partygoers, Anthony Eden, who was then the Under-Secretary for Foreign Affairs, thought it 'a Reichswehr triumph', as Heines and Röhm were intriguing against the army in order to establish the dictatorship of the SA, and he even reckoned that 'it means a more stable Europe'. By contrast Rob worried, 'How callous this generation is getting about human life.'[49]

That same day Bob Boothby and Philip Sassoon were at an air pageant at Trent Park, which was also attended by the undercover MI6 officer Frederick Winterbotham, who had been secretly buttering up Alfred Rosenberg, the self-designated Nazi 'philosopher' who still headed up the NSDAP Foreign Policy

Office, by feigning sympathy with the Nazi cause. Winterbotham was surprised when he showed one of Rosenberg's visiting staff members the headline announcing Röhm's death, as he thought the man was going to faint. Winterbotham wrote, 'He held onto my arm and said: "Thank God we got him before they got us."'[50] Bob and Philip were equally shocked. Bob wrote, 'One thing, we all agreed, had emerged from the shocking and squalid events of the day. The Nazis had been shown up for what they in fact were – unscrupulous and bloodthirsty gangsters. In future they should be treated as such.'[51]

From this moment on the NSDAP adopted an unambiguous campaign against homosexuality. Hitler wrote that he expected all SA leaders to assist in keeping the SA 'a pure and clean institution' by exactingly punishing all offences under Paragraph 175 with immediate expulsion from the SA and the party. As he put it, 'I want men as SA leaders, not ridiculous apes.'[52] That was not all. A new secret police or 'Gestapo'* unit was set up under the SS expressly to deal with homosexuality. At first it merely coordinated local police efforts to crack down on individuals on their 'pink lists', but on 1 September 1935 Hitler promulgated a new version of Paragraph 175, which made it far easier to get convictions for a wider range of 'lewd and lascivious' practices. Henceforth a mere touch on the arm or an amorous letter would suffice for an arrest, 'chronic homosexuals' were sent to concentration camps and chemical castration was introduced as a 'cure'. The personal prejudices of the Nazi leaders were given full rein. The head of the SS, Heinrich Himmler, believed that disposing of homosexuals was akin to digging up weeds and justified his position by arguing that 'a people of good race which has too few children has a one-way ticket to the grave'.[53] So in 1936 he created another special unit, the Reich Central Office for the Combating of Homosexuality and Abortion, which led to a significant increase in the number of arrests and convictions.

---

*'Gestapo' is an abbreviation of *Geheime Staatspolizei* (Secret State Police). It played a central role in the Holocaust.

These had been running at about four a day between January 1933 and June 1935, but from then on the figure leaped to fifty-four a day – 40,000 in total by June 1938. The Gestapo raided bars, seized notebooks and diaries, and bribed, intimidated or tortured individuals into informing on others. SS members who were caught were sent to concentration camps and shot 'while attempting to escape'.

The sense of fear this engendered was palpable. As one contemporary put it, 'in order not to mutually incriminate ourselves, we decided to no longer recognise each other. When we came across each other in the street, we passed by, without looking at one another.'[54] Overnight the words 'Street of the Lost' appeared on the walls of a subway that had formerly been a well-known homosexual meeting place – and queer men developed a gallows humour. Soon there were significant numbers in the concentration camps, where they were labelled with a large black dot or the letters '175'. Later they would be tagged with a pink triangle, which marked them out for even more vicious treatment. Many disappeared without trace, and thanks to the homophobia that was still prevalent for many years after the war, they had no family or community to remember them. Estimates vary, but roughly 100,000 homosexual men were arrested between 1933 and 1945, half of whom were convicted. Somewhere between 5,000 and 15,000 were sent to concentration camps and the scholar Rüdiger Lautmann has argued that roughly 60 per cent of them died in the camps. Depressingly, even the United States Holocaust Memorial Museum admits that 'there are no known statistics for the number of homosexuals who died in the camps'[55] and when Hans Zauner, the mayor of Dachau until 1952, was asked by a reporter in 1960 what he thought of the idea of a memorial, he replied with disdain, 'You must remember that many criminals and homosexuals were in Dachau. Do you want a memorial for such people?'[56]

Most people in Britain did not care in 1934 either, but the 'Night of the Long Knives' had a personal effect on Boothby,

Bernays and Nicolson, who now knew the brutal reality of what was happening in Germany at first hand. They had met several of those involved. Boothby had sat down with Hitler and Göring. Bernays had spent the best part of forty-eight hours with Heines and his aide-de-camp, who were both now dead. He had been shown round Berlin's queer bars by another young Nazi, whose fate was unknown. Likewise, Harold Nicolson was friendly with Walter Hummelsheim, a conservative Catholic who had worked for Papen and was present at the vice-chancellery when the SS stormed the building on 30 June. Hummelsheim witnessed them shoot Papen's head of press, Herbert von Bose, dead and cart the courageous anti-Nazi Edgar Jung off to be murdered elsewhere, after which Hummelsheim was imprisoned for several months in the Lichtenburg concentration camp. Harold noted, in a comment that was omitted from his published diary, that when they dined together at the Travellers Club in January 1935, 'his hands still tremble'.[57]

These events changed everything for this small group of men. From then on they knew that the Nazi attacks on Jews, homosexuals and socialists were all of a piece with Hitler's militaristic and territorial ambitions. As Rob put it, he no longer had faith in the statement, 'made to me by every Nazi with whom I talked, that Germany will only fight in a defensive war'.[58] Boothby agreed. 'How true and how right were our conclusions,' he wrote, before adding, 'Alas! In other quarters, a different view was taken.'[59]

9

A Masculine Assembly

Rob Bernays had begun to find his political feet, but he suffered a series of shocks in 1935. The first came courtesy of Frank Milton, who took on one of the highest-profile court martials of the era that July, representing Lieutenant Colonel L. Denis Daly, a 52-year-old, who had served at Gallipoli, and been garlanded with the Distinguished Service Order (DSO) and the Military Cross. After a prolonged spell in India, Daly had been given command of the 18th Field Brigade of the Royal Artillery, based in Brighton. Then came a series of allegations of 'conduct unbecoming an officer and a gentleman' and twelve charges of sexual impropriety with men in his employ. It was an enormous scandal. All the national and local newspapers reported the court martial. The prosecution case was weak. One of Daly's accusers was evidently a fantasist; another, Gunner Bertram Leyland, was a convicted thief and a blackmailer, and when Daly's defence lawyer told Leyland off for smiling throughout his evidence and the judge advocate asked him, 'Do you know that if your evidence is true Colonel Daly is ruined?' he coldly replied, 'Yes.'[1] Even the *News of the World* reckoned the case 'was begun out of blackmail and revenge'.[2]

Milton and his lead, St John Hutchinson KC, were convinced of Daly's innocence and mounted a stout defence. They argued that the very idea that 'these offences and disgusting acts' could occur in this 'fairly small house' night after night without the servants knowing was 'fantastic'.[3] A series of character witnesses 'spoke in the highest terms' of him, including his valet, who said that he had never seen anything untoward and that he would have known if anyone had been in the colonel's room at night.[4] It was to no avail. The judge advocate, Sutherland Graeme, said in summing up that the case hinged on whether one could accept the evidence of the three men 'with all their immorality and everything that could be said against them'.[5] Yet the court seemingly took exception to a letter Daly had sent to another soldier, Walter Andrews, which started with the words 'Dear Walter' and stated that since Andrews was getting married, he had lost a friend in Daly. 'Is that the sort of letter,' asked the prosecuting counsel, 'one would write ... unless there was something more in the relationship between master and servant?'[6] So on 6 August the court martial found Daly guilty on ten counts and sentenced him to seven years with hard labour. In addition he was to be cashiered out of the army and although the king cut his sentence to five years, he annulled his DSO the following February.[7] This was the total humiliation of a decorated war hero on the flimsiest of evidence. Milton and Hutchinson were so furious that the latter wrote to Duff Cooper at the War Office to beg him to prevent this hideous injustice. They were flummoxed though when Daly wrote to thank them for their work saying, 'It may be of some comfort to you to know that I have been homosexual all my life. Most of the really bad evidence never came out.'[8]

Frank and Rob must have discussed the case. The message was clear: rank, class and record were no defence. Prison, humiliation and social ostracism awaited even highly decorated war heroes if they transgressed. It was the Beauchamp saga all over again. The only answer was to lie. Rob had other worries, too. He constantly fretted about losing his seat. He had been elected in 1931 as a Liberal who supported the National Government, and when the official Liberal Party under Herbert Samuel crossed the floor over the National Government's imposition of tariffs in November 1933, he stayed put, but refused to join the group of Liberals led by Sir John Simon, who officially supported the government. Now he agonised about what to do. He disagreed with the government on tariffs and he regularly voted in the Opposition lobby, but he knew he could only aspire to ministerial office if he signed up to the government's programme by taking the government whip, and he feared that he would lose if the Conservatives put up a candidate. When the election came he persuaded the Tories to give him a clear run against Labour and stood as a Liberal 'independent of all groups in the party', but the sense of being isolated and impotent gnawed away at him. His overt attacks on fascism at home and abroad earned him some vicious new enemies. Several of his election posters were plastered with stickers proclaiming 'Jew'. He responded with admirable sangfroid. 'I am not, of course, a Jew,' he said, 'but even if I were, what would it matter? These stupid tactics leave me quite cold.'[9] But apart from that, the worst he faced was some robust heckling from a Labour-supporting pacifist at a meeting in Eastville three days before polling, which collapsed into pandemonium. As he tried to argue that he was 'against swollen armaments as much as anyone' and that all he wanted was 'enough armaments to fulfil our obligations under the League' she kept on bellowing at him, 'Our fight is not with Germany, it is home here … our argument is with you.'[10] It made little odds. Rob held on by 4,828.

Just days later he faced a family tragedy. His mother Lillian had been suffering from a severe mental health condition for several years, and in April 1934 she was admitted to the Mandalay nursing home in Staines. Although everyone was keen to stress that she had not been committed against her will, she was initially kept under very strict supervision. Her condition varied considerably over the next eighteen months. At one point family visits made her so anxious that they were curtailed. In November 1934 Rob wrote to his sister Lucy, 'You would not really have thought that there was anything wrong in the slightest degree. There seems so small a gap between her present position and complete recovery.'[11] But he found a visit to her at Christmas was 'rather sad' and in March 1935 he found her 'quite unutterably weary of life', and admitted that 'the sadness of the whole thing sometimes just crashes me and I can't make the effort to be bright and entertaining'.[12] She seemed to pose no risk to herself, so her doctors relaxed her security later that year and on 24 November she quietly slipped out of the nursing home. She was missing for weeks, during which the family feared the worst. Finally, the police dredged the Thames on 21 December and found her body a few miles away in West Molesey. Rob was keen to avoid any imputation of suicide and argued that it was just a very sad accident and that nobody was to blame, so he was relieved when the coroner returned an open verdict of 'found drowned'.[13]

Christmas at his father's rectory in Finchley was a sombre affair. Rob burst into tears when a kind letter arrived from his sister Lucy in Brazil. 'My trouble is,' he replied to her, 'that I remember Mother as she was in the plenitude of her strength and so I forget all the recent years. That is why I find it so difficult to comfort myself that it is for the best.' Tellingly, he added, 'The two great female influences on my life have been she and you and now she is gone and you are in Brazil. I am very lonely.'[14]

Loneliness was Rob's recurrent fear, but the 1935 general election provided Rob with three new parliamentary friends in the shape of Ronnie Cartland, Jack Macnamara and Harold Nicolson.

As young bachelors Ronnie and Rob had much in common. They were both imbued with a strong sense of right and wrong, they shared a degree of moral intensity, they believed that public service entailed making sacrifices, and they refused to follow convention. Unlike most MPs of the time, neither man was wealthy. Rob's rectory upbringing and his experience of living hand to mouth in India had left him deeply conscious of money, and with no independent means Ronnie often struggled to make ends meet on his £3 a week Central Office salary. True, his mother Polly was now living in the well-proportioned Littlewood House near Malvern and provided a small allowance, and his sister Barbara regularly topped up Ronnie's bank balance or paid off his bills when one of her books provided her with a healthy advance, but he was regularly hard up. At one point in 1929 he wrote to his mother, 'I continue to starve,'[15] and several years later his doctor attributed a bout of debilitating fatigue to the fact that he had not had enough to eat.

Both men were also exceptionally close to their elder sisters. In Rob's case that meant unburdening himself to Lucy, who had married Ashley Brereton ('a stuck-up landowner from East Anglia' according to her nephew Robert)[16] with whom she moved to Brazil. In weekly letters, which often had typed sections of his diary attached, Rob told her his political and personal ambitions, recounted his successes and fretted about his failures. She would be the first to hear of any new friend, whether male or female. And when it came to elections, Lucy would always be by his side, even if that meant an expensive trip back from Rio.

Similarly, Ronnie and Barbara were especially close. Most years they holidayed together in Europe at her expense and he spoke to her twice every day on the telephone, including every morning at 9.20 a.m. When Barbara moved to 37 Green Street she gave Ronnie a latchkey and he would often let himself in at the end of the day and sit at the end of her bed talking late into the night. The two were to become even closer when Barbara's marriage was soured by mutual allegations of infidelity in 1932. She later claimed – or admitted – that the real father of her daughter Raine was the king's bisexual son Prince George, but she bitterly and controversially contested the divorce and was grateful that Ronnie 'threw himself heart and soul into working for [her] interests'.[17] For a while they lived together in Green Street, but when she won her case and was forced to move to a maisonette in Half Moon Street, Ronnie took a tiny bedsit in Chelsea. They remained phenomenally close. As Barbara put it, Ronnie was 'like my other self. We thought alike, wanted identical things, and could almost have been one person.'[18] Every man she met seemed inferior to him and she claimed they were only 'perfectly happy' when they were together.

Like Rob, Ronnie had recently experienced a tragic loss. For years he and Antony, Viscount Knebworth, had been inseparable. When Knebworth was selected for the Tory seat of Hitchin in 1931, Ronnie spent the whole campaign at his side and when he was elected they regularly dined together at the Commons. They spent nights out on the town, too, although after one session at the Nightlight and Chez Victor in Soho, Ronnie pointed out to his mother that although they were nightclubs 'they were, of course, the ultra-respectable ones'.[19] Like many young aristocrats of the day, though, Antony took up aviation in a search for excitement and joined Sassoon's 601 Squadron in the summer of 1932. His mother worried about it, but Antony told her that flying was perfectly safe and 'supplies the two missing things in my life – a recreation which I enjoy and a kind of society which I love!'[20] He was not entirely telling the truth. Part of what attracted him to flying was the sense of danger. The Moth he bought was in such poor repair that colleagues joked that '*Some* of the cylinders fire *some* of the time.'[21] He loved it, though, and on Sunday 30 April 1933 he flew to Knebworth in his Moth with a fellow officer, Roger Bushell (who was later murdered after masterminding the Great Escape from Stalag Luft III). They played tennis, drank tea and chatted with Antony's mother before flying back to Hendon at eight in the evening. The next evening he took part in a practice formation flight. It was the last flight of the day. When the formation leader Flight Lieutenant Eric 'Hobby' Hobson dipped steeply over the aerodrome and held the dive for slightly too long, Antony suddenly found his machine slamming into a slight rise in the ground. His plane turned over and burst into flames. He died instantly and his gunner, Aircraftman Ralph Harrison, died moments later. A court of inquiry found Hobson guilty of an error of judgement and he was for ever inconsolable. Believing he had killed Antony, he shot himself a few years later.

Ronnie was distraught. He had remonstrated with his friend about the risks he took and now Antony was needlessly dead at just twenty-nine. What made it all the worse was that he could hardly express what he really felt. He pored over Antony's many letters to him before sending his condolences to Antony's mother. 'I was terribly upset,' he wrote, 'for tho' you know I have a complacent regard of death, K[nebworth] was one of the few men I really admired and respected.'[22] But then Ronnie always loved a daredevil.

Ronnie also shared with Rob Bernays an ambition to stand for Parliament, and not long after a walking holiday in Austria with Barbara, Ronnie learned in October 1933 that the Conservative MP for King's Norton, Major Lionel Beaumont-Thomas, would be standing down at the next election as a doubly adulterous affair (his second) had led to a messy divorce. It was a seat Ronnie felt he had a claim to, as his grandparents were buried in the local church and Major Howard Cartland's home, the Priory, occupied a large thirty-acre estate on the edge of the constituency. Yet Ronnie was full of self-doubt. He had no money and the election expenses would run to more than £1,000. Perhaps the Conservative Party would meet these centrally if he were lucky enough to beat off all the other candidates, but then he would be a party lackey beholden to the leadership. Besides, he told Barbara, he was only twenty-six. She would have none of it. She promised to support him financially by writing more books and columns and harangued him until he put his name forward. She went further. During a weekend house party at Ury House near Aberdeen, the home of Lord Stonehaven, who had become chairman of the Conservative Party after returning from Australia, she flirted with one of the other guests, Leo Amery. This was a crafty move. Amery was sixty and married, but he was a well-connected figure in the Conservative Party, having been First Lord of the Admiralty under Bonar Law and Colonial Secretary throughout Baldwin's 1924–9 government, and he held a neighbouring Birmingham seat. A passionate imperialist, he spoke fourteen languages and had Jewish antecedents. Consigned to the backbenches like his long-standing friend and sparring partner Churchill, Amery liked to be listened to. He was so taken with Barbara that he gently intimated that their rooms were remarkably close together and in a remote part of the castle. Perhaps they should take advantage of this 'unique opportunity'.[23] Barbara did seize the opportunity – but not for a sexual liaison. Instead she asked Amery to meet Ronnie and get him the nomination. A few days later Amery sent Barbara some passionate poems, together with an invitation for Ronnie to come and see him. The meeting went so well that Amery wrote a letter of commendation, and with the additional support of Bolton Eyres-Monsell, who was then First Lord of the Admiralty, David Margesson, the chief whip, and MP Sir Patrick Hannon, Ronnie was up before the seven members of the King's Norton selection committee just two weeks after Beaumont-Thomas's announcement. Here, too, he had rather unusual support, as Polly accompanied him and even answered questions on whether she was 'ready to open bazaars, help with the wards, speak and do everything that a wife would do if Ronnie had been married'.[24] Back in London, Ronnie wrote to her that night: 'I want you always to share in any triumph I shall have and I mean to have many. You are the most wonderful mother in the world.'[25] Two days later the selection committee told him they were recommending his adoption and on 23 November Polly watched with tears in her eyes as the King's Norton Executive adopted him as their candidate, the only stipulation being that he would pay the association £250 a year. Even then he fretted that he and Polly were giving members a false impression. 'The only pretence,' he wrote to her, 'is if we pretend we are richer than we are ... All I say is do not let us *volunteer* the information as to quite how poor we are.'[26]

The campaign was not going to be easy. The affable Labour candidate, G. R. Mitchison, also had a well-known novelist on his side, his wife Naomi, and he presumed he could rely on the thousands who worked in the local car industry. He was the bookies' favourite. The Cartland family threw themselves into it, though. Major Howard stumped up £500. Polly bought an Austin and had it painted black and white. She invited coachloads of ladies from King's Norton for cream-tea parties at Littlewood

House and became president of several local Conservative and Unionist branches. Barbara coached Ronnie on his speeches, toured the constituency with him, paid his bills and, when he threatened to stand aside for lack of money, bolstered him with her own optimism. She also took him on another summer holiday, this time to Germany, in 1935. They took the slow route – a boat with filthy cabins from Southampton to Bremen and then a train to Berlin. They both found it upsetting. There were anti-Jewish posters in the streets and men and women in Hitler Youth uniforms everywhere. Barbara was also incensed that there were signs telling women not to wear make-up. Ronnie returned convinced that the Germans would annex Austria and that 'sooner than anyone expected, they would fight Great Britain'.[27] To his surprise, an invitation from Hitler to the Nuremberg Rally that September awaited him in England. After all he had seen, he did not hesitate to turn it down.

As for Jack Macnamara, the *Bystander* had commented after his upset in Upton in 1934 (anonymously, but probably in the shape of Barbara Cartland), 'I hope he will fight again and be given a better chance to win,'[28] and in November that year he presented himself alongside eighteen other prospective candidates before the Conservative party in Chelmsford, where the MP, Lieutenant Colonel Sir Vivian Henderson, had 'found it necessary to retire, because of the strain of Parliamentary life upon his health'.[29] (He went on to live another thirty-one years.) Several factors counted in Jack's favour. Justice Wood Farm was not far from Chelmsford, he enjoyed the continuing support of Joseph Ball and he was a captain in the London Irish Rifles. What probably swung it for him, though, was the fact that the Chelmsford Conservative Association was already accustomed to queer or nearly queer MPs. In 1924 they selected Henry Curtis-Bennett, the successful barrister who defended a number of clients in importuning and gross indecency cases and was the first to advance the argument in court that homosexuality was a 'condition' that 'called for institutional rather than penal treatment'.[30] Curtis-Bennett stepped down in the autumn of 1926 to devote himself to the law, but when the *Essex Newsman* first spotted his successor as Conservative candidate, the national hero Lieutenant Colonel Charles Howard-Bury, who led the first reconnaissance expedition to Everest along with George Mallory, and supposedly discovered the 'Abominable Snowman' or 'Yeti', it reported that 'the Colonel has a pleasant smile and looks very fit', before pointedly adding that he was forty-three 'and a bachelor'.[31]*

Howard-Bury had met Jack at the Anglo-German Club exhibition and played a key role in securing him the nomination. He introduced him to the officers of the association and calmed any concerns they might have about the Upton debacle.[32] As usual, Jack refused to play safe. In a sharp deviation from the party script, he told the selection meeting that 'it was scandalous to tell anyone that we were safe from foreign aggression, because we were not'. He added that 'Göring might at any time sweep with his Air Force over France or London' and ended with a demand that with Germany and Italy uniting, Britain must 'decide on what side we should be'.[33] Despite this swashbuckling talk, Jack was unanimously selected.

By the time the general election commenced in earnest at the start of October 1935, Ronnie had been trudging up and down King's Norton for two years and Jack had been nursing his safe Conservative seat with a round of stump speeches about agriculture, livestock and licensing laws for a whole year, but Harold Nicolson had not even heard of the Leicester West constituency. Harold had half-heartedly and unsuccessfully offered himself for selection by the Sevenoaks Conservatives earlier that year, but lying in bed one night in August, he reckoned that he had made 'a fine muck of my life', what with working for Beaverbrook and his 'even more disastrous connection' with

---

*The code was accurate. In 1940, aged fifty-seven, he met and fell in love with a young actor from Yorkshire called Matthew Bowman, who subsequently changed his name by deed poll to Rex Bart Beaumont. The two men turned Howard-Bury's dilapidated Belvedere House into a magnificent country home and lived together for thirty years.

Mosley.[34] Yet on 3 October – the day after another aggressive move by the dictators when Italy invaded Abyssinia – he received an urgent phone call at Sissinghurst from Vita's cousin Herbrand Sackville, the 9th Earl De La Warr, commonly known as 'Buck', who had been the first hereditary peer to join the Labour Party in 1923 and now served as parliamentary secretary at the Ministry of Agriculture and Fisheries and chairman of the National Labour Party. Would Harold let his name go forward to stand 'in the National Labour interest' for Leicester West, a seat presently represented by an unpopular Liberal? Harold demurred. He had only ever visited Leicester in 1918 when he was having an affair with Victor Cunard, he had half-promised to stand elsewhere as a National Liberal candidate and he preferred to be a National candidate pure and simple, but after lunches with Rob Bernays, Cecil Beaton and Victor Cazalet (who was still close to another National Labour Cabinet minister J. H. Thomas), he agreed to present himself before the Leicester *Conservative* Club executive committee on 17 October, who selected him as the National *Labour* candidate, a normally inconceivable move only made possible thanks to Buck's intervention and the special circumstances of the National Government's political sheltering of Conservative, Labour and Liberal MPs under the 'national' umbrella. The meeting was all over so quickly that he reported that he was back home at his London flat by 9.10 that same evening.

It poured on election day, 14 November 1935, in Birmingham, Chelmsford and Leicester. Ronnie had worked hard, speaking at several meetings every evening, and Polly had run a military operation at the committee rooms, but they both feared that rain would assist Labour. Likewise Buck had promised Harold that this was a safe seat, but with the Labour candidate John Morgan calling him an 'ex-fascist', Vita refusing to appear on the hustings and a Liberal candidate threatening to split the vote, he feared defeat. All sorts of rumours started to spread at the Leicester count, so Harold's supporters glumly presumed a

Labour victory by at least 12,000 votes and Morgan patronisingly congratulated Nicolson on 'a rare fight for a first election'. Then came word from Harold's agent suggesting he was in by 150 votes and Morgan, who according to Harold was 'almost hysterical', demanded a recount.[35] The final result was tight, but Harold Nicolson was the new National Labour MP for Leicester West with a majority of eighty-seven. He seems to have been as surprised as anyone, although he wrote to Vita that it was such a personal triumph that he was 'overjoyed'.[36] Ronnie's fears had also been overblown. When the result came in at ten minutes to one in the morning, he had beaten Mitchison by 5,875. His supporters carried him aloft through the damp streets of Birmingham to the Conservative Club, where one of the first to congratulate him was Neville Chamberlain. As for Jack Macnamara, the *Essex Newsman* reported that a great cheer went up at 1.15 in the morning when the crowd outside the shire hall saw that Jack was standing immediately behind the High Sheriff, who announced that Jack had won with a very healthy majority of 16,624.

Things moved quickly for all three. Jack celebrated with Herbert and Paddy by holding a lively cocktail party at Kensington Court Place and immediately set about trying to find a suitable young man to act as his speech-writer and secretary. Within days Jim Thomas was showing Ronnie round Parliament, and Barbara had found him a 'nice and spotlessly clean' two-room bachelor flat in Albany Chambers in Petty France. Ronnie thought it 'rather small' and it was much less grand than the Albany bachelor apartments off Piccadilly, but meals came whenever he wanted at one shilling and threepence for breakfast, two shillings and sixpence for lunch and three shillings and sixpence for dinner, and he wrote home to Polly that he would be sharing a bathroom with another MP – Robert Bernays.[37] A week later Harold had lunch with Rob, who solemnly advised him to lie low at first on the grounds that the rather dramatic circumstances of his election 'might arouse some jealousy in that old hen the H of C'. Harold concluded, 'I must do the new boy for six months at least. That accords wholly with my own desire.'[38] This proved a rather forlorn ambition, as Harold already had a considerable reputation before he arrived in the House. When he tried to pass through the tea room looking nonchalant a few days later, Winston Churchill teasingly bellowed out to him that considering the state of the National Labour Party, he half expected to see Nicolson propelled onto the front bench immediately.

Rob probably gave Ronnie the same advice, but he refused to lay low. He had repeatedly said during the campaign that he would not just be lobby fodder for the Tory Party, and from the moment he arrived in Parliament – wearing his father's cufflinks – he bubbled with rebellious energy. He rebelled on where to sit in the Chamber, preferring the second row on the government side below the gangway, which was traditionally reserved for the older, sterner and less compromising sections of the Tory Party. His friend Dick Law thought his appearance 'slightly flamboyant' and added, 'The contrast between Ronald, slender, elegant and boyish, with his sleek black hair and his dancing black eyes, and the mass of the benches around him was both comical and alarming.'[39] He also fell in with a group of MPs who, as the *Daily Dispatch and Manchester Morning Chronicle* put it, seemed intent upon 'hotting things up' for the government. In his maiden speech he poured scorn on the government for merely trifling with the problem of unemployment and urged the House not to offer false hopes to 'those men and women in the depressed industries who for too long have held out, their craftsmanship disappearing, their faith vanishing, against growing misery and neglect'.[40] He was immediately commended from the Opposition benches for having been 'extremely courageous' by the Liberal MP Kingsley Griffith. This was a not-too-subtle warning. After all, Ronnie was criticising a bill presented by the Chancellor of the Exchequer, Neville Chamberlain, who was already the most powerful member of the Cabinet apart from the prime minister – and was known to harbour a grudge. It was not long before David Margesson summoned

Ronnie to explain himself and he had to face the sarcasm of the press, which proclaimed his speech 'The New Socialism, by a Conservative MP'.

Jack proved as rebellious as Ronnie. He hated the hierarchy of the Commons, he was deeply conscious of not having attended Eton, he inveighed against the nepotism and sycophancy that seemed to dominate the appointment of ministers and parliamentary private secretaries, and he resented the older members' suppression of the new arrivals, 'who should be prepared to fag and agree, but must never, never, in any circumstances, open their mouths, not for months and months and months'.[41] He found an early meeting with the government whips particularly depressing. They had summoned the new boys to a lecture on what he called 'playing the game'. They pointed out, with many dire threats, that 'we were now virtually monks, and could see a little of the outside world occasionally with their permission only. We must remain in the building all day, and, most probably, all night.' The whips would, of course, be guarding the exits. Before anyone dared ask any questions 'there was a flutter of old school ties and we realised that they had left the room'.[42] With such an attitude, Jack was a natural ally of Ronnie's – and, as he put it, it was not long before he too 'felt the lash of the whip'.[43] It was probably the idea that he should behave like a monk that most irritated him, as he was sailing extraordinarily close to the wind in his private life. There was the question of his relationship with Paddy, as there were rumours about what services Paddy provided. Some suggested he procured lovers for Jack. Others, that he was his lover – and Herbert Sharp's daughter Katherine reckoned that Paddy 'took care of all Jack's needs'.[44] But there was also the far closer and more enduring relationship Jack had with Herbert. On the face of things Herbert remained a respectable married clergyman who was made Archdeacon of the Aegean in 1935, but even Jack's closest friends must have questioned how Jack could afford his lifestyle on his £400 parliamentary salary, especially as Jack and Paddy moved to the well-proportioned 10 Holland Road in

Kensington soon after the election.* Many must have assumed that Herbert, who was a frequent visitor when he was not tending to his flock in Eastern Europe, was picking up the bill. They appeared together in public. In October 1934 they stayed together at the Grand Pump Hotel in Bath and when Herbert's local church in Minchinhampton held a fete and gymkhana in the grounds of Box House in June 1936, the rector welcomed Jack as the guest of honour and recalled 'previous events in the town in which he had played a valuable part'.[45] Jack and Herbert were careful to keep the relationship under wraps – they never appeared on the electoral register or in the *Kelly's, Post Office and Harrod & Co. Directory* under the same address and they took separate rooms in hotels[46] – but it would not have taken a determined private detective long to have established the truth.

Jack's boldest move, though, was his appointment of an obstreperously open homosexual 24-year-old ex-Etonian as his parliamentary assistant, speech-writer and general companion. The young man in question, Guy Burgess, was a mass of contradictions. He was intelligent, yet had left Cambridge with an aegrotat degree after a nervous breakdown. He was from a plush, well-connected background, yet he preferred the company of working-class young men. He had money, but contemporaries commented on his scruffiness. Victor Cazalet, for instance, turned up his nose at Burgess's filthy fingernails, and several of his pick-ups complained about the incredible disorder of his room. Yet when the Marxist journalist and academic Goronwy Rees, who was subsequently recruited as a Soviet spy by Burgess and later worked for MI5, first met him at an Oxford dinner party, he thought him 'very good looking in a boyish, athletic, very English way' even though he led 'a very active, very promiscuous and somewhat squalid sex life'.[47] Jack Hewit, who first met Burgess at the Bunch of Grapes in the Strand and was taken by him to a smart party in Whitehall before being installed as an on-and-off lover at his flat in Chester Square, was more impressed. 'He was

---

* It has been split up into three flats, but the next-door house sold in 2016 for £2.5 million.

the most promiscuous person who ever lived,' he wrote. 'He slept with anything that was going and he used to say anyone will do, from seventeen to seventy-five.' Jackie added, with some pride, 'If anyone invented homosexuality, it was Guy Burgess.'[48] Some attributed his sexual success to the air of danger that attended him, but others thought it boiled down to something far more basic. The poet and 'aesthetic bugger'[49] Brian Howard claimed Burgess's 'equipment was gargantuan – "What is known as a whopper, my dear"'.[50] And James Lees-Milne had it on good authority that Burgess 'was endowed with an asset which had to be seen to be believed. It was the secret weapon of his charm. Anyone so endowed could get away with murder, and he did.'[51]

One of the enduring mysteries is how and why Jack decided to appoint Burgess. He reeked of danger. He was loud and in your face. He drank too much and made indiscriminate passes at men who could easily have him arrested – as happened in a public toilet in Paddington in 1938. Despite being one of Guy's many lovers, Victor Cazalet's friend Micky Burn was embarrassed by Guy's 'brazenness'.[52] Even Burgess's Soviet handler reckoned that 'he had no internal brakes'.[53] Yet perhaps Jack, whom Katherine Sharp recalled as 'very brave and very masculine', was attracted to Burgess's lack of inhibition. Goronwy Rees bitchily claimed that Burgess's duties for Jack 'combined those of giving political advice and assisting him to satisfy his emotional needs'[54] but the episode in Tunisia proved that Jack was perfectly able to get himself into plenty of trouble without Burgess's assistance.

It is unclear how Burgess and Jack first met. In one version of events Harold Nicolson, who probably slept with both of them, toyed with appointing Burgess as his secretary before recommending him to Jack. As Harold's son Ben put it, 'He will look up a few things for Daddy and get political experience in exchange – no money transactions.'[55] Harold recorded in his diary that he regularly dined with Burgess, including on 31 March and 14 May 1936, but this was *after* Burgess started working for Jack, not before – and on the latter occasion Jack was present as well. In another version, Burgess applied to work at the Conservative Central Office through Victor Cazalet, and Sir Joseph Ball passed his name on to Jack. Yet Ball furiously denied this in the 1950s, when Burgess absconded to Russia and Goronwy Rees claimed in an article in the *People* that Ball had recruited Burgess to be part of his 'group'. Ball issued a writ seeking an apology and damages on the grounds that he had 'never heard of him until he fled the country'.[56] Ball was adamant on this point – repeatedly. In 1956 the Labour MP Tom Driberg, who was as unapologetically queer as Burgess and was a friend of Jack's, conducted an extensive interview with the now-exiled Burgess and threatened to publish the allegation that Ball was one of several homosexual British intelligence contacts Burgess had exploited. Ball insisted that his name be excised from Driberg's book and again demanded that it be made clear 'that I never met Burgess and never heard of him until he fled the country'.[57] This was a blatant lie, though. The records prove that it was only objections from the head of the Secret Intelligence Service, Admiral Sir Hugh Sinclair, that blocked Ball's suggestion that Burgess should work for the service and delayed Burgess's infiltration of British intelligence by a few years.

Ball had another secret. In 1914 he married the daughter of the landlord of the King's Head in Northam, Gladys Penhorwood, who was a school physical training instructor. Gladys died in 1918 aged twenty-three and within a year Ball married her half-sister Mary, with whom he had a son and a daughter in 1920 and 1924. That was not the whole truth, though. In his 1968 biography of Kim Philby, E. H. Cookridge claimed that Ball 'succumbed to the charm of Guy Burgess', that their relationship had 'a homosexual basis' and that 'Sir Joseph was known to have such tendencies'.[58] Ball was as secretive and as adept a liar as Burgess, and he knew as well as any other closeted man the danger of exposure. Of course he wanted to keep secret his relationship with Burgess.

Why did Burgess want to work for Jack? Many have claimed that it was because Jack was on the far right. It was certainly the view of some in the intelligence community. In his biography of Kim

Philby's Russian controller, Alexander Orlov, Boris Volodarsky called Jack 'right-wing'.[59] Another KGB handler, Yuri Modin, described him as 'extreme right-wing'[60] and Goronwy Rees maintained that he was 'so far to the right of the Conservative Party that it was quite reasonable to call him a fascist'. His Berlin speech must have added to that impression. Yet this was far from evident from Jack's speeches in Parliament. It is true that during his maiden speech (on his chosen subject of emigration) he sounded a Conservative imperialist to his fingertips. 'We must look back on that pioneer spirit, backed by capital, which went to these new lands and started building this Empire for us,' he declaimed.[61] Yet his days boxing in East End gyms had taught him something. He expected and demanded 'a very great deal of progressive and future planning' of the National Government, he praised the good intentions of the Labour Opposition and he implored everyone to work 'in a non-party spirit'.[62] He ended with a dark reminder of the political reality in Europe and the importance of the Empire to Britain's security. 'I am certain,' he said, 'that in the next four to six years the waters of this world are going to suffer such a storm that it would be as well for us and our Empire to start consolidating our anchorage now.'[63] This was hardly the talk of a fascist, and Jack's 'fine and boldly-spoken maiden' impressed even the new independent MP for Oxford University, the novelist and humourist A. P. Herbert.[64]

More importantly, Jack and Burgess were kindred spirits and they went on several continental trips that encompassed political and sexual adventures. Some of the stories that circulated about these trips may be apocryphal. There were tales of muscled cyclists draped naked across a table as an improvised table-tennis net, of visits to a male brothel where a handsome lad was lashed 'with leather whips'[65] and of louche meetings with queer pro-fascist French politicians including Edouard Pfeiffer, the Secretary General of the Radical Socialist Party, and Jacques Doriot, leader of the Popular Party. Rees's claim that Jack regularly joined Burgess's parties may or may not be true, but perhaps that was what Harold Nicolson was hinting at when he noted in his diary a conversation at his flat in King's Bench Walk with Jack at the end of May 1936, which went on until 1.30 a.m. (which sometimes meant it involved sex). That night Harold concluded, 'He seems the best of the new members, although he still requires much experience of public affairs *and public behaviour*.'[66]

Whatever Burgess's subterranean political motives, it is clear that he and Jack were close. The two were frequently together at smart dinner parties and receptions. They lunched with Nicolson, Boothby, Bernays and Cazalet at the Commons or at their clubs, and Jack regularly took Burgess – and other young men – to stay with Herbert and his family at Box House in Stroud, where Herbert's daughter Katherine recalled Burgess appearing in an elegant velvet dinner jacket and taking her sister to local dances. Katherine remembered hiding from her mother in the garden one day when she overheard Burgess talking to 'a left-leaning chap', who was trying to persuade him to join him fighting for the Republican government in Spain. His companion pointedly asked, 'I thought you were a communist?' When Burgess again refused to go to Spain, his friend called him a coward, to which Burgess replied, 'One day you will find out, there is more than one way of being a communist.'[67]

In bringing Jack, Ronnie and Harold into the Commons, the 1935 general election created a nucleus of queer and nearly queer MPs who knew each other and had first-hand experience of Germany. They met almost daily in one constellation or another. As they spread their tentacles within the homosocial world of Parliament they steadily became more rebellious. They were not yet a cohesive group – they often disagreed – but it would not be long before events on the Continent would force them to organise.

10

The Personal Becomes Political

Harold Nicolson was fuming. It was late November 1935, a fortnight after the election, and he had just learned that his friend Kurt Wagenseil had been arrested and despatched to a concentration camp without trial. Kurt had fallen doubly foul of the Nazis thanks to his celebrated translations of 'degenerate' works by Jean Cocteau, André Gide and André Maurois, and to his open homosexuality. The combination meant that in the Nazis' eyes, he had been 'promoting' homosexuality, which was a serious criminal offence. Kurt had also translated Vita's work, so Harold stormed off to the German Embassy and demanded to see Bismarck. They should either put Kurt on trial, he told him, or release him immediately. Bismarck took notes and said he would make enquiries, but confessed that 'they are "terribly severe" on homosexuality', which, Nicolson said amused him 'when one considers Röhm. What swine they are!' He came away fearing 'the man will die at Dachau'.[1]

Victor Cazalet was in a similar position thanks to his friendship with Gottfried von Cramm. The two men had first met when they played in the men's singles at Wimbledon in 1933. They had kept in touch when Gottfried defeated the American Don Budge to get through to the Wimbledon final in 1935, which he lost to the reigning champion, Fred Perry. Gottfried was by now an icon of Germanic sporting excellence. He was of noble stock, tall, slim, fair-haired and everything a good Aryan should be – except that, despite being married, he was homosexual.

Back in 1931 he had met an actor called Manasseh Herbst from the eastern European region of Galicia. Manasseh offended virtually every Nazi sensibility, as he was the star of a successful 'degenerate' operetta, *White Horse Inn*, he had met Gottfried at the Eldorado, and he was Jewish. By 1935 they were in severe danger. Hitler was desperate to use sporting heroes to bolster German patriotism and pride. For a high-profile aristocratic German to refuse to join the NSDAP was one thing, but for him to conduct a homosexual affair with a Jew was to add insult to injury. Knowing of Cazalet's connections in British-controlled Palestine, Gottfried approached Victor for advice. How could he protect his lover, who had changed his name to the more Germanic-sounding Manfred? We don't know what Victor said, but somehow Herbst was spirited out of Germany to Portugal and in February 1936 Gottfried wrote thanking Victor for his assistance: 'Even if I should not succeed in getting Manfred to Palestine in a near future I was so very glad that at least he is no more in danger to be put in a concentration camp.'[2] It seems certain that Victor had pulled strings to help Manfred out of Germany – and may well have helped financially. A week later Gottfried wrote again, saying that he had picked up some gossip in Monte Carlo from well-placed Germans who told him that he had a very bad reputation in Berlin, 'which forced the Gestapo to be interested in my dear person'. He claimed that these rumours made him laugh but added, 'I am sure that I am still in danger.'[3] Up until now Victor had been non-committal about Nazism. He had barely batted an eyelid when he visited Dachau. But faced with a close friend in mortal danger, he responded with courage and generosity and helped his friend's lover escape the clutches of the Nazis.

Many in Britain were still blind to the atrocities in Germany, but as every month went by the brutality of the Nazi regime was brought home in an ever more personal way to queer MPs. Harold Nicolson's fears were especially heightened when he sat next to Jack Macnamara at a lunch for new National Government MPs at Claridge's at the start of December and

Jack told him of visits he had paid to German concentration camps. It was, Harold wrote, 'by far the most convincing account I have yet received'.[4] Like Victor, Jack had remained broadly sympathetic to Germany even after the debacle of the Upton by-election. The Nazis continued to court him, too. When he visited Poland in early September 1934 and stopped off in Berlin on the way back, the Germans made a point of flying him to Nuremberg to witness the Führer in action at the 6th Party Congress. It was spectacular. Seven hundred thousand Nazis thronged the streets. Rows upon rows of uniformed SS men marched and saluted in perfect unison. For the grand finale, the Nazi architect Albert Speer created a 'Cathedral of Light' with 152 anti-aircraft searchlights piercing the night. The British ambassador in Berlin, Sir Neville Henderson, thought it was one of the most solemn and beautiful things he had seen, and one of Jack's fellow MPs, Arnold Wilson, claimed the ceremonies were 'so simple, so solemn, so moving and so sincere as to merit, better than many customary religious rites, the title of worship'.[5] For the first time, though, Jack was sceptical. 'Herr Hitler spoke for a long time,' he wrote. 'He waved his small hands as his voice grew staccato. The audience cheered, not, I felt, so much at what was being said as because they wanted to cheer.' He worried where it would all lead as he added, 'The audience was carrying Hitler along shoulder-high.'[6]

Then, just after dawn on Saturday 7 March 1936, Hitler made his boldest move yet, when he sent nineteen German infantry battalions into the Rhineland in direct contravention of the Treaty of Versailles. Harry Crookshank wrote in his diary, 'not unnaturally the world is upside down',[7] but the response in Britain was astoundingly muted. The strongest criticism that Anthony Eden, now foreign secretary, could muster was that Germany's actions 'complicate and aggravate the international situation', as he thought that there was no reason to suppose that the present German action implied 'a threat of hostilities'.[8] Duff Cooper told the German ambassador that the British did not care two hoots about the Germans 'reoccupying their own territory'[9] and although Victor Cazalet visited the German Embassy to 'beg them to make concessions', he believed the country would refuse to send a single man 'to turn Germans out of their own territory'.[10] Harold Nicolson concluded that 'the feeling in the House is terribly pro-German, which means afraid of war'.[11]

By chance, Jack Macnamara was the first British politician to visit the remilitarised Rhineland. Like so many other trips he undertook, it was a mixture of political reconnaissance and sexual adventure, as he travelled with Guy Burgess, Herbert Sharp and another handsome young homosexual, Tom Wylie, who after a conventional education at Westminster and Christ Church College, Oxford had landed the post of private secretary to the Permanent Under-Secretary for War, Sir Herbert Creedy. Tom was as much a target of Burgess's treasonable attentions as Jack. Kim Philby had studied with Tom at Westminster and contacted him the moment he started work at the War Office. Within months Tom was divulging secret British intelligence to Kim, who decided to exploit his indiscretion to the full by pairing him up with Burgess. He introduced them at an intimate cocktail party and left Burgess to work his magic. It did not quite work out as planned, as minutes later Burgess stormed over to Philby demanding to know 'who is that pretentious young idiot who thinks he knows all about Proust?'[12] Despite, or perhaps because of this initial antagonism, the Soviet agent Alexander Orlov confidently reported back to Moscow that Burgess was 'an adroit chap who could, according to the mysterious laws of sexual attraction in this country, conquer Wylie's heart'.[13] Orlov was proved right. Although alcohol killed Tom at the age of thirty-eight, by then he had trustingly allowed Burgess to see a vast array of secret government papers.

The precise details of the trip to the Rhineland are hazy. They told people they were travelling under the aegis of the Church of England's Council for Foreign Relations, of which Herbert was a council member, but there is no record of this in the council's papers at Lambeth Palace. Others have claimed – also without evidence – that they were accompanying youngsters to a Hitler Youth camp. One of the few verifiable facts is that at one point they visited a concentration camp. As Jack put it in his customarily oblique way, 'by a chance, which I need not go into here, it was almost a surprise visit'.[14] This was Dachau, which was still in theory a 'protective custody' camp for political prisoners but had become the exclusive fiefdom of the SS and held an increasing number of Jehovah's Witnesses, dissident clergy, homosexuals and people arrested under the recently passed Nuremberg Law for the Protection of German Blood. The regime Victor had witnessed under the first SS camp commandant Hilmar Wäckerle was tough enough, but when SS-*Oberführer* Theodor Eicke replaced him in 1933 terror became a systematic part of the operation, as Eicke instructed his guards that the inmates were enemies of the state, who should be beaten into submission, and that anyone who had a soft heart should retire at once to a monastery. Himmler explained the Nazi mentality in January 1937, when he encouraged soldiers to visit a concentration camp to see for themselves that they only held the 'offal of criminals and freaks … cross-eyed, deformed, half-Jewish, and a number of racially inferior products'.[15]

The guards resorted to daily gratuitous acts of cruelty. They made the showers so hot that prisoners were scalded within seconds and then forced them to shiver under a freezing cold stream for ages. They played vicious games with their inmates, snatching their caps and throwing them into the no-man's land between the compound and the electric fence – and then shooting them when they went to reclaim them. Many prisoners met the same fate as Erwin Kahn, who wrote to his wife Evi in March 1933 that the food was very good, that he was confident it was all a misunderstanding that would soon be cleared up, and that he was keeping his chin up and couldn't complain. Twelve days later he was shot five times at point-blank range in the woods outside the camp on the fabricated excuse that he was trying to escape. Jewish prisoners were treated with particular ferocity. Eicke tried to get the other prisoners to turn on them by placing copies of the hideously anti-Semitic magazine *Der Stürmer* everywhere; he also paid Jews to inform on each other, and when the Nazis' anti-Semitic atrocities made the news abroad, he confined Jewish prisoners to their bunks for months. One tall redhead from Bamberg called Wilhelm Aron was beaten so hard that his broken bones stuck out of his buttocks and he was whipped every day until he died. Another was so desperate that he bribed a nurse to pull out his toenails with pliers just so as to be sent to the hospital ward. And when Kurt Wagenseil was released, he told Harold Nicolson that he had been forced to watch prisoners being beaten with rubber truncheons and that a friend had died two days after a particularly brutal beating.

In 1934 Eicke was put in general charge of all the labour and concentration camps, but it was at Dachau that he introduced many of the elements that became synonymous with the camps. The blue-and-white striped pyjamas, the death's-head SS badges, the symbols for different categories of prisoner, the sign above the gate proclaiming '*Arbeit Macht Frei*', all started here. The rules were manifestly unfair. The penalty for anyone who 'makes ironical or jeering remarks to a member of the SS, who intentionally omits to salute as laid down, or who by his conduct shows that he does not wish to submit to order and discipline'[16] was eight days' solitary detention with twenty-five lashes administered before and after. For anyone who carried on 'politics for subversive ends', who told 'lies' to foreign visitors or secretly transmitted lies out of the camp, the penalty was hanging, 'as an instigator of subversion'.[17] Eicke even stipulated that a prisoner could be hanged for 'collecting, receiving, burying, or passing on *true or false* information about the camp' (my italics). It is scarcely surprising that many inmates chose to take their own lives by walking into no-man's land and waiting for the fusillade.

It is difficult to know what the Nazi authorities expected the British visitors to think of Dachau, but it was already a standard part of the political tourist itinerary. Perhaps they expected Jack to report back that all was well, just as Victor Cazalet and countless others had done. After all, Himmler's own report of a visit that year claimed that the 2,500 prisoners – one third of whom were political prisoners, the rest being 'professional criminals, a-socials and forced labour prisoners, homosexuals and about 200 Jews' – were 'well fed, clean and well clothed and housed'.[18] But they reckoned without Jack's intrinsic belief in personal freedom, which in no small measure stemmed from his own sexuality. He was horrified. 'I have never seen human beings so cowed,' he wrote, reporting that the young, black-uniformed SS guards herded their inmates into locked dormitories and swung their truncheons menacingly.[19] Even more disturbing was the reaction he got when he spoke to the inmates, as the answer was always the same and was addressed mechanically to the commandant: '"The visitor has asked about our conditions. I have replied that the food is ample, our facilities for exercise are excellent, that the Herr Commandant treats us most humanely."'[20] Even the patients on the hospital ward jumped out of bed and stood to attention as they entered. As an archdeacon, Herbert was struck to see so many clergy in Dachau – more than a thousand were murdered there by the end of the war – but all four men must have noticed the significant number of homosexual prisoners. Segregated from the rest (supposedly to prevent homosexuality from spreading), badged with pink triangles and treated with phenomenal brutality, they were difficult to miss. One thought must have run through Jack and Herbert's heads all day – 'There, but for the grace of God, go I.'

It is not clear which commandant they met, as there was a change of command at Dachau that spring, but all of them were psychopathic sadists. SS-*Oberführer* Hans Loritz had come from another camp at Esterwegen, where he repeatedly used torture to instil order, and he went on to run the camp at Sachsenhausen, where he executed 10,000 Soviet prisoners of war and selected 15,000 inmates to be sent to the euphemistically named Sonnenstein Euthanasia Centre to be killed as *Ballastexistenzen* ('dead weight' or 'ballast existences'). Perhaps the worst of the lot, though, was Rudolf Höss, who started as a SS-*Blockführer* at Dachau on 1 March 1936, just before Jack's visit and was promoted to SS-*Scharführer* a month later. While awaiting execution after the war for crimes against humanity for introducing Zyklon B and hydrogen cyanide into the gas chambers at Auschwitz, he detailed the brutality of the corporal punishment Eicke introduced at Dachau. A whipping block was placed in the middle of the parade ground and the whole company of armed sentries was lined up in an open square. Two block leaders led out two prisoners who had been sentenced to twenty-five lashes each for stealing cigarettes, while the commandant read out the sentence. The first prisoner, whom Höss described as 'a small, impenitent malingerer', was forced to lie across the block by two soldiers, who held his head and hands while the block leaders ran at him and delivered alternate strokes. This prisoner remained completely silent but when the second prisoner, 'a professional politician of strong physique', was strapped to the block, he screamed and tried to break free. Höss claimed that he was standing in the first row of the guards and 'was compelled to watch the whole procedure'. He explained, 'I say compelled, because if I had been in the rear I would not have looked. When the man began to scream I went hot and cold all over. In fact the whole thing, even the beating of the first prisoner, made me shudder.' It is not easy to have any respect for his account, but he added one point that rings true: 'Later on, at the beginning of the war, I attended my first execution, but it did not affect me nearly so much as witnessing that first corporal punishment.' [21]

The similarity between Höss's account of a beating at Dachau and Jack's own account of a beating at Haileybury is striking. By elevating the punishment into a ceremony, both spectacles inured the spectators. In Jack's account the dormitory classroom would be cleared of its inmates, who would hang about outside, listening through the keyhole. Two chairs were then placed back to back, the delinquent kneeling on one, bending his stomach over the two backs and grasping the legs of the other. 'Thus was his backside as taut as could be,' Jack wrote. The prefects who were to administer the punishment lined up at the other end of the room and, one after the other, gave their fellow pupil a stroke, each 'taking a run at it if they liked'.[22] No life was at stake at Haileybury and Jack claimed that a beating was 'better than many long-drawn-out punishments of copying down dates and the like'.[23] But he hated injustice. Just as he complained about being beaten unfairly at Haileybury, the violence, the menace and the bullying he saw at Dachau incensed him. The experience changed him. His views on Hitler and the Nazi regime thus far might have been ambivalent, but now he was clear: 'We do not want Germany to dominate.' Distrustful of demagoguery, he warned, 'Herr Hitler's methods may finally smash our civilisation beyond repair and leave us an exhausted wreck, an easy prey to the vultures of the East.'[24]

As with Jack's many other foreign trips with Herbert and Burgess, the spring 1936 visit was not all work. They visited Berlin and Hamburg and enjoyed the queer nightlife there, which, although muted, had not yet entirely disappeared. Years later it was claimed that Burgess had taken several supposedly compromising photographs of Jack and Herbert with their arms round some strapping young Nazi lads, which he then supplied to his grateful Soviet handler – and also, quite probably, to Joseph Ball. It is said that they still lie in the 'MÄDCHEN' ('GIRL') file, number 83792, in the Soviet intelligence-service archives, although these are now closed and I have yet to find anyone who has seen them.[25] Quite how compromising these were we will probably never know, but Herbert was certainly not embarrassed to be photographed in his swimming trunks with Jack, as he pasted several such photographs of their visit to Bad Weissee in the family album.

Dachau brought another change in Jack. The Nazis were throwing Jews and homosexuals into Dachau, so the battle against anti-Semitism was his battle too. In July he launched a considered attack on what he called 'Jew-baiting'. He put it in very moderate terms. 'It is very unfortunate,' he told the Commons, 'that this tendency has arisen in this country.' He called it 'ungentlemanly and very un-English'. His purpose was clear, though, as he stated more forthrightly than any other MP that he very much hoped 'that we shall all be able to use our influence, and, if necessary, *our force*, to stop a very horrid evil that seems to be creeping in'.[26]

Jack's remarks seem mild-mannered and understated, but he was confronting public opinion head-on. All sorts of prejudices had flourished in Britain for years. Jews supposedly had limitless wealth, they enjoyed excessive clandestine power, and they were uniquely gifted at intrigue. Despite their wealth, they were in league with revolutionary communism in a hideous 'Judaic-Masonic idea'.[27] They were deliberately engineering another war so as to enrich themselves. Newspapers carried letters asking, 'What has England done to deserve such a rabble [of Jews] as has flooded this country?'[28] When Sir Robert Bower angrily told the Labour MP Manny Shinwell to 'go back to Poland', he received a letter claiming the Jews were 'a creeping cancer in the soul of any country they fasten on to' and that Britain was being 'handed over to them'.[29] Fascists stirred up the mob with lines like 'Jews are the biggest owners of prostitutes in the West-end' or 'Jews stole your jobs and houses while you were fighting in the war'.[30] Jews were chased down alleyways and beaten with iron bars wrapped in paper; they feared for their lives. Books with titles like *The Alien Menace, The Jewish World Problem, Britain Under the Heel of the Jew, Israelite Finance, A Plot for the World's Conquest* and *Why are the Jews Hated?* abounded. One editor even claimed you could pick out Ashkenazi Jews 'by their broad, flat noses, their coarse lips, their high cheek-bones, their turned-down upper eyelids, and ... the great width of their heads between the ears'.[31] The fact that Welsh miners supposedly had similar features was proof enough for him that Welsh communism was inspired by international Jewry. If evidence were needed that virulent and vicious anti-Semitism was alive and well in Britain, thugs tore down the holy scripts and vandalised the rabbi's seat at the Gateshead synagogue attended by seven German refugees in two separate incidents in July 1935.

Anti-Semitism had plenty of advocates on the green benches alongside Jack. One Conservative MP, Edward Doran, urged the home secretary to prevent any 'alien Jews' from 'scurrying'[32] into the country and demanded that 'undesirable aliens' be given 'notice to quit'. Two other Conservative MPs sarcastically joked that 90 per cent of those accused of attacking fascists rejoiced in 'such fine old British names such as Ziff, Kerstein and Minsky', or 'Feigenbaum, Goldstein and Rigotsky and other good old Highland names'.[33] Another claimed 'we have lost the City of London to the Jews' and demanded that 'before long we shall have to declare war on them as they have done in Germany'.[34]

The sixteen Jewish MPs felt the brunt of it. Philip Sassoon had been Lloyd George's parliamentary private secretary when Rufus Isaacs, the Marquess of Reading, was appointed Viceroy of India in 1921, which led *Blackwood's Edinburgh Magazine* to carp about 'another Jew' being added to the 'many Jews' in the government, thanks to 'the hidden hand of Sir Philip Sassoon'.[35] The Clydesider Labour MP David Kirkwood shouted at Sassoon in a Commons debate that he was no Briton, but 'a foreigner'.[36] Harold Nicolson wrote Sassoon off as 'a strange, lonely, un-English little figure, flitting among these vast apartments, removed from the ordinary passions, difficulties and necessities of life'.[37] Ellen Wilkinson, another radical Labour MP, focused on Sassoon's foreignness – and effeminacy – when she wrote an otherwise affectionate pen portrait of him, describing him as wafting into the Commons 'on a magic carpet' and being 'too refined, too fastidious, too perfectly conscious of what is best in life'.[38] The Jewish minister Leslie Hore-Belisha received the same treatment. Doran taunted him by asking the number and nationality of all 'money-lenders' registered in the country and claiming that there were 3,000 fraudulent bankrupts in the country, who were 'mainly alien Jews'.[39] Viscountess Downe's objection to Mosley was that he accepted donations from Jews and liked to party with the likes of Lord Rothschild and the Sassoons.[40] Chips Channon's diaries are laced with similarly caustic anti-Semitism. Hore-Belisha was 'an oily man, half a Jew, an opportunist, with the Semitic flair for publicity'[41] or else '"the Jew boy", bungling and self-important';[42] and Sassoon was not to be trusted because of 'his Oriental mind with all its vanities'.[43]

Nancy Astor was no better. She greeted her brother-in-law Bob Brand as an 'actual or honorary' Jew solely because he was a director at the banking firm Lazard Brothers. She invited the Zionist leader Chaim Weizmann to dinner at Cliveden and astonished everyone by announcing that she had always disliked Jews – until she met Weizmann. As if to reinforce the slur, she added, 'Don't believe him. He's a great charmer. He will convert you to his point of view. He is the only decent Jew I have ever met.'[44] She continued in this vein even when news of Hitler's treatment of the Jews percolated through to Britain. Harold Nicolson witnessed one moment in the Commons in February 1938, when Captain Alan Graham, the Conservative MP for the Wirral, gently told her that he did not think she had behaved very well in the Foreign Affairs Committee that day and she immediately barked back, 'Only a Jew like you would dare to be rude to me.' Graham replied, 'I should much like to smack your face,' and Nicolson concluded that she was 'a little mad'.[45] In another account of this same episode Churchill replied 'I have never before heard such an insult to a Member of Parliament as the words just used by that bitch.'[46] A few weeks later the News Chronicle reported that Nancy had astounded dinner guests at the English Speaking Union with her 'emotions about the Jews'.[47]

The only Conservative MP to agree with Jack on 'Jew-baiting' in the Commons debate was Katharine Stewart-Murray, the Duchess of Atholl, who condemned the (British) National Workers' Party for claiming that Jews had deliberately produced war, civil commotion, crime and disease 'in their own interests' and denounced its leader, Colonel Seton Hutchison, who had said he would do everything in his power 'to prevent British men from again being sent to the shambles [slaughterhouse] in the interests of Jewish finance and the arrogant ambition of Jews to order and control the world'.[48] The extent of Jack and Katharine's isolation in the Commons was shown by the contribution from Sir Arnold Wilson late in the debate. It was not fascism that had led to 'Jew-baiting', so he maintained, but 'grievances long felt, and now becoming more serious in certain branches of administration of the law, such as hire purchase and housing rentals'.[49] In other words, the Jews had only themselves to blame.

Jack knew this was nonsense. He had seen the misery at Dachau first hand and his new friend Harold Nicolson had told him about Kurt Wagenseil, who had just been released from Dachau, but was absolutely convinced that Harold's intervention had saved his life, as 'one of the most terrible things about it all is that people without influential friends actually disappear in the camps'.[50] Jack now knew that prejudice and brutality had to be confronted – and as if to prove the point, when he went to the Carlton Club after the Jew-baiting debate, one of the members spat at him and called him a 'Jew lover'. He never visited the Carlton again. The double slur was obvious. This was now as personal for Jack as it was for Harold and Victor.

11

Hitler's British Friends

On 1 August 1936 the *Hindenburg* airship flew over the new 100,000-seat Olympic stadium in Berlin. Beneath it, the crowds roared when Adolf Hitler appeared. Military bands joined the Berlin Philharmonic and a 1,000-strong choir for Wagner's 'March of Homage', '*Das Lied der Deutschen*' and the SS marching song, the 'Horst-Wessel-Lied'. Once the athletes were gathered, all wearing straw boaters, the Olympic flame was lit and hundreds of pigeons were released. Hitler conceived of the games as a personal and national showcase, and many were impressed by the efficiency and showmanship, but it would have been all the more impressive if it were not for the birds shitting on the athletes' boaters throughout Hitler's speech.

Hitler had been waging a sustained public relations campaign aimed at wooing British politicians since 1933. This had suffered a setback when the Marquess of Reading resigned as president of the Anglo-German Association because of the treatment of the Jews and when his successor, the profoundly anti-Semitic Sir Ian Hamilton, was forced to close it down in April 1935, but by then Hitler had already authorised his confidant, ally and 'ambassador-at-large', Joachim von Ribbentrop to plot the formation of a new body, the Anglo-German Fellowship (AGF), using the merchant banker Ernest Tennant as his willing accomplice. This was launched six months later with the former Conservative MP Colonel Wilfrid Ashley, Lord Mount Temple, as chairman and instantly attracted large amounts of cash and dozens of Lords and MPs as members.

The AGF specified that 'membership does not *necessarily* imply approval of National Socialism',[1] and not all of the members were Nazi apologists. Ronnie Tree joined, as did Winston Churchill's son-in-law Duncan Sandys, Loel Guinness, and Commander Robert Bower. Many members, however, were out-and-out supporters of the Nazi regime. Mount Temple had to bite his tongue at the AGF annual dinner in 1936 when he nearly admitted that he hoped Britain and Germany would be on the same side against Russia if there were another war, and Bruce Lockhart was scandalised when the large ice centrepiece at an AGF dinner in 1938 (at which Mount Temple repeated that he hoped he would fight alongside Germany) featured the swastika entangled in the Union Jack and the cricketer C. B. Fry joked, 'Ah! *L'entente glaciale!*'[2] Ernest Bennett, the MP for Central Cardiff, repeatedly wrote to *The Times* in defence of Hitler's Germany. He found communist Russia 'infinitely more odious … than any features of Germany's domestic policy'[3] and wanted to give Germany back some of the colonies she demanded so as to avert another war 'to defend the last outstanding blunder of Versailles'.[4] Lord Brocket was so enamoured of the Führer that he attended his fiftieth birthday, along with the Earl of Erroll, who was George VI's Lord Steward. The Stockport MP Norman Hulbert attended the Nuremberg rally as Hitler's guest in 1938 and remained an active member of the AGF long after the Munich Agreement, while Viola Bathurst, the wife of Rob Bernays' parliamentary neighbour in Bristol, the Conservative MP Lord Apsley, defended Nazi labour camps because she had seen 'obviously happy young men' playing guitars and singing in the pine forests and gloried that they were 'all under twenty-four, working stripped to the waist in the glorious sunshine, of magnificent physique – like Norse gods in bronze'. She had as dim a view of the British as she had an exalted one of the Germans, as she complained that 'the majority of unemployed English men and women prefer to draw a dole and to do nothing until paid work is available'.[5] The Scottish MP Colonel Sir Thomas Moore backed her up, eulogising the games, lectures, excursions, picnics and healthy bodies he had also seen at a labour camp. 'One only wished,' he added, 'that we could see our own boys and young men developing their minds and bodies on the same fruitful lines.'[6] Moore spoke so ardently and frequently of Hitler's love of peace and justice that some speculated he was in the pay of the German government. In Moore's case this was just conjecture, but Ronnie Cartland must have been more upset by the behaviour of Sir Arnold Wilson, who succeeded Viscount Knebworth as MP for Hitchin. Wilson described himself as a 'left-wing radical Tory'[7] but he was so impressed when he met Hitler in 1934 that he wrote of him that the Führer was merely 'national by temperament, socialist in method, but, like our best conservatives, desirous of change'.[8] Harold Nicolson thought Wilson was 'a dangerous, well-meaning but slightly insane person'.[9] Even more remarkably, SS-*Oberführer* Wilhelm Rodde claimed that Wilson 'carried on intelligence work' for the Nazis.[10]

When Rob Bernays's friend the Liberal MP Geoffrey Mander angrily suggested that the whole point of the AGF and the *Anglo-German Review* was 'pro-Nazi propaganda and anti-Semitism', the Lewisham East MP Sir Assheton Pownall stated categorically that the sole aim of the fellowship was 'to promote good relations between us and Germany' and that it had received 'no official support of any kind' from the German government,[11] and Moore backed him up. This was patently untrue, though. In reality the AGF's programme of events, most of which were held at the fashionable St Ermin's Hotel in Westminster, was pure Nazi propaganda, as a British intelligence report made clear. 'The affairs of the Anglo-German Fellowship,' it reported, were 'arranged to a great extent' through Ribbentrop's unofficial alternative German Foreign Ministry known as his *Büro* or *Dienstelle*.[12]

The launch of the AGF was held on 5 December 1935, the night after a friendly football match between England and Germany, which had controversially been scheduled at the Tottenham Hotspur ground, White Hart Lane. Local Jewish groups and the TUC opposed the match (not least because of the significant number of Jewish Spurs supporters) and the *Jewish Chronicle* urged Jews to stay away, but *The Times* concluded that a ban would be 'abhorrent to the English spirit' and the Nazis must have been delighted to read the letters in the press. 'It's going too far,' wrote one reader, 'when the Jews try to dictate to us. It will be the Jews who cause another war between England and Germany.' Another went even further: 'The Jews apparently do not realise they are guests in England. They are only making things worse for themselves.' The *Daily Herald* even published a letter responding to the threat of a Jewish boycott under the headline 'England for England': 'I am in every way with them that they should walk out – but with a one-way ticket and not come back. The Spurs will always find enough English support without worrying about the "Yids".'¹³ The AGF was launched the following night with a dinner to welcome the Duke of Coburg and the organisers of the Berlin Olympics. The initial report back from London was encouraging. The organisation was apparently 'outstanding' and the German guests had been chosen 'with great sensitivity to English psychology. The Duke of Coburg in particular is a personality who ought to be attractive to English society members.'¹⁴ The only fly in the ointment, according to the German ambassador living in London, Leopold von Hoesch, was that all the British guests had talked about 'the Jewish problem' in Germany, to such a degree that Prince Otto von Bismarck had been forced to cut short the discussion with a curt suggestion that people should visit Germany so that they could see things for themselves. Hitler was so furious that he immediately demanded that all the German members of the AGF should resign forthwith. It was his least effective purge, as there were no German members, although a similar revenge was exacted on the sister body, the *Deutsch-Englische Gesellschaft*.

From the outset, then, the AGF was a willing tool of Nazi propaganda. At another AGF meeting, a Miss M. F. Bothamley enlarged upon the low moral conditions prevailing in certain sections in Germany before 1933, 'when liberty had become licence and healthy discipline and self-control were regarded as perversion of freedom'. She was clear: 'The women of Germany had rallied to the Führer to create of the state a great Christian institution.'[15] On Tuesday 14 July 1936 – which was deliberately chosen to rile the French, as it was Bastille Day – the AGF feted the Nazi-supporting Duke and Duchess of Brunswick. The Bishop of Salisbury said the grace and after dinner they toasted the king and the Führer. Another meeting was less ideological. It promised an instructive and artistic 'sound film with music … showing methods of production of German industry'. Tea would be served at 4.30 and sherry at 6 p.m. Some meetings were relentlessly dull. When Lord Brocket chaired a meeting with General Tholens, the deputy chief of the German labour camps, British intelligence reported that the speech 'was so dry and so boring that even the most enthusiastic member of the A.G.F. ceased to listen'.[16]

The culmination of this wooing of British politicians was meant to be the Olympics and the subsequent Nuremberg Rally, to which Hitler and Ribbentrop invited large numbers of MPs and peers. All the major press barons were there – Lords Rothermere, Beaverbrook and Camrose – as were Beaverbrook's son Max Aitken, the Marquess of Clydesdale and his younger brother, all three of whom flew themselves to Berlin. The lavish hospitality at competing parties held by Ribbentrop, Goebbels and Göring had its effect. Chips Channon thought the 'Horst-Wessel' had a good lilt to it and that the new regime 'are masters of the art of party-giving'.[17] He even admitted that he was more excited to meet Hitler than when he met Mussolini in 1926 'and more stimulated, I am sorry to say, than when I was blessed by the Pope in 1920'.[18] Even Sir Robert Vansittart, the married but predominantly homosexual permanent under-secretary at the Foreign Office, who was a renowned anti-Nazi, was impressed. As for the AGF's secretary Ernest Tennant, he was even more enthusiastic, as he bought in to the whole Nazi dream. 'Something is being formed anew,' he wrote, 'different from anything the world has seen hitherto.' Yes, it was troubling that 'unfortunately Germany in its birth pains is throwing out what it cannot assimilate, and the tragedy of the Jew in Germany is that he will not be assimilated', but even that 'tragedy' did not overly disturb him, as he unreservedly celebrated that 'if the present regime survives we are witnessing the birth of a super race'.[19]

Jack Macnamara was a notable absentee in Berlin – and although many might have expected him to be a member of the Anglo-German Fellowship, his name does not appear on any of the lists of its members or dinner guests in the archives.* The reason was simple. Jack had changed his mind on Germany. So too had Victor Cazalet. He had swallowed the Nazi explanation of the Night of the Long Knives whole. He had written in his journal that Hitler had 'done a great deal with the Germans and many of the social reforms are excellent',[20] and a month after the remilitarisation of the Rhineland he told constituents that 'the best thing to do is to let bygones be bygones and to take Hitler at his word, make him live up to each promise and come back to the League'.[21] But now he began to feel differently. The Nazis' atrocities against the Jews had revolted him and not long after staying with the Czech President Thomas Masryck in April, he wrote to Eden urging that Austrian independence had to be protected from Hitler's ambitions. According to Chips Channon, when Lord Beaverbrook's son Max Aitken turned up at Lympne and waxed lyrical about the stupendous Olympic opening ceremonies, Victor 'tactlessly flew at Max because he hates the whole Beaverbrook crew' and 'a dreadful discussion ensued during which everyone lost their temper'. This time Victor sided with Sassoon in arguing that the Nazis were not to be trusted.[22] Soon he would also be supporting rearmament as 'the shortest and certainly safest method of preserving peace in the world'.[23]

---

* Some have erroneously claimed that he was a member, almost certainly confusing the association with the fellowship.

The strongest emotion many ordinary citizens felt about Germany, though, was fear. H. G. Wells and Alexander Korda's science fiction film *Things to Come* sparked panic in 1936 with its convincing depiction of London flattened by bombers, but Baldwin had inadvertently set a hare running as early as November 1932. 'The bomber will always get through,' he told the Commons. 'The only defence is offence, which means that you will have to kill more women and children more quickly than the enemy if you want to save yourselves.'[24] This was a frightening and amoral concept, but as planes were being designed to be able to fly further and carry heavier bombs, the idea took hold in the public imagination that Britain was now vulnerable to attack from the air. Baldwin made the point explicit in July 1934. 'The old frontiers are gone,' he said. 'When you think of the defence of England you no longer think of the chalk cliffs of Dover, you think of the Rhine. That is where our frontiers are.'[25] One could draw two logical but contradictory conclusions. Either Britain needed significant air defences and a large offensive air force, or she should use every ounce of moral fibre to bring about a universal ban on aerial bombing.

This was played out in the annual Commons battle over the air estimates, the parliamentary allocation of expenditure for the air force, when Philip Sassoon, who was Under-Secretary for Air from 1931 to 1937, sought consent for the government's plans. It was always a tense affair. As an accomplished airman, Philip knew his brief inside out. He was an acknowledged master of the Chamber, too, who presented a complex argument with a stream of statistics entirely without notes. He knew, though, that the mood in the Commons could turn on a sixpence. In theory he could rely on a large government majority, but if he got the tone of his speech wrong he could easily lose the House. Besides, some MPs objected to the fact that Philip was only the under-secretary while his boss, the Secretary of State for Air, the Marquess of Londonderry, was in the Lords. More importantly, as became apparent every year, Philip was caught on the horns of a dilemma, as everyone demanded two mutually exclusive outcomes – disarmament and security.

When it came to the 1932 debate, Philip told T. E. Lawrence that he was going to 'get it in the neck from all sides' and urged him to 'come and see the fun'.[26] His prediction was accurate. The proposed cut of £700,000 was not enough for the Labour Party and was too much for those who feared German rearmament. At the same debate a year later – when he proposed a tiny increase – he tried to square the circle by suggesting that the Royal Air Force was involved in important humanitarian tasks. This drew the ire of Churchill, who pitched in with a sarcastic attack on the idea that 'the Air Force exists to fight locusts and it never drops anything but blankets' and argued 'we have to be strong enough to defend our neutrality'.[27] The same row was played out in the 1934 debate. Philip again presented his argument without notes: this time for an increase of £527,000, alongside increases for the Army and the Navy of £1.5 million and £3 million. Again he attempted to see off the arguments of those who objected to any money being spent on armaments by emphasising the humanitarian aspects of the RAF's work. With a nod to Churchill, he admitted that fighting locusts and dropping blankets were not its only work for peace, but that in safeguarding the life, liberty and goods of the Empire, 'the policeman goes hand in hand with the philanthropist'.[28] He was upfront about the failure of attempts at universal disarmament, and stated what should have been obvious to all: 'If other nations will not come down to our level, our national and Imperial security demands that we shall build up towards theirs.'[29] He was still in danger of pleasing nobody, though. The Labour leader, Clement Attlee, attacked the increase while Captain Freddie Guest, the Conservative MP for Plymouth Drake, claimed that since Germany had every intention of rearming as quickly as possible, and of annexing Austria, the increase was wholly inadequate.[30] At the end of the debate Baldwin stepped in to announce a major change in policy: henceforth he guaranteed that Britain would no longer be 'in a position inferior to any country within striking distance of our shores'.[31] It was a bold promise, which he followed up at the end of July with a pledge that the RAF would be half as big again as any German air force. In November he denied the rumour that Germany was rapidly approaching numerical equality with Britain and boldly predicted that 'so far from the German military air force being at least as strong, and probably stronger, than our own, we estimate that we shall still have in Europe alone a margin of nearly 50 per cent'.[32]

Despite all this grand talk, the government wavered, with fatal consequences. In the middle of talks with Germany about the possibility of establishing a legally binding balance of arms between the two countries, the government published a White Paper on defence in March 1935. Hitler pounced on its recommendation of another modest increase in British defence expenditure. Denouncing Britain's bad faith, he announced the creation of a new German air force and the reintroduction of conscription – both of which moves were expressly forbidden by Versailles. The Cabinet's response was yet another logically inconsistent decision. 'Our general aim,' so it claimed that April, 'should be peace achieved by some system of collective security under the League of Nations, without an acceptance of new commitments.'[33] Few other Cabinet minutes have so cruelly exposed a government's cowardly determination to will the ends but not the means.

When the new air estimates came up for debate, Philip was yet again at the crease. The atmosphere had worsened considerably. He knew his argument was weak. He was going to have to admit that Baldwin's claim about British air superiority was wrong. Britain had deliberately allowed herself to sink to fifth among the air forces of the world and had postponed a rearmament programme for ten years. He hoped that Britain might be narrowly ahead of Germany by the end of the year, but there was little or no prospect of outnumbering her by more than half. Some suggested that Baldwin had deliberately lied to Parliament. Yet again the government was in danger of angering everyone. Philip's strategy was simple – to garner sympathy for his personal predicament. He compared himself to St Sebastian, assailed by arrows from all sides, but lacking the comforting assurance that he would reap the rewards of martyrdom. 'From one side of the House,' he said, 'have come the clothyard shafts of those hon. Members who considered our provision for the air defence of this country inadequate; from another side the barbed bolts of those who would like to see the immediate abolition of all armed forces.' He was keen to point out that far from being 'warmongers', Britain had 'stripped our defences to the bone and the result has been that our weakness has not only become a danger to ourselves but a danger even to the cause of peace'.[34]

Philip's reference to St Sebastian was as bold as it was camp. Philip was a great art collector and a trustee of the National Gallery. He knew that many MPs, especially his friends, would recognise the insinuation behind his reference. In the many hundreds of representations of Sebastian's martyrdom, by Mantegna, Botticelli, Titian, Veronese, El Greco and others, Sebastian is shown as a paragon of male beauty, with defined, sinewy muscles, pert lips, a numinous air and little more than a loincloth to cover his dignity. His beauty is almost feminine and decidedly homoerotic, as many contemporary art historians acknowledged. The eponymous hero of Charles Kingsley's novel *Alton Locke* describes the first time he saw Guido Reni's *St Sebastian* in such terms. He admits being immensely impressed by 'those manly limbs, so grand and yet so delicate, standing out against the background of lurid night, the helplessness of the bound arms, the arrow quivering in the shrinking side, the upturned brow, the eyes in whose dark depths enthusiastic faith seemed conquering agony and shame, the parted lips'. He knew at once that this was a powerfully seductive image and felt he understood the heart of an Italian girl or Grecian boy excited by it 'to hopeless love, madness and death'.[35] Kingsley's sexuality is a matter of debate, but many homosexuals openly identified with Sebastian's agony. Oscar Wilde took the pseudonym 'Sebastian Melmoth' in exile in France and Evelyn Waugh named the tortured, alcoholic, sexually ambiguous anti-hero of *Brideshead Revisited* Sebastian Flyte. There was something spiritual about this glorification of masculine submission, too. When the married but homosexual German novelist Thomas Mann accepted the Nobel Prize for Literature in 1929 he confessed that Sebastian, 'that youth at the stake, who pierced by swords and arrows from all sides, smiles amidst his agony', was his favourite saint. He explained, 'Grace in suffering – that is the heroism symbolised by St Sebastian.'[36]

Philip's gloss did not pass unnoticed. Colonel John Moore-Brabazon, the Conservative MP for Wallasey, who was an accomplished airman and would remain a passionate opponent of war with Germany well into 1939, attacked Philip for putting 'a glamour over a sorry story with a regularity which is almost a danger to the community'.[37] That word 'glamour' sticks out. Despite its modern meaning, it then meant 'enchantment' or 'magic'. It implied something secret, foreign, seductive and supernatural. It had a similar double meaning to the word 'charm', implying beauty that cast a spell over one's eyes. Sir Walter Scott, whose novels were a staple of Conservative MPs' reading material, resuscitated the word in his poems and described glamour as 'the magic power of imposing on the eye-sight of spectators, so that the appearance of an object shall be totally different from the reality'.[38] It was a word normally reserved for women, who bewitched, beguiled, seduced and distracted men with their feigned beauty. Glamour was the name of Coco Chanel's new intoxicating perfume launched in 1933; *Glamour* was a 1934 American movie in which Constance Cummings played a scheming chorus girl who stalks and marries a successful composer and runs off with another man; *Glamorous Night* was the title of Ivor Novello's 1935 camp musical about a gypsy princess, which reached the silver screen in 1937, alongside the movie *Women of Glamour*, in which another ambitious working-class girl managed to snare a wealthy husband. Moore-Brabazon had chosen his word carefully. It sounded like a compliment, but he was really making a calculated but subtle insinuation that

Philip was a seductive liar, a spellbinding foreigner and a rank effeminate.

Two months after these exchanges, on the verge of becoming prime minister, Baldwin was forced to admit that he had been wrong about German air strength. One might have expected this would lead to a renewed national determination to beef up rearmament, but the reluctance of Conservative MPs to confront Germany and of Labour to countenance war combined with the traditional sentimentality of the House when anyone made a direct apology. Parliament merely sighed and moved on. Even days after the remilitarisation of the Rhineland, Philip still claimed in the 1936 air estimates debate that the government hoped to secure an air pact, but he confessed that events had left the government no option. Unless Britain had sufficient air power to stand by its commitments, international anarchy threatened and 'the whole fabric of civilisation may well be imperilled'.[39] Hence the increase in the air estimate to £43.5 million. Not everyone was convinced. Fred Montague, the Labour MP for West Islington, derided 'the perfectly futile, panic-stricken notion that by threatening anyone else you are going to achieve the defence and security of this country'.[40] His colleague Joe Tinker, the MP for Leigh, moved that there should instead be a ban on aerial warfare – and the vote was carried by 216 to 121.

Cabinet papers show the government's complacency. At one meeting on 4 November 1936, the foreign secretary 'expressed *some anxiety* as to the state of Europe and intimated that in his view some challenge was possible any time from next Spring onwards'.[41] This should have been a sharp warning. After all, they already knew that Germany and Italy had a clear advantage over France and Belgium, and successive reports in January and February 1937 warned that German rearmament had been proceeding throughout the year 'at a steady but rapid rate',[42] that the strength of the German army had increased and that the rate of production of armaments had 'accelerated'.[43] Against that background, Philip returned to the Commons in March 1937 asking for an even more dramatic increase in the air estimate, rising to £82.5 million. Many remained deeply antagonistic, though. Montague again asked him sarcastically whether he thought Germany intended to colonise Great Britain. 'Unless that is the idea,' he fulminated, 'then the fear of a sudden attack on this country, the kind of attack which is in many people's minds, an attack without warning from the air, is probably more or less a fantasy.'[44] Philip had gone much further than any other minister in laying out the dangers facing the country, but against such a barrage he still felt he had to justify the increased estimate with a pacifist argument: 'We think that a British Air Force, strong, ready and well-equipped, is the best contribution that this country can make to the peace of the world.'[45]

Meanwhile the march of the dictators had taken another major step forward on 17 July 1936 when Francisco Franco, an ardently Catholic Spanish general with a profound loathing for atheism, socialism and democracy, launched a military rebellion in North Africa against the elected Popular Front Spanish Republican government. Franco had hoped for a swift coup d'état, but the ensuing civil war brought German and Italian forces in on the side of Franco while Russia came to the aid of the beleaguered Republican government, which included far-left parties. For the British left this was a choice between democracy and dictatorship, but many Conservatives saw it as a battle against communism, so Baldwin's government opted for a formal policy of non-intervention.

The strength of pro-Franco feeling on the Conservative benches was remarkable. Patrick Donner thanked Franco for bringing law and order to Spain; Sir Alfred Knox praised Franco's humane attitude to the civilian population, while Edward Keeling attacked the Republican slaughter of civilians; Sir Henry Page Croft claimed that the 'Terror' in Spain was 'widely organised by large numbers of agents imported from Moscow';[46] Lord Redesdale said Franco was leading a crusade for everything that the British held dear; Victor Cazalet wrote that he trusted and prayed that 'General Franco will win a victory for civilisation over Bolshevism';[47] Chips Channon told *The Times* he was 'very pro-Franco, and I hope he wins';[48] Alan Lennox-Boyd wrote that he could not understand the argument that it was in Britain's interest 'to stop General Franco winning';[49] and Winston Churchill, while publicly supporting neutrality, condemned the Republican government for its 'nightly butcheries ... [which] had robbed the Madrid Government of the lineaments of a civilised power'.[50] As Harold Nicolson noted, the enormous majority of Conservatives were 'passionately anti-Government and pro-Franco'.[51]

Yet again Jack Macnamara swam against the tide. In early November 1936 he joined a cross-party group of MPs who were unconvinced by the government's handling of the situation and organised a visit to Spain. They did so with some trepidation, as stories abounded of indiscriminate aerial bombardment and violent retribution being exacted on supposed opponents. So nervous were they that Jack persuaded a reluctant Harold Nicolson to write to Robert Vansittart asking him to alert Franco to the visit and promising that the group would express no political opinions 'whatsoever' while in Spain. The Labour MP Fred Seymour Cocks followed this up two days later with a letter to Eden in which he assured him that 'nobody had any desire to cause any embarrassment'. This was not particularly reassuring, however, as he continued, 'one or two of us are quite prepared to sit ... in a hospital, unarmed of course, and to say to any invaders that if they want to kill wounded patients they can only do it over our dead bodies'.[52] The group, consisting of three Labour men (Seymour Cocks, Dai Grenfell and the young Labour-supporting Earl of Kinnoull), three Conservatives (Jack Macnamara, Wing Commander Archie James and Crawford Greene) and the Liberal Wilfrid Roberts, left for Valencia on the morning of 20 November.

It proved to be a hair-raising visit. Churchill had asked Jack to try to save the life of the young aristocratic leader of the Spanish Falange movement, Primo de Rivera, who had been arrested for the illegal possession of firearms by the Republican government and was in prison. This proved abortive, as de Rivera was found guilty and executed on the day the group left Britain, but Jack and another member of the group did secure the release of four men and a woman who had been acquitted but feared for their lives by turning up unannounced at the prison and claiming they were taking vital insulin to diabetic inmates and persuading the guards to release them on compassionate grounds. They also experienced Franco's air assault on Madrid at first hand. While two squadrons of Nationalist bombers rained down bombs on the north-west suburbs of the city, Jack and Crawford Greene came under fire standing outside the gates of the British Embassy. That evening they sent an angry telegram to Franco through the embassy protesting against the bombing of areas 'known to be inhabited wholly by the civil population'.[53]

On their return Jack and Wilfrid were clear in the Commons. Yes, it was true that there was not much to choose between the two sides when it came to the atrocities that had been reported in Spain. Both were fighting ruthlessly, prisoners were being shot, hostages and the wounded were being murdered. But Jack had seen German barrack rooms in Munich earlier in the year plastered with notices asking for volunteers for Spain, he knew that Germany was shipping whole divisions out to Spain and that it was no secret that Germany was 'very actively engaged' in the war on the Nationalist side.[54] Yet again Jack was in a minority on the Conservative benches – even Crawford Greene took a diametrically opposite view – but when he was attacked in the press, he repeated his assertion that German tanks, aeroplanes and 30,000 troops were fighting on Franco's side. Both sides had committed horrors – the only difference was that Franco had from the start 'taken the trouble to let us know of his enemy's misdoings'. He ended the year deriding the tendency to treat Germany differently from every other nation. 'She is excused as might be a hysterical child. But why?' he asked.[55]

The war in Spain inspired Jack's compassion for another reason. As Franco pushed forward to Bilbao with ruthless force in the spring of 1937 and stories filtered through to Britain of the saturation bombing of Guernica that April, large numbers of Basque children found themselves separated from their parents. Although he had become closer to his mother in later years, Jack had always called himself 'an Empire orphan' and knew what it felt like to be passed from pillar to post. He immediately signed up with David Grenfell and Wilfrid Roberts as the three honorary secretaries of the Basque Children's Committee (BCC) and the National Joint Committee for Spanish Relief. Yet again, this was a brave move for a Conservative, since the only other Conservative involved was the Duchess of Atholl. Although the trade union movement was clamouring for the government to take the evacuee children and there was strong public revulsion at the blitzkrieg vented on Guernica, Baldwin was desperate not to get involved and came up with the weak excuse that the climate in Britain would not suit the refugees (he was presumably unaware that the Basque country's climate is remarkably similar to that of Wales). Jack was determined, though.

Eventually Baldwin relented (on the proviso that the BCC would guarantee ten shillings a week for each child) and the steamship *Habana* docked at Southampton on 23 May. Designed for 800 passengers, it had 3,886 children, ninety-six teachers, 118 assistants, and sixteen Catholic priests on board and the proposed tented accommodation at North Stoneham, which was originally prepared for 2,000, could barely cope. Jack's rudimentary Spanish proved useful, as the children panicked when they heard that Bilbao had fallen to the Nationalists on 19 June and immediately jumped to the conclusion that their parents had been killed. Jack was able to calm them with news that many inhabitants of Bilbao had fled for Santander, although he admitted to *The Times* that 'about 200 children got over-excited and some preferred to cry in secret in the woods'.[56] He felt so strongly that he lobbied for the children's safe return as soon as it was practicable and wrote to Eden from Corfe Castle, where he was training with the London Irish Rifles, to say that if necessary he would go to Bilbao in person to help find the children's parents. In the end the BCC managed to persuade the

American Friends Service Council to represent them in Bilbao and the majority of the children were able to return home in safety. Four hundred were farmed out to children's homes and 250 or so made their lives in Britain either because their parents were dead or in prison or because they were old enough to choose for themselves.

Jack's position on Spain did not endear him to the government whips. One of the few Conservatives to sympathise with him was Bob Boothby, who appeared at a 'People's Front' rally at Friends House in Euston Road in December 1936. This too was bold, as both the government and the Labour Party fervently objected to the inclusion of the Communist Party in any anti-fascist campaign. The rally collapsed in chaos as the Labour firebrand G. D. H. Cole demanded that the National Government be 'smashed', which prompted Bob to storm off the platform and officially dissociate himself from the movement. That same week Eden secured headlines in the press along the lines of 'Mr. Eden Warns "Hands off Spain"',[57] but in Bob's mind Britain's policy of non-intervention was unbalanced. 'We never raised a finger,' he later wrote, 'to help the Spanish government, and allowed Hitler and Mussolini to win the war for Franco by the most brutal methods without protest.'[58] At least Jack had helped save the lives of hundreds of young Basques.

Hitler's attempts to win over individual members of the Conservative Party bore fruit as he had plenty of British friends by the end of 1936. Some were committed supporters of the policies he, Franco and Mussolini advocated. Others were just keen to avoid war. Public opinion was similarly inclined against making too many military commitments to Britain's allies. But Jack was happy to swim against that tide, whatever that might cost him.

PART THREE

What Price Peace?

12

Getting On

It was just before 6.30 p.m. on 17 November 1936, a Thursday. Most MPs were gossiping about King Edward's affair with Wallis Simpson, but Ronnie Cartland was building up for a fight. He had always been concerned about poverty and unemployment, but since his maiden speech he had been roped in as secretary of the Special Areas Committee, which Viscount Wolmer had set up to 'press for more vigorous action in the gloomy areas'.[1] Touring depressed parts of the country that were unfamiliar to most Conservatives, including the Rhondda and Merthyr Tydfil, Ronnie had grown impatient with the government's inertia. He and others had been pressing for an ambitious Special Areas Act and major investment, but that afternoon Chamberlain had announced a paltry amount of cash, and when the debate opened it became clear that the government was engaged in parliamentary jiggery-pokery designed to prevent any discussion of the government's feeble measures. Wolmer joined Labour MPs in attacking the Speaker, who seemed in cahoots with the government, but got nowhere, so Labour moved that the House ditch the government's business by adjourning the House. Then Chamberlain made a patronising speech that utterly infuriated Ronnie. He sat there fuming until he was finally called at ten o'clock, when he launched a direct attack on the Chancellor, declaring that he was 'seriously disappointed' in Chamberlain's speech, which sounded as if the Chancellor had only just considered the problem of poverty and unemployment in the industrial heartlands for the first time. Ronnie ended with a challenge:

> You can either do nothing or you can do something. If you are going to do something, you have got to spend money. If you are going to do nothing, I beg the Government to say so with complete and appalling frankness, because then at least we who support them, will know where we stand.[2]

Chamberlain visibly seethed, as Ronnie was effectively accusing him of dishonesty. The debate continued raucously through the night until Labour called a vote at 5.30 in the morning. Tempers were strained but the whips persuaded Wolmer to abstain. Ronnie refused to back down, though, so he and Jack Macnamara joined two other Conservatives in the Aye Lobby with Labour. Chamberlain won comfortably enough − by 155 to eighty-six − but the chief whip Margesson stared stonily at Ronnie, and the Labour Clydesider MP, James Maxton, told him 'the only trouble with you is you're on the wrong side of the House'.[3] Ronnie had been making a name for himself. *The Times* even singled him out along with his neighbour Bernays for having 'made their mark'.[4] But plenty of friends warned him that he wouldn't get on if he kept on attacking his own government.

Yet just a few weeks later, Philip Sassoon invited Ronnie to his house party at Trent Park − an event normally reserved for bachelor friends − and tried to persuade him to be his parliamentary private secretary (PPS), the traditional first step on the parliamentary career ladder. It was unpaid. It entailed little more than being Philip's bag-carrier and his eyes and ears within Parliament. Yet most MPs would have leapt at the chance. When R. A. Butler, for instance, suggested to Chips Channon that he should be his PPS at the Foreign Office in 1938 Chips could barely conceal his excitement. Since Butler and he would be the only two MPs at the Foreign Office, he reckoned 'it would be a position of power, great power', adding, 'If I got

it, I might play a great role.'[5] The role of Sassoon's PPS was in
the same league. Philip was at the fulcrum of one of the most
important debates of the decade. He was a known ally of the
foreign secretary, Anthony Eden, and regularly hosted Churchill
and Lloyd George. Yet Ronnie turned him down. It is difficult
to know why. Ronnie was by now convinced that war with
Germany would not be long in coming and that MPs should be
open with their constituents about the real and present danger
posed by Hitler. He was prepared to put his own safety on the
line, too. Even though he had a gammy leg and he had just
celebrated his thirtieth birthday, both of which factors should
have precluded him from being accepted into the Territorial
Army, he had pulled a few strings to make sure he did not have to
undergo a medical and had joined his father's old regiment, the
Worcestershire and Oxfordshire Yeomanry, in January 1937. All
of which suggests that as PPS in the Ministry for Air he would
have been in an ideal position from which to 'play a great role'.

Yet Ronnie confessed that something in him baulked at
Philip's 'fantastically beautiful and comfortable' lifestyle. Philip's
guest list that weekend may not have helped, as the atmosphere
must have crackled with misfiring sexual energy. Philip was at
the time obsessed with one of his guests, the well-proportioned
up-and-coming civil servant Ian Wilson Young, but that was
going nowhere. The wealthy and adventurous widow Venetia
Montagu was engaged in an on-off affair with another guest,
the much younger Rupert Belleville. Four other guests were
dancing a very complicated quadrille. Malcolm Bullock was the
MP for Waterloo and had been a faithful husband who grieved
in manly fashion when his wife Victoria died in 1928, but had
'soon afterwards sought discreet consolation from members of his
own sex'.[6] For a while that had included an intense relationship
with Rex Whistler, whose homosexual friends all 'held that he
was one of them, if only he would face it'.[7] Rex had broken off
the relationship in 1931 and left Malcolm with little more than
a painting, *Ulysses' Farewell to Penelope*, but he was now engaged
in a frustrated relationship with Patricia Douglas, and Malcolm

was trying to avoid the attentions of his dead wife's sister-in-law, Portia Stanley. To add heat to an already spicy mixture, Philip had invited the unashamedly homosexual Lord Berners and the more demure but nonetheless very confirmed bachelor Lord Stanmore. At least half the guests were queer, and while Ronnie liked the bright set, this was just a bit too heady a mix for him.

One other experience may have played a part in Ronnie's decision to decline Sassoon's offer to be his PPS. On 10 February 1937 he initiated a Commons debate on 'the trend of population'. It is difficult to imagine today, but in the 1930s Britain feared depopulation far more than overpopulation, as thousands of British families decided to emigrate to Australia, New Zealand and the wider Empire, and the British birth rate was in steady decline. It was brave of Ronnie to lead on such a contentious subject. From the moment he started, members jeered at him that he was a bachelor. Even his friend Duncan Sandys argued that Ronnie was 'not in a particularly strong position to preach on this subject'.[8] He was meaning to be jocular, but others took the matter more seriously. Sir Richard Pilkington, the MP for Widnes, who did not marry until 1946, claimed that he was horrified to see that the Commons had nearly 200 bachelors, 'a situation which hon. Members should take immediate steps to remedy'.[9] Speaking for the government, Austin Hudson quipped that the debate would have been much better led by the MP for West Nottingham, Arthur Hayday, who had seven children. The former miner, George Griffiths, lambasted the bachelors. 'It is no use the hon. Member opposite, a bachelor, telling us how to go on,' he said with a sneer, claiming that he was 'going to speak from experience, not from theory'.[10] That day the *Daily Express* – part of the Beaverbrook stable – sent Ronnie a peremptory telegram demanding that he explain why he was still unmarried at the age of thirty. It was difficult to avoid the unnerving hint of an accusation about that word 'bachelor'.

Rob Bernays's life was in flux, too. He had long debated what side of the House to sit on, and finally decided in 1936 to take the National Liberal Party whip on the grounds that he had found himself in agreement with the government on all the main issues for several months and felt, as he put it to the party leader, Sir John Simon, 'I have no justification any longer in maintaining my isolation.'[11] His private life was equally turbulent. He fretted about being single. 'I sometimes wonder,' he wrote, just after visiting Beauchamp in Paris, 'whether, even if I fulfil all expectations and ambitions, I shall not be rather lonely in old age if I do not marry; and at present there is no one in the world with whom I could contemplate spending the rest of my days.'[12] He had several women friends, including Nancy Astor and Sibyl Colefax, but the woman he really confided in, his sister Lucy, lived in Brazil. He wrote to her two days before Christmas that he was bored. Nothing seemed to have happened in politics since the king's abdication 'and nothing seems likely to happen again'.[13] He was even less convinced about his own prospects, having come to the conclusion that he had long since passed the stage where he could have 'a really passionate flirtation'.[14] But six days later he was telling her that he was infatuated with a sassy comic actress called Leonora Corbett, who had just starred opposite Richard Tauber in the musical film *Heart's Desire*. It had started when Leonora appeared in the opposite pew in his father's church on Christmas Day. Rob was smitten. 'I thought she was one of the most glamorous things I have ever seen,' he wrote. The moment the service was over he ran over to invite her for a drink – and two days later they had a long lunch at the Ivy, which carried on until five o'clock. 'It is all very school-boyish,' he admitted, adding, 'I do not suppose it can last but it is fun while it lasts.' The only problem he could foresee was that 'an actress has a great facility for playing a part but I was impressed with how sincere and intelligent she was behind all the glamour and glitter'.[15]

It was unfortunate timing. Rob was due to set sail for East Africa a few days later on a ten-week trip looking at colonial education. Buck De La Warr led the delegation, but the real interest for Rob lay in the fact that Harold Nicolson was going. They had known each other before Harold was elected, but the new Parliament had brought the two men closer; they had become frequent dinner companions and he would occasionally stay over at Harold's flat at King's Bench Walk. They had a lot in common. Neither was a Conservative, but they both sat with the government. They mixed in similar circles. They believed that politics was a noble profession and they enjoyed gossiping about who was in and who was out. Their relationship took on a new intensity on this trip, as they spent the ten weeks, in Rob's words, 'sharing the same experiences, interested in the same things and bored by the same people'.[16] The two men thoroughly enjoyed their time together. Frequently they peeled off from the rest to spend time alone. Night after night they dined together in exotic locations. They confided in each other. Rob recounted the Beauchamp saga, Harold teased Rob about his stutter, Rob posed for Harold's cine-camera in front of architectural wonders like the Colossi of Memnon at Luxor and teased Harold back when it turned out that he had loaded all thirty reels of film in the camera the wrong way round, so all the posing had been for nought. Often they got so close it was almost painful not to touch each other. It seemed to Rob as if they had almost identical minds and outlook, although he admitted that Harold's brain was 'infinitely more trained and better stocked'.[17] By the time they returned to England Rob was mildly infatuated – and rather confused. He admitted, 'I suppose that what I really want in a woman is that kind of mental affinity which I get from someone like HN. And yet that is probably an impossibility, or if it exists it must surely be better than the powers of physical attraction.'[18]

The tussle in Rob's head became more intense when he took things up again with Leonora, whose career was blossoming as she starred in the long-running comedy *Dusty Ermine* and in the film *The Price of Folly*. At first he told Lucy that things were going well, although he reported that Leonora was more than a bit surprised when he announced that his career must come first. But by the middle of July his ardour seemed to be cooling. Rather than seeing Leonora and himself as passionate lovers, he wanted them to be 'two independent creatures proposing to conclude a formal alliance'. Perhaps with Harold and Vita's relationship in mind, he admitted to himself, 'It is not as though the dashing male is carrying off a shrinking adoring woman. I want my wife to be reasonably independent. That is what I desire.'[19] This reflected almost exactly the sentiment Harold expressed in his own diary about his relationship with Vita, who, he reckoned, did not really care for domestic affections. 'She would wish life to be conducted on a series of *grandes passions*,' he wrote. He was sceptical, as he reckoned that if he had been more passionate, she would have been more jealous, there would have been endless scenes 'and we should now have separated'.[20] There was another problem, though. Rob wanted Harold to approve of Leonora, but Harold thought that she was dreadful, so when Rob put him on the spot about her one evening on the Commons Terrace, Harold tried to keep things vague and merely said that she seemed very pretty. Rob persisted. 'But you did not like her,' he said, daring him to agree. Harold was keen not to be rude, but his answer cannot have pleased Rob, as he told him that what really mattered in a marriage was not people's 'outside' but their 'inside' and that to be completely frank he did not think Leonora's inside was 'sufficiently interesting'. Of course, he added, if Rob insisted on marrying her he must completely forget his unkind remarks.[21] Rob felt crushed, but adopted a philosophical approach when he wrote to Lucy that 'Harold says she is not good enough for me! But then he is very fond of me as I am of him.'[22] A few weeks later, though, Rob wrote that something had suddenly snapped inside him and he had put an end to the relationship with Leonora. The excuse he gave was that he had given her a watch for her birthday and she had not even remembered his, but the words he wrote to Lucy betrayed a deeper unhappiness: 'I saw her for what she really is – a spoiled, vulgar, gold-digging chorus girl, sprung from a bitch in Finchley and quite unable to stand any degree of criticism.'[23]

It is not difficult to see why Rob was keen to marry. Lone-liness was the constant fear of every homosexual man – and

society demanded that men marry. Two of his closest friends –
Harold Nicolson and Ronnie Tree – were married yet had
extramarital relations with other men. He also got especially
keen on marrying when others around him got married. He was
delighted to act as best man at his father's wedding to Evelyn
Bolton, the daughter of a former parishioner in a deliberately
low-key ceremony in Chorley Wood on 24 April 1937 – and
gave the happy couple a chest of drawers. Besides, the matter
of Rob's unmarried status returned to haunt him publicly time
and again. Later that year he took part in another debate on the
subject of depopulation and received similar taunts to Ronnie
Cartland's. They both tried to laugh it off. Ronnie replied to
the *Express*'s telegram, 'Regret have no statement to make as
to future intentions'[24] and Barbara later claimed he had had
several offers of marriage from complete strangers. Rob likewise
attempted to head the question off at the pass, starting his speech
in the debate with a half-hearted joke: 'I was attacked tonight for
having committed the atrocious crime of being still a bachelor,
but surely there is still plenty of time. I am not an old man yet.'
When that was not enough, he added another long-prepared
'light' comment: 'If I may give the House a little secret on this
question of my bachelorhood, it is that I have always heard that
really great men are the sons of elderly parents, and I want a son
of whom I can be proud.'[25] Those who knew him best must
have stared at their boots with embarrassment. A year later his
local newspaper provided yet another sharp headline. 'Bachelor
Bernays MP Lives in Hope', it read, while reporting that Rob
had told the Women's Public Health Officers Association that
although he had 'led eight young men to the altar' (a curious
phrase in itself) he had yet to persuade any of the bridesmaids
to marry him.[26]

Despite their breeziness, one can imagine the panic in both
Ronnie and Rob's hearts, but this first shot across Ronnie's bows
from a hostile Conservative press did not stop him telling people
the unpopular truth about Germany: that 'we can[not] stand
aside in this country and see these battles going on without

saying "Is it going to be our turn next?"[27] At another event he raised a laugh by drawing a parallel with the unfortunate young lady of Riga 'who smiled as she rode on a tiger./At the end of the ride the girl was inside/And the smile on the face of the tiger.'[28] It seems likely, though, that it made him very wary of allying himself to another very prominent bachelor, especially one so ostentatious as Philip Sassoon.

Such anxiety was understandable.The national hysteria around homosexuality had escalated. The number of prosecutions for gross indecency, importuning and buggery in London alone rose above 200 for the first time in 1937 and the raids on queer bars and clubs continued. One in particular received considerable press attention. When Billie's Club in Little Denmark Street was raided after several months of surveillance, its proprietress Billie Joyce was prosecuted along with an American music-hall artist called James Rich and thirty-four others. The trial, which started at the Old Bailey on 12 January 1937, was harrowing.The defendants had to run the gauntlet of a baying crowd outside the court and there were so many of them that they were given numbered chairs. As part of the prosecution Detective Sergeant George Miller reported that the 'majority of the males present were of the nancy boy type. They used make-up and their hair was waved or dyed.'[29] Twenty-one were convicted, including a floor layer, an author, an actor, a pianist, a bricklayer and a paint sprayer. The Common Serjeant of London, Cecil Whiteley KC, was horrified that 'these premises have been for many months a meeting place and resort of sexual perverts'.[30] He gave ten of them two years in prison each and called for Rich to be deported. Billie Joyce collapsed in the dock. Newspapers up and down the land published the story and even defendants who were acquitted had their names, ages and occupations published in the *Illustrated Police News*.

Another case arose at the end of the year, closer to Ronnie's Birmingham constituency, when two men, Clifford Hardy (twenty-three) and Wesley Reeve (thirty-one), were charged with gross indecency, which had supposedly occurred at a

Dudley Town Hall dance. The police officers – who were later proved to have lied – claimed that they had clearly seen the two men together in a doorway with a glass partition and a light shining through. In the initial magistrates court hearing, one of the constables described chasing one of the defendants along a corridor, on to the stage, where the band was playing, through hundreds of people dancing on the floor and up several flights of stairs into the kitchens before apprehending him. The magistrates recognised that Hardy occupied a significant position in the town and that 'the whole of his future and his life rests upon the outcome of this case', but despite the inconclusive evidence they committed the two men for trial.[31] After a four-day hearing in which the vicar of St Luke's and the Archdeacon of Dudley gave evidence for Hardy, another witness said he had seen Reeve shaking Hardy because he was so drunk and Hardy claimed that he was 'out cold' because he had been drinking his beer through a straw. Hardy was sent to prison for three months and Reeve for six. Mr Justice Lawrence, sentencing, complained that he understood 'offences of this kind' had been prevalent in Dudley and recognised that whatever sentence he passed would add but little to the men's punishment. 'But,' he pronounced, 'offences of this sort cannot be passed over, especially in cases of two men like you who have had some education.'[32]

Queer men had always known they were walking a tightrope, but as more stories of arrests appeared in the press, they became ever more anxious. This was also true for bachelors in the public eye, and Jack, Ronnie and Rob always had to bear in mind that defying the whips could be dangerous. It was the whips' job to pick up gossip, rumour and tittle-tattle and deploy it when necessary. Any member who wanted to get promoted, join an influential committee or go on a trip overseas had to be loyal, and disloyalty could lead to a quiet phone call to a journalist. As long as Baldwin was prime minister, they had a useful ally in the shape of his son Oliver, who was living with a man and campaigning for British rearmament. In February 1936, though, Harold Nicolson wrote that 'Baldwin is getting deaf and will have to leave', and predicted that the Chancellor, Neville Chamberlain, would soon take his place.[33] Fifteen months later his prediction came true when Chamberlain, who was now sixty-eight, formed a new National Government on 28 May 1937. As always with government reshuffles, there was plenty of gossip about who might get posts. Philip Sassoon had worried about being sacked – but was promoted to First Commissioner of Works and set about redesigning Trafalgar Square and redecorating the Members' Dining Room in the Commons (Nicolson thought the green carpets and brocaded green curtains were 'quite effective').[34] Rob Bernays and Harold had speculated that one or other of them might be promoted and Jack Macnamara had told Harold he had heard Harold was in line for a post at the Foreign Office, but in the end Rob was the only successful one, as he became under-secretary at the Ministry of Health.

13

The New Prime Minister

Colleagues liked affable, self-deprecating Baldwin. He knew how to play the House. On his last outing in the Commons, just before travelling to Buckingham Palace to resign, he announced that MPs' salaries would increase from £400 to £600 a year 'at an early date'. Not surprisingly, everyone cheered, but when a member pressed him on whether he would 'consider the propriety' of leaving this to a free vote of the House, his answer had everyone in stitches. 'I am not certain,' he said with a twinkle in his eye, 'that it would be an act of propriety on my part to consider *anything* that this House might do *next week*.'[1]

Views about his successor, Chamberlain, by contrast, were mixed. Chips Channon was besotted with him. He was 'so calm and yet so sensible and determined'; he was 'the shrewdest prime minister of modern times'.[2] Others were more critical, though. The senior civil servant Sir Horace Wilson reckoned Chamberlain took time before making up his mind, but that 'when that course was settled he did not wonder whether it was right and whether it would have been better to decide to try something else'.[3] Sir Alexander Cadogan, who was permanent under-secretary at the Foreign Office from 1938 to 1946, saw him as a 'man of one-track mind. If, after much reflection, no doubt, he decided on a certain move or line of policy, nothing would affect him.'[4] Likewise the Italian ambassador, Dino Grandi, claimed Chamberlain was 'not a politician, but a man of simple ideas and strong character, particularly sensitive to an act of personal trust and friendship'.⁵ Harold Nicolson considered there was something darker going on, as he noted that in becoming prime minister, Chamberlain had triumphed over the bullying of his father, Joe, and the 'subtle hostility' of his half-brother Austen, neither of whom had achieved their life goal. In short, he was complex. Distrusting others, he relied to an unhealthy degree on his own resources. He hated his judgement to be questioned. Once committed to a course of action he would deploy all necessary means to see it through, including deliberately provoking his opponents. It led the Labour Party to despise him just when the nation would have benefited from a unifying prime minister. It also led him to develop a secretive network of loyalists upon whom he could utterly depend.

This was especially apparent in international diplomacy, which was rapidly acquiring a new urgency. On the night Chamberlain took over, Bob Boothby found Baldwin warming himself in front of the fire in the Commons lobby and suggested it was a sad occasion. 'Not for me,' replied Baldwin. 'It is time I went. There is only one thing I regret. I never took any interest in foreign affairs.'⁶ This clearly weighed on his mind, as he told Chamberlain, in his customarily languid way, 'It will be a wonderful thing for you if you can bring about European peace. I hadn't the energy to do it during my last two years.'⁷ By contrast Chamberlain was so sure of the power of his own personality that in November 1936 he wrote to his sister Hilda that 'by careful diplomacy I believe we can stave off [Germany], perhaps indefinitely'⁸ and within days of becoming prime minister, as he boasted, he said 'a few kind words to Germany which might have a far-reaching effect'.⁹

This combination of overreaching self-confidence and distrust of others was to lead to a visceral antagonism between him and any Conservative who criticised his foreign policy. Inevitably, the foreign secretary would be caught in the middle of that row, but everything started promisingly when Chamberlain appointed Sir Anthony Eden. Born the third son of a grumpy County Durham baronet in 1897, Eden had been at Eton with Victor Cazalet but had enjoyed a much faster rise since he was first elected for Warwick and Leamington in the 1923 general election. He had deliberately cultivated a reputation for being a foreign affairs expert. He had been PPS to Austen Chamberlain as foreign secretary, Under-Secretary for Foreign Affairs, Minister for the League of Nations and Lord Privy Seal in MacDonald's National Government, and Baldwin had made him at thirty-eight the youngest foreign secretary since Pitt, when Hoare was forced to resign in 1935. Chamberlain rated him and in large measure agreed with him, as the scars of war had left Eden determined to avoid another war if possible. Both his older and younger brothers had been killed in action and although he was awarded the Military Cross, he felt that he would never forget the devastation he had seen at the Somme. Appeasement, he believed, in the sense of bringing peace, had to be the central aim of British diplomacy, and he was prepared to make considerable concessions to the German and Italian dictators.

Chamberlain and Eden were therefore largely of one mind in 1937, but one of the first things Chamberlain did as prime minister was bring Sir Joseph Ball into Downing Street, and charge him with two new tasks, both of which had to remain secret: black operations against his critics and private diplomatic missions to the Italian and German dictators. Often these two tasks merged into one. Ball had already been cultivating close personal contacts in the press, the BBC and the British film industry. He had courted all the newspaper barons. Now he provided pliable journalists from supportive newspapers with twice-weekly briefings away from prying eyes at the St Stephen's Club opposite Westminster Bridge on the completely deniable understanding that he knew the PM's mind. He rewarded those who filed supportive copy with titbits of gossip and bullied critics into rejecting derogatory articles. He also wrote to Chamberlain that he was certain he could count on most of the film industry, whose newsreels reached 20 million people every week, 'for their full support to any reasonable degree'.

In practice this meant downplaying atrocities committed by Franco's troops and presenting Germany in a positive light. Ball had considerable success. Geoffrey Dawson, the editor of *The Times*, wrote that he did his utmost 'night after night, to keep out of the paper anything that might have hurt [the Germans'] susceptibility'.[10] On the rare occasion that anything did slip through – such as the paper's report in April 1937 that German planes had taken part in bombing Guernica – Dawson expected and received a stern rebuke.

Ball had one other trick up his sleeve. He wrote to Baldwin in late 1935 that 'the *Daily Mail* and the *Daily Express* attack us more frequently than they support us, while, although *The Times* and the *Daily Telegraph* are admirable papers and give us their full support, their circulations are so small … that their influence among the masses is almost negligible'.[11] His solution was to buy 'a suitable weekly publication' and staff it with writers who would do his bidding. He had his eye on *Truth*, which had been founded in 1877 by the MP who introduced the 'gross indecency' clause, Henry Labouchère, as a popular weekly magazine that exposed fraud, corruption and malfeasance of every kind. Under its early editor Horace Voules it enjoyed a readership of over 1 million. After Labouchère's death in 1912 the majority shareholding passed to a trust, which was ripe for purchase when the magazine's circulation subsided. So as to preserve the myth of the magazine's editorial independence, Ball drafted in Lord Luke of Pavenham, who was heir to the Bovril empire, owned shares in several gold mines in West Africa and was chairman of the fundraising arm of the Conservative Party's National Publicity Bureau (which was also run by Ball), secretly to purchase the 1,902 shares on his behalf. Within months Ball and Luke took over the board, appointed Ball's deputy at the Conservative Research Department, Henry Brooke,[12] as a director and installed a pliable new editor, Henry Newnham, whose only editorial post thus far had been at the *John Lewis Partnership Journal* and had little to recommend him other than his personal loyalty to Chamberlain.

Thus, even before he became prime minister, Chamberlain had a respected weekly magazine at his beck and call, which, so he admitted to his sister Ida, was 'secretly controlled by Sir Joseph Ball'.[13] Once Chamberlain was installed in No. 10, it was to prove an invaluable secret asset, as Ball used it to conduct vendettas against rebel MPs and bring them to heel. When Lieutenant Colonel Gilbert Acland-Troyte, who had been Conservative MP for Tiverton since 1924, mildly criticised the government's agricultural policy, *Truth* waded in, accusing him of being no more than a 'nominal' supporter of the government. Entirely ignoring his impressive military record in the Boer and First World Wars, it derided him for being a man whose name 'would not naturally occur to anyone invited to make a list of twenty well-known British politicians', and accused him of having 'blimp blood in his veins' and of having been 'overtaken by a rhetorical bilious attack'.[14] One can only imagine the fury Acland-Troyte would have vented if he had known that his own party's director of research was directly running the magazine.

Ball's second task of opening up a secret channel with Mussolini was even more controversial, as it involved deliberately circumventing Eden, who was adamant that no further concessions should be made to Italy unless and until she verifiably withdrew her support for Franco and abandoned her claim to Abyssinia. Yet again Ball relied on some shady characters, in particular a lawyer of Maltese-Italian-English extraction called Adrian Dingli, whom Ball engaged to provide secret information 'about Italian Diplomatic moves'[15] and to enable a completely deniable avenue to the Italian ambassador, the newly ennobled Count Dino Grandi, and through him to Galeazzo Ciano, who was Mussolini's son-in-law and his Minister for Press and Propaganda. Chamberlain doubtless thought he could exploit Ciano's known scepticism about Germany, but the Italians had a motive of their own for encouraging this surreptitious backchannel, as they hoped, as Grandi told Ciano, 'to drive a wedge into the incipient split between Eden and Chamberlain and to enlarge it more if possible'.[16]

It did not take long for this split to become apparent, as there were several moments of high farce. On one occasion Grandi had to pretend to read out a non-existent letter from Mussolini to Chamberlain. Then Chamberlain tried to exploit Eden's absence on business in Geneva in January 1938 by arranging a private meeting with Grandi, but Eden was so anxious to prevent Chamberlain from committing Britain to open-ended talks with no preconditions that he returned early and Grandi had to flee to the golf course at Wentworth in order to to avoid meeting him. In a subsequent meeting with Grandi, Eden and Chamberlain spent all their time disagreeing with each other. When the Italians seemed to blow cold on the whole idea of bringing Chamberlain and Mussolini together, Ball arranged a surreptitious brush-past meeting with Dingli and an Italian Embassy official at Waterloo station behind the back of an unsuspecting Cabinet member who was hailing a taxi. Ball then delivered the message that Mussolini approved of the British plan to open public talks to Chamberlain, who told the Cabinet at 3 p.m. It was the first Eden had heard of it and he was furious. As he told Malcolm MacDonald, he could not defend a policy that he was convinced was wrong, nor could any foreign secretary tolerate such freelance diplomacy. So, when the Cabinet reconvened at 7.30 p.m. he tendered his resignation, along with that of his under-secretary, Viscount 'Bobetty' Cranborne.

Chamberlain's cronies had been deliberately undermining Eden for months. When Eden was ill the previous November, Ronnie Cartland told Eden's PPS Jim Thomas that both Hoare and Simon had been briefing the *Sunday Times* that his flu 'was the beginning of the end for A. E., that the strain was too great and he would soon go'.[17] Ball went into overdrive when Eden resigned. In the words of another rebellious Conservative MP, Paul Emrys-Evans, Ball and the whips 'took good care to conceal as far as they could the extent of [Eden's] support'.[18] Ball boasted of it in a letter to Chamberlain, when he claimed to have taken 'certain steps privately' with the press to destroy

Eden and Cranborne's case.[19] He persuaded the BBC to relegate Eden's resignation to the second story on the evening bulletins and to say nothing at all about Germany or Italy. The *Daily Mail* attacked Eden for being in thrall to the League of Nations, the *Evening Standard*, the *Daily Express* and the *Daily Telegraph* all sided with Chamberlain and 'his policy of appeasement, which is also the policy of peace'.[20] The *Manchester Guardian*, which was one of the few newspapers not in thrall to Ball, noted that although a double resignation of this kind might have precipitated a major government crisis, the press had 'preserved a unity of silence that could hardly be bettered in a totalitarian state'.[21] Ball was so proud of this comment that he pasted it in his cuttings book. That was not all. In advance of Parliament sitting, he and the government whips put it about that Eden had resigned out of pique brought on by ill health, and *The Times* carried a fictitious story that Eden had been contemplating taking a three-month 'holiday'. The insinuation was that he had had a nervous breakdown.

From this moment on Ball sought to exploit all of Eden's foibles. Top of the list was the meticulous way Eden presented himself. After all, the one thing everybody knew about Anthony Eden was that he was immaculately turned out. Unlike many of his colleagues he remained slim and there was something of the movie star about the way he trimmed his moustache and slicked back his hair. He was particular about his attire. He liked to wear double-breasted waistcoats with single-breasted jackets. He mixed pale waistcoats with dark suits and was never without a casually perfect pocket square at his breast. He so popularised his black homburg that it came to be known as an 'Anthony Eden' and even American newspapers looked out for it. When he became Lord Privy Seal in 1933 the *Bystander* commented that 'Captain Eden ... is excessively good-looking and swell-elegantly tailored. In France they talk at length about the Eden silhouette – particularly the trousers.'[22] In 1938 a group of French tailors even voted him the world's best-dressed man, ahead of the actors Douglas Fairbanks Senior and Gary Cooper.

These were compliments, but it was all too easy to insinuate something untoward about Eden's sartorial elegance, as the anonymous writer Anomaly had warned homosexuals back in 1927 not to be too meticulous about their clothes lest they give the game away. Many of Eden's opponents derided his attention to detail as effeminate vanity. Eden was likened to Count Vronsky from *Anna Karenina* or the Regency dandy Beau Brummel. Mussolini called him the 'best dressed fool in Europe', Rab Butler described him as 'half mad baronet, half beautiful woman'[23] and the elderly Earl of Crawford and Balcarres dismissed him as 'vain as a peacock' with 'all the mannerisms of a *petit maître*'.[24] Few went as far as Sir James Grigg, Eden's permanent under-secretary at the War Office, who described him as a 'poor feeble little pansy',[25] but Ball's allies questioned why Eden habitually called everyone 'my dear', including men. They gossiped that he had propositioned Eddie Gathorne-Hardy at Oxford and that his marriage was on the rocks – and casually noted that all his friends were bachelors.

In this last regard Eden's critics had a point. Apart from Cranborne, virtually all the politicians he relied on at this key moment were queer or nearly queer and, ironically enough, the snide barbs helped create out of Eden's friends an alliance of like-minded spirits, who loathed the dictators and distrusted Neville Chamberlain. They were friends, colleagues and allies who met informally all the time, but they fought shy of constituting themselves as an official group, and they remained necessarily secretive.

The group never had a fixed membership list, but some men were constant friends and allies. Eden's PPS Jim Thomas was a genial, suave and discreet unmarried 34-year-old at the time and remained a close ally of Eden's for the rest of his life. Later that year the *Sketch* carried a fetching photograph of Jim in black tie with Bob Boothby, Ronnie Cartland and Noël Coward at the Curzon premiere of Charles Boyer's louche melodramatic film *Le Bonheur*, which featured Michel Simon as a homosexual artistic director. Having been closely involved in every twist and turn of the preceding months' battles with Chamberlain, Jim resigned with Eden and sat at his feet during his resignation speech in the Commons. Likewise Harry Crookshank helped Eden with his resignation speech and considered resigning with him, and Ronnie Tree went at it hammer and tongs with Nancy Astor when she accused Eden of being 'vain and obstinate' at a party at Ditchley Park.[26] Harold Nicolson also argued Eden's case in the private meeting of National Labour MPs, which Malcolm MacDonald addressed on the Monday afternoon prior to the House sitting, and when Eden and Cranborne took their seats on the upper back benches in the Commons, 'both looking pale and self-conscious', Harold yelled and yelled and waved his order-paper.[27] After the two personal statements, Harold made one of his best speeches, arguing that Italy's negotiating technique was

> that of the corkscrew. The tip of the corkscrew is placed gently, charmingly, sweetly upon the top of the cork. Nothing happens. The bottle is placed in the right position. That manoeuvre is called 'good relations'; it is called 'ending a vendetta'. Suddenly, the corkscrew is given a twist and the cork begins to squeak.

The corkscrew would go in and in and in, which was why it was so foolish to enter negotiations with Italy without concrete guarantees.[28] Afterwards Harold had dinner at the Reform Club with Jack Macnamara before joining Rob Bernays in popping round to the house of another Liberal National MP, Bill Mabane, who was also then single. As Nicolson wrote in his diary, 'They are both glum. Rob feels he ought to have resigned. Mabane feels he ought to have spoken.'[29] At the end of the day Eden and his private secretary Oliver Harvey went to dinner at Philip Sassoon's Park Lane mansion. There the three of them discussed how Eden should play the next few days.

The debate continued the following day, by which time the Opposition had tabled a motion deploring the circumstances in which Eden had been obliged to resign and declaring no confidence in 'Her Majesty's present advisers in their conduct of foreign affairs'.[30] In the ordinary course of things such a motion would have rallied all Conservatives, Unionists and National Government MPs, but during the debate Ronnie Cartland, Jack Macnamara and Ronnie Tree met with Harold Macmillan, Vyvyan Adams and Edward Spears to agree their strategy. Should they vote for the motion or against – or abstain? Ronnie Cartland, who had organised a successful rally for Eden in Birmingham Town Hall two weeks earlier, was Eden's staunchest defender in the debate. When Sir Alan Anderson parroted the Ball line that Eden had resigned 'on account of ill health', Ronnie intervened to correct him, only to be further infuriated when Anderson repeated time and again that the foreign secretary was 'overworked and his judgement was not quite normal' and that his 'mental balance … was wrong'.[31]

Later in the debate Ronnie derided the Chancellor for insinuating in *The Times* that Eden had 'felt the strain of recent events and was far from well'.[32] Quite the contrary, he argued. Eden had taken the decision to resign 'in the full possession of his powers and faculties, and … he had never been better in health since he went to the Foreign Office'.[33] Ball must have smiled at this. The very fact that Ronnie and others were defending Eden's sanity showed that his shafts had hit home. But Ronnie went much further. He attacked Chamberlain's dubious diplomatic methods and argued that in questions of foreign policy 'right should always come before expediency, whether it be dangerous, difficult or foolhardy'.[34] He ended by claiming that Chamberlain was 'employing methods, which are not in keeping with our traditions and which, even if they are successful, must spoil our good name'.[35] This was about as close to challenging his party leader's integrity as an MP could get, and at the end of the debate he joined Nicolson, Macnamara, Thomas, Tree, Macmillan, Bracken, Churchill, Eden, Cranborne, Emrys-Evans, Adams and Spears in abstaining, along with about seven other Conservatives. This was brave. In effect they were declaring themselves indifferent as to whether their own party were thrown out of office. The whips must have been roaming the lobbies, the tea room and the dining rooms, determined to crack down on dissent. Ronnie Cartland was the most exposed, as he was the only Birmingham MP not to support the prime minister, who considered the city as his family fiefdom. Even Ronnie's relative by marriage, Malcolm McCorquodale, snidely suggested in the debate that Eden should 'take a rest and be restored to health and strength'.[36]

Ronnie soon felt the wrath of the party hierarchy. He was pointedly excluded from any involvement in a neighbouring by-election and faced vigorous heckling when he addressed his next constituency meeting. He stuck to his guns, though. Chamberlain had adopted a policy of 'peace at any price', which would put half the world in slavery. Ronnie could now envisage Britain in the years to come as isolated, alone, and faced with a colossal Germany asking: 'Now what are you going to do about it?' Great Britain would then turn anxious eyes towards the nations who would help, only to find that Germany had 'gobbled them up'.[37] It was not until the end of March that Ronnie felt that 'the whips have come out of the refrigerator', as far as he was concerned.[38] Eden rightly acknowledged Ronnie's 'great courage' in a note that pointed out that 'nothing is more difficult than to disagree with one's political associates at a critical time'.[39]

One other person Eden hoped to count on was Rob Bernays. Eden had spoken for Rob at a rally in Bristol in the 1935 election, Rob had returned the favour with a lengthy puff piece in *Good Housekeeping* calling him 'the brightest new jewel in the Conservative crown',[40] and Eden had invited Rob for a quiet chat back in 1936 as he 'was getting together two or three of us as a team to support him in the country'.[41] Rob was by now convinced that the only way to deal with Germany and Italy was to 'make ourselves so strong' that they 'just would not take the risk', so he should have been a ready ally, but he felt torn. His party, some of whom had objected when he was appointed as a minister, intended to vote with the government en bloc. Many of his close friends, though, were going to abstain. He had a lot to lose. Unlike many others he had no other source of income. If he followed his friends he would have to resign as a minister – and there was no sign that any of the other junior ministers were minded to do so. What was he to do? 'Resign alone,' he asked himself, 'take my political life into my hands and bring upon myself the whole crushing weight of the government machine?' He was mulling things over on the morning of the vote when he bumped into Harry Crookshank, who revealed that he felt equally unhappy. After a long chat and with many misgivings they decided, according to Harry, that it was 'quixotic of 2 of us who were not in things to go out when ministers in the Cabinet who might hold our view did not. So we left it.'[42] But then came Chamberlain's speech, which so infuriated Harry that he searched Rob out, determined to resign. By this stage Rob was in a bit of a panic, as rumours of his supposedly imminent resignation had found their way into the *Evening Standard*. He wrote to his sister that his conscience had been 'lulled to rest' when he heard Chamberlain speak, but he told Harry that he had not been in the Chamber for the speech. Would Harry mind if they waited to see the text in *Hansard* the next morning? Harry did not press him and they both voted with the government that night (as did Sassoon).

When they met up again the next morning, though, they were still incensed that Chamberlain was 'throwing over the League altogether'[43] (a phrase they both used), and decided to send the PM a stiff letter demanding an assurance that Britain was still supporting collective security under the League. Chamberlain played them beautifully. The next day they received cordial letters from Downing Street asking them to see him that afternoon at 4.20. Of course, he reassured them, there had been no change of policy. They were happy to be pacified and Harry noted, 'With this we have prima facie to accept his statement but I still remain worried about it all, but obviously we can't move at the moment. It may be we have shown him the red light and done a public service if we make him more careful.'[44] They were probably right. Chamberlain was unassailable at this stage, but if the two men had resigned the prime minister might have proceeded more cautiously. As things were, they were reduced to sitting throughout the debates looking, as Oliver Harvey noted, 'most uncomfortable and sheepish'.[45]

Rob's mind may well have been swayed by his financial position. His son told me that Rob's side of the family was always 'very conscious of money' and that he had hated the hand-to-mouth experience of writing daily copy in India without a contract.[46] As an under-secretary, though, he was paid £1,500 in addition to the £600 he received as an MP, the equivalent in 2018 prices to an additional £100,000 a year. It afforded him a comfortable life. In 1940 it enabled him to move to a new flat at Allington Court, just behind Buckingham Palace, which had three bedrooms, two bathrooms and two reception rooms. When he held cocktail parties, he employed a barman/butler and a Mrs Green helped with coats. According to the chauffeur/valet who came to work for him in 1939, he was 'not only very fussy as to his own appearance (pressed trousers and shining shoes)' but he insisted on his staff wearing a smart uniform with gleaming buttons at all times. He could be quite strict as an employer, too. Rob might finish the day inviting his valet to a fireside chat to discuss the events of the world over a glass of whisky, but he never wanted to see his valet in 'civvies'. And when the two men stopped off at Rob's brother's house near Petworth, he objected in the strongest of terms when his sister-in-law Sylvia invited his chauffeur to take tea with them, even though they had known each other as children.[47] Rob had done well for himself and he was reluctant to throw that away unnecessarily.

One other thing may have weighed in both men's minds. Chamberlain made sure, through Ball in the Conservative Research Department and David Margesson and James Stuart in the whips' office, that the rebels faced open hostility in the Chamber and the tea room and tough questioning in their constituencies. Cranborne, whose resignation speech was more incendiary than Eden's, was fearful of how his association would see things in South Dorset. 'All my prominent supporters are furious,' he wrote to Eden, adding 'my executive have asked to see me, and I get the general impression that, at one or all of a number of meetings that I have next week, I am likely to be stoned.'[48] Considering he was the eldest son of the Marquess of Salisbury and grandson of a three-time Conservative prime minister, he might have expected a degree of old-fashioned deference, but Chamberlain's dirty tricks team was not interested in such niceties. Cranborne decided to face the cannon fire head on. Addressing his association at Weymouth a week later, he defiantly argued that he was not there to apologise or excuse his actions, as he had never been more certain that he was right. It worked. The association backed him this time. Meanwhile Jim Thomas received such rough treatment in Hereford that Cranborne wrote to sympathise with him: 'I am fed up with the Tory machine, which becomes both more short-sighted and wrongheaded.'[49]

In Harold Nicolson's case the pressure was exerted in quite a different direction. Soon after arriving in Parliament his reputation as a former diplomat had helped him secure the important role of vice chairman of the Commons Foreign Affairs Committee, but Jack Macnamara had warned him that there was a move against the National Labour MPs in the Conservative ranks, and after Harold's performance in the Eden debate, the whips conspired to remove him and the chairman, Paul Emrys-Evans. Harold survived a first attempt, when just 'one little vicious hand' – that of Nancy Astor – was raised against him, but the pressure grew so strong that when he and Emrys-Evans were asked whether they were 'pro-Chamberlain or pro-Eden', they felt they had no option but to resign. On their way to the committee in Committee Room 14, another MP, Jock McEwen, angrily told Emrys-Evans that he was about to be ousted, to which Emrys-Evans responded that this would not be necessary as the two men had already tendered their resignations. When Churchill made an impassioned plea on their behalf, though, Harold and Emrys-Evans said they would stay if they could issue a press release saying they had been asked to remain in post. This prompted another bout of anger from loyalist Conservatives, which led Churchill to whisper to Emrys-Evans that they might have to resign after all. A couple of weeks later McEwen, who had initially denounced appeasement, replaced Emrys-Evans as chairman of the committee and joined the government payroll as a junior whip.

Jack Macnamara's local executive also gave him a hard time over his abstention. Jack was fortunate, though. His association president, the wealthy owner of Danbury Palace, John Wigan, had served valiantly in the First World War, was seriously wounded four times, awarded the DSO and made Brigadier-General. Most significantly, after retiring from the army, Wigan had served as MP for Abingdon for three years. He knew what it was to be under attack from opinionated party members who did not bear the responsibility of facing the wider public. So when a motion was discussed at the Divisional Executive on 3 March, Wigan argued that Jack had been unwise to abstain but refused to make the discussion public.

The Ball/Margesson campaign worked. The resignations were limited to Eden, Cranborne and their parliamentary private secretaries, Jim Thomas and Mark Patrick. Even Ronnie Tree remained in post as PPS to Robert Hudson. Those with fewer qualms about Hitler and Mussolini were promoted. Chips Channon got Mark Patrick's post as PPS at the Foreign Office and Alan Lennox-Boyd (who had told the Commons that it was the height of folly 'to deny that the king of Italy is now Emperor of Abyssinia')[50] was controversially made parliamentary secretary to the Ministry of Labour. Others were flattered into loyalty or visibly cowed. As Oliver Harvey put it, the 'Conservatives in H. of C. were hysterically behind the P.M. ... as the man who had preserved peace in face of the dictators'.[51] By the second week of March many were claiming that the whole affair had been a storm in a teacup and the *Bystander* announced that 'the country seems, on the surface, at any rate, to have settled down in characteristic English fashion "to give Mr. Chamberlain a chance"'.[52]

Chamberlain had won, but he had also sown the seeds of his own destruction. In pushing Eden out and waging a dirty tricks campaign against him, Chamberlain and Ball had forced those who supported Eden to coalesce as an informal group of allies. They would be loyal to Eden even when he disappointed them and the fact that most of Eden's closest supporters were queer meant that they would be loyal to one another, too, because they knew precisely what Ball and the Chamberlain machine were up to with their none-too-subtle slurs against Eden for being too well presented and glamorous.

14

The Insurgents

On the day that Eden resigned, Hitler made a much-heralded speech to the Reichstag. For the first time he publicly pronounced that Germany was no longer willing to tolerate the suppression of 10 million Germans *outside its borders*. It should have set every alarm bell in Downing Street ringing. After all, the whole aim of Chamberlain's behind-stairs diplomacy had been to tame Hitler's territorial ambitions, but Hitler was casting an envious eye over Austria, Czechoslovakia and Poland. Nor was the Führer merely speculating. On the morning of 12 March 1938 the *Wehrmacht* – the combined forces of Germany's army, navy and air force – crossed the Austrian border and that evening Hitler was given a hero's welcome in Linz. By the end of the month Austria was incorporated into the Reich, Austrian Jews were being driven out, Jewish shops were being plundered and thousands of Austrian gypsies were being despatched to Dachau. The *Anschluss* was complete.

The reaction in Britain was embarrassingly muted. Chips Channon was typically flippant, recording in his dairy, 'An unbelievable day, in which two things occurred. Hitler took Vienna and I fell in love with the Prime Minister.'[1] Yet Victor Cazalet called it 'a real Black Letter day. The invasion of Austria – the country we all love, by those bloody Nazis.' Like many others he admitted that he felt 'overwhelmed by news. Furious, raging, impotent.'[2] Three days later Chamberlain told the Commons that Eden's replacement as foreign secretary, Lord Halifax, had given his German counterpart 'a grave warning', that the British ambassador had 'registered a protest in strong terms' and that he personally had made 'earnest representations' to the German foreign minister, but admitted that 'the hard fact is that nothing could have arrested this action by Germany'.[3] He implied that he was terribly saddened by the turn of events – but it felt as if he was making little more than a token fuss.

In fact, he had expressly detailed Sir Joseph Ball to undermine any criticism of Hitler. The pages of *Truth* betray Chamberlain's real views. In February it attacked the rest of the press for issuing dire forebodings about Austria and doing its best to sensationalise Hitler's demands 'as if determined that its readers' flesh should creep'.[4] While Hitler was threatening Austria, it was firmly of the view that 'Germany's domestic affairs are her own business'.[5] After the *Anschluss* it pointed out that this could easily have happened ten years earlier and added with an approving flourish that 'Herr Hitler has a flair for the right moment'.[6] It repeatedly found means of praising Hitler. It described him in glowing terms at the Nuremberg rally: 'To-day he looks ten years younger than he did four years ago, when he was a tired, worn and harassed man. Now he is fresh-complexioned, often smiling, the worried expression replaced by one of quiet confidence.'[7] Without any irony, it claimed that 'the outstanding fact in German constitutional history is that, before Hitler, the masses counted for nothing'.[8] In May, it poured scorn on the growing number of stories of atrocities against the Jews in Austria. Anti-Semitism in Germany had, so it claimed, 'weakened of late'.[9] In June it claimed that if anti-Semitism ever assumed an uglier aspect in Britain, it would be 'the Jews' own fault', because although there were just 350,000 Jews in Britain at the time, 'this is difficult to credit when one walks through the West End on a Saturday night'. It resorted to the customary calumny, too. Without offering a shred of evidence it stated that it was 'no exaggeration to say that of every ten swindles that come under the notice of TRUTH, an unduly high proportion are operated by Jews'.[10]

These views were sanctioned by Ball, acting on the express wishes of the prime minister, who had fixed on a course of appeasing Hitler. He had plenty of allies. *Time* had said in February that the ban on the incorporation of Austria was 'one of the least rational, most brittle, and most provocative artificialities of the peace settlement'[11] and now Lord Mount Temple defended Germany on the grounds that 'the dynamic of National Liberation' would not exhaust itself until the question of German unity was resolved – but illogically added that this philosophy posed no danger to the territorial integrity of other neighbouring countries.[12] The Conservative MP for Hull North West, Sir Lambert Ward, who was a lieutenant colonel in the Territorial Army, went further. Having studied at a German university and visited Germany and Austria every year since the war, he reckoned he could claim, 'without boasting, to know as much as anybody in the House about the conditions and what has been going on there'. He doubted reports that thousands were being driven into 'hastily-constructed prisons and concentration camps'. He insisted that people should 'face facts as they are' before forming a judgement and added that if Germany were to invade Czechoslovakia, a third of the Czech army would desert to the German flag. When Labour MPs tried to howl him down, he questioned whether those who demanded that Britain take a strong line had the stomach for war.[13]

This at least was a point with which Jack Macnamara would have agreed. The state of the army's readiness for war had become his constant obsession. He was angry that despite the fact that hundreds of thousands of unemployed men were willing to accept almost any job offered to them, the army could not fill its ranks. But he reckoned he knew why. Soldiers were not held in high enough regard. Bars and dancehalls regularly refused admittance to men in uniform and the army was full of 'pettifogging restrictions and nursery punishments' such as the ludicrous practice of giving men their last meal of the day at 4.30 in the afternoon. 'If officers need an evening meal,' he pointed out, 'so do soldiers, who are also human animals.'

Politicians should take this seriously, because 'at any time in the near future England may find herself alone in a hostile world'.[14] He regularly returned to the unjust treatment of soldiers and complained about the way new recruits were used as skivvies. 'Expecting to be ennobled, he becomes debased. He is a given a bucket and a rag and put on washing the dank passages of an officer's mess.'[15]

He knew what he was talking about, as he devoted many hours to his Territorial regiment, the London Irish Rifles (LIR), which had been founded as the London Irish Volunteers in 1859 and had gained its first battle honours in the Boer War and at Loos in the First World War, when Rifleman Frank Edwards nonchalantly dribbled a football in front of the troops as they crossed no-man's land and scored a 'goal' when he booted it straight into a German dugout. More than a thousand of the regiment's riflemen laid down their lives in the war, but drastic peacetime cuts to the Territorial Army had left it a shadow of its former self. It was based in the grand but dilapidated Duke of York's Headquarters in Chelsea; Prince Arthur, the Duke of Connaught, was its honorary colonel, and many well-heeled Anglo-Irishmen found their way to its drill hall. By the time Jack joined in 1934, numbers and morale were low and the linoleum was in need of repair, but it was still the centre of a select circle of mostly single men who lived between Chelsea and Westminster, played rugby for London Irish, and drank, dined and drilled together. So, brimful of energy, determined to face the Nazi challenge and half in love with the male camaraderie of the regiment, Jack privately set himself the task of revitalising the London Irish and, as the official history of the regiment put it, 'his enthusiasm and cheery comradeship with all ranks helped to put a new zest and energy into the battalion'.[16] It helped that nobody in the regiment seemed to care that Jack was openly attracted to men. As Captain Nigel Wilkinson who joined the LIR after the war told me, 'Several of the senior officers were gay and it never seemed to bother anyone, not least because they were often the bravest of the lot.'[17] Another of Jack's fellow officers was

Lieutenant (later Acting Lieutenant Colonel) Charles Wegg-Prosser, who joined the LIR straight out of Oxford – after a brief flirtation with the British Union of Fascists – expressly so as to fight fascism. According to his daughter, Anne Gibbins, Charles's political conversion had already begun when he met a beautiful girlfriend of Jewish Ukrainian descent, Betty Shapiro, when he was speaking at a pro-Republican demo at Hyde Park Corner, but the couple were avowedly anti-fascist and had many gay friends, including the broadcaster Gilbert Harding and James MacColl, who was later a queer Labour MP, who persuaded Charles to join the Labour Party. Clearly Jack had little to fear at the gay-friendly LIR.

Nor did Jack worry that his sexuality might get in the way of his promotion, as he endlessly came up with new ideas. His first suggestion for smartening things up by putting the riflemen in kilts did not impress his commanding officer, the Ulsterman Colonel Edward Gribben, but when Jack proposed replacing the regiment's standard service dress cap with a distinctively Irish piper-green beret or 'caubeen' and a matching feather plume or 'hackle', his idea was taken up so enthusiastically that Jack was allowed to be the first member of the regiment to wear it at the Speaker's well-attended annual reception in the Commons on 19 February 1937. He was still just a captain, but he insisted it be worn sloping jauntily to the left rather than to the right, as was common among the other Irish regiments. He took the lead when it came to old-style recruiting, too. At the end of 1937 he got kilted pipers to lead the regiment on a march through Sloane Square and Pimlico. The regiment's Old Comrades accompanied a series of armoured vehicles with riflemen carrying machine guns and wearing gas masks and steel helmets. At the rear was a lorry covered in Union flags, from which Jack delivered stirring calls for men to enlist when they stopped in each of the squares in Chelsea. A few men joined up, impressed by the razzmatazz – or by Jack's reminder that: 'Aggressors sound no warning bells ... time is no longer necessarily on our side.'[18] But still the regiment was short of more than 150 men, so, having been promoted to major in January 1938, Jack was back on the stump in March. A few more trickled in, but the problem was far larger than one regiment could tackle, so that spring Jack took up the cudgels in Leo Amery's Council of the Army and Home and Empire Defence League, which sought to help lacklustre recruiting offices do a better job. This drew the ire of Liberal Chief Whip Sir Percy Harris, who called on the government to disown the league, as otherwise anyone could band together to promote recruitment in His Majesty's Forces,[19] but Jack was determined to inject a degree of urgency. As he pointed out in the league's monthly magazine *Rising Strength*, the flower of the British Army was still in India. If war came, the front line would be the Territorial Army, because enemy bombers would be overhead even before war was declared. Yet the Territorials were 45,000 men short and had completely out-of-date 'old lumbering monsters' for tanks. His answer was simple: 'There is no reason why every fit young man should not be a Territorial.'[20] His logic was impeccable. Britain was going through a very dangerous time. 'If we decide on isolation we shall have to stand on our own legs alone. If we decide on commitments, limited or general, we may be called on to carry them out.'[21]

Jack's friends felt the same. Bob Boothby leapt to print, demanding 'a national effort, on a far greater scale than anything hitherto contemplated, to provide ourselves with adequate air forces'.[22] He attacked what he described as the worst of all possible worlds, when Britain had 'a maximum commitment to the defence of other countries and the minimum of actual security'.[23] Ronnie Tree agreed. The *Anschluss* had persuaded him that conversations with the German government would not only be useless, but dangerous. The government should be reformed immediately, bringing in Churchill, Eden and the trades unions. What was more, every citizen, male and female, should be registered, with a warning that it might be necessary for them to undergo military training at some point, for the simple, ominous reason that 'every day of drift adds greatly to our danger'.[24]

Harold Nicolson proclaimed himself thoroughly depressed. 'How can I continue to support a government like this?' he asked. His mood deepened as the year wore on and he took to unburdening himself on his new neighbour, Victor Cazalet, who had bought Swifts Place, which lay less than a mile from Sissinghurst, back in 1936. Not content with its eighteen bedrooms, Victor had commissioned Tray Mortimer's boyfriend Paul Hyslop to tear the whole thing down and replace it with a neo-Gothic mansion with seven bedrooms, each with an en suite bathroom. Hyslop had scoured architectural salvage for antique wood panelling, a rococo chimneypiece and an eighteenth-century staircase, so by the middle of 1937 Victor had taken up residence and his friend, the writer and committed Zionist Baffy Dugdale, was rejoicing in its central heating and profusion of orchids. Often, Harold and Victor would travel up Westminster together and in May they paced around Rodin's gaunt statue of the Burghers of Calais in Embankment Gardens after lunch with his former diplomat colleague Gladwyn Jebb. What could they possibly do to avoid war? Jebb's only solution was to 'cut off any controversy at almost any price until our air-defences are in order'[25] but that felt like capitulation. Things didn't seem any better when Victor and Harold sat out in the gardens at Sissinghurst. Nicolson feared that Hitler would force the leader of the Sudeten Germans in Czechoslovakia, Konrad Henlein, to make ever-greater demands of the Czech government, which they could not possibly accept. In the end Hitler would intervene, that would bring in France, and Britain would be faced with the alternative of abandoning France or having a disastrous war.[26] As if to add to the sense of despair, Victor had spoken to the famous young American airman Charles Lindbergh, who had leased Long Barn from Harold for the summer. Lindbergh had told him that the German and Italian air forces were infinitely better than Britain's, and that 'we have not a chance in a thousand'. Victor came to the depressing conclusion, 'He is rather Nazi.'[27]

The opponents of appeasement started to organise themselves. Eden's resignation had been the catalyst for the first rebellion against the government's handling of foreign affairs, but Eden was reluctant to form an official grouping. On 22 March, though, Chips Channon wrote that 'the H. of C. is humming with intrigue' and claimed that 'the so-called "Insurgents" are rushing about, very over-excited'.[28] The next day Ronnie Cartland wrote to Jim Thomas that the Commons had been in almost continuous uproar since Jim left for France and that 'there's a lot of talk (tho' it's not more than talk yet) of a group, Winston etc., having a campaign in the country'.[29] Chips named seventeen 'insurgents'. In addition to the former Cabinet members Churchill and Amery, he listed Tree, Cazalet, Macnamara, Nicolson, Boothby and Cartland; the Churchill allies Brendan Bracken and Duncan Sandys; plus Godfrey Nicholson, Derrick Gunston, Paul Emrys-Evans, Edward Spears, Vyvyan Adams, Leonard Ropner and the Duchess of Atholl.[30] The Chips list was far from definitive. It left out Eden, Cranborne, Jim Thomas, Mark Patrick, Harold Macmillan, Malcolm Bullock, Ronnie Tree's cousin Anthony Crossley, Hubert Duggan, Hamilton Kerr, Dudley Joel and Richard Law among the Conservative backbenchers and the National Liberal MPs Herbert Butcher and James Henderson-Stewart, MP for East Fife (who joked up until his marriage at the age of forty-two in 1940 that the reason he was still a bachelor was that he was blessed with a superb mother 'in comparison with whom it seems impossible to find a modern young woman fit to be a wife').[31] Chips also failed to recognise that several government ministers agreed with the insurgents. Bernays, for instance, was far from convinced by the speech Chamberlain made on 24 March, which he thought was like 'our old drawing room clock emitting the strokes of doom'.[32] He was somewhat mollified by a tougher speech a week later, but reassured himself that Harry Crookshank and he had stiffened the PM's resolve.[33] With Duff Cooper and Philip Sassoon equally unimpressed by Chamberlain's strategy, the 'insurgents' totalled about two dozen. However one composes the list, at least a third of them were queer or nearly queer.

There was another factor in play. Each of these men knew personally what the Nazi regime was up to. This was brought home especially forcibly to Victor Cazalet in the spring of 1938. Gottfried von Cramm had told Cazalet in 1936 that 'the only thing which might save me is my sport. The better I play the more they will be afraid to catch me.'[34] He was right. The deciding match in the 1937 Davis Cup inter-zonal stage between Germany and America – between Cramm and Don Budge – had been particularly tense. Gottfried had just defeated Fred Perry in the French Singles and *Time* had plastered him over its front cover. People spoke of an existential battle between democratic America and dictatorial Germany. As Gottfried walked on court, Hitler rang to demand victory, even though many expected Budge to walk off with the honours, as he had defeated Gottfried in straight sets on the same court just a few weeks earlier. The match was described by the German coach 'Big Bill' Tilden (who was queer and American) as the greatest he had ever seen, as Gottfried came out fighting and took the first two sets with ease, and when they came to the fifth set he was 4–1 up. Budge rallied, taking it to 7–6, but even then, as evening fell, Gottfried fought off five match points before Budge took the match. Hitler was said to be incandescent, but Gottfried told Budge that this was the finest match he had ever played and that he was very happy to have played it against a man whom he liked so much. Gottfried and his fellow player Henner Henkel then toured the US, Japan and Australia for several months before returning to Germany on 4 March 1938.

Unbeknownst to Gottfried, Hitler had been further infuriated. Maybe it was the endless praise lavished on Gottfried by the international press that wound the Führer up. He had 'the best manners on the tennis court of any player', he was 'one of the best-looking boys I have ever met',[35] Germans apparently 'loved this unassuming champion',[36] he was 'sleek, slight and beautifully built' and his 'fine, aristocratic features, clear skin, and easy confidence of bearing' made him a true 'cosmopolitan'.[37] In Hitler's mind, he should be the poster boy for the New

Germany, but Gottfried consistently rejected Nazism. One of his oft-repeated pointed comments was that his full name was Gottfried *Freiherr* von Cramm because as a 'freeman' he owed no allegiance to any king.[38] In January he went to see the top-grossing film of the year, *The Road Back*, and had to ask photographers to destroy pictures of him entering the cinema because the film, which was directed by James Whale with a screenplay by Charles Kenton and R. C. Sheriff, warned about the rise of Nazism and was banned in Germany.

Gottfried suspected nothing when he arrived at his mother's castle near Hanover on 4 March, but the Gestapo had discovered that Gottfried's wife was the great-granddaughter of a Jewish banker and that he had had affairs with the Englishman Geoffrey Nares and with Manasseh Herbst. The next day two Gestapo agents turned up to arrest him for 'sex perversion' under the revised and more draconian version of Paragraph 175. For days there was confusion about what had happened to him. The German Tennis Board initially claimed that he was 'in a hospital, where he is suffering from neurosis of the heart'[39] but when his family contacted his cousin Prince Bernhardt, husband of Princess Juliana of the Netherlands, the authorities admitted that he had been arrested and was awaiting trial. This was kept secret in Germany, but as soon as the news hit the international press Gottfried's many friends started lobbying Hitler for his release.

The subsequent trial was a farce. The carefully selected judge had not acquitted anyone for more than four years, the press were excluded and proceedings were almost entirely conducted in secret. The few snippets that reached the foreign press suggested that Gottfried had been forced to allege that his affair with Herbst had only started because his wife had slept with a French athlete soon after their marriage – and that he had only sent Herbst £2,000 in Palestine as a form of blackmail because he was 'a sneaky Jew'. These accounts seem unreliable considering Gottfried's punctilious honesty, but the outcome was never in doubt. On 14 May the judge declared that he had 'damaged the reputation of German sport'[40] and sentenced him to a year's imprisonment. The story was covered in every national newspaper outside Germany. Victor must have been painfully conscious that his friend had written in 1936, 'I do not fear anything as I have your promise to pay me a visit in any concentration camp.'[41] In the back of his mind he must also have worried that the 'bribe' received by Herbst was the money Victor had sent to help him escape to Portugal and Palestine.

So many of the 'insurgents' had first-hand knowledge of atrocities in Germany that it was perhaps inevitable that they became the most vocal oponents of appeasement, but when Chamberlain and Ball humiliated Eden and attempted to isolate opponents, the insurgents began to coalesce. They were already friends, but at first they were so nervous that, as Nicolson put it, 'we decided that we should not advertise ourselves as a group or even call ourselves a group'.[42] Yet they appointed Mark Patrick, Cranborne's former PPS as the unofficial secretary of the non-group and began to meet regularly but informally. When the House was sitting they met roughly once a week either at Jim Thomas's house at 17 Great College Street behind Westminster Abbey, or at Ronnie Tree's mansion overlooking St James's Park at 28 Queen Anne's Gate, or at Brendan Bracken's home at 8 North Street[43] – all three of which were within walking distance of the Commons in time for a vote, as long as the division bell in Ronnie's house was working. On other nights, or when there were not going to be any divisions, they would gather in Mark Patrick's drawing room at 15 South Street behind the Dorchester, which until 1920 had been the home of the last great Victorian courtesan, Catherine Walters.

Eden later claimed that he used to preside over these meetings, but the composition of the group remained very fluid, no minutes were kept and considering who attended, it is highly likely that the discussions wandered. Ronnie Cartland was always the most earnest and determined. He cared not a fig for what the whips thought and was happy to say so. He wanted real action in the depressed areas and a clear defence of democracy over dictatorship. Jack Macnamara agreed about the depressed areas and the whips, but like Leo Amery was more focused on rebuilding the armed forces – and would often turn up in uniform. Ronnie Tree was equally certain about the need to rearm, but tended to defer to others. Brendan Bracken, tall and flame-haired, chain-smoked and made rapid interjections laced with reference to his great friend Winston or his own, largely invented past. When Winston was there, they quarrelled like a happily married couple. Paul Emrys-Evans was as eager to talk as anyone, but often preferred 'masterly disdainful silence' to get his point across.[44] Harold Nicolson played the elder statesman, casually dropping the names of international leaders he had dealt with over the years and frequently making the most astute points. Harold Macmillan came up with the most radical, almost socialist policies – but was the most socially inept. Duff Cooper would turn up looking as elegant and raffish as Eden. Edward Spears, older than most, insisted on the need to bring France into the equation. Ever the congenial host, Jim Thomas puffed on his pipe and cracked jokes when things got too serious, but he and 'Bobetty' Cranborne repeatedly urged Eden to be more outspoken. Mark Patrick would bring the group back to practicalities – how were they going to vote in the next division, how were they going to win over more allies and should they allow Bob Boothby (who several thought was unreliable) to join them?

An opportunity to flex their muscles came on 23 June when the Commons debated the motion 'that this House do now adjourn', which Labour had tabled in the middle of the debate on the Finance Bill so as to embarrass the government about the bombing of two British ships off Valencia by planes flying out of Franco's Nationalist bases in the Balearics. The motion seemed innocuous, but Chamberlain gave an angry and highly personal defence of his policy of non-intervention, prompting at least ten Conservative MPs, including insurgents Cartland, Nicolson, Boothby, Henderson-Stewart, Churchill and Sandys, to make a point of staying in their seats while the government whips drilled MPs through the Noe Lobby. The vote was merely symbolic – only a handful voted Aye – but it was a dress rehearsal for debates still to come.

By now Ronnie Cartland was very clear who the enemy was. Sitting in the Commons library one evening in April, he had a long conversation with the Etonian Labour MP Hugh Dalton, who was apparently monogamous but had briefly fallen in love with Rupert Brooke at Cambridge and enjoyed adopting bisexual young men like Hugh Gaitskell and Tony Crosland as his protégés. In a foretaste of a speech Ronnie would make a year later, he held forth about the state of the Conservative Party. It 'now had a Führer … The P.M. was getting more and more dictatorial. It was astonishing how the bulk of the Party followed him blindly.'[45] When Dalton asked who influenced Chamberlain, Ronnie replied that none of his colleagues in the Cabinet did, much. 'But,' he added, 'there was a queer figure, Sir Joseph Ball, now in the Conservative Head Office, who had been in M.I.5 during the war, in whom the P.M. had great confidence.'[46] It is impossible to know what Ronnie meant, or Hugh understood, by 'queer', but one can imagine the ambiguity hanging in the air.

Much of life continued as normal in 1938, though. Philip Sassoon hosted a couple of art exhibitions at his Park Lane mansion and was commended as 'the most hospitable man in London'.[47] The 'season' of royal courts, presentation parties and garden parties proceeded as usual, with hopeful mothers taking large houses in London or setting up headquarters in West End hotels in preparation for their daughters' coming out, when they would queue down the Mall in their gold and silver lamé dresses to be presented at the court of the new King George V. Hoardings asked 'Have you Macleaned your teeth today?' and advertised suits from the 'fifty-shilling tailors'. Magazine adverts urged those who couldn't sleep, 'Drink delicious Ovaltine and note the difference!' Oxford won the boat race and Flares won the Gold Cup at Royal Ascot. Rob Bernays went to see Noël Coward's new show, *Operette*, with the Sieff family, who along with Simon Marks built Marks & Spencer into a thriving national business. It was not Coward's best, but it included

'The Stately Homes of England' – a potent end-of-era symbol. Ronnie Cartland became a regular presenter of the BBC Home Service radio show, which was produced by Guy Burgess, *Week in Westminster*; he went on his annual holiday on the Continent with Barbara – this time in Switzerland – and Barbara produced two more novels, *Broken Barriers* and *The Bitter Winds of Love*. Benjamin Britten premiered his piano concerto at the Proms – and he and his lover Peter Pears had a long after-dinner political debate with Rob Bernays. Victor held a housewarming at Great Swifts, with a firework display watched by scouts and two local choirs camping in the grounds, when 'the woods were filled with echoing booms and crackles as rockets screeched heavenwards and spattered the night sky with multi-coloured stars'.[48] Ronnie and Nancy Tree also held a grand house-warming party at their finally refurbished Ditchley Park, at which the designer Oliver Messel decorated a white muslin marquee with busts of Africans sporting feathered headdresses and ropes of pearls, the orchestra played in a rose-covered birdcage, all the ladies dressed in red or white, and Ronnie reported that the smell of the lilies in the drawing-room 'was almost overpowering'. The only embarrassment was when Messel turned up in the *ladies'* dress code, in a white suit and a red tie. One outraged guest was heard to mutter, 'Fellow ought to be thrown into the lake.'[49]

Harold Nicolson's life was not much changed, either. Vita still allowed him considerable sexual freedom and he spent much of his time with former lovers like the young writer James Pope-Hennessy and Victor Cunard, who was back after a ten-year spell as the *The Times* correspondent in Venice. In the summer Harold visited Willie Maugham and Gerald Haxton in the south of France without Vita and enjoyed sailing with Gerald and two friends, Lulu and Jojo. Harold wrote that the latter 'is brown and big and rather plain', while Lulu was 'pure nancy boy, at present basking in the attentions of the chief pilot of Nice'. Despite being a former miner from Lens, near Lille, Harold thought him 'beautifully dressed and very soigné'.[50] He saw the Duke and Duchess of Windsor a couple of times and spent the rest of his holiday camping with his two sons in the Outer Hebrides. He dined with Chips Channon and Paul Latham in the Commons or at Boulestin with Ronnie Cartland and Will Mabane, but his most frequent companion was Rob Bernays. They went to Sibyl Colefax's party together after a Commons vote and heard Cole Porter playing 'his little tunes', they dined together at Pratt's, Rob had him and Jack Macnamara round for lunch at Albany Chambers, and Rob and Harold motored up to Finchley to meet Rob's newly remarried father for dinner.

A further change had come over Victor Cazalet, however. Now Czechoslovakia and Poland were in Hitler's sights, Victor was a firm opponent of appeasement. He knew Central Europe well and worried that Poland was vulnerable. Although not Jewish himself, his close friendships with Baffy Dugdale and Chaim Weizmann had led him to take the Jews' plight to his heart. In July 1937 he helped set up a cross-party group in the Commons to look at the problem of anti-Semitism in Eastern Europe with Jack Macnamara, the Duchess of Atholl and the Labour MPs D. N. Pritt and Tom Williams. He was convinced that Britain had to help create a Jewish homeland – and after a visit to Palestine in January 1938 he wrote, 'I am 100% Zionist now, but understand the Arabs' point of view perfectly; partition seems the only way out.'[51] All this took on a new urgency for him as 1938 wore on. When he visited Vienna in April he met countless Jews who were so desperate that they pleaded with him to take them as 'a gardener, valet, anything', to get them out of Austria. New stories of hideous atrocities against the Jews spewed out of Central Europe on a daily basis and in May he wrote to *The Times:* 'It is inconceivable that the world can look on much longer and see what amounts to the extermination of the European Jews without finding among the empty spaces of the earth some asylum for them.'[52] It was the first time the word 'extermination' had been used in this context.

Yet few in Britain seemed interested and the government was reluctant to accept more than a handful of refugees, so on the last day before Parliament broke for the summer, Victor made his most moving speech. He started in apocalyptic terms. 'Never since Milton immortalised the slaughter of the Albigenses has a whole community been in such danger,' he told a stunned House of Commons. He talked about the atrocities and the wholesale indiscriminate arrests of Jews in Vienna. He did not want to accuse anyone in Britain of complacency, as he felt that most people simply could not envisage the situation in Germany. 'We can all understand one act of cruelty,' he said, 'but what we cannot conceive is a definite official policy that is driving thousands of people to choose suicide as the only release from their problems.'[53] That led him to the refugees. He spoke prophetically of up to 5 million Jews and 'non-Aryans' who were being hounded out of their own country and having every penny stolen from them. They would need a new, permanent home. Of course Britain should do all it could to help – after all, Britain had always been 'an asylum for the persecuted'. He ended with a challenge to the government, who, he predicted, would do everything it could to prevent Europe from suffering from the horrors of war. 'Is it too much to hope,' he asked, 'that they will be equally successful in mitigating what may be justly termed one of the horrors of peace – the persecution of the Jews in Central Europe?'[54] It was a theme he returned to in September when he questioned why Jewish refugees from Germany were being interned. Would it not make more sense to use their services either in the armed forces or in other war-effort work? 'After all,' he wrote, 'that would give them the opportunity to join everyone else in hastening the arrival of that day when they will be able freely and peacefully to return to the land of their birth.'[55]

This was brave talk. Anti-Semitism continued to flourish in Britain, as Philip Sassoon knew only too well. In September 1937 his home at Trent Park had been daubed with vast letters spelling out one of the anti-Semitic war cries, 'Perish Judah'.[56] Guards were put on the house, but anti-Semitism was so run of the mill that no national newspaper published the story. In July 1938 large swastikas were daubed in red paint and tar over the walls of the Finchley District Synagogue. The local rector, Rob

Bernays's father Stewart, presumed 'this was done by the same fools who write the name of Mosley on walls and pavements'.[57] Likewise the Stoke Newington Synagogue could not be used for the Passover in April 1939 when a pig's head dripping with blood was found nailed to the front door, and a month later a pig's head was thrown over the gate at the Stepney Synagogue.[58]

Anti-Semitism was also on the rise on the Conservative benches, as the activities of Captain Archibald Ramsay proved. Ramsay had been the MP for Peebles and South Midlothian since 1931 and was almost a caricature of a Conservative MP. He had all the accoutrements – an Eton and Sandhurst education, a Scottish castle, a private income and an aristocratic wife. He also had a pronounced loathing of communism and a vivid imagination. He had become convinced by 1938 that the Russian Revolution, the Republican Government in Spain and all the subversive societies in Britain 'were part and parcel of the same Plan, secretly operated and controlled by World Jewry'.[59] He was obsessed with this conspiracy theory. Atheism, agnosticism, communism and Judaism were all wrapped up in a single 'Plan' in Ramsay's twisted logic, so when a group of humanists who described themselves as 'free thinkers' announced that they were considering holding an international conference in London in April 1938, he was incensed. This was clearly part of the 'Plan', so he demanded in the Commons that these 'godless aliens' be banned from entering the country. Other like-minded MPs took up the cudgels. Commander Arthur Marsden fulminated that this 'League of the Godless' congress would lead to 'riot and disturbance' and Sir Cooper Rawson and Sir Frank Sanderson huffed their indignant agreement.[60] They returned to the crease when a new date was announced for the congress. The government must ban the meeting because it was being organised by the 'International Godless Movement at Moscow' and ministers must take new powers to ban all such foreigners. This sounds like the wild ravings of the terminally unhinged, but Ramsay was a persuasive speaker and he was popular with National Government colleagues, many of whom shared his prejudices. One of his friends and neighbours, for instance, was Colonel C. I. Kerr, the MP for Montrose Burghs, who was the Liberal National chief whip and alleged that the great bulk of people pushing communist propaganda were 'of the Jewish race'. As if aware of the prejudice inherent in this speech, he added, 'I have many Jewish friends and those with whom I have discussed this menace are as concerned as I am at what is going on.'[61] Kerr was forced to apologise, but when Ramsay brought forward a Private Members' Bill on 28 June, which sought to ban 'godless aliens' (i.e. Jews) from entering the country, so many Conservative MPs backed it that it was carried by 165 votes to 134.

Ramsay did not leave things there. Convinced that the press was dominated by Jews (and therefore, in his logic, by communists) he produced the equally xenophobic Companies Act (1929) Amendment Bill, which attempted to prevent the 'manipulation and control of "news" for their own ends ... by big finance', on the grounds that the press 'could be used to thrust this country into a war'.[62] Yet again this was based on the old stereotype of rich, sneaky Jews running the press and conspiring to enrich themselves by dragging the world into a new war. It was a subject *Truth* harped on about, as it persistently insinuated that Jews ran and owned the *Daily Mirror*, and a week after the debate it declared that the paper was 'to be held up as a typical example of the manner in which Jews debauch the minds and standards of a community'.[63] A few Labour MPs voted for the Bill because they disliked the influence exerted by the press barons like Beaverbrook and Rothermere, but yet again a swathe of Conservative MPs carried the bill by 151 to 104.

The public mood was equally unpleasant. The British Medical Association complained in July 1938 that there were too many German doctors coming to Britain as refugees – the coded reference meaning that they were Jewish – and the aristocratic MP for East Toxteth, Patrick Buchan-Hepburn (who was painted rather beautifully by Glyn Philpott), objected that German refugee doctors were 'taking the bread out of the mouths of our medical practitioners'.[64] Even the German ambassador, Herbert von Dirksen, was struck by a widespread resentment against the Jews, which, he reckoned, had 'already assumed the form of hate'. He added, with a tinge of suppressed delight, 'The view that the Jews want to drive Britain into war with Germany finds widespread belief.'[65]

Against such a landscape of public opinion, Victor stood out as a rare and courageous friend of the Jews. His political career had never really taken off, but at least he could be proud that he had stood up for what he believed in. The time was coming when such courage would be needed.

15

Peace With Dishonour

There was much excitement when the genial leader of the German Sudetens in Czechoslovakia, Konrad Henlein, visited London in May 1938. Would he insist on total secession from Czechoslovakia or was he prepared to compromise? Gossip had been circulating for some time that Hitler had been behind the arrest of Henlein's close ally Heinz Rutha, who had taken his own life in prison when facing charges of homosexuality, so was Henlein now entirely beholden to Hitler? With Downing Street and the Foreign Office mired in mutual suspicion, different agencies competed in their attempts to garner intelligence on him. This put Guy Burgess back at the centre of things. He had already been simultaneously freelancing for Joseph Ball/Chamberlain on the one hand, and for MI6 and the Foreign Office on the other when he discovered that Henlein was staying in the Goring Hotel, where Guy's lover Jack Hewit was working as a telephonist. Four £5 notes later, Guy had a list of all the numbers Henlein had rung, plus details of his secret assignations. At the same time Sir Robert Vansittart, whom Chamberlain had sidelined as the chief diplomatic advisor at the Foreign Office, persuaded Harold Nicolson to invite friends to meet Henlein over tea at King's Bench Walk. It was not a large party – just Macnamara, Spears, Sandys and Godfrey Nicholson, who came from a family of gin distillers and was MP for Farnham – but Harold put on a substantial feast, with five heaped-up plates of sandwiches, four pyramids of scones and a Dundee cake. It was unseasonably hot, so Harold kept the windows open, which meant journalists could catch snatches of him giving Henlein a lecture, telling him he had a grave responsibility: only he could prevent a second European war – and he should think again if he presumed that British soldiers would refuse to fight Hitler over Czechoslovakia. Harold was actually mildly impressed by Henlein, but Hitler had already issued strict instructions that Henlein was to be as obstructive as possible in the hope of provoking the Czech government and providing a pretext for Germany to invade.

That was in May. By the time Bob Boothby visited Prague with his association chairman, Colonel Gardie Duff, at the end of July, a German invasion felt imminent. They saw Henlein in demotic action and were shocked to see Oswald Mosley's sister-in-law, the socialite Unity Mitford, sitting on the platform with a swastika brooch pinned to her bosom. The President of Czechoslovakia, Edvard Beneš, told them that the 9 million Czechs would fight to the death to defend their freedom. When they visited the Škoda factory at Pilsen, which was churning out tanks and munitions for the Czech army, they feared it would soon be commandeered by Hitler. (They were right.) They tried to impress the urgency of matters on Chamberlain when they met him on 24 August, but he was adamant that he would make no commitment to defend Czechoslovakia. Four days later Bob wrote again, warning Chamberlain that a group of German industrialists had told him at dinner that 'they estimate Prague can be captured and Bohemia occupied within three weeks and bargain on our persuading the French to remain neutral'.[1] Chamberlain dismissed the letter as alarmist, but Hitler had already issued secret orders for an invasion to start no later than 1 October.

Rob Bernays had come to the same conclusion as Bob. He spent the recess visiting another bachelor MP and fellow minister Sir Anthony Muirhead at his expansive but lugubrious Oxfordshire country home, Haseley Court, and on 26 August he arrived at the much more elegantly appointed family home of the Earl and Countess of Carlisle, Naworth Castle, where he joined a ten-day house party including Buck De La Warr and the up-and-coming young actor James Mason, who had just appeared in the Armada-based film *Fire Over England* and would be a conscientious objector in the war. Rob had visited Naworth twice before, but this time he was intrigued by his bedroom window, which had originally been used for pouring cauldrons of boiling oil on the enemy a hundred feet below. With similar defensive measures in mind, he wrote to Lucy on 29 August that he was certain that 'if Hitler now ignores all the danger signals and plunges into Czechoslovakia it will be war'. Britain would at least have to blockade Germany and that, he imagined, 'would mean the instant reprisals of an air attack on London'.[2]

Ronnie Cartland and Jack Macnamara were only too aware of what that meant. Ronnie told Harold he was so fed up with Chamberlain that he was thinking of joining the National Labour Party in July, and spent two weeks in August with his Royal Artillery regiment, which had been redesignated as the 53rd Anti-Tank, in a major training exercise on Salisbury Plain, which was led by Tony Muirhead. It was hard work, with all-night operations followed by artillery training and long lectures on military strategy – about as different from anything Ronnie had ever experienced as was possible – but he told Barbara that he enjoyed being a carefree young man of thirty-one for a fortnight. Jack likewise spent much of the summer training with the London Irish Rifles. Both of them knew that if and when war came, they would be on the front line. So too the 41-year-old Ronnie Tree had joined the 9th Lancers on a training exercise on Salisbury Plain, 'attempting to understand in passable degree the intricacy of tanks and machine-guns'. The experience heightened his frustration. 'I was horrified to discover,' he said, 'how deficient was their equipment.'[3] The tanks broke down every hundred yards and the machine guns could not be fitted on the armoured vehicles. Even Nicolson, who at fifty-four was well over the age for active service, was conscious that Sissinghurst was vulnerable. A gas-proof air-raid shelter was fitted out – though Harold declared that he would prefer to die lying in his bed with all the windows open.

On 14 September, with German troops massing on the Czech border, Chamberlain surprised everyone by announcing that he would visit Hitler at his mountain home at Berchtesgaden the following day. He had never flown in all his sixty-seven years, but he was convinced that he could do business with the Führer. His supporters welcomed the move in exuberant terms. Chips Channon was in Geneva at the time but thought Chamberlain's announcement was 'one of the finest, most inspiring acts of all history' and proclaimed that 'History must be ransacked to find a parallel'.[4] Once Chamberlain had already set off, he added, 'Of course some Jews and many of the more shady pressmen who hang about Geneva are furious. No war. No revenge on Germany.'[5] Harold Nicolson admitted to feeling a mixture of relief and disquiet. 'I shall be one of his most fervent admirers,' he wrote, 'if he brings back something which does not constitute a Hitler triumph.'[6]

The three-hour meeting produced nothing of substance. Hitler merely reiterated his demands with added vitriol. Chamberlain returned to Britain and reported back to the Cabinet, which then met with the French prime minister, Édouard Daladier. Their joint proposal – that Beneš should surrender the Sudetenland in exchange for a guarantee of the territorial independence of the rest of Czechoslovakia – pleased nobody, but Chamberlain flew to Cologne for a second meeting with Hitler on 22 September. By this stage it was clear to many that Hitler was determined to dismember Czechoslovakia, and that was effectively what Hitler told Chamberlain. Along with a barrage of histrionics about invented atrocities against Sudeten Germans, Hitler claimed that Czechoslovakia was merely a 1918 invention and should be parcelled out to Germany, Poland and Hungary. Chamberlain was astounded. This was a wholly new set of demands and was accompanied by an ultimatum. The Czechs must withdraw from the Sudetenland by 8 a.m. on 26 September or Germany would mobilise. This infuriated Chamberlain, but he quibbled about the date, not the concept, of the deadline – and it was pushed back to 1 October, which was the date Hitler had pencilled in months earlier for the invasion. But when Beneš stepped aside, a new Czech government was formed under General Syrový and a million Czechs enlisted in the army in just twenty-four hours, Hitler brought the deadline forward again – to 2 p.m. on 28 September.

Parliament was summoned to meet that day at 2.45 p.m. The mood was very dark. The deadline had already passed. Nicolson reckoned that 'war is almost on us'[7] and noticed an ominous poster in the Strand: 'City of Westminster; Air Raid Precautions'.[8] Boothby, who had also been in Geneva, rang him to report 'complete demoralisation' at the League of Nations. He predicted that Britain would be 'in for four years'.[9] Eden was reported to be in the depths of despair. Even Channon thought the war 'still looms'.[10] As Rob Bernays made his way to the Commons, he noted trenches being dug in the parks and sandwich boards announcing where to get gas masks. When he tried to make a joke about it all, a woman overheard him and shouted, 'Damn you! Can't you realise that we may be dead next week?'[11] In Whitehall a silent, anxious crowd stared at MPs as they arrived at Parliament Square 'with dumb, inquisitive eyes'.[12] War, invasion and aerial bombardment seemed imminent.

Things were even tenser in the Chamber, which was so packed that members were standing at the bar of the House, sitting on the floor in the gangways and spilling over into the gallery. The Peers' Gallery was so crowded that a microphone had been placed on the despatch box to relay Chamberlain's words to an overflow room. As if to heighten the solemnity of the occasion, the Speaker read out the names of four MPs who had died since the House last met and there was a brief set of questions about a national insurance scheme in preparation for war.

There was a cacophony of frantic cheering from the Tory benches when Chamberlain arrived in the Chamber, but when he started his calm, measured speech, laying out, step by step, the events of the last two months in chronological order, there was that sudden dead silence that can seize the Commons in an instant and evaporate just as fast. MPs hung on every word as they tried to interpret what it all meant. Chips Channon, just back that morning from another visit to Brdo Palace, the refined summer residence of Prince Paul, Regent of Yugoslavia, whom he adored, had heard a rumour that Chamberlain had sent an 'SOS letter' to Mussolini and Hitler, but nobody knew where the speech was going to lead. At one moment the prime minister seemed to be veering towards confronting Germany as he criticised Hitler, which prompted Anthony Crossley, who was sitting next to Channon, to cheer lustily. 'Why don't you cheer?' he pointedly asked Channon. 'How are your friends the Huns?'[13] Much of what Chamberlain said stuck in the insurgents' throats, though. He looked a little too pleased with himself when he referred to his 'first flight', and his justification of his own actions was patronising. Dealing with totalitarian governments was difficult, he explained. He knew that he courted criticism by visiting Hitler, but in such a crisis, he felt, rather piously, 'such considerations should not be allowed to count'.[14] Only his most loyal backbenchers nodded at this. But when he stated that the Führer had categorically declared that rather than wait he was prepared to risk a world war, a shudder passed across the whole House and when he added that 'Honourable Members will realise the perplexity in which I found myself', everyone murmured in sympathy.[15]

He had been speaking without interruption for nearly an hour and twenty minutes when members noticed a rustling of papers in the officials' box to the right of the Speaker's chair. Chamberlain had just explained that he had approached Mussolini about the possibility of another meeting with Hitler and that Mussolini had passed on the message. This was clearly intended to be his peroration, but as a note on Foreign Office paper was passed down the row of PPSs to Sir John Simon, he slowed down. Simon tugged Chamberlain's coat-tail and handed him the note. Chamberlain paused and adjusted his pince-nez.

The House waited. Suddenly his whole body seemed to change and as the light fell from the ceiling full on his face he appeared to Harold to be 'ten years younger'.[16] Chamberlain resumed his speech, now without notes. 'That is not all,' he said slowly and deliberately. 'I have something further to say to the House yet. I have now been informed by Herr Hitler that he invites me to meet him at Munich to-morrow morning.' Mussolini and Daladier had also been invited. With a flourish he added, 'I need not say what my answer will be.'[17] The sense of relief was palpable. Channon felt sick and longed to clutch Chamberlain, as 'Peace must now be saved, and with it the world'.[18] One MP shouted out, 'Thank God for Neville.' Others were seen to weep. Members across the House rose to their feet and started cheering and dozens of Conservatives stood on the green benches, waved their order papers in the air and shouted until they were hoarse.

Except for the insurgents. Tree, Cartland, Macnamara and Boothby sat with Churchill, Sandys, Bracken and Eden – sullen and silent. Nicolson remained seated until Walter Liddall hissed at him, 'Stand up, you brute!'[19] Barbara Cartland recorded that Ronnie stayed in his seat, too, 'calm, silent and aloof in the midst of what was to him undignified emotionalism'.[20] As for Bernays, he told Nicolson at dinner at Boulestin that night with Buck and Sibyl that he 'had lost all faith in the government and that nothing will restore it'. Afterwards Harold went on to broadcast his account of the day's events on the BBC, only keeping back his private view that in his vanity Chamberlain seemed to believe that Mussolini had made his gesture 'out of friendship for the Chamberlain family'.[21]

The next day Sassoon dutifully joined the whole Cabinet at Heston aerodrome to send Chamberlain off to Munich for round three, while wits chanted, 'If at first you can't concede, fly, fly, fly again.'[22] At 1.30 the next morning Hitler, Chamberlain and Daladier agreed a proposal, theoretically proposed by Mussolini, that ceded the whole of the Sudetenland to Germany by 10 October on the sole promise that Hitler would go no further. The only hitch for Hitler was that his inkwell was dry when he came to sign. It was left to the French and British to notify the Czechs that if they chose to fight Germany they would fight alone – whereupon General Syrový reluctantly and bitterly acceded, and started evacuating the contested territories. At the last minute Chamberlain ran back to Hitler to ask him to sign a separate three-paragraph Anglo-German Agreement. It included the words that this would be 'symbolic of the desire of our two peoples never to go to war again'. Hitler nonchalantly signed the scrap of paper, which Chamberlain proudly flourished and read out to the assembled crowds after stepping out of the aeroplane back at Heston. After his hero's welcome came a ninety-minute victory parade through streets lined with people on his way to Buckingham Palace, where he joined the king on the balcony. 'My good friends,' he said, recalling Disraeli's return from the Congress of Berlin, 'this is the second time there has come back from Germany to Downing Street peace with honour. I believe it is peace for our time.'

Plaudits showered down on his head. The *Daily Express* declared that 'Britain will not be involved in a European war this year or next year either'. The *Daily Mail* carried a staged photograph of German girls kissing Chamberlain's hand, it rhapsodised that the premier had returned with peace 'at the summit of his valiant endeavours' and reported that countless readers were calling for an annual 'Chamberlain Day'.[23] *The Times* pronounced that 'no conqueror returning from a victory on the battlefield had come adorned with nobler laurels'.[24] Channon called him 'the reincarnation of St George – so simple and so unspoilt ... I don't know what this country has done to deserve him'.[25] Collin Brooks reported that at a Livery Guild dinner in the Painted Hall at Greenwich the 'whole assembly spontaneously sprang up, crying the name of Chamberlain and toasting him, and singing "For He's a Jolly Good Fellow"'.[26] Sara Taylor, the mother of the actress Elizabeth, went even further. 'Thank God,' she wrote to Victor Cazalet, 'Mr. Chamberlain['s] broadcast speech from Downing Street on Tuesday night was the most marvellous thing I've ever heard ... it was divinely

Christlike in its compassionate understanding.'[27] Hugh Walpole's driver and companion Harold Cheevers was more nonchalant when he brought Hugh his breakfast. 'Peace,' he announced, before adding, 'I hope you're not tired of fish cakes.'[28]

By contrast the insurgents were depressed and infuriated. Noël Coward punched Ivor Novello when he caught him crying at Chamberlain's speech and told Ronnie Cartland that Chamberlain had 'just discovered what every chorus boy discovers his first year on the stage – the heady quality of applause'.[29] When a very disconsolate Bernays conferred with Crookshank, the latter wrote in his diary that the two of them were going to leave the government even though it would create difficulties for them personally 'when the world thinks Neville so great'.[30] Rob maintained that he then submitted a letter of resignation and was only persuaded to withdraw it when Chamberlain made another set of private assurances. We do not know what these amounted to, but his letter to Lucy reads like an excuse. 'I feel,' he wrote, 'that if a junior under-secretary can, in fact, have such influence on foreign policy as I appear to have had, it is really madness for him to resign.'[31]

Chamberlain's account was very different, as he claimed that Crookshank alone sent in a letter of resignation and demanded the opportunity to make a personal resignation statement on the Wednesday. Margesson persuaded him that he should at least meet with Chamberlain first. After half an hour Chamberlain got Crookshank to delay his resignation until he had spoken in the House again – and subsequently Harry asked him to burn his resignation letter. As for Rob, Chamberlain, interestingly, reckoned that Bernays was indeed another 'doubter' but claimed that he did not hear of Rob's doubts until they were both in the division lobby at the end of the debate when Rob laid out his concerns, 'but added that my speech had put everything right'.[32] Yet again Rob persuaded himself that it was better to argue from within the government than without. By the end of the year he was even arguing in a speech that he delivered several times that 'there is an increasing tendency to criticise the PM's actions at Munich and to forget how overwhelming was the sense of relief that his personal intervention had given us peace'. He also persuaded himself that he had an important role in preparing the nation for war as junior minister at the Department of Health. He argued time and again that 'you cannot defend liberty merely by making perorations about it'. The days were over 'when the walls of Jericho will fall before the blast of a trumpet. You need guns and the men to man them. You need air raid posts and the nurses to staff them, you need stretchers and the people to carry them.'[33] He persuaded himself that he was indispensable and kept his doubts to himself, so the only resignations were those of Duff Cooper (which even Chips Channon thought was brave, as he had very little private income) and Duff's PPS, Victor's unmarried close friend and travelling companion Hamilton Kerr.

The four-day debate ending on 6 October was a protracted but sullen affair. Chamberlain found it 'a pretty trying ordeal', as he had to fight all the time against the 'defection of weaker brethren'.[34] The insurgents were seething, but Colonel Sandeman Allen conveyed the tone of most Conservative MPs. 'I feel that I must start,' he pronounced, 'by paying my tribute of praise, admiration, and thanks to the Prime Minister for the pertinacity, patience, and courage which he showed and by which he brought peace to this country, peace, too, as he said, with honour.'[35] Conservative after well-drilled Conservative made the same point. From the government benches the only opponents of the agreement who were called to speak were Leo Amery, Winston Churchill and Harold Nicolson, so other insurgents were reduced to muttering and making pointed interventions. Churchill faced constant barracking. When he claimed 'we have sustained a total and unmitigated defeat', the House erupted in jeering and Nancy Astor screamed 'nonsense' at the top of her voice.[36] Harold was even tougher. He referred to 'this defeat, this humiliating defeat, this terrible Munich retreat'; and claimed that the 'Munich capitulation' was 'one of the most disastrous episodes that has ever occurred in our history'. Above all, he complained, 'By that capitulation we allow Herr Hitler to make it perfectly clear to the whole world, or at least to the whole of Europe, that the dominant Power in Europe to-day is not Great Britain, but is Berlin – or rather the Führerhaus in Munich.'[37] Ronnie Cartland kept on trying to catch the Speaker's eye, but was not called, so he rang up the editors of his local papers instead. 'Surely,' he told them, 'no one can regard the Munich agreement as a triumph for peaceful negotiation, while the circumstances in which the Anglo-German declaration was signed appear to many in the light of presenting a testimonial to a gangster.'[38] Ronnie agreed with Duff Cooper, who told his friends, 'It was "peace with honour" that I couldn't stomach. If he'd come back from Munich saying "peace with terrible, unmitigated, unparalleled dishonour" perhaps I would have stayed. But peace with honour!'[39]

Throughout this period the insurgents met constantly. They dined together in private rooms at the Savoy or the Carlton Club; they held weekly meetings at Ronnie Tree's, Jim Thomas's, Brendan Bracken's or Mark Patrick's. At one meeting they tried to draft a joint telegram to Chamberlain from Churchill, Eden and Attlee demanding that he step back from giving Hitler everything he wanted. Sometimes the meetings got heated. Cartland, Thomas and Macmillan all wanted the group to be far more overt in their criticism of Munich and urged that they should all vote against the government, but Eden demurred and eventually it was decided that it was better for them all to abstain, so they sat in their seats during the division, which according to Nicolson enraged the government, 'since it is not our numbers that matter but our reputation'.[40] Some insurgents, like Jack Macnamara, Godfrey Nicholson and Ronnie Tree, decided to give Chamberlain the benefit of the doubt this time, which prompted Sandys to write the word 'rat' against Ronnie Tree's name.[41] But the former Cabinet ministers Eden, Cooper, Churchill and Amery were joined by Boothby, Thomas, Cartland, Nicolson, Kerr, Cranborne, Wolmer, Sir Roger Keyes, Sidney Herbert, Spears, Macmillan, Law, Sandys, Crossley, Bracken and

Emrys-Evans in sitting it out. In all some forty Conservatives abstained. Ronnie was again the only Birmingham Tory to defy the whip.

It made little difference. Chamberlain won by 222 votes, whereupon the House rose 'as by one thought … shouted its cheers at full pitch, flourished its order papers in an abandon of affection and loyalty'.[42] Yet again the insurgents had to suffer in silence, sullenly slinking out of the Chamber. They were downhearted. It was a bitter moment for Jack Macnamara. 'There is not a Briton,' he told his local paper, 'who does not feel a cold shudder at the thought of what has happened now, and instinctively they know that we were beaten.' He added, 'We cannot escape the fact that we … have given in to force.'[43] It is not surprising that Jack felt 'a deep sorrow, a deep and justified spirit of foreboding'.[44] Just a few days later the commanding officer of the London Irish Rifles announced he was leaving to join the RAF, in whose ranks he had made his name in the First World War. On 1 November Jack took up the reins as the new lieutenant colonel.

In the aftermath of the Commons vote, the Ball dirty-tricks machine stepped into action. Chamberlain even boasted to his sister that Churchill and the Czech ambassador Jan Masaryk were 'totally unaware' that he knew everything they were up to. 'I had continual information of their doings and sayings,' he admitted, before bragging that this merely demonstrated 'for the nth time … how completely Winston can deceive himself when he wants to.'[45] The insurgents were easy to pick off. When Hugh Dalton joined a meeting at Brendan Bracken's house, the Conservatives all talked about how they had been 'victimised by their whips'.[46] Barbara Cartland reported she had been told that people like Churchill and her brother should be shot. Leo Amery hoped that his previous record of being unpopular 'and right afterwards' might protect him from the trouble he feared in his constituency, but he was furious to hear that Jim Thomas thought he was 'in grave danger' and that Anthony Crossley, who had only stood in 1935 when the Conservative Association in Stretford persuaded him to abandon plans to retire from the Commons to devote himself to a literary career, now worried that the executive might 'even go to the length of firing him for his abstention'.[47] Likewise Boothby was forced to explain himself to his constituency association the following Saturday. One heckler claimed he had in effect denounced the whole of the government's foreign policy, to which he responded that if the vote 'had simply been a vote of thanks to the Prime Minister for what he did I would have given it with a full heart. But it was more than that. It was a vote approving the policy which led up to that act.'[48] In the end the executive unanimously approved his action and expressed the hope that he would 'ginger up' the government on rearmament.

One thing remains unclear. What did Harry Crookshank mean when he said that he and Rob would face 'difficulties … *personally*'? They certainly both knew that it was as dangerous as ever to be considered homosexual, that the whips collected colleagues' secrets and that Downing Street would stop at nothing. It is not surprising that queer MPs feared rocking the boat with the subtle threat of political blackmail in the air. What is more surprising is that so many were prepared to risk everything.

On the Wednesday evening after the Munich votes, Marjorie Maxse, the petite and forceful chief operational director at Conservative Central Office, had dinner with Oliver Harvey at the Foreign Office. She was the first woman to rise to the top of any party's organisational structure and had done so thanks to sheer determination and single-minded devotion to the cause. Yet she was sceptical about her own party leader, as Harvey recorded that they frankly discussed 'the P.M.'s dictatorship in the Cabinet' and she pronounced that she believed him to have 'a sort of infatuation for Hitler and … no serious intention of drastic re-armament'. Despite this, she refused to accept that party headquarters were in any way responsible for attacks on the insurgents.[49] Maxse was wrong. She might have been aware that on the eve of the Munich vote Lord Rothermere was so sure that an election would clear out Chamberlain's critics that he had written to her immediate superior, Sir Douglas Hacking, demanding one immediately. 'He was very frank,' wrote Collin Brooks, who was deputed to deliver the message. 'He says there are 40 Tory malcontents.'[50] What Maxse could not possibly know, though, was that Ball and the whips office were still running a secret dirty-tricks operation against those '40 Tory malcontents'.

Ball knew the importance of naming his enemies. For a while the term 'insurgents' sufficed. But by the end of the year he had adopted a more subtly derisory term, 'the glamour boys'. It first appeared in print in an article by one of Ball's preferred journalists, Charles Graves, who took a pop at Churchill's son-in-law Duncan Sandys in his daily gossip column in the *Daily Mail* at the end of June.[51] Under the headline 'The "Glamour Boys" of the Commons', he referred to Sandys as the 'smoke-screen for Mr. Churchill's barrages' and pronounced that: 'He is in fact one of the "glamour boys" of the House of Commons.' He went on to explain that the nickname had circulated for some time in the House of Commons 'to signify seven or eight youngish Members of Parliament, nearly all of them good-looking'. He only named Sandys, Cartland, Nicolson and Bracken, but he made clear the source of his intelligence: 'they are viewed with some suspicion by the party heads'.[52] It was a successful tactic. The word 'glamour' struck a particularly vibrant chord. The *Sketch* used it, for instance, to describe the bisexual poet Byron as 'half a charlatan and wholly a cad'.[53] It seemed to contain a compliment, but it insinuated something disturbing. It suggested that these men were vain and overly fastidious, effete if not actually effeminate, and easily distracted by glitter and fashion. The implication of deviancy was subtle, too. While nobody suggested that Duncan Sandys was anything other than heterosexual, Cartland and Bracken were unmarried and rumoured to be homosexual, Eden was thought to have had a queer phase at university and Nicolson's extramarital exploits were the subject of society gossip. The aim was to tar all Chamberlain's opponents with the same innuendo-laden brush.

Chamberlain's supporters took up the nickname with relish. The Canadian-born Conservative MP for Wood Green, Beverley Baxter, for instance, was a convinced supporter of appeasement, so when he was asked to address the Empire Tea Centenary Committee luncheon at the Commons in December he teased that you could identify an MP's allegiance by what they drank. Anyone drinking milk was bound to be a Liberal, those sipping crème de menthe were likely to be 'contemplating joining Churchill's glamour boys' and only if they were drinking tea could you be sure 'they will vote like gentlemen for their party – even if they do not know what they are voting about'.[54] Yet again the insinuation was that the glamour boys were engaged in conduct unbecoming a gentleman – the ultimate slur.

In response, the Glamour Boys' sense of moral outrage rapidly intensified. Ronnie Cartland was particularly frustrated. Inspired by a conference led by Rom Landau at Windsor Castle, he despaired of the fripperies of the State Opening of Parliament in November. 'So much is happening these days off stage,' he wrote to Barbara, 'that the Chamber has taken on the appearance of a backcloth against which the old favourites do their turns while the audience wait for the great transformation scene.'[55] He could not have realised how percipient these remarks were, but the next two nights (9–10 November) saw the worst Nazi violence yet, when government-sponsored thugs ran amok throughout Germany and Austria, smashing the windows of Jewish-owned shops and businesses, supposedly in reprisal for the murder of the 29-year-old German diplomat Ernst vom Rath by a Polish Jewish teenager. Oliver Harvey reckoned these were 'the most ghastly anti-Jewish riots in Germany since the Middle Ages'[56] and this *Kristallnacht* even shocked *The Times*, which had thus far repeatedly downplayed anti-Jewish attacks. 'No foreign propagandist,' it argued, 'bent upon blackening Germany before the world could outdo the tale of burnings and beatings, of blackguardly assaults on defenceless and innocent people, which disgraced that country yesterday.'[57] Even Lord Mount Temple was prompted to resign from the Anglo-German Fellowship. Terrified Jews were hunted down by mobs led by members of the SS, the SA and the Hitler Youth. The main shopping streets in Berlin and Munich were devastated, shops were ransacked and 267 synagogues were burnt to a shell. Roughly 30,000 Jewish men were arrested and despatched to concentration camps along with dozens of women. When, after forty-eight hours of rampant violence, Goebbels finally demanded that the entire population desist from further 'demonstrations against the Jews', he cynically lauded the 'justified and understandable indignation of the German people at the cowardly Jewish assassination' and ominously announced that 'the final answer ... will be given to the Jews by legislative means or by decree'.[58]

The protection of the Jews was now a moral imperative for the Glamour Boys. Jack Macnamara had come to loathe every aspect of the Nazi regime. He warned children at a school speech day against the authoritarian trend in Germany, where young people had abandoned their right to say 'Yes' and 'No' and had given the state their blind trust. 'I hope', he said, 'we shall never ourselves get to that state of things.' He added, 'I hope that because there is something much higher – there is the right to be individuals.'[59] A week after *Kristallnacht* he drew attention to the plight of 30,000 German Jews living in tents on the border with Poland. Whatever Chamberlain had hoped for out of Munich, the truth was that Germany was 'arming day and night colossally' and the next war would be 'a totalitarian war in which every man, woman and child would be involved'.[60]

This was to become the Glamour Boys' constant refrain. When Ronnie Cartland launched a brutal attack in the Commons on his own front bench for having no policy on unemployment, he too argued that what was lacking was leadership. After all, 'when you get leadership, you will get the country responding to sacrifices, but unless you face up to your difficulties ... you will go down to disaster and destruction.'[61] That meant reconstructing the government and setting up a

Ministry of Supply, as Churchill advocated in an amendment to the King's Speech on 17 November. Chips Channon reported that this was 'the day when the Glamour Boys hoped to damage us', as Churchill urged fifty Conservatives to follow him into the Lobby, but all bar four of the Glamour Boys decided to keep their powder dry and voted with the government.[62] The backlash continued. A few weeks later Jim Thomas received a letter from a 'former supporter', accusing him of impertinence for not supporting Chamberlain when he was clearly 'less able, less gifted and with less experience than the P.M. and Foreign Secretary'.[63]

Ball's secret campaign took its first casualty in December, when Patrick Blair and the deputy chief whip, James Stuart, organised to oust Katharine Stewart-Murray, the Duchess of Atholl, who had been MP for Kinross and West Perthshire since 1923. She was a trailblazer as the first female Conservative minister who served as parliamentary secretary to the Board of Education from 1924 to 1929. She never fought shy of controversy. She had repeatedly voiced her concerns after Eden's resignation and she joined the insurgents in abstaining over Munich. The whips had been hovering for some time, but retribution came swiftly, as James Stuart organised a vote of no confidence in her by her local party, meaning that she would not be able to fight the seat as a Conservative in the next general election. Katharine decided to fight back. On 24 November she resigned her seat by taking the office of Crown Steward of the Chiltern Hundreds and prompted a by-election, which her supporters expected she would win, as she had a majority of 5,000 at the last election. Stuart swung into action again, clamping down on any insurgents who were thinking of supporting the duchess and signing up seventy Conservative MPs for a leaflet calling on voters to support the official candidate. Katharine asked Churchill if he would speak for her, but he was so frightened of being deselected in Epping that he declined. She tried Boothby. He had only just delivered a coruscating attack on the government in the Commons. 'We have been continuously and grossly misled by Ministers ... as to the true state of our defences,' he said.[64] But when Katharine asked him to speak for her, he ignominiously stayed away. All he offered was a miserable letter of support, which she spurned. It was the same with every other Tory MP. Katharine might nevertheless have hoped to win. Sandy Lindsay, the master of Balliol, had nearly taken the Oxford by-election on 27 October on an anti-Munich platform; and just before Katharine resigned her seat Vernon Bartlett had won the Bridgwater by-election as an independent candidate supporting Eden's position in a straight fight against a Conservative. But when Katharine's by-election came, in a blizzard on 21 December, she lost by 1,400 votes. In typically boorish fashion, James Stuart's brother-in-law, Ivor Cobbold, sent her a five-word telegram: 'Am delighted you are out.'

The Glamour Boys failed to stand by Katharine. Several had tried to persuade her against forcing the by-election. Yet they continued to campaign for faster rearmament and a reconstruction of the government in the face of the Chamberlain machine. On 8 December they launched a weekly broadsheet, the *Whitehall News*, out of temporary offices in Kensington. Short, sharp and to the point, it had a small but influential readership in the UK, in America and in Europe. It argued that Munich had been a bitter humiliation and it demanded that Hitler must surely see 'that the recent Jewish Pogrom in Germany with its attendant abominable and arrogant disregard of all Christian justice, is the very last way in which Germany can hope to regain British goodwill'.[65] Its articles were anonymous, but one can hear the well-turned phrases of the individual Glamour Boys in every edition. It derided the tendency of the British 'to cling to pleasing delusions', it attacked the reception Chamberlain had received on his return from Munich as 'disgustingly hysterical' and it denounced the prime minister for having 'left his soul and his country's honour in Munich'.[66] Its second edition carried the headline, 'No More Surrender to Hitler and Mussolini!' It hoped that with luck Britain might still have a few months in which to prepare for 'the coming European holocaust'. But it was certain that the only way to guarantee peace in Europe was for Britain to build a vast military machine.'[67] The first edition of 1939 screamed, 'Wake Up, Britain! Our Only Hope of National Salvation is to Arm! Arm! Arm!'[68]

16

The 'Glamour Boys'

One morning in January 1939 Ronnie Tree received a phone call from one of the two joint editors of the *Whitehall News*, a plucky thirty-year-old American journalist called Helen Kirkpatrick. Did Ronnie know that his phone was being tapped by the security services? Yes, now he thought about it, he had heard some odd clicks when he picked up the receiver. He was outraged, but in a way it was a compliment. Thus far the Glamour Boys had seemed relatively harmless. All they had done was abstain a couple of times. Yet the government machinery was clearly worried and if Ronnie's phone was tapped then the same was almost certainly true for the rest of them, who now found themselves at war on two fronts – with the dictators and with Chamberlain.

The feeling was mutual. The home secretary, Sir Samuel Hoare, bullishly denounced anyone warning about Hitler as 'jitterbugs' and 'scaremongers'. 'These timid panic-mongers are doing the greatest harm,' he declared. They were undermining public confidence and creating a fatal feeling of the inevitability of war. 'Worst of all,' he added, 'they are showing cowardice in the face of a potential enemy.'[1] The press largely echoed the view expressed in the *Hartlepool Evening Express*: 'These spineless scaremongers are doing infinite harm by their wailings'.[2] Such patronising and complacent claptrap irritated Ronnie Cartland beyond measure. 'The jeers of the Nazi Press-hounds grate on our ears,' he wrote. Britain had to hold itself in readiness for 'the decisive struggle', but he feared that 'the mass of our people are quite unaware of the determination and vigour of the tyrant across the sea'.³ Bob Boothby was yet more direct. Hoare was 'the pygmiest ... of all the political pygmies.'⁴

But in truth the sense of urgency had dissipated. Parliament took six weeks off from 22 December 1938 to 31 January 1939. Jack Macnamara took a long break, too, sailing to New York on the *Paris* on 4 January and returning on the *Aquitania* on 10 February. He was by now something of a celebrity. He was (at thirty-four) one of the youngest battalion commanders in the British Army, his recruitment drive had brought the London Irish to full strength faster than any other Territorial unit and he had already published his memoirs, *The Whistle Blows*. So he was invited to speak on foreign affairs in Toronto, Ottawa and Montreal and was given a warm reception by the Queen's Own Regiment of Canada. On his return he went straight into training exercises with the London Irish. Then came an episode that confirmed Jack's change of views about Germany. One of his fellow officers in the LIR was the lanky Captain George ('Geordie') Lennox-Boyd, whose younger brother Alan had entered the government in the immediate aftermath of Eden's resignation and had just got married (much to Alan's friends' surprise). At the end of March 1939 Geordie and another Lennox-Boyd brother, Donald, who was an officer in the Scots Guards, travelled to Stuttgart, supposedly on a reciprocal mission with the Germans to investigate air-raid provisions in their respective countries. Somehow the two brothers were arrested and although Geordie was released, Donald died in custody on 5 April. According to the official version of events Donald died of a heart attack, but the Germans had hastily cremated Donald by the time Alan and his new wife Patsy arrived in Germany; and back in England rumours abounded that Donald had been arrested in some kind of homosexual situation and had either been murdered by the Nazis or had taken his own life. Geordie must have known the truth and may well have talked about it to Jack, who would have recognised the stench

Ronnie Cartland lost his father in the First World War, but was especially close to his mother Polly (above left, seated with Ronnie), his brother Tony (above right) and his elder sister, the novelist Barbara (right), who provided an entrée into London society and regular invites to extravagant parties.

Most MPs spent their time exclusively in the company of other men, at their club, their bachelor's apartment or in the Commons. Yet many feared being asked why they were 'bachelors'. Ronnie Cartland, Bob Boothby and Jim Thomas are seen here with Noël Coward.

It was not just Jack Macnamara's support for Germany that got him into trouble in the Upton by-election in 1934, when he was accused of being a 'friend of Hitler' and the press ran a strange headline.

MR. BEN GARDNER canvassing in the Division.

UPTON TORY GOES FASCIST

Wants Blackshirts in Territorials

QUEER ANTICS BEWILDER THE ELECTORS

CANDIDATES

Mr. Ben Gardner (Lab.).
Mr. J. R. J. Macnamara (C.).
Mr. Fenner Brockway (I.L.P.).

Nominations to-morrow; Polling May 14.

By Our Special Representative

UPTON electors are becoming bewildered by the antics of the Tory candidate, who announces a policy one day and denounces it the next.

Although the campaign has been in progress for only a few days, he has made so many statements and denials that, as the Cockney said, "E dunno where 'e are!"—and certainly the electors do not know.

It may be that Mr. Macnamara, in his impulsiveness, has forgotten the policy laid down by the Conservative Central Office. At any rate, he found it necessary last night to introduce many qualifications to his support of the Empire Free Trade of which, on Tuesday, he declared himself an ardent advocate.

"STAGGERED"

But the most surprising turnabout was in regard to his attitude to Fascism.

Upton was staggered yesterday to read in the "Stratford Express" that, at his adoption meeting, he had declared that—

"He could find nothing in Fascism that was not in the Conservative programme."

"I would like to see the Fascists in the Conservative ranks," he was reported to have said, "with the blackshirts changed to the uniform of the Territorial Army."

Upton has already heard of Mr. Macnamara's interest in the Nazi movement in Germany, but this, of course, is the first time that a candidate has suggested that the Conservative Party should become a camouflaged Fascist organisation.

It was not surprising that many people wanted to know last night whether the suggestion had official support.

When questions were put to Mr. Macnamara, however, he performed his familiar act as a political gymnast and denied that he had made the statement.

The independence and accuracy of the local newspaper are, however, well known throughout the division, and the revelation, apparently intended only for the inner circle of the local Tory Party, has become awkwardly public.

Meanwhile, Mr. Ben Gardner, who addressed his first meeting last night, is going steadily on with his campaign. He is standing for the Labour Party programme and, as an associate of Keir Hardie, the first Labour Member for West Ham, whose election agent he was, he claims that he alone can represent the workers' interests.

"Keir Hardie was a great Socialist and he would have been on my side to-night," Ben told an enthusiastic audience at Holbrook-road School.

"I stand for the Labour Movement, not as an individual, but as a believer and an active worker for that cause.

"Every vote given to split that cause is a vote of encouragement to the Tory Government to carry on its policy and is a vote against yourselves."

But the "unkindest cut," Mr. Gardner

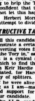

Mr. H. Morrison

MR. BROCKWAY'S ONLY HOPE

"IT is necessary that the role of the I.L.P. in this byelection shall be made abundantly clear to Labour voters.

"The I.L.P. candidate has no hope of winning. He knows that he will be fortunate if his deposit is returned.

"The real thing that the I.L.P. hopes to achieve in this byelection is to demonstrate a certain destructive power by diverting votes from Labour's candidate and letting the Tory candidate in.

"It is all they can hope to do."

Mr. Herbert Morrison at Upton last night.

continued, was the intrusion of Mr. Brockway—"doing here what the Communist failed to do at Hammersmith—trying to help the Tory to get in, but I am confident that the people of Upton will not let this happen."

Mr. Herbert Morrison also deplored this attempt to divide the Labour vote.

DESTRUCTIVE TACTICS

"All this candidate hopes to do is to demonstrate a certain destructive power by diverting votes from Labour and letting the Tory in," said Mr. Morrison.

"It is a cynical and tragic situation in which to find the organisation with which Keir Hardie was so prominently associated, for Hardie was always the enemy of splitters.

"If he were alive to-day he would be doing as I am—making an appeal for united support for Ben Gardner, the Labour candidate.

"The I.L.P. candidate represents the half-baked Communist point of view, and I would sooner have an honest Communist than one who has not the courage of his convictions.

"It means that Labour supporters must work harder for the purpose of defeating Toryism in this election, for the real fight is between Socialism and the capitalist view of Toryism."

"Given adequate work on the part of all London Labour men and women in this election, Ben Gardner and the Labour Party will achieve a handsome victory for Socialism over the Tories."

(Editorial, Page Ten.)

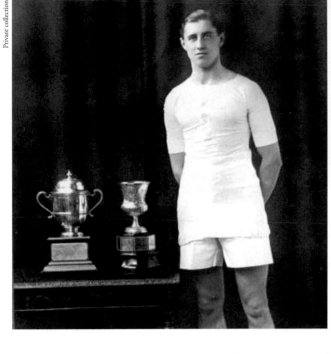

Society magazines speculated about 'bachelors'. Ronnie Cartland's close friend Anthony, Viscount Knebworth (above), was a successful boxer and was elected MP for Hitchin in 1931. When Sir Paul Latham MP (below left) got engaged, *Bystander* said it was surprised, as 'he wasn't the marrying type'. Rob Bernays (below right) regularly faced questions about why he was still unmarried.

An Engaged Couple   *A Black Cat for Luck*

Bachelor Bernays M.P. Lives in Hopes

MR. R. H. BERNAYS, Parliamentary Secretary to the Ministry of Health, M.P. for Bristol North, who was twitted on being a bachelor during a recent Commons debate on the decline of the birth rate, said on Saturday night, "I cannot say that I have done very much to arrest that decline.

"Although I have now led eight young men to the altar (he was best man at a wedding on Saturday) I have not yet succeeded in persuading any of the bridesmaids to go with me up the bridal steps— but I live in hopes"

Mr Bernays said this at the annual dinner of the Women Public Health Officers' Association in London.

Sir Paul Latham and Lady Patricia Moore, daughter of the Earl of Drogheda and Kathleen, Countess of Drogheda, announced their engagement about ten days ago. Sir Paul Latham is M.P. for Scarborough, and on the L.C.C. He succeeded his father in 1931

at the door, with the result that they both saved themselves £1 16s.

OTHER regular Newmarket enthusiasts were Sir Christopher and Lady Magnay. Lord and Lady Playfair came in their party, as also did Lady Marjorie Erskine. I also saw Lord and Lady Weymouth. Most of the women seemed to be dressed in blue and green, while the men wore their bowler hats tilted over the eye.

Mr. Francis Baring and Lady Rose McDonnell, the elder sister of the Earl of Antrim, who were married at Godalming, found a determinedly-asleep black cat on the steps of the Church as they came out. It had already been removed once by the police, but had come back

Anti-Semitism was rife in Britain (above left, the broken window of a Jewish tailor's shop in Bethnal Green, London, after an anti-Semitic attack in 1936), and Hitler found sympathetic British ears in the Anglo-German Association, whose chairman, General Sir Ian Hamilton (above right), was profoundly anti-Semitic. Membership of its successor, the Anglo-German Fellowship, did not 'necessarily' imply support for Nazism, but when a friendly match between England and Germany was played at White Hart Lane, the German team gave the Nazi salute (below).

Neville Chamberlain, the architect of appeasement, recruited the former intelligence officer Sir Joseph Ball (above) to run a black-arts operation for him, denigrating his opponents as 'The Glamour Boys', having their phones tapped and buying up the influential weekly magazine *Truth* (above) to act as his secret mouthpiece.

Ronnie Cartland enlisted in the Royal Artillery (right). In one brave attack on Chamberlain he told the Commons, 'Within a month we may be going to fight, and we may be going to die.' In 1940 he was part of the courageous defence of Cassel, as British forces evacuated at Dunkirk.

The London Irish Rifles, which Jack Macnamara joined in 1934 and led from 1938, was a safe haven for single men. Below, Jack drinks with the French military attaché whose flight prompted the air-raid warning on the day war was declared in 1939.

Victor Cazalet, seen above in uniform walking back from parliament to the Dorchester Hotel with Lord Halifax, led an anti-aircraft battery known as the 'monstrous regiment of gentlemen', but spent most of the war as liaison officer with the Free Poles under General Sikorski. Rob Bernays joined the Royal Artillery, married Nancy Britton (below left) and they had two sons. Early in 1945 he went on a morale-boosting visit to troops in Italy (below right).

PRIME MINISTER

10, Downing Street,
Whitehall.

6 January, 1945.

Dear Mrs. Stewart Orpen,

I send you my deepest sympathy on the
death in action of your son. I knew him and
greatly admired him. In 1942 he wrote to me "I
feel that as an M.P. I should give a lead in Battle,
and that I sincerely want to do as soon as possible".
I am sure that he would have played a notable part
in public life after the war. Now that cannot be;
but I hope that in these sad days you will find
comfort in the thought that he served his country
well and without regard of self. The House of
Commons, the Army and the Country have lost a good
servant.

Yours sincerely,

Winston Churchill

P.S. I grieve for him greatly. He was all
that a man should be

Mrs. Stewart Orpen.

Winston Churchill was particularly moved by the loss of his parliamentary colleagues. He wrote to Jack's mother that her son 'was all that a man should be' (right) and insisted after Victor's swift burial in Gibraltar (below left) that the new Commons Chamber carry shields commemorating them all. It is difficult to know what the *Chelmsford Chronicle* meant by its headline (below right).

COLONEL
V. A. CAZALET, M.C., M.P.
ROYAL ARTILLERY
4TH JULY 1943

"WELL DONE
GOOD AND FAITHFUL SERVANT"

He Loved Men

By T. N. Benson

This tribute to Colonel Macnamara is from the pen of the Rev. T. N. Benson, M.C., who won that decoration as a platoon officer in the last war.

Mr. Benson is the rector of Little Waltham, the parish in which Col. Macnamara lived.

Col. Macnamara inspecting the Essex Regiment in the Mediterranean theatre of war

ON THE EVE OF HIS RETURN

General Wigan's Tribute

of a government cover-up. After all, the family would have been ashamed to acknowledge that Donald was homosexual and the British government, in which Alan was an ardent and ambitious minister, did not want to upset the Nazis. One of Donald's closest friends, the travel writer Freya Stark (who later married Stewart Perowne), reckoned that Donald was 'the first victim of this war'.[5] Jack almost certainly agreed.

As for Rob Bernays, he vacillated. He privately threatened to resign again in December, but then wrote to Lucy just before Christmas that he had purposely not joined a revolt by four other junior ministers, including Harry Crookshank and Robert Hudson (whom Ellen Wilkinson described as 'handsome, young, rich and generally regarded as one of the "glamour boys"'[6]). With a direct reference to Ball and Chamberlain's love of fishing, Rob added, 'If I go it will be at my own time and on my own initiative and because I dislike fishing-rod men! "I travel alone."'[7] When the New Year broke he reckoned that although Hitler would soon provoke another crisis, British morale was strengthening. 'They are not nearly as afraid of war as they were', he wrote on 5 January, 'and the nation that is not afraid of war … has taken the first step to avoiding war.'[8] A month later, though, he dissuaded his friend and ministerial colleague Walter Elliot from proclaiming that 'spring had come' precisely because he was convinced that 'all that has happened is that the winter is less intense'.[9]

Rob had other matters on his mind, though. For some time he had been involved with another young woman, Clementine Freeman-Mitford. By all accounts she was a beautiful young woman and although her father's early death had left her relatively impecunious, she was well connected. The aristocratic Mitford sisters were first cousins on her father's side, Clementine Churchill was her mother's cousin, and her great-aunt the Marchioness of Salisbury had brought her up at Hatfield House. Rob admitted that she was a bit young for him, at just twenty-three, but she was 'pretty, unpretentious, charming and very,

very keen on politics' and unlike her uncle Lord Redesdale, she was 'fanatically anti-Hitler', so Rob and she struck up a friendship.[10] Things moved very slowly, though. They met in the spring of 1938. In May they went to the theatre. In July they had dinner together – when she told him she was going to New Zealand for six months. In August it transpired that she was not going after all. It was only in December that Rob took her to Finchley to meet his father, which prompted a 'great fluttering in the dovecot' even though Rob had heard tell that she had slept with Winston Churchill's womanising son Randolph and turned down Nancy Astor's son Bill 'and £40,000 a year!'[11] Rob later confessed to Lucy that 'when you are thirty-six and have had one disaster, you cannot rush your fences' and he complained that Clementine's one failing was that she had no sense of humour, but Clementine picked up on his diffidence or anxiety. It was only when they were alone in the countryside in March 1939 that he came close to making his feelings clear – and that proved a difficult meeting. He gently intimated in a roundabout way that a man might need some encouragement from a girl, but she was quite firm about the propriety of these things – it simply wasn't decent for a girl to 'give encouragement'. Rob tried beating about the bush in a different direction. With some men, he suggested, love was a plant of as slow a growth as in women, but it needed some sunlight and rain. 'You mean,' she said, 'that without warmth and water the plant may just stop growing or wilt away.' Rob was then as direct as he could be. 'Yes, that is exactly what I do mean.' It made no odds. As he told Lucy, 'And then there was silence.'[12] In April it was all over, as Clementine announced her engagement to the heir to a South African diamond fortune, Sir Alfred Beit, who had a large house in Belgrave Square, a great art collection (he proposed to her underneath Goya's 1805 *Portrait of Doña Antonia Zárate*) and a seat as the Conservative MP for St Pancras. Yet again Rob feared a lonely old age. 'I feel in despair,' he wrote to Lucy, 'and may be a victim to anyone on the rebound.'[13]

The national mood of complacent confidence continued well into March, when the Anglo-German Fellowship held a grand dinner at Claridge's for Hitler's personal nominee as 'leader of the German women', the 36-year-old mother of four, Frau Gertrud Scholtz-Klink. The AGF pulled out all the stops for this dinner, which was organised by the young president of the Women's League of Health and Beauty, Prunella Stack. Her involvement in the AGF was significant. She had married Lord Douglas-Hamilton, the Nazi-loving youngest son of the Duke of Hamilton, in Glasgow Cathedral the previous October. *Life* claimed that she had the most-photographed legs in Britain. She was regularly referred to in the press as Britain's 'Perfect Girl'. Chamberlain had asked her to serve on the National Fitness Council and she had led a British delegation to a Congress of Physical Fitness in Hamburg in 1938. Every women's voluntary group attended the AGF dinner and the *Sketch* declared in a whole page of photographs, 'We Take Our Hat Off to Frau Gertrud Scholtz-Klink for being Hitler's "Ideal Woman"'.[14] Some were infuriated by the visit, though. Nancy Astor refused to meet Scholtz-Klink on the grounds that the Nazis refused to countenance women playing any role in public life. A band of twelve feminists marched from Tottenham Court Road to the German Embassy carrying banners reading 'Clear out Scholtz-Klink' and 'Hitler Wants War, We Want Peace' and one poster that made an even sharper point in German: 'Freedom for the Women of Hitler's Concentration Camps'.[15] Less subtly, the journalist Richard Baxter resorted to claiming that the woman Hitler called 'the perfect woman' was actually 'a dour, irritable Hun' who had 'the biggest pair of feet I had ever seen on a woman'.[16]

On the day the *Sketch* printed its adulatory piece about Scholtz-Klink, Hitler took his next decisive step. Early that morning he bullied the new Czech president, Emil Hácha, who had a heart attack during the meeting, into ordering the complete surrender of the Czech army under threat of heavy aerial bombardment of Prague. That day German troops completed the takeover of

Czechoslovakia and on 16 March Hitler, speaking from the Czech capital, proclaimed Bohemia and Moravia a German Protectorate. The Glamour Boys had been predicting this ever since Munich, and Rob Bernays, who wrote to Lucy that 'the country is really stunned by it all' reckoned war was now a probability and appeasement was 'definitely "down the drain"'.[17] Victor Cazalet was not so sure. Hitler's 'unspeakable' actions had 'roused the man in the street as nothing else had' and with Hitler seemingly determined to dominate Europe, 'we seem very near war', he wrote in his journal on 18 March. Two days later he equivocated, though. 'Is it war?' he asked. But later that day he wrote in a different pen, 'It looks like war for a certainty.'[18] Despite his personal affection for Chamberlain, he too was now done with appeasement. 'If a single German soldier crosses the border of Romania, Poland, Yugoslavia or Holland,' he declared, 'we are in with all our forces. Perhaps that might prevent a European war!'[19]

Even though they had now been vindicated, the Glamour Boys were still under attack from Chamberlain loyalists and closet Nazi-supporters. When the Conservative MP for Hulme, Sir Joseph Nall, addressed a concert held by the Lowdham Men's Conservative Association at the end of March, he declared that 'the German aggression into Czechoslovakia … can only be described as a sheer act of treachery' and claimed that Hitler's actions had taken everyone by surprise, but went on to attack the very people who had bravely predicted it. 'At Westminster we call them "The Glamour Boys",' he said, 'people who always know better, but who did not know it sufficiently well when they were in office.'[20] He was speaking just a week after one of the Glamour Boys, Sir Sidney Herbert, the jovial 48-year-old MP for the Westminster Abbey constituency, had died quite suddenly in Cannes. The newspapers noted that he left £555,968 and was a bachelor. None mentioned that he had been a committed opponent of appeasement and regular attendee at Glamour Boys meetings.

The invasion of Czechoslovakia stirred the Glamour Boys into more urgent action. As Harold Nicolson put it, the 'gang' who met at Ronnie Tree's thought 'we must fight if [the government] surrender and support if they fight'.[21] At the end of March some of them met with Eden in Philip Sassoon's ministerial office in the Commons, where they drew up a Commons resolution calling for three things: conscription, a 'national effort to meet present dangers' and the creation of a new National Government 'on the widest possible basis'. Forty MPs signed up,[22] but the whips retaliated the next day with an amendment condemning any attempt to undermine the prime minister signed by 208 Conservative loyalists. It proved the Glamour Boys were still in a small minority, but they responded with derision. Amery signed what he called 'the whips' office round robin of unqualified support for Chamberlain' as well as the main motion it contradicted, on the grounds that, 'I thought it better to make the thing ridiculous.'[23] The Glamour Boys were gaining allies, though. The wealthy, philandering Anglo-Argentine Hubert Duggan had joined the insurgents in abstaining after Eden's resignation and over Munich, so he was already a likely signatory of the original motion, but now the list gained Sir Ralph Glyn, Robin Turton, Ernest Makins, William Duckworth, Viscount 'Tops' Wolmer, Sir Brograve Beauchamp, Fred Macquisten and two more bachelors, Ernest Shepperson and the eighty-year-old former Eton schoolmaster Annesley Somerville, both of whom were prevailed upon by the whips to sign the amendment but refused to take their names off the original motion.

With the growing confidence of numbers, the Glamour Boys added their names three weeks later to another motion calling for 'the immediate acceptance of the compulsory mobilisation of the man, munition and money-power of the nation'.[24] This meant conscription, which had also been contentious within the Conservative Party, as Chamberlain resisted anything that might antagonise Hitler. But Jack Macnamara had been arguing for a year that some form of mandatory national service was necessary because he knew from the London Irish Rifles that 'our strategy at home relies, in the first place, on somebody else's line abroad, and secondly on a very small army of very young men'.[25] Again

Jack was lucky that his association president, General Wigan, agreed, but the two men were given a hard time at the association AGM in May 1938 because their members fretted that any suggestion of national service 'virtually meant conscription' and they 'did not consider the country would accept it'.[26] In April 1939, though, the Glamour Boys were allying themselves with a wider range of Tories, especially among former members of the armed forces. This time sixty-two Conservatives signed the rebel motion. They were still in a minority out of a vast phalanx of 386, but there was a sense that the tide was beginning to turn, as Chamberlain reluctantly and unexpectedly introduced a limited measure of conscription on 26 April. All 26-year-old men would have to undertake six months' training – and the Territorial Army would be doubled in size. For Jack that meant recruiting a whole second battalion of the London Irish.

Throughout this period the group made every effort to keep its meetings secret. This was never straightforward. Meetings were held close to the Commons, but that meant it was easy for other MPs to spot colleagues arriving and departing, especially as Chamberlain's ally J. C. C. (now Viscount) Davidson lived next door to Jim Thomas. There were other problems. The group was constantly on the lookout for new recruits, but complete secrecy was only feasible if they remained small and tight-knit. New recruits might have mixed loyalties and an excitable plotter might have a loose tongue. Some were so distrustful of Bob Boothby, for instance, that they deliberately excluded him from meetings. When Eden later wrote that his memory was that Boothby was a 'dubious character', Paul Emrys-Evans readily agreed, stating that Bob was 'far too unreliable in private conversation and in his public actions'.[27] Jack Macnamara also picked up from one of the friendlier whips that 'the powers that be' were obsessed with the Glamour Boys' activities. The group's very existence and the secrecy under which it operated rattled them. Joseph Ball and the whips were keeping very close tabs on them, watching their every move, listening to their phone calls and keeping dossiers on them. As Jack told Harold Nicolson,

'They know that we meet, and what they do not like is that we do not attack them in the House. If we came out into the open they would know where they stood. What they hate is this silent plotting.' As for the individual MPs, they respected the 'big bugs', Eden, Churchill and Cooper, and they patronisingly thought of Nicolson 'as an able man gone astray', but the people they really suspected were Ronnie Tree, Ronnie Cartland and Paul Emrys-Evans.[28]

Ronnie Tree felt the lash of the whips in May at a meeting of the East Midlands Imperial League. He had a perfectly pleasant chat with one of the assistant whips, Captain Charles Waterhouse, the MP for South Leicester, when he bumped into him on the railway platform at Leicester. But Waterhouse launched a vicious attack on Ronnie at the meeting. He and his friends, he said, were warmongers determined to make as much trouble for the PM as possible. Waterhouse then suddenly pulled out a motion declaring the meeting's full support for Chamberlain in an obvious attempt to embarrass his colleague. Ronnie saw off the ambush with ease, as Waterhouse's motion was almost unanimously rejected and the captain left the room 'very angry and red in the face'. A few days later Waterhouse approached Tree in the Commons and made a half-hearted apology, but Ronnie wrote in his memoirs, 'I was incensed, and told him what I thought of him in no uncertain terms.' He added, 'My only reason for recounting this faraway incident is to show how bitter were the feelings and divisions in the country – indeed in the Conservative party – as we edged closer and closer to war.'[29]

Despite the dirty tricks being waged against them, the Glamour Boys felt they were achieving something. Leo Amery wrote to Boothby in June, 'One sometimes feels weary of playing the Cassandra part, but in the present issue it does look at least as if our warnings have borne fruit. Possibly even in time.'[30] Although the rebels were as one on the need to defy Hitler, they were far less united on parliamentary tactics. Harold Macmillan thought that Eden and his supporters were too soft and gentlemanlike. He hated the fact that the Tories were so sycophantic. 'If Chamberlain says that black is white,' he claimed, 'the Tories applaud his brilliance. If a week later he says that black is after all black, they applaud his realism. Never has there been such servility.' For that reason alone, so he told Harold Nicolson, they should have been clamouring for Chamberlain's removal. After all, 'no man in history has made such persistent and bone-headed mistakes'.[31]

Boothby was angry that the group was too mealy-mouthed. He wrote a scorching letter to this effect to Nicolson who sent a disarming reply. 'I have slipped out of gear in the House of Commons,' he confessed.

> The real fact is that old queens like myself are capable of hysterical heroism but are not good at the constant fight. I lack (as do many of my kind – those of what we might call a literary temperament) a lust for battle. We have no combative qualities.

The one point where he took issue with Bob was his charge of insincerity.

> You do not accuse me of that but you imply it. The real accusation would be that, having discovered that by being sincere I expose myself to awkward situations in my own constituency, I keep silent and cover up my silence by a rather silly pose of aloofness.

He signed his self-effacing note, 'Bless you Bob.'[32]

Philip Sassoon had been absent from these debates for weeks. The press reported on 19 April that he was suffering from influenza and had been advised by his doctor to cancel his engagements for a least a fortnight.[33] A month later the news was that he was still confined to bed 'with a high temperature' at his Park Lane residence[34] and on the morning of Saturday 3 June he died. He was just fifty and the newspapers reported that he was a bachelor who died without an heir to his baronetcy or his estate. Some added that he was 'reputed to be "the foremost Jew in society"'.[35] A friend, the local Baptist minister John Charles Carlile, wrote that Philip was lonely and 'recent events deepened his sadness, his sensitive spirit was hurt, bruised and wounded'.[36] Chips Channon recorded 'what a loss to the London pageant. No one infused it with so much colour and personality.'[37] Philip's cremation was held quickly and privately at Golders Green, and the following Monday 601 Squadron circled, dipped and roared over Trent Park while his ashes were scattered from a Lipton's tea box. All the press noted that he was one of the country's richest MPs, and had left just short of £2 million, but there was a poetic irony in the subsequent by-election, as St John 'Jack' Philby, Kim's father, who was a pronounced anti-Zionist who admired Hitler, stood as the first parliamentary candidate for the pro-Fascist British People's Party on a platform that he wanted to 'give the inarticulate supporters of Peace an opportunity of expressing their strength'[38] and to show that they emphatically 'disapprove of European alliances and war commitments'.[39] Philip would have been delighted that Philby got just 576 votes and lost his deposit.

When summer came it felt as if the nation was back in denial. As Ronnie Tree put it, 'the summer of 1939 was, by all standards, a very gay one. There were a great many balls, there was much entertaining and many foreigners were in London.'[40] One day he hosted a lunch for the German General of the General Staff, Count von Schwerin, and asked 'a group of the toughest-minded MPs I could muster to meet him, among them Ronnie Cartland and Jack Macnamara'.[41] The next he was at a grand ball thrown by Lord and Lady Ilchester at their magnificent residence, Holland House, which was floodlit for the occasion. The king and queen were the guests of honour and Rob Bernays attended in court dress after a dinner party in Regent's Park.* The grandest ball

---

* The Ilchesters set up a broadcasting system for summoning chauffeurs when guests were ready to leave, but when it broke down cars had to pass the front door on a continuous loop in the hope that their owner would be ready. Rob Bernays was not reunited with his chauffeur till 2.15 in the morning.

of the season, though, was given by the Duke and Duchess of Marlborough for their eldest daughter Sarah's coming-out on Friday 7 July. No expense was spared for the 17-year-old. The *People* claimed that it would be 'the biggest party ever' with more than a thousand guests and that an aerodrome had been hired for guests arriving in their own aeroplanes.[42] Ambrose and his band played in the ballroom and Don Carlos and his Strolling Players wandered the grounds in Tyrolean costumes. Ronnie and Nancy Tree hosted a dinner party beforehand and attended with Eden and Churchill. Ronnie wrote, 'The house and gardens at Blenheim, floodlit down to the lake, looked lovely and we all danced until the dawn came up over the trees. It was the last of the great parties to be given before the war.'[43] The only hiccup was that even though a hundred police officers were deployed in evening dress, thieves stole seventeen of the finest coats, capes and furs while their owners partied.

That summer Harold Nicolson became closer than ever to Jack Macnamara. Jack's situation had changed considerably. In 1938 he moved into another grand house, 25 Palace Street in Westminster, probably also at Herbert's expense, but at some point that year Paddy Kennedy left him to marry Ivy and to run the Star Tavern behind Belgrave Square also. Jack's stepfather had died in the summer of 1938 and Jack had bought a house for his mother in Little Waltham near Chelmsford called Windmills, which he renamed Justice Wood in memory of the farm he had shared with Paddy. As commanding officer of the London Irish Rifles, Jack now devoted much of his time to preparing the regiment for what he presumed would soon be active service on the Continent but that still allowed him time to buy a yacht that spring and to join Harold on his yacht, the *Mar*. The two men met up in Dover very early in the morning of 29 May and spent the day strolling round the town before dinner at the Lords Warden and taking in a 'rather good … movie about the Navy and spies and things'. As they tumbled into bed on the *Mar*, Harold concluded that Jack was 'a good companion', an impression confirmed the next day as they sailed to Boulogne, took a taxi to Étaples, sipped vermouth and cassis by the beach and enjoyed 'a truly marvellous dinner'. Once they had clambered back in the dark, the *Mar* was 'all quiet and peaceful inside' and Harold wistfully noted it was 'the end of a lovely day'.[44] Foul weather prevented them from sailing to Le Havre the next day, so Jack took the train to Paris and back home. The short holiday had been intimate and five weeks later Harold and Jack were back messing about on boats, although another bout of bad weather meant that Jack failed to get his boat up the Solent and had to drive from Bursledon to find Harold in Lymington Harbour. This time Jack had intended to meet up with nine men from the signalling section of the London Irish Rifles, but when he and Harold found them drenched to the skin, Jack insisted that seven of them come back to his boat, and two joined Harold on the *Mar*. The next day they all joined up and drove back to London – the men singing in an army lorry all the way and Jack and Harold following in Jack's staff car. From the genial way Harold wrote all this up in his diary it is clear that he had taken a shine to the younger man. Harold, who was now fifty-two, claimed, 'Why I like young men is not really that I am homosexual but that I have a passion for my own youth.'[45]

The first half of 1939 felt like politics was in the doldrums. Everyone feared war, but nobody dared make a first move, so Britain hovered between action and inaction. Only the Glamour Boys readied themselves for what they thought was both inevitable and necessary – a wholesale confrontation with Nazism.

17

At War With Germany

Neville Chamberlain found Parliament an inconvenience and admitted that he salivated at the idea of suspending it for a couple of years when he was told that his French counterpart was contemplating doing the same. The parliamentary summer recess, though, was a well-established tradition. In 1938 it had run from 29 July to 28 September and in 1937 from 30 July to 21 October, giving the government two hassle-free months every year. The only problem was that he had to get the Commons to agree. That meant tabling a motion that could be amended and voted on.[1] So on 2 August Chamberlain opened the debate on a motion to adjourn the Commons until Tuesday 3 October. This was normally a formality. Nobody had seriously opposed a recess motion for years. But the Glamour Boys were not happy. After all, the previous year had seen Hitler take advantage of the summer months to provoke the crisis in Czechoslovakia and now Hitler was demanding that Danzig, which had been made a semi-autonomous 'free city' by the Treaty of Versailles, be restored to Germany, along with road and railway access via a corridor of Polish land. It was true that Chamberlain had unexpectedly issued a British guarantee of the territorial integrity of Poland in March, but the rebels did not trust him. He had betrayed Czechoslovakia – what was to prevent him doing the same to Poland? After all, Commander Bower had overheard two Tories on the bench behind him during a debate in early May. When one said, 'I suppose we *shall* be able to get out of this beastly guarantee business?' the other had replied, 'Oh, of course. Thank God we have Neville.'[2] So when the group met at Ronnie Tree's house on 19 July they feared 'another Munich over Danzig' with Chamberlain portraying himself as the 'Great Appeaser' and stigmatising them as 'war-mongers'.[3] Harold Nicolson felt strongly that the House should not adjourn for the whole of two months. Labour had tabled an amendment, which was supported by the opposition Liberals, bringing the return of Parliament forward to Monday 21 August. That seemed far more sensible – but to support an Opposition motion was to court anger in the party again. Eden thought they should toe the party line, but when Churchill refused to do so, the group resolved yet again on abstaining.

Conscious that trust was in short supply, Chamberlain offered a minor concession to his critics, as his recess motion provided for an early recall of Parliament if the government deemed it necessary. His opening speech was humdrum, though. He barely mentioned Germany or Poland. He suggested that he knew MPs would criticise him for trying to avoid 'interrogation by the House'.[4] The Glamour Boys decided to pile in and several of them took advantage of the convention that House matters such as recess dates were not considered subject to party discipline, so MPs could vote with their conscience. Churchill said he would 'regret' it if members were to agree to scatter themselves to the winds till October, but made it clear that this was not for him a matter of trust in the prime minister. Sir Derrick Gunston expressly made the point that this was not a party matter, but a national one. Vyvyan Adams sarcastically thanked the whips for not putting a mandatory three-line whip on the vote. Dick Law tried to quash the rumours in the press that anyone who wanted to limit the prime minister's power to adjourn Parliament was plotting against him. Leo Amery pointed out that 'we are in a state of what is, if not declared war, very near war. Every day some act of aggression is being committed in Danzig which might at any moment precipitate a struggle.'[5]

At 7.10 p.m., presuming that the House was 'probably prepared to come to a decision' after three hours of debate, Chamberlain spoke again. This time the control freak in him came to the fore. Members had claimed there was no three-line whip, but that did not mean that members who were 'supposed' to support the government would be free to take any line they liked. Besides, since the Opposition had made it clear that the root of the matter was their distrust of the government, it was irrelevant whether there was a three-line whip. 'A vote against the Government on this occasion must', he declared, 'be a vote of want of confidence.' As if suddenly changing the terms of the debate was not enough to rile his critics, he went on the offensive. Many of the speeches he had heard had given him the impression that his critics were 'very badly in need of a holiday [as] their reasoning faculties wanted a little freshening up'. It was bad form. It reminded the Glamour Boys of the way Eden had been treated. Ronnie and Jack shook their heads. But Chamberlain ploughed on, ending his twenty-seven minutes with a sharp dig. The amendment was nothing but a vote of no confidence. 'And I confidently expect my honourable Friends to defeat it,' he ended, as if to make clear that anyone who voted the other way was neither honourable nor a friend.

Chamberlain's attempt to curtail the debate failed. He had expected an immediate vote, but Geoffrey Mander, a passionate anti-appeaser who was PPS to the Liberal leader Archie Sinclair, immediately lambasted Chamberlain. The prime minister had just missed one of the greatest opportunities of his career, he claimed, as he had made a narrow, bitter, partisan speech, which 'shows him to be … the greatest single obstacle to unity in this country'.[6] During Mander's speech the Glamour Boys left the Chamber and gathered in the Members' Lobby. Ronnie Cartland was especially disconsolate. For some months he had been arguing that it was a terrible indictment on Parliament that 'policy is so closely bound up with personality'.[7] Yet Chamberlain's intervention had deliberately bound the two together. He found Chamberlain's attitude towards the Labour Party partisan and undignified. Neville could afford to be generous, and as prime minister he should be in a position, should the need arise, to call for unity and get it. But by continually rubbing salt in the wound he so infuriated the Opposition that they would never support him 'even if the Germans were landing in Dover!'[8] Yet now, at a vital moment in the destiny of Europe, Chamberlain had indulged all his worst habits. It was enough to make Ronnie despair. As the others continued discussing what to do, he went to the toilet, just as Vyvyan Adams came rushing out of the Chamber. Adams grabbed Nicolson and told him, 'You must speak at once, the thing is blowing up for a real gale.' Harold had promised not to speak, though, and told him so. 'We must get Ronnie Cartland,' said Adams, and when Nicolson told him where to find him, Adams dashed into the toilets, where Ronnie had had a few moments alone with Churchill.[9] 'Well,' Ronnie had said, 'we can do no more.' Churchill was not impressed. 'Do no more, my boy?' he echoed. 'There is a lot more we can do. This is just the time to fight – to speak – to attack!'[10]

With that advice, Ronnie turned on his heels and went back into the Chamber, determined to speak his mind, even though he had not prepared a speech. Moments later, with loyalists expecting a vote any moment and the dinner hour almost upon them, Ronnie was called. He felt he had to apologise for detaining the House, but there was a glint in his eye. He was not going to be silenced, however much the whips glowered at him. At first he seemed to agree with Chamberlain. The Opposition had shown that they had no confidence in the government. This provoked heckles from both sides of the House. But, he pointed out, the Opposition had every right to have no confidence in the government. The point was, though, that all the Conservatives who had spoken for a shorter recess had put forward a completely different argument. They expressly did *not* see this as a matter of confidence. He then turned directly to Chamberlain's second speech, which, he confessed, had 'profoundly disturbed' him. As things stood, MPs were going to part until 3 October. The majority would be going to their constituencies, where he warned they would find that there was a common impression that the prime minister had 'ideas of dictatorship'. It was a deliberately inflammatory phrase. Ronnie mitigated it by saying twice that this was 'a fantastic and ludicrous impression', but it provoked fury. Members shouted 'nonsense' at him and his neighbour Sir Patrick Hannon tried to interrupt him. He persisted. He had addressed dozens of meetings over the last year and time and again he had had to dissuade people of the 'ludicrous' impression that Chamberlain had ideas of dictatorship. The problem now was that Chamberlain's 'absolute refusal to accept any of the proposals put forward by members on both sides of the House will make it much more difficult for those of us to try and dispel that idea'. The whips and their allies were furious. But challenged again by Hannon, Ronnie repeated his allegation and added that he had received a letter from a Conservative-voting constituent who said she was very upset because 'so many people think the Prime Minister is a friend of Hitler'. Yet again the House was in uproar, but Ronnie pointed out that the prime minister only had to ask his chief whip (he called him the 'Patronage Secretary') and he could get anything he wanted through the Commons. It was a mystery to him that Chamberlain refused to defend democracy and resist aggression.

His mind turned to the last month, which he had spent in training with the Royal Artillery. Thus far nerves had made him speak louder than usual. His sister Barbara thought it was as if the loudspeaker was on full volume. But for a moment he spoke more softly and there was a catch in his voice. 'We are in the situation,' he said, 'that within a month we may be going to fight, and we may be going to die.' This brought a sarcastic laugh from Hannon.* Ronnie was not to be put off, though. He turned on Hannon with a flame of indignation and said with all the energy he could muster,

---

* *Hansard* suggests members said, 'Oh', but Nicolson reported Hannon laughing.

It is all very well for hon. Gentlemen to laugh. There are thousands of young men at the moment in training in camps, and giving up their holiday, and the least that we can do here, if we are not going to meet together from time to time and keep Parliament in session, is to show that we have immense faith in this democratic institution.

It was a bit pious, but it silenced his detractors. He ended on a sad rebuke to his colleagues. 'I frankly say that I despair when I listen to speeches like that to which I have listened this afternoon.'

His speech was just twelve minutes long, but it hit home. Churchill thumped him on the back and said, 'Well done, my boy, well done!' Nancy Astor shouted, 'The spirit will out.' But when Ronnie had left the Chamber, Hannnon made a nasty speech claiming that since he was partly responsible for getting Ronnie his seat, he wanted to apologise to the House for the poisonous speech Ronnie had delivered. When pressed by other MPs, Hannon restated his line. 'I want to make clear,' he said, 'my regret and disappointment that I had anything to do with his selection as a Member of Parliament.' Tempers got even more fraught. The Glasgow Maryhill Labour MP J. J. Davidson accused Hannon of lying and was forced to apologise. An hour after Ronnie had spoken, John Morgan paid tribute to him for a speech

such as I do not expect to hear again in this House for some time. It was not the speech of a man who was stabbing his own party in the back … [but] the speech of a man who has consistently … tried to gather together all the elements in this House … for the purpose of facing the situation which we have to face.[11]

In the end Ronnie was right, though. Chamberlain and the chief whip could drive anything they wanted through the Commons. Roughly forty Conservative MPs abstained, but the government won by 250 votes to 132.

Ronnie knew full well what he had done. He was kissing goodbye to any hope of promotion. When Sidney Campion of the *Star* had picked out eight MPs he thought might become famous that May, he had placed 'tall, slim, handsome bachelor Mr. Ronald Cartland' top of the list, predicting that he would be a future home or foreign secretary and commenting that 'his finely chiselled classical features and jet black hair brushed well back make him a striking figure'.[12] Others predicted great things for him. But although he knew this speech put paid to all that, he felt that above all 'I can't act a lie'.[13] The moment the vote was over he went to telephone Barbara and Polly to warn them that the newspapers might be grim reading over the next few days. In fact, things were even worse than he expected. Several of the Glamour Boys had been vocal in the debate, and the following day the *Evening Standard* ran the headline: 'Premier Calls for List of MPs Who Did Not Vote Last Night. They will all be blacklisted.' But it ominously added 'the indications are that they will not be disciplined beyond being remonstrated with by the Whips. I understand, however, that the case of Mr. Ronald Cartland is regarded as being different because of his criticism of the Prime Minister.'[14]

Harold Nicolson reported the following day that MPs were all still 'bubbling about last night' and that 'the whip point of view is that Ronnie Cartland has done himself in'.[15] Different lines from Ronnie's speech made it into the headlines of all the local and regional newspapers, many of which had large readerships and carried significant clout. For the *Leeds Mercury* it was accusing Chamberlain of being a 'Friend of Hitler', for the *Yorkshire Post* 'Ideas of Dictatorship'. The front page of the *Birmingham Gazette* the next day ran the headline 'Premier Attacked by Supporters' with photographs of Cartland and Hannon along with the words '"Pettifogging party speech" says Cartland'.[16] The paper claimed that Ronnie had been 'moved by emotion', 'profoundly disturbed' and 'labouring under some emotion' and predicted the repercussions of the debate would be felt in the constituencies. A few supporters wrote to the *Birmingham Mail* defending him. J. F. Bramley, for instance, said he preferred a member 'who does not cringe under the party whips' and described him as 'one of the few bright spots in that depressing spectacle of a huge Conservative majority'.[17] But within days there were calls for Ronnie to be hanged as a traitor, expelled from the party and removed from Parliament. A week later the *North Devon Journal* reported that twenty Tory MPs were trying to get Ronnie expelled and a supportive colleague wrote to say 'there will be an organised attempt by Government supporters to prove their own virtue by assailing yours'. Ronnie told Barbara, 'I regret nothing – I would say it all again to-morrow – I stand by everything I said.'[18] He knew a moment of reckoning might be coming in the King's Norton constituency, as the chairman wrote to tell him there would be a meeting to discuss the matter on 4 September.

Chamberlain was directly behind all this. He wrote from Chequers to his sister Ida, 'As for Master Cartland I hope he has effectually blotted his copybook in King's Norton and I am taking steps to stimulate local opposition.' Claiming that Ronnie had always been 'a disloyal member of the team', he was infuriated by the personal attack. He thought the Party might lose the seat if Ronnie was ousted, but added, 'I would rather do that (temporarily) than have a traitor in the camp.'[19] Not that Ronnie cared. Immediately after the debate Rob Bernays had told Nicolson that Ronnie 'has ruined his chances with the Party but he has made his Parliamentary reputation'.[20] Ronnie would have settled for that.

Life carried on for others, of course, with its highs and lows. Harry Crookshank had resented what he called the 'v. acrimonious debate', as it went on so long that he missed the party Victor Cazalet hosted for his sister Thelma, who made history the next day by being the first woman MP to marry in the crypt chapel at Westminster. Bob Boothby had written her a sarcastic letter from the French House the moment he heard of her engagement. 'Normally,' he wrote, 'I hesitate to congratulate anyone in getting engaged to be married, holding as I do somewhat jaundiced views about the whole business.'

Nevertheless, he ended, 'as a cynical and embittered mysogenist [sic], I send my warmest congratulations'.[21] The press suggested that the wedding was a quiet affair out of deference to the national mood, but the king and queen gave a china dessert service, the MP for Anglesey, Megan Lloyd George, acted as Thelma's bridesmaid, the colonial secretary, Malcolm MacDonald, was her groom David Keir's best man and Chamberlain, Margesson and Lloyd George attended. Crookshank noted in his diary that 'all the greats were there', as both best man and best girl were prime ministerial children 'and Neville there too'.[22] The couple decided to honeymoon in Britain rather than on the Continent, but a few days later a very relaxed Victor was filmed playing cricket at Shipbourne before travelling to Deauville, where he played in a two-day parliamentary tennis tournament against France until heavy rain ended play.

As for Ronnie, he spent a couple of days at his mother's Worcestershire home, and welcomed Viscount Carlow and his wife, who were visiting for the Malvern Festival. He took part in another week of army training at Burley Manor, joined Barbara and her children for a holiday at Caister-on-Sea, and toyed with another trip, this time to Swanlake Bay with his childhood friend from Pershore and frequent travelling companion, the unmarried aristocratic farmer Marcus Stapleton-Martin. But on Tuesday 22 August Hitler signed a Non-Aggression Pact with Russia. It confirmed Ronnie Tree's worst fears and Victor thought history would look on Hitler's volte-face 'as the most remarkable travesty of international decency ever committed'.[23] Two days later Parliament was summoned. The recess debate had been utterly futile.

The recall brought MPs back from all over the country. Chamberlain moaned that he had been dragged back from fly-fishing in the far north of Scotland, where he was staying at the remote fifteen-bedroom Lochmore Lodge. Ronnie Cartland had been bathing in the sea at Caister, Ronnie Tree had been sailing on the Isle of Wight, where he had taken a house for the month, and Harold returned from sailing the *Mar* off the north coast of Scotland. Victor motored up from Kent, Harry Crookshank returned from Gainsborough, where he had been sunbathing on the roof, and when Jack Macnamara left the London Irish Rifles at Burley at the crack of dawn and arrived in London before breakfast, he went straight to Brigade Headquarters to be given new orders to prepare the company to mobilise.

According to Jack, the mood was less hysterical when the House gathered at 2.45 that afternoon than it had been during the Munich crisis, 'when it displayed such uncreditable mass relief because we had bought peace with dishonour. This time it was grim, steely.'[24] Ronnie Cartland thought the 500 MPs were 'more silent than usual, more serious, but without any sign of fear'. After weeks in the open air he found the Chamber 'almost unbearably stuffy' and the whole scene unreal. Everything was out of kilter. 'The words one listened to did not register, as one's thoughts did, the horrors of war. The speeches seemed out of focus to the picture one's imagination so easily, so terribly conjured up.'[25] Crookshank noted that Cartland had effectively been vindicated. 'I always said it was likely we would meet this week,' he wrote.[26]

The session started funereally, as the Speaker announced the death of another of the Glamour Boys, Anthony Crossley, in a plane crash. Chamberlain, who looked extremely grave, announced the government's intention to take an Emergency Powers Bill through Parliament that day and proceeded to tell the House that 'the international position has steadily deteriorated until to-day we find ourselves confronted with the imminent peril of war'.[27] Following the escalation of enmities between Germany and Poland, Britain had been forced to notify Hitler that the Cabinet was resolved to employ all the forces at its command. 'This issue of peace or war does not rest with us,' he asserted, 'and I trust that those with whom the responsibility does lie will think of the millions of human beings whose fate depends upon their actions.'[28] For once he called for unity, in the nation and in the House, and he got it. The rebels bit their tongues and offered not a word of criticism as they trooped through the Aye Lobby for the new laws. Only four MPs – all Labour – voted against the new measures; 427 voted for. Not everyone was convinced, though. Captain Archibald Ramsay, who had formed the Right Club earlier in the year expressly 'to oppose and expose the activities of organised Jewry', was a notable absentee.

Sitting in the smoking room afterwards with Churchill and Lloyd George, Victor Cazalet reckoned that Chamberlain's speech had been 'good but not very impressive'. The guarantee to Poland was all very well – but it meant little without bringing the Russians on board. Other Conservatives were more sanguine, though. When Ronnie Tree was having dinner in the Members' Dining Room with his fellow insurgents, he was astonished that a member he did not know leaned across and interrupted them with a categorical assertion that there would be no war. Ronnie later wrote, 'When I asked him how he had obtained his information, he announced that Hitler had told him so in Berlin a week before!'[29]

That was not how things looked in Germany. Gottfried von Cramm wrote to Victor the following Monday. He had been released from prison after six months and had visited Victor at Great Swifts in June with 'a young cousin' and the two men had played a match on the new court with Victor and Anthony Eden. It had all been very enjoyable. Baffy Dugdale described the Germans as 'two of the most charming young men, and violent anti-Nazis'[30] and Bob Boothby and the Belgian and Romanian ambassadors joined them for lunch. Five days later Gottfried gave 'one of the finest exhibitions of his career'[31] beating Bobby Riggs 6–0, 6–1 in the men's singles semi-finals at Queen's Club and the following day he won the finals, producing 'winning shots whenever he wanted them'.[32] Many expected him to go on to win Wimbledon, but the German Lawn Tennis Federation had refused to enter him, unusually preferring the Jewish player Danny Prenn (who was already exiled in Britain) to a convicted homosexual. Wimbledon's officials did not encourage him to apply in an individual capacity, probably due to his conviction for 'moral turpitude', but he was such a gentleman that he refused to make a fuss. That same sense of honour remained with Gottfried as he wrote to Victor from his hotel room in Budapest. Since this might be the last time he could write, he wanted to thank Victor for all his help, especially with securing Manfred's safe passage to Palestine. Victor had been a wonderful friend, but he was now going back to Germany, as he thought it was wrong for him to play tennis in safety overseas while his six brothers could be called up at any moment. 'I loathe war and pray for peace,' he wrote. 'But if the catastrophe comes I must not be where the cowards are.' He ended with a bleak line that reflected how many people felt: 'God has turned away his face from Europe.'[33]

On Thursday 31 August the government decided to evacuate roughly 3 million women and children from areas like Rochester, Chatham and Southwark, which were reckoned to be most at risk of an air attack. War suddenly became very real for Jack, who heard the order to mobilise the army, including all territorial units, which were now fully incorporated into the general army, when it was broadcast on the radio at four o'clock that afternoon. Immediately he felt a sense of purpose. His recruiting work had been so successful that the London Irish Rifles had completed its second line, so Jack was now the commanding officer of the 1st Battalion, which formed part of the 1st London Infantry Brigade within the 1st London Infantry Division. He had imbued them with a new fighting spirit thanks to an assiduous training schedule. As one newspaper noted during a training exercise in Burley in August:

> There are no troops in the British Army of more striking appearance that the London Irish Rifles. Their distinctive headgear, the 'Caubeen', with its green hackle or plume, is most picturesque, while their pipers, in Irish kilts and cloaks, have the most romantic air that any maiden could desire.

Thanks to Jack's comprehensive regime, their physique and their military bearing gave the lie to the belief that they were 'too beautiful to be true soldiers'.[34]

The division had been tasked with assisting the Metropolitan Police during air raids, and Jack's battalion was to be based at Brixton police station. So when the mobilisation order came, Jack leapt into action and there was little need to send out summonses, as 'men in uniform started coming in almost at once. They passed the doctor, signed various forms and drew their arms and ammunition.' Every half an hour a batch marched off from the Duke of York's Barracks in Chelsea to take up their new duties in south London, as the regimental band played the Irish ballads 'The Wearing of the Green' and 'Minstrel Boy' and the crowd applauded.

There was almost a carnival air to these military preparations, but that evening the BBC broadcast, without comment, Hitler's sixteen-point demands on Poland. That night the Nazi Gauleiter in charge of Danzig announced the city's incorporation into the Third Reich and, as Jack put it, 'Germany invaded Poland in the early hours of the morning, after announcing that the "peace" terms she had offered Poland had been ignored.'[35]

Duff Cooper had just finished a particularly bad round of golf at Goodwood when the club secretary told him that 'Hitler started on Poland this morning'. Back in London he enjoyed a fine luncheon of lobster and cold grouse washed down with Montrachet 1924 and Château Yquem 1921 before making his way to Parliament.[36] Likewise, Harold Nicolson was sitting out in a deckchair in the sun in the garden at Sissinghurst when he heard the news. He had deliberately planted himself near the phone, but at 10.45 Vita came out to tell him 'it has begun'. It was the same in Worcestershire, where Ronnie Cartland was staying with Polly. Just after breakfast she came to tell him that she had heard on the radio that Germany had invaded Poland and that Parliament was to be summoned for six o'clock that evening. From different ends of the country Harold and Ronnie jumped into their cars and drove to London. On the way up, Harold saw yet more symbols of the imminence of war and possible invasion or aerial bombardment: schoolboys filling sandbags, soldiers in khaki uniforms and a row of silver barrage balloons hanging over London.

Anxious crowds gathered in Whitehall and around Parliament throughout the afternoon, but with all the activity setting up his new battalion headquarters, settling his four companies in and requisitioning the Avondale Dance Hall in Landor Road for A Company, Jack was so busy that he only had time to glance in to Parliament, which he noted was for the first time heavily sandbagged in preparation for the air raids that everyone expected at any minute. Regulations had been issued stipulating that all homes, offices and public buildings should operate a strict blackout from that night on, and blinds had been fitted on some of the thousands of windows in the Palace of Westminster, but where that was not practical light bulbs had been removed or replaced with low-wattage bulbs, which cast an eerie blue glow. The effect was such that when Harold arrived at the Commons at 5.30 he reckoned that the lobby was 'extremely dark, and the Chamber, which generally seems like a dim aquarium, appear[ed] quite garish in comparison'.[37]

The session began at six o'clock. The Chamber was rammed, hot and tense as a long order of business was read out. There were half-hearted cheers when Chamberlain arrived, accompanied by Arthur Greenwood, deputy leader of the Labour Party, who was standing in for Clement Attlee. A few people waved their order papers but sat down feeling a little silly, realising that with the Polish ambassador sitting in the gallery, this was not really the moment for triumphalism. There were splashes of khaki among the dark suits of members. Jack had come straight from Brixton in uniform. Horace Trevor-Cox and Somerset Maxwell wore the uniforms of the Welsh Guards and the Middlesex Yeomanry and Robert Grant-Ferris was in air-force blue.[38]

The prime minister started by admitting that he did not have much to say. But anyway, he pointed out, the time had come when action was needed rather than words. Ronnie Cartland, Harold Nicolson and Ronnie Tree nodded. It felt as if Chamberlain had finally seized the enormity of the situation. Yet even at this stage he seemed to prevaricate. When he told the House that he had issued an ultimatum to the German government demanding 'satisfactory assurances that the German Government have suspended all aggressive action against Poland and are prepared promptly to withdraw their forces from Polish territory', members heckled him about a time limit.[39] Some newspapers reported that Chamberlain's voice rang with a strong note of resolution, but to Jack, Ronnie and the other rebels it was as if he was offering Germany yet another get-out clause. He had said this was a time for action, but all he had offered was yet more words. Jack was already furious that the government had delayed the evacuation of children for far too long, but he was now incandescent that it was still delaying the declaration of war. If Britain carried on like this, he argued, 'the Poles and others will lose confidence in us'.[40] Greenwood's response for the Opposition was far more effective. He did not use the word 'war', but he stated that the die was cast and he complained that Chamberlain had appeared to allow Hitler a loophole. 'There is in the human spirit,' he said, 'something which may be tortured and which may be temporarily suppressed but which can never be destroyed, and that is its determination to keep alive and keep fully aflame the lamp of liberty.' He ended, 'However great the suffering, however poignant the agony and whatever the sacrifice may be, I know in my heart that freedom and mankind's hope for the future cannot be quenched. I know that liberty will prevail.'[41] Yet even Greenwood's words could not obscure the fact that Chamberlain had not yet truly committed Britain – and for the rebels that spelt dishonour. Members hung around the House for a while but soon melted away to their clubs. Churchill and Duff and Diana Cooper went to the Savoy Grill, where they agreed that Britain must declare war the next day – and were given a lift home in the Rolls-Royce of the Duke of Westminster, who complained that the Savoy was full of Jews. Nicolson dined at the Beefsteak and then went to Ronnie Tree's, where he and Harold Macmillan awaited Eden, who had been with the prime minister. At 2 a.m. Ronnie Cartland rang his mother to say that war was now inevitable, even if the prime minister did not yet recognise it, and packed his bags to join his battery at King's Heath exactly a month after he had issued his chilling prophesy to the Commons.

The House gathered again the next day, Saturday 2 September, at 2.45 in the afternoon. It was another hot, sticky day – the kind of day when the Palace of Westminster feels like a fuggy, airless prison and everyone prays for a thunderstorm. Rob Bernays noted 'an unwonted stillness on the packed benches'.[42] Normally the House would feel restless and irritable when it gathered for a great controversial issue, 'but that afternoon, all were united and the quiet was that of a cathedral'.[43] Everyone was expecting Chamberlain to make a new announcement. But silence gave way to grumpy exasperation as Sir John Simon told the House that it was going to proceed with emergency legislation first. So one by one the war measures were considered. As each was agreed, members expected the prime minister to appear, but the clerk of the House popped up to read out yet another measure. Members sat about in the tea room or the smoking room, they watched the news from Poland as it poured out of the ticker-tape machine, they moaned about being kept waiting, they smoked and they drank heavily. When it was rumoured that Chamberlain was on his way, they made their way to the Chamber, only to be told that there would be another delay. Just after 6.20 the Speaker adjourned the House and said the bells would ring when the prime minister was ready. Frustrated, members returned to their gossiping and drinking. Above all, they kept on asking themselves, when was the declaration of war coming? What did the delay mean? Had Mussolini or America come up with a new proposal? Had the French caved in already?

Rob Bernays was so concerned at this last rumour that he sauntered out onto the Terrace to get some air. When Jim Thomas appeared the two of them decided to help the workmen laying sandbags 'for want of something better to do'. They joked that they might spend the whole night laying bags, but finally came news that Chamberlain would address the House at 7.30 and the division bells started ringing, so Rob and Jim joined the throng of members as they trooped in and took their seats in the overheated Chamber. Twelve minutes later Chamberlain and Greenwood appeared. Expectations were even higher this time. This must surely be the moment when the PM would admit that appeasement was dead, that there could be no more postponements and that Britain was at war. Nicolson thought it felt like a court waiting for a verdict, and that when Chamberlain spoke he 'betray[ed] some emotion as if he were sickening for a cold'.[44]

When he started, though, MPs could hardly believe what they were hearing. Chamberlain still put no time limit on his ultimatum, and he limited his speech to just four vacuous minutes. Bernays described it as 'one of the most painful scenes the House can ever have witnessed'[45] as Chamberlain seemed to be making excuses for the delay and even referred to yet another Italian proposal for a meeting of France, Britain, Germany, Poland and Italy. The Glamour Boys feared another Munich and even Crookshank reckoned it left the House aghast because 'it was very badly worded & the obvious inference was vacillation or dirty work'.[46] Dusk was descending when Chamberlain sat down in what Bernays called 'deathly silence', followed by murmurs of barely suppressed anger. Two of Chamberlain's closest allies stumbled along the benches to be sick in the lavatory.[47] The eerie pall of the blue bulbs accentuated the gloom. Jack Macnamara and Harold Nicolson wondered whether anyone would challenge Chamberlain. Churchill perhaps? Or Eden? But when it became clear that the only other people to speak that evening would be the leaders of the two main opposition parties, they felt everything depended on what Arthur Greenwood would say.

Greenwood stood up and leaned, tall and lanky, against the despatch box. As usual, Labour MPs roared their support for their deputy leader – but suddenly there was a second wave of approval, from the government benches. One booming voice could be heard through the din, although nobody could agree who it was or what he said. Either Boothby shouted, '*You* speak for Britain,' or Amery begged, 'Speak for England,' as Greenwood, who was normally an indifferent speaker, arranged his notes. As Bernays put it, 'the cry was taken up and the Chamber rang with "Speak for England, speak for England"'. The words cut like a whiplash. Bernays thought Chamberlain was staggered by his reception and that senior ministers looked like men in the dock. Nicolson agreed, 'It was an astonishing demonstration. Greenwood almost staggered with surprise.'[48] Greenwood blinked for a moment, waited till the shouts died down and admitted that he was a bit flummoxed. He had been expecting to welcome the government's declaration of war – but it had not come. Unlike the day before, he had no prepared speech. He was reduced to saying, 'I am speaking under very difficult circumstances. I have had no opportunity to think about what I should say; and I speak what is in my heart at this moment.'[49] Devoid of rhetorical flourish, the central point of his eight-minute speech was simple, though: 'An act of aggression took place 38 hours ago. The moment that act of aggression took place one of the most important treaties of modern times automatically came into operation.' The implication was clear. There was a brief altercation when the pacifist Independent Labour Party MP for Glasgow Shettleston, John McGovern, shouted at Greenwood, 'You people do not intend to march – not one of you.' A furious Labour MP who was sitting on the other side of the gangway lashed out at him but only landed a punch on McGovern's arm. Greenwood carried on. 'Every minute's delay now means the loss of life, imperilling our national—' he said, only to be interrupted by Boothby, who shouted, 'Honour!' Greenwood stood his ground. 'Let me finish my sentence,' he said. 'I was about to say imperilling the very foundations of our national honour.' He turned to Chamberlain. Labour hoped that they would know the mind of the British government the next day, 'and that there shall be no more devices for dragging out what has been dragged out too long'.[50]

When he sat down the Chamber erupted again. This was the speech everyone had wanted to hear. Greenwood was resolute, determined and unflinching. His plain speaking matched the need of the moment and even the most loyal Chamberlain supporters started cheering at the top of their lungs, leaving the government front bench looking like 'they had been struck in the face'.[51]

The government was in danger. Chamberlain tried to pacify the House with another short speech, but when he had finished, half-a-dozen members rose to speak. A debate began between the pacifist Jimmy Maxton and the Conservative backbencher Sir John Wardlaw-Milne, but when Margesson saw the government was in danger of losing control of the House, he jumped up to move that 'this House do now adjourn'. The compliant Speaker took advantage of the dark to pretend he had not seen anyone else wishing to speak and before anyone knew what had happened the chair was empty and the debate closed at nine minutes past eight o'clock.

As the police shouted the traditional question 'Who goes home?' and the Speaker processed back to his residence, members stumbled out into the corridors and lobbies, which were so dark that 'a single lit match shone like a beacon',[52] and gathered in little knots in the 'dim ghostly glimmer of the new emergency lighting'.[53] The argument continued. Backbench rebels and junior ministers alike were fuming. As Jack put it 'we have sent what is virtually an ultimatum to Germany, but there is no time limit'. Yet again the prime minister appeared to have left a loophole. But there could be no get-out clause now. Britain was honour bound to Poland. The only explanation they could come up with was that France was ratting on Poland – and that meant disaster for Britain. Some members openly asked, 'Can we go on?' Others argued, 'We cannot fight Germany alone.' When others shouted, 'We cannot let Poland down,' it felt as though members were going to come to blows, and the doorkeepers started putting out the remaining lights in an attempt to send them home.

When they groped their way to the exits they found that the storm had burst 'with daemonic fury. Rain lashed the pavements and the roofs with the clatter of falling shrapnel.'[54] It was the second night of blackout but London was illuminated through the night by flashes of lightning. Nicolson reckoned that 'the PM must know by now that the whole House is against him', but what Harold did not know, as he set off to the Travellers Club for dinner with Gladwyn Jebb, was that immediately afterwards the Cabinet dragged a reluctant Chamberlain into Simon's room in the House and forced him to hold a Cabinet meeting there and then, and that Margesson, the chief whip, told Chamberlain in no uncertain terms that he would have to announce that he had declared war the next time the House sat – or face being removed from office. It was only when Harold bumped into a very unhappy Buck De La Warr that he discovered what had happened. He noted in his diary that as he left the club, 'The black-out is complete. I creep carefully. I foresee that once the habit of order leaves us, there will be a recrudescence of footpads and highway robbery.'[55]

The answer came in the morning newspapers. Chamberlain had sent a final note to the German government stating that, unless Britain received an undertaking from Germany by eleven o'clock in the morning on Sunday 3 September that they were prepared at once to withdraw their troops from Poland, a state of war would exist between the two countries. Churchill's closest friends, including Boothby, Cooper, Eden, Sandys and Bracken, had met in Winston's flat the night before, when they discussed whether Churchill should accept the seat Chamberlain now offered him in the Cabinet, and on the Sunday morning the Glamour Boys met at Ronnie Tree's house, where Eden told them that the Cabinet had been furious not to have seen an advance copy of Chamberlain's statement to the House. Unable to do or say anything constructive, they watched the clock tick down to eleven. Cranborne was too ill to attend, Ronnie Cartland was already with his battery and Jack Macnamara had processed to Brixton Parish Church at the head of his battalion with pipes and drums leading, but most of the leading Glamour Boys were there. They even allowed Boothby along this time, despite the friction between him and Harold Macmillan. Suddenly they realised that they didn't have a radio to listen to Chamberlain's broadcast at 11.15, but after scouring the house they discovered that the housemaid had one, which was brought down from the attic and set up in the drawing room just as Chamberlain said the fateful words: 'Consequently this country is at war with Germany.'

PART FOUR

Into Battle

18

Removing the 'Old Limpet'

The rebels were not the only ones to be pleased that Britain had finally taken the plunge. So too was Rob Bernays, who was attending his first war committee at the new Ministry of Supply when the chairman Colonel Llewellyn read out the news. 'The crisis was over,' he wrote. 'War had been declared. Indeed there was every reason to believe that it had already begun.'[1] Jack received a message to the same effect halfway through a church service. After breaking the news to the congregation, the vicar finished the service with special prayers for Divine guidance and protection in time of war, and the soldiers who had bowed their heads in silence formed up and marched back to their posts while Jack made his way to Parliament, where Chamberlain was due to make another speech.

The rebels at Ronnie Tree's house also made their way to the House. It was just a few hundred yards away, but as they set off, an air-raid siren started to wail. At first they refused to take it seriously. Leo Amery even complained that it was irresponsible to test the sirens like that when people had only just heard Britain was at war. But suddenly it dawned on them that this was real and they started running to the nearest shelter. When Edward Spears overtook them in his car, Amery, Nicolson and Eden piled in and ended up sitting on one another's laps as they careered through the crowds in Parliament Square and into New Palace Yard. A policeman ushered them to Parliament's newly improvised air-raid shelter where Cabinet ministers, backbenchers, doorkeepers, cleaners and chefs huddled together and waited for the enemy aircraft to appear.

The same air-raid warning disrupted Bernays's ministerial meeting and he admitted that he was really afraid for the first time since Munich. He had been closely involved in the hospital preparations for air-raid casualties, so he knew the Air Staff had increased its estimate of likely casualties every month and was now predicting up to 18,000 dead a day. So Rob was convinced that within months London would see 'the roar and swoop of the German bombs, the crash of falling masonry, the scream of carnage and confusion'. When the committee gathered in the shelter, a Cabinet minister turned to him. 'Is not this typical of the Germans?' he said. 'They must have sent off their bombers before the ultimatum expired.' Rob replied, 'I should not be surprised if this was the worst air raid of the whole war.' At that moment the all-clear was sounded. As Rob walked down Whitehall to the Commons he felt 'wholly irrationally that I had had my first taste of war, that I had been blooded and that I had somehow or other not betrayed the terror in my heart'.[2]

When the House convened, the atmosphere was completely different from the night before. Not only was there the feeling that Britain could now look the world in the face, but the false air raid had also given MPs a sense of relief that Britain had thrown down the challenge and the skies had not fallen in. If anything, Rob felt, 'something like gaiety had returned',[3] and when the sirens began again during prayers and Margesson asked his opposite number whether they wanted to adjourn, everyone shouted back 'carry on'. This time, even though Chamberlain's words were as self-pitying and lugubrious as his broadcast, he was cheered in full measure as he announced the declaration of war and the creation of a new nine-man War Cabinet, including Churchill as First Lord of the Admiralty. After some more emergency legislation the House adjourned at 4.36. As Boothby put it, 'Thus we tumbled into Armageddon without heart, without songs, without an ally except France (and she lukewarm), without sufficient aircraft, without tanks, without guns, without rifles, without even a reserve of essential raw commodities and feeding stuffs.'⁴

Ronnie Tree went to lunch with the Edens at their house in Fitzhardinge Street and then drove to Ditchley to prepare a wing of the house for a nursery school, which was being evacuated from the East End. Nicolson and Cazalet drove back to Kent together. The signs of war were everywhere. They passed dozens of army lorries and a few trucks evacuating refugees from the East End. Harold spotted an elderly woman in one of the trucks shaking her fist at them as they passed in their grand car and shouting that the war was all the fault of the rich. 'The Labour Party will be hard put to it to prevent this war degenerating into class warfare,' Harold wrote, and when he reached Sissinghurst, he found that the flag had been pulled down.⁵ Victor returned to his anti-aircraft battery and was soon frustrated. 'The W[ar] O[ffice] makes it very hard to get on with the job,' he wrote. 'We are told to do one thing one day, and it's invariably altered the next. We have had about four contradictory orders in the last week.'⁶

From the moment war was declared Ronnie Cartland was full-time with his regiment, the 53rd (Worcestershire and Oxfordshire Yeomanry) Anti-Tank Regiment of the Royal Artillery. It was a good fit. Two of the regiment's batteries were based at King's Heath, near Ronnie's constituency, his ninety-year-old great-uncle Major Howard Cartland had been in the regiment's predecessor, the Queen's Own Worcestershire Hussar Yeomanry, and in September 1939 his friend and colleague Anthony Muirhead became the new commanding officer. War gave training a new urgency. Within a fortnight Ronnie had started a course at the Small Arms School in Hythe. It hardly felt like war, though, being billeted in an expensive hotel at Folkestone and it gave him an opportunity to pop over to Sissinghurst for dinner with Harold Nicolson and his son Ben. Ben wrote in his diary that Ronnie arrived 'plus boyfriend',⁷ whom Harold named as Michael Shewell, a nineteen-year-old second lieutenant in the Oxfordshire and Buckinghamshire Light Infantry who was just out of Wellington College. Harold noted that Ronnie was 'brave but gloomy. He thinks they will all be killed for nothing.'[8] Ronnie had certainly grown impatient with the Royal Artillery's appalling lack of equipment and instructors. Back at King's Heath he was furious when nine supposedly new vehicles arrived and turned out to be so clapped-out they were fit for nothing but driving instruction, and he agreed with the regiment's first inspection that prospects 'could look considerably brighter'.[9] He was so infuriated that he wrote to Basil Liddell Hart, who was advising Hore-Belisha at the War Office, to complain that officer after officer had to explain to their instructors 'that they have never seen – nor heard – of the sort of training tackle which the training instructors were telling them to train their recruits with'. He was caustic about the Ministry of Information and hoped Liddell Hart might be able to get things moving in the High Command, but ended on an elegiac note by wishing him well 'before the clouds of war finally envelop us'.[10]

At dinner with Harold Nicolson, Rob Bernays, Sibyl Colefax and Guy Burgess at the Savoy Grill, Ronnie admitted that he was so angry about the shortage of ammunition in every branch that he would 'like to see Margesson [who was sitting at a nearby table] and Chamberlain hung upon lamp-posts' before catching a train back to Hythe.[11] He found Parliament equally frustrating. 'The general atmosphere in the House,' he wrote to his mother, 'would strike any visitor as almost Gilbertian for the Parliament of a nation at war – bombs will have to fall before the House appreciates the vast changes which itself and the Nation will have to undergo if we are to win.'[12] He grew ever more fatalistic. He told the *Birmingham Post*'s parliamentary correspondent that he did not expect ever to return; he surrendered the lease at Albany Chambers, sent his furniture into storage and wrote to his secretary that his old life was over. 'Don't think I'm not happy,' he urged her, before adding, 'I'm a soldier now – it doesn't do to think. That indeed is fatal. So I train and instruct and, I hope, inspire.' He claimed to be fairly content, but he knew that this was not really his life. 'As you know, I'm not exactly sociable and even an Officer's Mess makes me long for solitude – or the companionship of a few chosen friends.'[13]

In October came a sudden shock. The regiment had been training at the Royal School of Artillery at Larkhill when he heard the news. The initial details were patchy, but the press reported that Colonel Muirhead had returned home to Haseley just before dinner on Saturday when he told his butler of sixteen years' standing, A. W. Bondfield, that he would go to Winchester the next day, so he was to lay out his civilian clothes and prepare lunch for 12.30. Bondfield told the coroner that when he came to bring Muirhead his tea at eight the next morning he could see the top of his head on the pillow, but thinking he was still asleep, he left the room, to return at 9.15 when he discovered that the colonel was lying in a pool of blood. He summoned Muirhead's doctor, Dr E. C. Cooke, who pronounced him dead at 10 a.m., recording that 'over the right temple was a penetrating wound and in the right hand was gripped a revolver'.

Muirhead had left no suicide note – and people scratched around for a reason. Cooke claimed that he had worried about the possible recurrence of a painful bout of phlebitis of the leg and hated the thought of having to wear a stocking. Jim Thomas told Harry Crookshank that there had been 'insanity in the family', although there is no evidence of this.[14] Others said he feared his age and ill health would exclude him from active service. Few people credited these stories. As General Stamford Cartwright of the Worcestershire Yeomanry told me, 'Military men don't take their life over things like that.'[15] Inevitably, people had other theories. There had been bad blood over Muirhead's appointment and his reformist plans for the regiment. He was still unmarried at forty-eight. Perhaps a scandal was about to break. Whatever the reason, though, Muirhead had shot himself and the coroner brought in a verdict of suicide while the balance of his mind was disturbed.

Ronnie was upset. He had seen Muirhead on the Friday when he seemed the same as always – and then this. 'One sighs and passes on,' he wrote, 'but life is never quite the same afterwards.' Ronnie hinted at a deeper friendship between them, too. 'Those who were privileged to have revealed to them in friendship the quality of his mind and affections realised that his public life and his military duties were the inevitable outcome of the pattern of existence which he fashioned for himself and determined to follow.'[16] This was to be a theme throughout the war. Men who were of serviceable age often yearned for active service – and felt depressed, resentful and discarded when they were denied it. Suicide was still then a sacrilegious crime, but Muirhead was awarded a funeral with full military honours at Haseley on 8 November. Among the crowds, Ronnie and Jim Thomas watched Muirhead's coffin pass by, shrouded in a Union flag and bearing his cap and sword as the regimental band played the majestic, drumbeat-driven 'Dead March' from Handel's *Saul*. Ronnie asked himself, was this the first victim of the war? Yet in a more optimistic vein, he wrote, 'I've figured out the whole business of living now. This war is a tremendous opportunity. It is a colossal mental jerk for which really we should be deeply grateful. We have just got to think out everything anew.'[17]

Ronnie was about to come face to face with the reality of war. At the end of the year the *Birmingham Daily Gazette* noted that he was unable to send his customary New Year greeting to his constituents as he was serving with his regiment, and five days after his thirty-third birthday, which fell on 3 January, he rang his mother and sister. He could give no details, but Barbara wrote 'they knew it was good-bye'. At 9.30 a.m. on Monday 8 January, a cold and sunny winter's day, he and the regiment's four batteries, 'all excited like a Sunday School treat',[18] set off by train from Wantage to join the British Expeditionary Force in France under General Gort as part of the 48th (South Midland) Infantry Division. A shopkeeper gave Ronnie a St Christopher medal at the railway station, but the only person to wave them off was the wife of Muirhead's replacement, Colonel Edgar Medley.

It was not an easy journey. They boarded ship in Southampton, on which, according to the regiment's *War Diary*, conditions 'were not too good, there being considerable overcrowding'.[19] They had to wait for five hours before they set sail, there was 'an acute shortage of latrine accommodation'[20] and Ronnie had a nasty abscess on his heel, but the following morning they disembarked at Le Havre and the colonel took Ronnie in his staff car to their first billet in the chateau at Valliquerville, which sounded grand but proved to be 'a summer residence with [a] proverbial lack of sanitation'.[21] The men's initial accommodation was even more rudimentary, as they were sleeping in damp, draughty barns and there was a shortage of blankets. It was bitterly cold and several men came down with flu, which 'affected throats in a very unpleasant manner'. Despite the terrible pain in his foot, Ronnie's entrepreneurial skill and his love of the finer things in life rapidly kicked in, as he sorted out a battery officers' mess in a small café.

After three days they were on the move again – this time travelling 170 miles north-east towards Lille and the Belgian border, their convoy made all the more difficult by the coldest winter in many years and a lack of antifreeze, which meant several trucks froze up and had to be towed. They made an overnight stop at Blangy-sur-Bresle and arrived on the thirteenth at Noyelles-Godault, a small town of about 5,000 people near Douai, which Ronnie described as sitting in a 'sort of Black Country mining district'. Again the first accommodation was dire – the men were in 'low-down dance-halls' and the officers in 'a sort of villa' without water – but within days Ronnie managed to get his men sorted at a mine near Hénin-Liétard, with hot pit-head baths every day and the officers billeted in cottages with a bathroom within a hundred yards of the battery. His own accommodation was plush, as he stayed with the director of the company, whose 'magnificent house [was] superbly furnished'. He dressed for dinner every night, sipped champagne, enjoyed an en suite bathroom and slept in linen sheets.[22] In many ways it was difficult to imagine that this was really war. In theory they were to be ready at two hours' notice, but day after day the war diaries of both 53 Anti-Tank Regiment and 145 Brigade, which was headquartered six miles away at Ostricourt, read 'nothing to report' or 'quiet day'. The men were training every day – and there was a brief two-day visit to the firing ranges at Calais at the start of February – but the most interesting aspect of most days was a visit from a senior officer or the changing weather: 'Variable easterly wind. Sky overcast. Mild. Slight Showers.' The only excitement was when the owner of a large chateau left the keys to his wine cellar with the regiment as he fled, urging them to drink as much of it as possible so that the Germans would not have it.

Ronnie had one piece of good fortune. He was a second lieutenant and second in command of 210 Battery when they arrived in France, but his battery commander, Major Richard Wiggin, was one of six officers who contracted flu and was forced to spend three weeks in hospital in England, so Ronnie was made temporary captain in command of the battery. Ronnie admitted to Barbara that he couldn't be enjoying the war more and the only snag (apart from his heel) was that he felt a fraud when he got a letter from home. He added, 'It's more fun, naturally, being in command,' and boasted that his battery was not just by far the best run, but the best fed. 'In fact our reputation for hospitality is almost embarrassing,' he wrote home. 'I've a small dinner party tonight. I'm writing this at 7:30 pm in bed after a hot bath! We all change for dinner.'[23] To cap it all, he was pleasantly surprised to get a letter from Sibyl Colefax and promptly replied that he was being 'very busy and martial and I hope efficient', although he gently complained that he had been sitting around 'in a most insalubrious mining district' and that although he did at least have a bathroom he was only allowed to use it 'once a day at any time except in the morning when I most need it'.[24]

All the champagne and hot baths in the world, though, could not make up for the government's incompetence, which increasingly irritated Ronnie. People might think this was 'phoney war' back in England, but Ronnie feared it could get very real very quickly. Colonel Medley was 'first-rate' and Ronnie loved his men, but when Wiggin returned to duty on 6

February Ronnie found him hidebound and stuck in his ways – just the kind of diehard he had come to loathe in the Commons. The new anti-tank guns required new thinking if they were to be deployed effectively, but every suggestion Ronnie came up with was met with stony silence. After a long chat with the adjutant, Ronnie asked for a transfer to another battery, even if that meant returning to being a second lieutenant. He had other complaints. The battery was still hopelessly short of ammunition. When eight new two-pounder guns arrived in mid-March they only took the regiment up to thirty-two guns out of a full complement of forty-eight and, as the adjutant noted, 'At this rate of supply we will not be up to establishment till 1941!'[25] Ronnie complained that this might still be a 'phoney war' but there was a chronic shortage of small-scale maps, the army was manifestly wasteful and, worst of all, the country's whole attitude to the war remained lackadaisical. He wrote to Sibyl that 'the doings of parliament [were] wonderfully remote', but people needed to know that 'there are innumerable scandals out here. We want another Miss Nightingale, another LL[oyd] G[eorge] and every soldier I've spoken to wants Churchill in place of Chamberlain.'[26] Although he was unable to join a group of serving MPs who were invited to dinner with Chamberlain on 21 February, organised by Victor Cazalet and Hamilton Kerr, and he missed the christening of Barbara's son Glen in April, events back in England were not entirely out of his mind. Time and again he referred to himself in letters home as 'more revolutionary then ever'. He told his mother that 'after the war – if Chamberlain still reigns – the revolution for me – one last desperate chance to save England'.[27] And he wrote to Paul Emrys-Evans, 'Incredible as it may sound I'm very busy and when the day's work is done I fall animal-like into sleep. Twice a week we're up all night – my Parliamentary training at last comes in useful! Seriously I think I'm through with political life.' He ended, 'I am quite convinced never to support the Tory *Party* again.'[28]

With these thoughts burning away – and on the strong advice of Colonel Medley, who thought he should tell the Commons that Chamberlain must go – he sought special leave to attend a secret session of Parliament, which was scheduled for the second week in April, and left France on Tuesday 9 April, the day Hitler invaded Norway and Denmark. By the time he arrived at Barbara's flat in Grosvenor Square the secret session had been abandoned, and when he dropped in on the Commons to see Jim Thomas and Dick Law, he got even more depressed about the attitude back in Britain. He spent the Thursday with friends and only got back to Barbara's after midnight, when he sat at the foot of her bed and told her he was terribly depressed. 'The complacency – apathy – ignorance everywhere is even worse than I feared,' he complained.[29] He predicted that with Neville in charge the war would last eight years, that there was 'every chance of us losing it' and that Hitler would take Norway, Belgium and Holland. Barbara worried about her tired-looking brother, but she knew he had an uncanny knack of being right. He had intended to go to Birmingham the next day to see his mother and great-uncle, but woke to newspaper headlines proclaiming the imminent invasion of Belgium, so he rushed his breakfast, packed his few belongings, said his hasty farewells, rang his mother, hired a car to Dover and hurried back to his battery.

On his arrival back in Noyelles-Godault, Ronnie received two pieces of news. The regiment was to 'stand to' in readiness for a German invasion of Belgium; and Medley wanted Ronnie to take over 209 Battery as temporary major. Ronnie was delighted. He even thought for a brief moment that the action was starting in earnest when they were moved to Flines-lez-Raches on 13 April. But yet again it was a false start, as 145 Brigade was to see no action for three weeks, and ten days later Ronnie was back where he had started, living a 'complacently peaceful war existence' at Noyelles-Godault. Here the men filled their time with more training exercises and Ronnie gave lunch parties and dined out with officers from other batteries twice a week. The brigade even held a sports day on 3 May, at the end of which Ronnie gave everyone champagne 'so there was much jollification and everyone in very good humour'. A week later Germany invaded Belgium.

Ronnie was not alone in feeling frustrated at the dawdling during this 'phoney war'. Others were exasperated by the government's lack of energy. They heard tell of doubts around the Cabinet table and rumours that it might be better to negotiate with Hitler. They noted that arms factories were running half-days on Fridays. Even ministers like Rob Bernays thought that Britain was being mollycoddled. He thought the country needed to be told far more firmly how unpleasant life was going to be, but the only man who was straight with the British people was Winston. The worst of it was that the Commons had become a very unlovely place, as the cream of the young men had gone off to war and 'we are left with the worst elements on both sides'.[30] By March Rob was even more certain that the country had to throw everything at the war. He inveighed against 'business as usual' at a smart luncheon at the Savoy for the Electrical Development Association, 'We are fighting powers of darkness that have mobilised to their aid the total resources of the most highly disciplined nation the world has ever witnessed. Against such a foe we must throw all that we have into the struggle.'[31]

Jack Macnamara agreed. The London Irish Rifles expected to be deployed overseas at any moment, but he briefly returned to Chelmsford to address his association on 23 February. 'We are fighting a difficult war against the whole German people,' he told them. 'I am entirely against any form of complacency. Do not in any way minimise the extent of the struggle.' He called for the rich and the wage earners alike to make sacrifices in the common cause and urged people to welcome 'the hardships and the toughening'. It was, he promised, going to be a long war.[32]

Even Victor Cazalet was aware that there was remarkably little war going on. At forty-three he was nominally over the conscription age, but he had volunteered just before the war started and was in charge of the newly created 83rd Light Anti-Aircraft Battery at Sevenoaks, with ten officers and 156 other ranks. He loved it. He interviewed and recruited many of the men personally – often at the Ritz or the Dorchester, where he was a director – and thought they were 'a very remarkable collection of men', not least because three-quarters of them were former public school boys who would in ordinary conditions have been commissioned officers. One recruit, Elwyn Jones, who was later a Labour MP and Lord Chancellor, recorded that it was 'a remarkable collection of publishers, lawyers, actors, stockbrokers, landowners, grooms, bus-drivers, labourers'.[33] Victor's brother Peter was one of the battery captains, as was the very successful amateur steeplechaser Anthony Mildmay, who joined the Welsh Guards with Peter, inherited his father's title as Lord Mildmay and died unmarried in 1950. Other recruits included the architect Denys Lasdun, the novelist Hammond Innes, the dystopian novelist John Mair, Bombardier Thomas, the handsome first cellist in the Philharmonic Orchestra, and Ivor Novello's close associate, the actor and poet Christopher Hassall.

What was more surprising, though, was that many recruits were queer or nearly queer, including Harold Nicolson's son Ben, who became a lance bombardier and telephone operator in November, Harold's former lover James Pope-Hennessy, the literary editor John Guest, and the aristocratic society photographer and gossip columnist Brodrick Haldane (who only allowed his sexuality to be revealed posthumously). Haldane expressly wrote to Victor to offer his services because he had heard that the battery was for 'backward boys' like himself and was vetted by Victor at the Dorchester. Likewise Ben Nicolson was delighted when a new recruit sidled up to him after morning parade and said he was an artist and had been to one of Ben's parties in London. Ben later learned that the man in question, Rowland Pym, had spent three glorious weeks in Salzburg with Pope-Hennessy's equally gay elder brother, the art historian John, who was later the director of the British Museum. Ben noted 'that is the sort of agreeable fact which occurs in this battery – it's so civilized, friendly, incompetent'.[34] It was all very informal. No uniforms arrived until the middle of October – and even then there were only dungarees, caps and overcoats, leaving Ben Nicolson looking like 'a Prussian officer'.[35] James Pope-Hennessy took his typewriter onto the gun emplacement to work on a book while they were watching for the enemy, while Haldane 'created a rock garden'[36] and Pym painted a sub-Whistler mural in the HQ featuring Victor and others in Napoleonic costumes astride a mound of Lewis guns. After one visit from a senior officer the official report merely stated 'the officer was an absolute charmer'.[37] Victor would inspect the men every week, send his regards to their parents or lovers, and chat with everyone before getting back into his Rolls-Royce. As Haldane recalled, he would always be in a rush and would make some excuse such as, 'I have to hurry. I'm having tea with Queen Mary.'[38] The battery acquired a reputation. Some called it 'the Monstrous Regiment of Gentlemen', others 'a sissy A. A. battery', and Philip Toynbee, who tried to join the battery to be with his closest friend Ben Nicolson, wrote to Churchill's nephew Esmond Romilly that it led to all sorts of 'amusing things, such as well-known pansies mincing into the Café Royal in battle-dress'.[39] This explains why Toynbee was bribed into joining the Welsh Guards instead by his father-in-law, the former MP Lieutenant-Colonel Evelyn Powell, who asked his wife to leave the room so that he could explain what he thought of his son-in-law joining 'a bugger's battery'.[40]

The Café Royal was not the only venue for uniformed queers. Le Boeuf sur le Toit opened as a smartly decorated predominantly queer nightclub in Orange Street, behind the National Gallery, in 1939. The opthalmic surgeon Patrick Trevor-Roper (who was later a prominent campaigner for gay rights) described it as 'an eye opener', as officers would come back 'hoping to dazzle with their uniform'.[41] Two years later it gained a neighbour, the Arts and Battledress. By then the Swiss Hotel in Old Compton Street and the Crown and Two Chairmen in Dean Street also had an almost exclusively queer clientele – and were warned by the police that people thought they were 'harbouring … sodomites'.[42] Not far away the Regent Palace Hotel opened its men–only Shake Up Bar. As one young officer, John Alcock, put it,

> I was sitting at the bar and I became aware of the amount of officers that were standing around, including two from my own battalion in Portsmouth, and all the officers were homosexual and it gave me a tremendous lift to realise that other ranks were queer the same as I was.[43]

The same was true of the basement bar at the Ritz Hotel, which rapidly became known as the 'Pink Sink' when it was redesigned during the war and formally renamed, L'Abri du Ritz (the Ritz Shelter). Fitted out with 'sandbags galore, struts, cross-beams and all that would delight an architect or builder' and lit by 'endless dead bottles with candles stuck in their necks', it looked like the set of *Journey's End*. As the *Bystander* archly commented, 'the dug-out décor may perhaps account for the large number of bemedalled Allied generals who seem to come here to relax'.[44] Here officers and men mingled through to the early morning. When the liberal-minded poet Louis MacNeice visited in 1940, he commented that the bar was 'noisy and crowded with officers in uniform, but all of a peculiar kind, shimmying their hips and speaking in shrill or velvety voices – "My dear! My dear! My DEAR!"'[45] The clientele at the Pink Sink was said to include a senior man from the War Office with a penchant for young junior officers who was known as 'Colonel Cutie', and a renowned shoplifter, nightclub hostess and singer, Edomie 'Sod' Johnson, who was nicknamed 'the buggers' Vera Lynn'.

Whether or not Victor ever ventured into any of these venues, he loved being the commanding officer of his 'buggers' battery'. Three days after war was declared he wrote in his diary, 'No wonder many people enjoy a war.'[46] A month later, after hosting a battery party at Great Swifts, with Bombardier Thomas in regular attendance, he added, 'my Battery counts far more than anything else'.[47] And that Christmas he had seven unattached battery men to stay and was delighted to report, 'So far no privations except not quite all the butter we want.'[48] He had doubts about the War Office, complaining that 'all real Army folk seem terrified by the thought of offending some clerk', and noting 'an incredible amount of fuss over everything and such muddle as beggars description'.[49] Yet his overall impression was that there was 'so little War going on' that he hardly dared mention it to Halifax when he came to stay.[50]

Neville Chamberlain, meanwhile, was determined to hang on to power and continued to use Joseph Ball to do his dirty work. *Truth* became even more vitriolic about Chamberlain's opponents. When he was given a hard time in a secret session of the Commons just before Christmas, he complained to his sister that 'the "glamour boys" turned up in force and were very noisy so that at one time things were rather ugly'. His arrogance was barely dented by the attacks. As he put it, 'What I had to say was necessarily put together very hastily and in presentation was largely impromptu but I'm glad to say it was very successful.'[51]

He reserved his harshest treatment for the war secretary, Leslie Hore-Belisha, whose attempts to reform the army and his frequent interventions in military affairs had earned him enemies among the generals. His demands in Cabinet for a more energetic prosecution of the war had incurred Chamberlain's wrath. His attire and the fact that he was still unmarried at the age of forty-seven raised eyebrows, and his Jewishness offended Hitler (and therefore embarrassed Chamberlain). One satirical ditty (which Hore-Belisha banned in October 1939) that was doing the rounds made clear the nasty combination of anti-Semitism and homophobia involved:

Onward Christian Soldiers
You have nought to fear,
Israel Hore-Belisha
Will lead you from the rear.
Clothed by Monty Burton
Fed on Lyons pies,

Die for Jewish freedom,
As a Briton always dies.[52]

By the end of 1939 Chamberlain was determined to remove him from the War Office and shamelessly told the Palace that 'as I had told him repeatedly before, there existed a strong prejudice against him for which I could not hold him altogether blameless'. Chamberlain's prejudice was not unique. When Halifax told his permanent under-secretary, Sir Alexander Cadogan, of the plan to get Hore-Belisha out of the War Office and into the Ministry of Information, Cadogan wrote in his diary that he found the idea 'exquisitely funny', but that on consideration he had come to the conclusion that 'Jew control of our propaganda would be a major disaster'.[53] Likewise, General Henry Pownall, the chief of staff to the British Expeditionary Force (BEF), reckoned that it was inevitable that General Gort should fall out with Hore-Belisha. After all, the former was 'a great gentleman', while the latter was 'an obscure, shallow-brained, charlatan, political Jewboy'.[54]

Truth had continued peddling its anti-Semitism. In July it had declared in an editorial that 'if we set aside the ideological passions of Mr Gollancz and his tribe in the tents of Bloomsbury, the truth is that no appreciable section of British opinion desires to reconquer Berlin for the Jews or see the Vistula run red with British blood'.[55] In a strange fit of hypocrisy, immediately after war was declared *Truth* had urged that 'it would be a profound mistake if we were to indulge in hate propaganda'.[56] It meant anti-German hatred, of course, as it defended Nazi anti-Semitism on the grounds that such views were 'liable to flare up without warning, wherever Jews cluster thickly'.[57] In other words, the Jews were the architects of their own misfortune.

Hore-Belisha was aware that he was in danger in December and summoned Jack Macnamara for advice, which meant Jack had to cancel dinner with Harold Nicolson.[58] The climax came on 4 January, though, when Chamberlain summoned Hore-Belisha at 4.30 p.m. and offered him the post of president of the Board of Trade, outside the War Cabinet, and told him to consider it overnight. Hore-Belisha was astounded. He sought advice from Churchill, who inadvertently let on that he was aware of the plan to move him, and he told Cazalet that Neville had told him, 'There is prejudice against you – I don't agree with it, nor do I think it is deserved, but because of it I want you to accept the Board of Trade.'[59] Smarting from the insinuations and furious about Chamberlain's duplicity, Belisha scornfully resigned that night. The ensuing furore saw several newspapers indulge in what Harold Nicolson thought was less 'a pro-Belisha than an anti-Chamberlain outburst'.[60] *Truth* swung into action. The 12 January edition launched what was later described as 'a deliberate attempt to kill Belisha once and for all as a political force'[61] in the shape of an article entitled 'Belisha is No Loss', which accused him of all manner of financial misconduct and incompetence. Its author, Henry Newham, was caustic. 'Mr Belisha's resignation is a minor episode,' he wrote, 'because he is a minor man whose most conspicuous talent is for getting his photograph into the newspapers.' In addition, *Truth* blamed the 'hysteria' surrounding his resignation on 'newspapers controlled by Mr Belisha's co-religionists' and the 'racial sympathy' he had elicited.[62] The following week Newham went further. The *Daily Mirror*, which had defended Hore-Belisha, came 'from the Jew-controlled sink of Fleet Street'.[63] Just to ram home the message, these two editions of *Truth* were sent unsolicited to the homes of all MPs and peers and a large number of journalists and senior civil servants. Nancy Astor started whispering to all and sundry the totally unfounded allegation that Hore-Belisha had enriched himself on army contracts; and the next edition of the *Free Press*, the journal of the Militant Christian Patriots, lauded *Truth*'s determination to show that 'Britain has had the distinction of having a company-promoting Jew for a War Minister'.[64]

Chamberlain's double standards did not go unchallenged. The ranks of the Glamour Boys had been diminished by Crossley's death, by Ronnie and Jack assuming full-time army commitments and by Eden, Churchill and Jim Thomas joining the government payroll, but a group of rebels continued to meet every Wednesday at the Carlton Club with Leo Amery in the chair. Victor Cazalet and Hamilton Kerr set up a committee of members serving in the armed forces, which largely consisted of insurgents, and in April 1940 Lord Salisbury formed a 'Watching Committee', which deliberately included Chamberlain loyalists like Patrick Spens and Joseph Nall, in the hope that moderate backbenchers might join the cause of throwing everything at the war. By now they were convinced that the war could only be won with a change of leadership at the head of a coalition government, and Chips Channon predicted 'a first class political struggle between the Chamberlain men and the "glamour" group'.[65] It certainly felt as if the rebels were limbering up for the fight. The Watching Committee and the Amery Group met separately several times in April and so strong was their belief that this was their most important contribution to the war effort that Amery's allies invariably went straight from a Watching Committee meeting to their own dinner, where they discussed the same issues all over again.

It came to a head in May, when an ill-conceived campaign in Norway saw Hitler victorious and Britain humiliated. The strategic mistakes had largely been Churchill's, but the blame stuck to Chamberlain. A two-day debate on the seemingly innocuous motion that 'this House do now adjourn' started on 7 May and although Churchill summed up in the government's defence, large numbers of Conservative MPs remained unconvinced that the prime minister had the energy, the determination or the strategic wherewithal to prosecute the war to success. The mood was fraught enough on the first day, when Amery ended his stinging speech with the words of Oliver Cromwell, 'In the name of God, go,' directed straight at Chamberlain. That night the Amery Group met to organise speakers for the second day – and to gather as many votes as possible in case there were a division – and according to Harold Nicolson the next morning Salisbury urged Watching Committee members 'not to vote against the Government if a Division came'. Labour announced at lunchtime that it would be forcing a vote at the end of the day and when Herbert Morrison spoke in the Chamber he explained their reasoning. 'Before the war and during the war,' he said, 'we have felt that the whole spirit, tempo and temperament of at least some Ministers have been wrong, inadequate and unsuitable.'[66] In the meantime Victor Cazalet and Hamilton Kerr had met with twelve other members of their Service Members' Committee, all bar one of whom said they wanted to vote against the government and most said they were going to do so, 'whatever happened'.[67]

Chamberlain's arrogant response in the Chamber was to raise the stakes. 'I say this to my friends in the House,' he said, before adding limply 'and I have friends in the House. No Government can prosecute a war efficiently unless it has public and Parliamentary support.'[68] By calling on his 'friends' to support him in the Lobby that night he again turned the motion into a confidence vote. The rebels had long grown used to this trick. Many had abstained before – and were joined by Victor Cazalet and Malcolm Bullock in abstaining again.[69] Yet even more courageously, forty-one Conservative and National Government MPs trooped through the Noe Lobby with Labour, including Bob Boothby, Harold Nicolson, Jack Macnamara, Ronnie Tree, Harold Macmillan, Dick Law, Hamilton Kerr, Duff Cooper, Derrick Gunston, Godfrey Nicholson, Mark Patrick, Roger Keyes, John Profumo, the recent by-election victor, Rob Bernays's friend Hugh Molson, and Nancy Astor. Many of them were in uniform and if Ronnie Cartland had not been in France he would have joined them. The only resignation proved an embarrassment for Rob Bernays, as his PPS, Herbert Butcher, suddenly announced that he had come to the conclusion that 'unless the war is conducted with greater speed in decision and increased resoluteness of action, peace will be delayed and the price of victory in life and treasure will be higher than is necessary'.[70] It was what Rob was saying in private – but he chose to stay put. Hardly any Jewish Conservative MPs supported the PM, as Hore-Belisha, Daniel Lipson and Leo Amery voted with the rebels, and Dudley Joel, James de Rothschild, Alfred Beit and Abraham Lyons abstained, leaving just the virulent anti-communist Marcus Samuel, Sir Isidore Salmon, who was catering adviser to the army, and Henry Strauss, who was a PPS, as Chamberlain's Jewish 'friends'. The same was true of the queer and nearly queer MPs. Only the ministers and PPSs (Bernays, Crookshank, Lennox-Boyd and Channon) voted with the government. Chamberlain won by 281 votes to 200, but it felt like a victory for the Glamour Boys. The atmosphere was toxic. Several of Chamberlain's supporters came up to Ronnie Tree and told him, 'You've got what you've been working for – I only hope you will regret it for the rest of your life.'[71] In response, Harold Macmillan and Josiah Wedgwood started singing 'Rule Britannia' and shouted 'Go!' at Chamberlain as he left the Chamber.

Many thought that the prime minister would resign immediately. Even Victor, who had a personal affection for Chamberlain, could see that the 'story of discontent against the PM [was] a long one'. He blamed it all on Margesson 'and the Whip hostility to all who voted against or criticized Govt. at time of Munich'.[72] The young members 'could have been won over by tactful handling' but had been treated as traitors.[73] Boothby agreed. He wrote to Margesson: 'If the House of Commons has failed in its duty during recent months and years, it is largely due to the extremely effective control you have exercised over it.'[74]

Yet Chamberlain was in no mood to cede control. Instead he set about trying to reconstruct the government. He told Victor there would be major changes in the Cabinet. He offered up Simon, Hoare and Kingsley Wood to appease his critics. He even put out feelers to the Labour leaders, whom he had repeatedly and unnecessarily alienated for years. The Glamour Boys despaired. They met on the Thursday morning and decided to tell Labour that they would not support any government that did not include the other parties. This, they hoped, might deliver the premiership to someone who could create a true National Government. Still Chamberlain hung on, though, bolstered by arch-loyalists and his own self-belief. One Glamour Boy described him as 'a dirty old piece of chewing gum on the leg of a chair'.[75] Brendan Bracken thought he looked like a 'tough old gentleman' who would fight with all his might to stay at the helm,[76] and Labour's Hugh Dalton compared him to 'an old limpet'.[77] And in the midst of it all, the whips ensured Ronnie Tree was blackballed from membership of the Royal Yacht Squadron.

However, as Thursday wore on Chamberlain looked more and more haggard. He was running out of options. The Glamour Boys and their allies were implacable. As Boothby said in the Commons that afternoon 'the events of yesterday proved that the Government, as at present constituted, do not possess the confidence of the House and of the country in sufficient measure'.[78] Labour spurned Chamberlain's offer, some of his old allies were secretly abandoning him and he had gained no new friends. So he arranged to meet with Halifax, Churchill and Margesson at 4.30 in the Cabinet Room and told them he was minded to resign. The precise details of that meeting are contested. Victor, who had dined with the foreign secretary on Wednesday, had always thought Halifax would take over rather than Churchill, and Churchill had initially encouraged Chamberlain not to give up after the vote, but when the four men left the Cabinet Room it was agreed that Churchill should try to form a National Government. The next day he became prime minister.

19

The Stand at Cassel

Ronnie Cartland felt the wind of change almost immediately. On 10 May, the day Churchill received the seals of office, Hitler invaded Belgium and the Netherlands and Ronnie joined Colonel Webley driving into Belgium – the first MP to cross the border. He felt like royalty as hundreds of Belgians greeted them, cheering, throwing flowers and waving good luck, but eight bombs were dropped on them that day and one civilian was killed. After so many weeks of hanging about, he was suddenly caught up in the chaos of war. For the next few days the 53rd were spread out along a seventy-five-mile road between the Forêt de Soignes and the Bois de Hal, to the south of Brussels, providing anti-aircraft cover for the 48th Division's deployment up to the River Dyle. The regiment's war diary noted that 'it was a pretty problem to do this with but 50 guns', yet they managed to bring down at least six enemy aircraft.[1] Then there was a change of mind and Gort ordered the withdrawal of Allied forces in three overnight stages – to the River Senne, the River Dendre and finally to the River Escaut – during which the 53rd were to guard the eastern flank near Waterloo. This also proved challenging, as the regiment was constantly digging itself in and then moving again in thick darkness without maps. In the midst of this, Ronnie's battery was attached to the Armoured Reconnaissance Group and had to hold a gap in the line on its own, which led to his first engagement with the enemy when they were attacked by a flight of Stuka bombers on Friday

17 May. Ronnie had a natural friend in the battery, Second Lieutenant Bob Hutton-Squire, who had been at Charterhouse with him, but like many well-to-do officers, Ronnie became attached to his men in a way that society would never normally have allowed in peacetime. As he put it, 'the intimacy of one's own men is remarkable. My driver and despatch rider have a curious relationship with me that can never be explained in the language of peace or translated into peace-time terms.'[2] Now he lost the first of his men, as four were killed outright and two received such heavy shrapnel wounds that they had to be repatriated. That evening he and the junior officers wrapped the men in white sheets and buried them. Two of the corpses were unrecognisable. War had become very real.

With the Luftwaffe in control of the skies, the next stage of night-time withdrawal to the line of the River Dendre saw several units split up. Ronnie was lost for a while and yet again poor equipment let them down, as one of the guns lost a wheel when it went into a ditch and the spare did not fit properly, so one of the companies spent hours improvising a repair with some large nails from a deserted café near Tournai. It took Ronnie forty-eight hours before he made it to the new brigade headquarters and two more days before the company was reunited with the rest of the battery. Ronnie was amazed when he finally spotted his men, as he confessed that he had already reported them missing in action.

By this stage there was an element of chaos in British planning at every level. The 145th Infantry Brigade, which incorporated the 2nd Battalion, the Gloucestershire Regiment ('2 Glosters'), the 4th Battalion, Oxfordshire and Buckinghamshire Light Infantry ('Ox and Bucks' in which Ronnie's 'boyfriend' Michael Shewell served) and the 145th Infantry Brigade Anti-Tank Company, had been led by Brigadier Archibald Hughes, but like many senior officers he was now considered too old at fifty-four to take the men into the heat of battle and he returned to England on Wednesday 16 May, when his place was taken by the commanding officer of the 2 Glosters, the Hon. Nigel Somerset, the 46-year-old great-grandson of Lord Raglan (of the Charge of the Light Brigade fame). Somerset's orders kept on changing. First, 145 Brigade were moved away from its positions on the River Scheldt (the Belgian part of the Escaut) on the night of 22 May and were briefly based on the border near Rumegies, where they were to be relieved by French troops. Ronnie found himself at nearby Orchies during 23 May, where he wrote several letters home. One was to Eden to congratulate him on his new Cabinet appointment. Another was to his mother, in which he mused that it was 'a rum war' as he was now precisely where he had been ten days ago. 'The last week or so while we've been on the move,' he told her, 'we've been in these evacuated houses. They must have been left in a great hurry … the most intimate things left as they must always have been.' It all felt unreal as they commandeered houses as if they were guests. He was getting just four hours sleep every night. He wrote again to Sibyl Colefax, telling her he was still furious about the feeble prosecution of the war and complaining that the anti-tank guns were most disappointing. He ended on a contemplative note. 'War is a terrific experience,' he claimed, 'as such I wouldn't forsake this – but it would be nice (I often think) to drop in say now about 6 o/c and see you and all our friends again. Love to you, Ronnie.'[3]

In his letter to his mother he noted, 'We live in a state of being ready to move anywhere at any time,' and that night the brigade retreated three further miles to Nomain, where they arrived at dawn. Virtually the moment they arrived there, they were given new orders at 7 a.m. to relieve the siege at Calais, which was a hundred miles away. Troop transport would apparently arrive that afternoon. Within hours – and before they could even set off – that order was countered with another – to take on the defence of Hazebrouck and the hill town of Cassel as part of the protective perimeter for Dunkirk. En route it was decided that the Ox and Bucks would stay at Hazebrouck, which meant that Ronnie and Michael Shewell were parted, but at least, Ronnie concluded, Cassel was on the way to Calais.

Ronnie was remarkably calm. The brigade chaplain, David Wild, later recalled meeting Ronnie on the evening before they set off for Cassel. He was 'ever-cheerful' and invited him to a picnic supper, which his batman had laid out on a spotless tablecloth spread out on the grass in a field. As they tucked into cold duck in aspic, 'specially good tinned fruit', a bottle of commendable wine and some Cointreau, German planes were constantly passing to and fro overhead, a steady stream of despatch riders called at HQ on the other side of the hedge, and some soldiers sang 'all their most sentimental favourites' around a piano they had dragged out of a farmhouse 400 yards up the road. Despite these harbingers, Wild thought they might have been lying by the banks of the Cherwell in Oxford and Ronnie was in his element as a genial host.

It was a brief respite.

Cassel was an ideal site for one of Gort's strongpoints, designed to protect the 15- to 23-mile-wide corridor that stretched thirty miles inland from the Channel. The town sits on the top of a steep hill with unimpeded views across Flanders. Its ancient arched stone gateways were designed to keep out invaders and its narrow streets would be difficult to breach. There was a chateau, a town hall, a couple of hotels, a well-defended keep, some municipal air-raid shelters, plenty of billets and lookout posts – and a statue of General Foch, who had used it as his headquarters in the First World War. Most importantly, it lay at the intersection of the key roads to Calais and Dunkirk and all Somerset knew at this point was that they were to halt the German advance.

The march up into Cassel on Friday 25 May was ominous enough. As Wild acknowledged, 'for all I knew, we were driving straight towards the enemy, supported by (just) two lorries of signal equipment and two trucks full of dry rations, cooks and typists'.[4] After passing through thickly wooded foothills – which could easily hide a German advance – they climbed a series of zigzags up into the town itself. Turning a sharp corner, Ronnie and his men saw the first of many scenes of gory devastation.

The town had been heavily bombed the previous day. Artillery carriages, trucks, men and horses had been hit and the wreckage and corpses 'were still blocking the road'.[5] A pony lay with his jaws apart and its shining teeth still betraying the agony in which it had died. A French soldier lay by the side of his dead horse 'one hand on the animal's forehead, the other holding the reins'.[6] Things got worse the further they went into town. A six-wheel lorry lay burnt out, several townhouses were just shells and in the main square several of the largest buildings now lay in ruins, their contents cascaded into the street. There was silence everywhere and although the British soldiers stopped to check if any human or animal was still alive, there was none. As Colonel Robert Bridgeman noted, the Hotel du Sauvage had been hit by a shell 'and the staff had evidently bolted the day before, leaving the cloths of the tables in the dining room … [and] a deserted bottle of Armagnac'.[7] Worst of all, as Captain E. Jones of the 2 Glosters put it, 'Over the whole area occupied by the battalion were distressing sights to be seen by weary men with the knowledge that they had to clear up the mess.'[8]

The immediate job was to make the town defendable. Roadblocks were placed at the gateways on the north and south entrances to the town, barricades were set up in the narrow streets, buildings were shored up and Ronnie's anti-tank guns were dug in at strategic outposts where any German arrivals could be spotted and halted. The next day they buried the French dead and were relieved to find that what they had thought was a river of blood was just spilt red wine.

On Monday 27 May some of the most senior generals in the British Army met with the French Admiral Fagalde at Cassel, but it soon became clear that the Wehrmacht recognised the strategic importance of Cassel, as the meeting was broken up by heavy German artillery and strafing from the air. At 10.30 a.m. one of the brigade's outposts at Zuytpeene was attacked and a score of German tanks appeared with a hundred or so soldiers. Soon it was overrun and that evening German troops made their first attack on another outpost, a blockhouse where a platoon held out for three days against overwhelming odds. By this stage the road to Bergues could no longer be used and Cassel was virtually cut off.

Ronnie was in full command of the anti-tank unit at Cassel, but with just four companies, plus a troop from 211 Battery led by Major Henry Mercer, it was a small force with which to face a relentless assault by the 6th Panzer Division. They did not have long to wait. When Ronnie spotted the first of a couple of dozen German tanks appearing through the woods to the west of the town some 600 yards from where Bob Hutton-Squire's troop was dug in with a two-pounder, he alerted the company, who fired their first round. It missed and the German commander swivelled his turret to aim back. It was only after fifteen rounds, with the Germans advancing to within a hundred yards, that the British finally hit the first tank's tracks, disabled the turret and forced the now defenceless German crew to flee. Moments later Ronnie's men scored direct hits on two other tanks, which exploded. Shells continued to fall virtually every minute throughout Monday and the brigade took significant casualties, but at dusk eighteen German tanks lay abandoned by their crews in front of the town and the acting commanding officer of the Glosters, Major Maurice Gilmore, noted that 'as the evening wore on, the attack and the mortaring died down, and things became quiet'.[9] The only new problem was that when the quartermaster appeared with new rations, he was fired at and his vehicle was written off when it drove into a shell hole. From then on the troops would have to rely on what they could forage from the town itself, although Captain Jones proudly noted that 'although Brigade repeated their orders concerning the looting of wine shops, there was not a single case of intoxication in the battalion'.[10]

Somerset's men were in real danger now. Eden had already cabled Gort with instructions to evacuate the BEF and the Germans had twice demanded that Godfrey Nicholson's older brother Claude surrender as the commanding officer at Calais. He had twice refused, and Churchill's telegram to him on 25 May was unambiguous: 'Every hour you continue to exist is of the greatest help to the BEF. Government has therefore decided that you must continue to fight. Have greatest possible admiration for your splendid stand. Evacuation will not (repeat not) take place.'[11] Churchill felt sick when he sent it, but Nicholson knew he could not breathe a word of this to his men as they resolutely followed orders. The following day, though, the Germans overwhelmed British troops at Calais and captured Nicholson, who later died as a prisoner of war. Had Somerset and his men been aware of this they might have quailed at their own prospects.

Ronnie, however, managed to keep morale high, as he and Major Mercer made a makeshift headquarters in one of the cellars at the top of the town. Anyone could see the Germans were slowly surrounding Cassel and cutting off their retreat, and the town's elegant squares were now scarred by German artillery. When Lieutenant Tom Carmichael of the East Riding Yeomanry arrived in the town on Tuesday 28 May, he noted trees that had been shattered, 'a little heap huddled under a groundsheet [which] marked the remains of one of the crew' of a two-pounder that had taken a direct hit and the remains of a three-ton lorry carrying personnel whose 'mangled remains [were] ghastly'.[12] The Germans dropped leaflets telling the garrison to give up, as 'your generals are gone'. But when Colonel Medley appeared on 28 May, Ronnie and Major Mercer gave him an excellent lunch of bully beef, black cherries and champagne and they both presumed – or hoped – that Medley's presence meant a British counter-attack was imminent. Somerset had been forced by German artillery attacks to move the brigade HQ to the keep, but as the brigade's war diary noted, 'Everything was very quiet that evening and though perhaps out of place here, we must record that we dined most excellently that evening and celebrated our arrival at the Keep with a bottle of champagne.'[13]

At this point accounts differ. According to Barbara Cartland, Medley left Cassel at three o'clock on the Tuesday afternoon, intending to call in on his other gunners at Wormhoudt, but had to take a detour when he learned that it had fallen. On his arrival at divisional headquarters at 2 a.m. on the Wednesday he learned that 48 Division 'had sent an armoured car to Cassel with a message to the Brigadier ordering him to retire that night' and to make his way to HQ for immediate evacuation via Dunkirk.[14] That afternoon Medley gathered his other troops ready to leave at 4 p.m. and was perplexed when the men from Cassel failed to materialise. Eventually he gave up and set off without them at 9.30 that evening. In Captain Jones's account, instructions were issued on the Tuesday 'but the motorcyclist lost his way, and only reached Cassel on the twenty-ninth after spending most of the night in a ditch'.[15] By contrast, 145 Brigade's war diary claimed that '*permission* was given for 145 Inf Bde to withdraw' (my italics) and added that 'whether this withdrawal was carried out or not was left to the discretion of Comd 145 Inf Bde'.[16] According to this version it was only at 8 a.m. on the Wednesday that Somerset received a separate order, by wireless, to withdraw. Somerset's account differs, too. He maintained that a written order to withdraw had been sent the previous evening, but that the driver had been unable to get through, owing to enemy tanks, but had managed to elude the Germans in daylight. He pointedly added, 'Had the message been sent by wireless, which was always open – withdrawal the previous night would have been fully possible, but to withdraw in daylight while in contact was out of the question.'[17]

It is easy to smell a rat in this confusion. Clearly Somerset did. 145 Brigade could only leave Cassel with any degree of safety under cover of darkness, but by the time the news reached them, morning had broken and another day was lost, during which the brigade would face a further onslaught. It may be that Gort expected 145 Brigade to set off during Tuesday night, but since the order was not issued until the evening, the brigade would have been hard-pressed to destroy their artillery and move out with anything like enough time to make a clean getaway before dawn. It seems likely that High Command deliberately delayed sending the order until the last possible moment, because it was worth risking the lives of the men at Cassel to prioritise the mass evacuation of tens of thousands of men at Dunkirk under Operation Dynamo. Somerset stated as much later, when he wrote to the *Daily Telegraph* that, 'I now fully realised that we were the "Joe Soaps" of Dunkirk. That we were being sacrificed so that as many British and French could get away from Dunkirk, and get all the kudos for that.'[18] There was some bitterness in his comments, but the defence of Cassel and Gort's corridor helped 371,000 men evacuate to England.

Either way, Somerset received his orders early on the Wednesday morning and from eight o'clock the brigade was under constant attack. Mortars landed in the town's *gendarmerie*, whose cellar had been commandeered as the Ox and Bucks' and the East Riding Yeomanry HQ, decapitating the second in command, Major Joe Thorne. At noon Somerset alerted the men that they would be moving out that night. At 2.30 p.m. he sent an armoured patrol from the East Riding Yeomanry along with anti-tank guns led by Major Mercer to reconnoitre a possible exit route through Winnezeele. They never returned and Mercer was captured. At 4 p.m. Somerset issued more detailed orders for their departure. 'All kits would be left behind. All transport would be abandoned; vehicles would be put out of action; anything that could not be carried would be destroyed … Nothing should be burnt except papers and these with precautions against smoke rising.'[19] As the 53rd's war diary states, the order came 'as a great shock to us all. We were furious about it.'[20] So they did their best to show contempt for the Germans by putting on their best uniforms and vigorously shining their brass buttons. At five o'clock the German artillery went silent. At 7.30 p.m., following an incoherent radio message from divisional HQ, the men started destroying their guns and vehicles by drilling holes in their petrol tanks. Somerset noted, 'elements of the enemy – particularly tanks – were all around us & I began to doubt if we should be able to get clear of Cassel – let alone to the BEF'.[21]

At nine the Glosters started their withdrawal from the west of the town. At 10.30, on a dark but warm night, the rest of the column left Cassel with Ronnie at the head of the anti-tank gunners, aiming to march as silently as possible cross-country towards Watou and to rendezvous at Hondeschoote on the perimeter of Dunkirk. It was every man for himself. All were convinced that they were already surrounded and that only a miracle could get them through. As they left they could see a dense black pall of smoke hanging in the sky, which they presumed to be oil tanks burning at Dunkirk. The only nearby light came from the Hotel de Ville, which was still burning. The road was so pockmarked by artillery that they had to pick their way single file down the hill, and so many farms were on fire that they had to skirt round them so as to avoid their silhouettes being framed against the flames. They made good speed through the night, though, and even when the sun began to rise at 3.45 a.m. they had the added protection of a thick mist. Somerset noted, 'The only event – other than constant feelings of continually walking into an ambush – was the usual lunatic who let his rifle off by mistake during a short halt.'[22] However, when an enemy reconnaissance plane appeared, the men threw themselves into ditches, but were spotted and when the Ox and Bucks bumped into the enemy at Winnezeele at 5.30 the column splintered and each unit was forced to work out its own salvation. Some decided to lie low during the day and travel at night, but that was slow and laborious. Ronnie avoided the roads and lanes and led his battery through woods and along ditches, slowly and steadily making their way to Watou. All that kept running around in his head as he tried to work out a way of getting back to Dunkirk were the words that he had written home: 'I will never surrender. I will fight to the end. If I am captured I shall give a false name as it does no good for an MP to fall into the enemy's hands.'[23]

As the day wore on, the far superior German forces steadily captured or killed many of the men from 145 Brigade. Thirty-seven officers from Cassel became prisoners of war, including Somerset. A trickle of men made it to Dunkirk and onto ships back home, but barely half the Ox and Bucks' officers and only five officers and 284 men from Ronnie's 53rd Anti-Tank Regiment were spotted getting onto British ships and boats. Ronnie's friend Michael Shewell was safe – and received the MC for his courageous defence at Hazebrouck – but there was no sign of Ronnie.

Then began a hideous waiting game for Ronnie's family. Polly received two letters at Littlewood House on 6 June. One recorded that 'Captain J. A[nthony]. H. Cartland, the Lincolnshire Regiment, is reported by his Unit as missing'; the other, that 'the Major J. R. H. Cartland M.P., R.A., is missing'. That meant both brothers were unaccounted for. Polly wrote in her diary 'Tony *and* Ronald – it's too terrible'.[24] She had been through all this when she had at first received good news about her husband Bertie in 1918, only to discover months later that there had been a mistake. The only thing that she and Barbara had to console them was a letter from Ronnie in which he wrote, 'Don't be anxious if there is a long silence from me – the fog of war is pretty impenetrable. We shall win in the end, but there's horror and tribulation ahead of all of us.'[25] Polly got in touch with Colonel Wiggin, who feared Ronnie was missing, and with Tony's colonel, who was in hospital in Liverpool, and thought Tony had been captured. Jim Thomas, who was now PPS to Eden at the War Ministry, rang every week with whatever news he had managed to glean from the Army. They waited and hoped.

It was not until 4 January 1941, Tony's twenty-eighth birthday, that news came, when a letter arrived from Lieutenant Derek Woodward, a member of Ronnie's battery, who was now a prisoner at Oflag VII-B at Eichstätt. He had been in a ditch bordering a lane with Ronnie, Bob Hutton-Squire, Lieutenant Harold Freeker and about fifty men when they saw German tanks engaging British troops ahead of them at about 8.30 a.m. Ronnie called Woodward forward and since they had no anti-tank weapons, they decided to hide. When the tanks converged on them, though, they had little choice. Hutton-Squire started firing at the Germans with a Bren gun and shouted, 'They won't capture me!' as he ran off into a small plantation where German machine guns mowed him down. Other men were shot or captured as they tried to clamber into neighbouring fields. As for Ronnie, the accounts vary slightly. Harry Munn, who was a hundred yards away with Hutton-Squire, claimed that, 'Very heavy casualties were inflicted on our battery and to save further losses Major Cartland gave the order to surrender. At this point heavy firing was going on and Major Cartland was killed.'[26] Derek Woodward, though, who was just five yards from Ronnie at the time, did not mention any attempt to surrender but wrote that as Ronnie rose 'he was hit in the head by a bullet and killed instantly'.[27] He was thirty-three.

Polly still believed that Tony was a prisoner, and refused to believe the famous medium Estelle Roberts, who told her during a 'consultation' that he had been killed the day before Ronnie, but finally in February 1942 Jim Thomas rang with incontrovertible evidence that Tony had also been killed when he refused to surrender. The medium had even been right about the date. Finally able to hold a memorial, Polly added two lines to the monument to her husband Bertie in the grounds of Tewkesbury Abbey. For Ronnie she put, 'I will not cease from mental strife, nor shall my sword sleep in my hand,' and for Tony, 'I will surrender only unto God.'

Heartfelt tributes flooded in. Churchill sent his deepest condolences to Polly on the loss of 'so brilliant and splendid a son, whose exceptional abilities would have carried him far'.[28] Dick Law wrote in *The Times*, 'It was too much to hope that Ronald Cartland should be spared, and all who enjoyed his friendship must, I think, have known – although we could not bring ourselves to admit it – that he had fallen.' Liddell Hart from the War Office expressed the terrible sense of wasted opportunity: 'Of all the younger men in parliament whom I met during the last few years before the war he impressed me as the most promising.'[29] Perhaps the best tribute came from the enemy, as Somerset recorded an extract from a German broadcast in his notebook while he was in captivity. It read, 'We must recognise that the British fighters [at Cassel] were magnificent. We must assume that these were their crack regiments. Each soldier was of marvellous physique and full of fighting spirit.'

As Somerset put it, 'By holding on at Cassel we not only deprived the Germans of one of the main roads to Dunkirk, but enabled many British detached units and individuals to reach the bridgehead.'[30] In other words, Ronnie died that others might live. The stubborn and courageous defence of Cassel saved many thousands of Allied lives. That extra day, vitally, bought more time for Operation Dynamo to succeed. Churchill and the High Command knew the risk to which they were exposing 145 Brigade, but Ronnie would not have complained.

There is another sadness behind Ronnie's death. When Barbara put together a short book in Ronnie's honour, she included all of Law's words, apart from a single sentence: 'I think that his appearance, slightly flamboyant as it was, must have told against him in the House.'[31] Barbara hated what that coded word 'flamboyant' signified, yet courage ran through Ronnie like a golden thread. It equally inspired his decision to stand out from the crowd in Parliament, his acceptance of his own true nature and his refusal to abandon his post at Cassel.

20

Itching for Action

Churchill did not have a free hand when he formed his new government in May 1940. He was still beholden to Chamberlain, who remained leader of the Conservative Party, and with several of the architects of appeasement still in the Cabinet – including Chamberlain as Lord President of the Council and Halifax as foreign secretary – it was not yet the vigorous government for which the Glamour Boys had been clamouring. Churchill kept Harry Crookshank as financial secretary to the Treasury, though, and he brought several of the Glamour Boys into government. Eden was initially war secretary and Jim Thomas returned as his PPS. Amery was minister for India and Burma, Cranborne was paymaster-general, and Duff Cooper took over the under-performing Ministry of Information, with Harold Nicolson as his deputy and Ronnie Tree advising him on American affairs.

For a while the old guard acted as a brake on Churchill, repeatedly questioning his determination to fight an all-out war. Joseph Ball secretly continued to advise Chamberlain, too, impressing on him that it was 'certain that the "Glamour Boys" [would] be well organised' at meetings in the House – and that Chamberlain's supporters 'must be equally well organised'.[1] Things changed in July, though. First *Guilty Men* appeared on British newsstands. Published pseudonymously, it angrily pointed the finger at Chamberlain, Halifax and Simon for Britain's ill-preparedness for war and it swiftly sold 200,000 copies.[2] That same month Chamberlain discovered that he had terminal bowel cancer and retired. He died that November. Churchill took advantage of Chamberlain's retirement and Lord Lothian's death in December to move Halifax to Washington as ambassador, thereby allowing Eden to become foreign secretary.

There would be many more reshuffles before the war was out. After fourteen months Duff Cooper moved to the Duchy of Lancaster, Brendan Bracken took over Information and Nicolson was gently eased out. Later Crookshank was moved to postmaster-general and Jim Thomas took over from him at the Treasury, and Paul Emrys-Evans, Duncan Sandys, Richard Law and Harold Macmillan were all given ministerial posts. But from the end of 1940, the insurgents finally had the government they wanted.

The main problem for several of the queer Glamour Boys, though, was finding something useful to do in the war, not least because, as Eden told Victor Cazalet, all the generals were 'terribly against' MPs being soldiers.[3] Jack Macnamara found this infuriating. He expected the London Irish Rifles to be deployed overseas at any minute, but for months he found himself kicking his heels in London. As he wrote in his diary on 12 October, 'The London Irish are, meanwhile, still in Brixton,' with a heavy emphasis on the word 'still'.[4] It was not until May 1940 that the battalion finally moved out of London. Yet again their duties felt more like policing than soldiering, as they were sent to prevent air landings in Kent and on the Isle of Thanet. At least there was a sense of danger, as everyone believed that the threat of invasion was real and 'the order was to fight to the last man and to the last round'.[5] Moreover, life was not unpleasant, as Jack had a very congenial set of officers. Viscount Stopford was in charge of headquarters company, both A and B companies were led by queer men, John Cantopher and Paddy Mahon, and Jack recruited as second lieutenants Cantopher's partner, E. M. Grace of the Grace Shipping Line, the unmarried Liberal MP Stephen Furness, and the vivacious and queer Mervyn Bonham Carter, who ran the battalion concert party known as 'the

Liricals'.[6] But Jack felt guilty that, unlike his friends, he had still not been anywhere near danger. Ronnie Tree's London house was bombed (consigning him to the Ritz for the duration of the war), another bomb, which landed on the Café de Paris in Covent Garden, killed one of the young men Jack had taken to Box House, the poet Charles Dooley, and in May 1941 came the news that the 37-year-old Dudley Joel, who had attended many of the Glamour Boys' meetings, had drowned when the converted steam merchant HMS *Registan* was bombed off Cape Cornwall. Yet for Jack the only moment of danger came when two members of the Chelmsford Conservative Association came to visit. They were standing by Jack's car on the road between Dungeness and Littlestone when a German Messerschmitt treated them to a burst of its guns. According to the *Essex Chronicle*, 'Mrs Wakefield took shelter under the running board and Mr Wakefield disposed himself full on his face on Mother Earth.'[7]

There was one other form of danger for queer men. War provided many opportunities for sex, but the law had not changed, and in June 1941 its long arm reached Parliament. Eddy Sackville-West's former lover Sir Paul Latham, who was still the MP for Scarborough and Whitby, had enlisted in the 70th Searchlight Regiment of the Royal Artillery the moment war was declared. He was made captain the day Churchill became prime minister and found himself overseeing defensive operations on the Sussex Downs, where he was billeted not far from Jack Macnamara at Hove. Latham was lonely. He had had affairs with men both before and after his wedding, but his wife Patricia had grown sick of the lies. She sailed to America in July 1940, taking their son with her, and the following year she sued for divorce from Palm Beach. Paul relished the newfound freedom this brought him, as he openly admitted that he had only really married to bring forth an heir, and his wife told the court that he had told her 'marriage is a device to shackle a man to a woman he is tired of'.[8] He was still a wealthy man, with two country mansions and a flat in London, so when military duties allowed he would pop round from Hyde Park Garden Mews to the Pink Sink, where he met young men like the anti-aircraft gunner Gilbert Bradley, whom he took home. If the Pink Sink failed him there was always one of the nearby parks, St James's, Green or Hyde Park.

Then, on 24 June, one of his fellow officers, Captain MacDonald, warned him that a letter to him from a gunner had been opened in his absence. It had been referred up to his brigadier and charges would almost certainly be brought. His heart sank as MacDonald added that the letter included a phrase about how the gunner did not want to be messed about again. 'I want to be a man,' he wrote, according to MacDonald, 'or I want to be treated as a man.'[9] Latham knew how this could be interpreted and immediately said, 'There's only one answer − a motor-cycle.'[10] Realising that Latham intended to take his own life, MacDonald told him that it would be more courageous to stay and face it out, but later that day Latham drove his powerful motorbike at full pelt off the road with the intention of killing himself. He said in court that he had not intended to take his own life, but he was deliberately reckless, as his artificial leg made it difficult to brake, and he admitted that he looked on it as 'Providence … I might die or I might not'.[11] Found with nothing more than some superficial head wounds, he was immediately arrested and charged with thirteen separate offences of disgraceful conduct with three Royal Artillery gunners and a civilian, plus a further charge of attempted suicide. Latham pleaded not guilty, but he resigned his seat while he awaited his court martial. Latham's lawyer, Sir Patrick Hastings, told the jury in summing up that, 'Whatever your decision is in this case, Sir Paul Latham's life is now pretty well damned,'[12] but they found him guilty and the court sentenced him to be cashiered (that is to say, dismissed and dishonoured) and imprisoned for two years. Every queer man in Parliament must have shuddered.

In February 1942 Jack's battalion was finally notified that it would be starting intensive training for a major deployment overseas – and in the same breath Jack was given a promotion of sorts. He was to be a member of the General Staff of the new RAF regiment in charge of all the regiment's squadrons in Northern Ireland. He was furious. Britain was still just 'pottering',[13] he resented being parted from the battalion and he came to the conclusion that the army was wasting his time in Northern Ireland, as he felt he was eating his soul out staring at Irish aerodromes all day. Eventually he wrote to Churchill's PPS, George Harvie-Watt, 'I am a soldier at heart and I want to do some soldiering – and as soon as possible.'[14]

Churchill tried his best, but his chief military assistant, 'Pug' Ismay, and the War Office came up with all sorts of excuses[15] and it was only after several notes from Downing Street that it was agreed Jack could have a 'special vacancy' on the next Senior Staff College course in the palatial stately home, Minley Manor.[16] Jack could finally see his way to a fighting command, but a week before Christmas he wrote again to Churchill from 25 Palace Street, hoping that when he finished the course in April he would be posted to some formation that had at least 'a sporting chance of going abroad'.[17] Jack's frustration continued, though. He was so desperate he even agreed to join the Council on Foreign Relations at the suggestion of Herbert Sharp (who was by this stage openly giving his London address as 25 Palace Street, while Jack normally pretended to stay at the Athenaeum).[18] Jack's course ended in April, but nobody had any idea what to do with him when it was over. In June he wrote to Churchill again: 'No one is more anxious to go and lead troops in battle than myself, but, although I left the Senior Staff College nearly two months ago I am still no nearer to it!!'[19] Then, finally, came a deployment overseas. He was to sail to Cairo on 12 August, where he was to join the Middle East Command under General Sir Henry 'Jumbo' Wilson. Jack was excited but apprehensive. He asked Tom Driberg, who was now the Independent MP in neighbouring Maldon, to look after his constituency correspondence and wrote one final letter to Churchill, 'I just want to take my humble share leading troops in action.'[20] Yet again he was disappointed, as he was appointed to another training job as assistant commandant of the Combined Training Centre, Middle East. Even Ismay acknowledged that it would not 'give him his heart's desire for action'.[21]

There were occasional moments of high drama – at one point he wrote that he had 'nearly been blown up twice in the last few days' and in April 1944 he was indirectly involved in Patrick Leigh Fermor's daring (although ultimately foolhardy) capture of General Heinrich Kreipe, the German commander in Crete – but Jack found himself filling time as a military tourist. He spent Christmas in Jerusalem and Nazareth. He visited Edward Spears, who had been appointed minister of state in Beirut, and he went to Syria. Then finally, in the summer of 1944, General James Gammell, Wilson's chief of staff, gave Jack a new role as General Staff officer at the newly created Land Forces Adriatic (LFA). This new 9,500-strong unit was part of the Balkan Air Force based in Bari, near the heel of southern Italy, and was responsible for raiding operations out of Vis. This 'new and mysterious command in Central Mediterranean'[22] was a real military role, as in the words of the LFA's new commanding officer, Brigadier George Davy, their instructions were 'to do as much damage to the Germans within reach as possible'.[23] Jack was in his element. For the first time he was a central part of an adventurous establishment, which included No. 2 Commando Brigade, the Long Range Desert Group, the Special Boat Service and the Raiding Support Regiment.

In October he led an amphibious landing of his own. The background was complex. Relations had been tense with the head of the Yugoslav partisans, Marshal Tito, who repeatedly played the British and Americans off against the Russians. Tito insisted that he did not want British troops landing in Yugoslavia without his permission, 'because we already have our own military and civil government'.[24] But, conscious of his own lack of firepower, Tito encouraged the British to send artillery and a commando unit to assist with forcing the Germans into a chaotic retreat. Davy put Jack in charge of the preliminary reconnaissance prior to landing a substantial British commando force, so, on 21 October, Jack landed with fifteen men in a small boat near Dubrovnik. He wrote back to a relative, 'We were told it was a heavily mined coast so we went in close to avoid them.'[25] They managed to get ashore undetected, but a mine exploded on the beach, wounding Jack's batman, Alfred Savage, in the face and legs, though not too seriously. Savage was evacuated, but Jack stayed in Yugoslavia, where he reported that the Germans had left a trail of devastation. He wrote that one could journey for miles without seeing a single house intact, as all the homes were 'burnt-out, roofless, gaunt skeletons like their former owners'.[26] Davy also recorded that Jack had seen a pile of naked corpses being disposed of by partisans, which probably means that Jack witnessed the aftermath of the infamous Daksa massacre, in which partisans dragged forty-eight compatriots accused of collaborating with the Germans to the ancient monastery on the island of Daksa and shot them. Apparently the partisans stripped their victims before execution 'because they wanted the clothes'.[27]

In December Jack decided to pay a visit to his old battalion of the London Irish Rifles. They had seen fierce action in Iraq, Egypt and Tunisia, and had formed part of the Eighth Army at Sicily, Monte Cassino and the Anzio beachhead. They had sustained more than 600 casualties and endured two harsh Italian winters. Now they were engaged in holding the line on the floodplains of the River Senio. It was a miserable task. The weather was so atrocious that communication with forward positions became impossible. The Germans pounded Allied forces across the river and chunks of the riverbank collapsed into the swollen waters. It had always been Jack's ambition to lead the LIR in battle, so he insisted on visiting them when he had four days leave in the run-up to Christmas. They were in reserve at Faenza when Jack arrived late on 21 December, but they received a message that night that they were to take over from 10th Gurkha Rifles on the river by 12.30 the following day. Jack was exhilarated to see so many old faces and insisted on seeing the forward companies. Just after 11 o'clock Jack was on the roadside outside C Company's HQ talking to their South African officer, Major Martinus Boswell, when the Germans started a new mortar bombardment. Jack, Boswell and a thirty-year-old Scottish platoon commander, Lieutenant John Prosser, were caught in the attack. Prosser died of his wounds later that day. Boswell was wounded but went on to lead an extraordinarily brave and victorious advance across the river three months later. Jack, though, was killed outright and was buried at the British Military Cemetery in Forlì the next day. The adjutant wrote: 'Although it was felt by those who had known him that it was the death he would have chosen, the death of Col. Macnamara who had done so much for the Battalion came as a great shock.'[28] The official regimental history recorded that it was particularly tragic that Jack had died 'while for the first time he was watching in action the Regiment of which he was so proud'.[29]

The tributes were generous. Churchill sent his deepest sympathy to Jack's mother and added in a postscript, 'I grieve for him greatly. He was all that a man sh[oul]d be.'[30] The *Sunday Mirror* described him as 'one of the most colourful figures in politics … young and dashingly romantic'.[31] The most effusive words came from another homosexual of Irish extraction, Flight Lieutenant William Teeling, who had helped in Jack's by-election in 1934, had been stationed in Hythe at the same time as Jack, and was elected for Brighton in a by-election in 1944. Teeling described Jack as 'lonely … silent, shy and extremely modest' and dropped a hint when he noted that he had only recently realised 'how few family ties [Jack] possessed'. Teeling concluded, 'I know of none in Parliament who is there so completely to work for other people.'[32] Remarkably, the *Chelmsford Chronicle* headline read 'He Loved Men'.[33] The article was a sentimental tribute from the vicar of Little Waltham, but the double entendre was almost certainly intentional.

Chelmsford Cathedral was packed for Jack's memorial service on Saturday 6 January. His mother Natalie sat in the front pew with her other son Brian, who was now a wing commander, and his wife. The only sour note came later from Brian. Jack had made Herbert Sharp and Richard Wilson (a bachelor solicitor and soldier friend) the executors of his will, in which he left £500 each to his batman Alfred Savage and his godson Peter Robson, and the rest of his £23,000 estate to Brian, but his brother so disapproved of Jack's homosexuality that he refused to accept a penny and the rest of the money went to Alfred and Peter.

A few weeks later a memorial service was held at St Margaret's Westminster, with twenty-three of Jack's parliamentary colleagues in attendance. It must have been particularly difficult for Herbert Sharp, who helped lead the service. Jack was praised for never accepting opinions ready-made and finding it difficult to toe the line, for his transparent honesty and unswerving loyalty. At the end of the service, just as in Chelmsford Cathedral, two pipers from the London Irish Rifles took their places on the chancel steps. The congregation stood as the pipers played the 'Skye Boat Song' and the regimental march, 'Garryowen'. The congregation trooped out in silence. Everyone – even Natalie – kept saying that Jack had intended to return home in the New Year to take up his duties in Parliament. 'If only' was on everyone's lips.

Herbert's family reckoned that he was never the same again.

Victor Cazalet had a similarly frustrating time as Jack, as he suddenly found himself with 'practically nothing to do'[34] when the War Office decided to split his battery in two in July 1940. By luck, though, he had joined a delegation to the Free Polish Army's celebration of the 149th anniversary of the Polish Constitution in France on 3 May and had met the Polish commander-in-chief, General Władysław Sikorski. He was impressed. Sikorski was charismatic, brave and articulate. In his youth he had been strikingly handsome, with a strong military bearing, high cheekbones and full lips. Now aged sixty, he retained that virile energy and his determination and vanity were a mix that turned many heads. He had formed a Polish government in exile and was now its prime minister and commander-in-chief with 66,000 troops at the disposal of the Allied forces.

Victor had a strong interest in Poland. His family had traded extensively with Eastern Europe out of St Petersburg, he had spent time with the White Russian Army after the war and he had visited Poland more than once. The two men established an immediate rapport, so when Sikorski arrived in London in June, Victor put him up at the Dorchester and they dined together the following night. There were other dinners and meetings – and Sikorski came down to Great Swifts for the weekend of 6–8 July. There they came up with an idea. Relations within the Free Polish community and between the Poles and the British government were strained. If Cazalet could persuade Churchill and Eden to appoint him as the official liaison officer with the Free Polish Army, they could kill two birds with one stone. The plan was put to Downing Street and on 9 July Victor received official confirmation from Eden. Victor noted 'I think it will be interesting and I can do a useful job. I hate leaving [the] Battery.'[35]

From then on this was Victor's primary war effort. He held parties at the Dorchester and Great Swifts so that the British establishment could get to know Sikorski, he hosted fetes to raise money for Polish relief, he eased the way to a new Anglo–Polish Agreement, he accompanied Churchill, Eden and the king on visits to Sikorski's men in Scotland and Ireland, he smoothed ruffled Polish feathers, and when rows erupted between Sikorski and Britain or Russia he deployed his considerable charm to bring about a second Polish accord with the Allies. For substantial periods this took him overseas. In March 1941 he and Sikorski travelled to Canada and the US, where Victor lobbied senators and congressmen for support and caught up with old friends. He was still in the US when Hitler attacked Russia on 22 June, but suddenly his liaison role became even more complex and important, as Polish interests were subsidiary to Russian might, and Polish hatred of the Russians, as Victor acknowledged, 'goes back 150 years'.[36] Victor also accompanied Sikorski that autumn on a nine-week trip that took in Gibraltar, Malta and Cairo before a secret night-time visit to Tobruk, where they delivered twenty-five cases of whisky to the Polish Brigade. From there they went on to Baghdad, Teheran, Baku (where they enjoyed two gargantuan feasts and an opera), Astrakhan (where the arrival of caviar mildly mitigated the horror of a filthy and foul-smelling lavatory) and Kuybyshev (now Samara), the temporary home of much of the Russian government. There Victor stagnated while Sikorski went alone to Moscow to negotiate with Stalin.

Victor's life back in England, by contrast, was strikingly mundane. His diary regularly noted 'no invasion' and during the Blitz he reported that the Dorchester had been shaken to pieces by gunfire, a bomb and a plane had fallen in the park at Great Swifts, Parliament had been bombed several times and the Commons had a new home in Church House. Yet even when he slept one night in the gym at the Dorchester, he commented, 'Very quiet and as safe as can be. It's an amusing and exciting world.'[37] When he helped bring in the harvest at Great Swifts, his diary made everything seem idyllic: 'July 19th: A quiet day – church, croquet, gardening. A long walk.' He was only too aware of his privileged position. When he spent a night at a bomber station near Newmarket he felt guilty for being safe and warm for the five hours they were out, but he felt even more ashamed when they all returned safely and one of them apologised for not having hit his target. 'What humility I feel!' he wrote. 'All I want to do is unlace their boots if they'd let me.'[38]

One political concern particularly dominated his thoughts, though – Palestine and the plight of the Jews. As far as he was concerned, 'Deliverance of the Jews from persecution was as important an issue as any for which we are fighting.'[39] He was infuriated at what he saw as the government's reneging on historic promises and argued more forcibly than anyone for a Jewish homéland. He was uncompromising on the issue in the Commons. He had just received news of further atrocities in Poland: 'The Jews are being exterminated to-day in tens of thousands. The stories of the horrors of the massacres at a camp called Treblinka would put to shame the massacres of Genghis Khan or the sufferings of the Albigenses.'[40] He was ashamed of growing British anti-Semitism, which he saw as a measure of Goebbels's victory. 'Unless,' he said, 'our final victory includes the defeat of anti-Semitism it will be a sham victory.'[41]

In May 1943 Victor and Sikorski set off on a tour of Polish troops in the Middle East in the midst of a new political row over the German discovery of mass graves of Polish officers in the Katyn Forest, for which the Russians angrily denied responsibility.* This Middle Eastern tour also gave Victor an opportunity to make a detour to Palestine, where he addressed a large meeting with the Jewish leader David Ben-Gurion. He went further than any other British politician thus far. 'I would gladly give my life for the establishment of a Jewish state in Palestine,' he said, 'as I am ready to give my life for the preservation of the British Empire.' He added 'Whatever happens, the Jews *must* have a permanent home.'[42]

A few days later Victor joined Sikorski on the journey home to England. On Saturday 3 July they stopped off in Gibraltar. Most of the population had been evacuated and the town was devoted to the military effort. Vast barrage guns were ranged across and inside the Rock to protect British waters for troopships. Despite the military situation, there was an air of jollity about the place. The governor, General Noel Mason-MacFarlane, was a friend of Sikorski and would later be a Labour MP. He also loved the theatre and had recruited several actors to his staff, including Anthony Quayle and Quayle's friend John Perry, who was theoretically a flight lieutenant in the RAF but had never managed to master the art of flying, so was nicknamed 'Wingless Victory' and consigned to unspecified intelligence work. Mason-MacFarlane had even enticed John Gielgud to perform for the troops at the head of a cast of stars earlier in the year, largely because Perry, who was tall, fair-haired, amiable, good-looking, low maintenance and discreet, was the star's lover. Perry and Gielgud had a pleasant

---

* It was only in 1990 that the Russian state admitted that the massacre had been ordered by the head of the Russian secret police, Lavrentiy Beria.

time. They toured the Rock, sat up drinking in Gielgud's room after curfew, and Gielgud wrote home to his mother that he had enjoyed 'some quite gay parties'.[43] Victor was equally delighted to see Perry in July, as he was an old friend and the two men spent the Sunday morning together. That afternoon Victor played tennis with Anthony Quayle before joining the rest of the party at the American Independence Day reception at Government House.

After the reception, Perry drove Victor to the airfield, where Sikorski's Liberator aircraft was parked on the runway next to the plane of the Soviet ambassador to London, Ivan Maisky. After a few moments they were joined by the rest of Sikorski's entourage, including another unmarried British Conservative MP, Brigadier John Whiteley,[44] all of whom were, according to Mason-MacFarlane 'in very good spirits'. The group had had a narrow escape when they flew to Canada in November, as both the engines on their Hudson had conked out just as they got twenty feet up in the air. The pilot had then crash-landed just twenty yards from the edge of the airstrip. They were not so lucky this time. Their Czech pilot, Eduard Prchal, took off at 11 p.m., but sixteen seconds later Perry noticed that the Liberator's navigation lights seemed to dip. Clearly the plane was in trouble. The airport's emergency vehicles rushed to the edge of the runway and pointed their searchlights into the sea, where the aircraft could just be seen sinking into the water. The bodies of Sikorski and Tadeusz Klimecki, chief of the Polish General Staff, were found fairly quickly but it took thirty-six hours before Victor was found, still strapped to his seat. Perry was asked to identify him, and Victor's body was buried in Gibraltar at 7 a.m. on 12 July. All sixteen passengers were killed, but the pilot survived. When Churchill was asked in the Commons if he was able to give any indication what had caused the crash, he simply shook his head. Despite several inquiries, rumours persist to this day that the Russians sabotaged the plane. Suspicious minds have pointed out since that the Iberian head of British intelligence at the time was the Soviet double agent Kim Philby.

Victor was forty-seven. Tributes poured in from around the world. Bob Sherriff sent his condolences to his mother Mollie, who replied, 'no one can ever take his place as his loving never failed me'.[45] A thousand trees were planted in Palestine in his honour. Chaim Weizmann called him 'one of the few precious friends of the Jewish people in modern times who never was moved from his devotion to the cause'.[46] *The Times* commended his 'almost boyish zest'[47] and the Marquess of Londonderry called him 'a most lovable character'.[48]

One casualty of Churchill's creation of the coalition government in 1940 was Rob Bernays, who was surprised and angry to be sacked until he was made deputy regional commissioner for the Southern Civil Defence Region on an annual salary of £1,200 at the end of May. This was no sinecure, as Rob spent the next two years flitting between his constituency in Bristol, Reading, where he was based, and Southampton, which he effectively ran under emergency powers.

The war brought somebody new into Rob's life, a young woman called Nancy Britton, who was the only daughter of George Britton, a former Liberal MP. Rob had met Nancy, or 'Nan', as he called her, when he stayed with her parents during the election in 1931, but it was only when they were reintroduced at one of Nancy Astor's weekend parties at Cliveden in 1939 that they hit it off. Nan embodied many of the characteristics Rob most admired in others. She was interested in politics. She was a good listener. She was practical, assertive and independently minded. Her strong sense of public duty had led her to volunteer for the Auxiliary Territorial Service (ATS), the women's branch of the British Army, in which she had risen to be a senior commander – and her father's death had left her and her elder brother Jack wealthy. She was equally attracted to Rob, with his mixture of confidence and self-doubt, earnestness and sociability. Even his manifest hesitation when it came to matters emotional or sexual was appealing and came as a pleasant change from the attitude of so many other men.

Nan coincided with other major changes in his life. Rob was a writer, a journalist, a politician – a man who used words, not force, to get his way. Tall and lanky, with a thirty-six-inch chest, his bearing was academic rather than soldierly. But as the war ground on, he knew that he might have to enlist in the ranks. After all, at thirty-seven he was still well under the upper age limit for conscription. Besides, as he revealed in a speech in the Commons, he was angry that the public was being mollycoddled by the Ministry of Information. 'They suggest that alarm creates despondency,' he said. 'It does not. Alarm is the spur to endeavour.'[49] He was effectively preaching to himself – and when he left the Chamber Walter Elliot told him he was taking his life in his hands, 'that conscription would follow and perhaps a sticky end in a tank in Libya'.[50] Despite his public nonchalance, Rob vacillated privately and that spring he paid a doctor six guineas to give him a 'thumpingly adverse report', which concluded that he was 'quite unfit for general service'.[51] Rob told Nan that the doctor had certainly been worth his fee, but he seems never to have deployed the report, not even when a summons came from the Reading Medical Board in August 1941.

At the start of August Rob's father was so dangerously ill that he did not recognise his wife for a couple of days. He put up a fight for a while and rallied a little, but in the end his seventy-four years were against him and he died at the end of the month. Rob wrote to Nan, 'He was to me a great rock and under his shadow I found a calm anchorage from the sufferings of the world.' Like many people when they lose their second parent, he confessed that he felt 'strangely unprotected now'.[52] Then in December he received news that his eldest brother, Jack Bernays, was missing, presumed drowned, having returned to his sinking ship to save others. His brother's act of heroism finally helped Rob make up his mind. A few days later he wrote to Nan that the decision had been taken. The home secretary had agreed to allow him to resign as deputy commissioner so as to enlist.

A month later Rob took another plunge. He had always been slow on the uptake with women, and his courtship of Nan was conducted almost entirely by letter. He could be tactless and maladroit. On several occasions he implied that she did not come first in his affections. In the midst of apologising for not writing to her, he admitted that he hadn't written to his 'beloved Lucy' in five weeks either and added, 'As soon as that was done to-day I said "Nan comes next."'[53] Yet he repeatedly claimed that he was infatuated. 'I always write to you with my face contorted into a faint giggle. I don't know why. Do you do the same?' he asked.[54]

So, with the prospect of army life on the horizon, he asked Nan to marry him while on leave in Salisbury in February 1942. As ever, he was not in a rush. He thought she should think it over for a month before replying and three days later he explained that there were all sorts of things that she needed to know about him. 'I am not a "hubby" in any sense of the word,' he wrote, 'sitting at home in his "den" with his old "smoking jacket" and his row of pipes and his Saturday afternoon gardening, content only to have "the Missus" around.' He admitted that he knew nothing about 'gynaecology' and wondered whether Nan's job was 'quite unsuited and painful to starting a baby'. He seemed genuinely besotted, although he pointed out that even with the £2,000 he had just inherited from an uncle she was far wealthier than he, so 'I should never have to pay your income tax!'[55] Many a woman might have questioned this apparent ambivalence, but Nan found it endearing or convenient and said 'yes'.

The big day came on Saturday 25 April 1942. Wartime restrictions meant that 'there was an absence of pageantry, and the bride, dressed with exquisite simplicity, was attended by one little bridesmaid'.[56] Yet it was a joyous occasion. Walter Elliot acted as best man, Harold Nicolson, Will Mabane and Ernest Brown attended from the Commons, Bristol Cathedral was full and many had to wait outside. The only downside was that just days later, while they were on their honeymoon at Walter and K Elliot's house in Hawick in the Scottish borders, Rob received his enlistment notice, requiring him to appear at Longmoor two weeks later.

Rob found army life every bit as tedious as he had feared. He hated the endless nights of guard duty, the nonsensical rules and the constant shouting. At times he erupted with fury when an officer berated him or prevented him from taking the leave he reckoned he was entitled to as a married man and as an MP. Yet he was commissioned as a second lieutenant in January 1943 and appointed as a railway transporter officer based at Preston that February. This was a particularly dull appointment, as he was effectively an unpaid stationmaster, conducting colonels to their carriages or answering commanders' questions about the next train to Chesterfield. As he complained to Nan, 'In the ranks humble duties had their dignity. As an officer they only seem ludicrous.'[57] But a chance invitation to address the Officer Cadet Training Unit about the life of an MP was such a success – he wrote to Nan, 'I was given an ovation such as I cannot think I have even been accorded by you. It was deafening'[58] – that in December he was transferred to a more suitable post. Officially termed 'entertainment officer' at No. 3 Anti-Aircraft Group, based at Horfield Barracks in Bristol – and promoted to captain – Rob was to spend the next year addressing troops up and down the country.

The long absences from Nan made him more effusive and sentimental in his daily letters, which would start 'My darling – oh my Darling!' or 'My Own Sweet Darling'. He shared everything with her – his worries about money, his frustrations with army life, and his hope that the Conservatives would not stand against him if there were a general election. Clearly Rob loved Nan, yet they spent remarkably little time together during their three-year marriage. He was absent when their first son Richard was born in February 1943 – so Nan brought him up with the help of a nanny at her brother's home, Shortwood Lodge. But he also took the extraordinary decision in August 1944 to spend the whole of his leave not with his wife and son but with the Elliots. Nan might have been pleased to hear that he had thought of her when he climbed the mountain that they had trekked up during their honeymoon, but she was less than amused, not least as she was then pregnant with their second son, Edward, who was born after a long, hard labour on 7 October. At least this time Rob was able to sit and hold her hand while she recuperated.

The family was yet again apart at Christmas, because Rob chose to spend it with Frank Milton, who was now a major in the Royal Artillery, had married in 1940, but was already separated from his wife and was living in a flat near Piccadilly Circus. Rob visited the devastation in the East End, he went to the opening night of Terence Rattigan's latest play, *Love in Idleness*, which he thought rather scurrilous, as 'adultery is after all a very wicked thing', and he complained that it was going to be a very dark Christmas, with nothing but Frank, another friend, Philip Ross, and 'the forced jollity of complete strangers'.[59] The only time he had with the family was forty-eight hours leave on 30 and 31 December, much of which he spent on trains. Nevertheless he was upbeat when he wrote on House of Commons paper on 2 January about the new house they intended to move in to. Above all he looked forward to Nan 'being my wife instead of nurse, being grand and charming about the constituency and coming up to stay for a week at a time'.

Rob ended that letter, 'We never know what the next 3 months will produce,'[60] but he was excited that he was about to join a cross-party group of MPs boosting the morale of British troops in Italy. The trip was meant to last three weeks, and after an uneventful journey they arrived on 6 January in Naples, where Rob gave his first talk to troops. On 7 January they motored up through Cassino to Rome, where, although they stayed in the grandest suites in the Grand Hotel, he was reduced to writing in pencil by the light of a candle, as there was no ink or electricity. A day later he was driven up into the forward lines ('towering mountains, driving snow and warm-hearted companionship'[61]), where he saw Charlie Morpeth, the son of the Earl of Carlisle, whom he had last seen at Naworth Castle, lying in a field hospital.

The highlight, though, was when he left the rest of the group and was driven in a Jeep for four hours into the mountains in a snowsuit to visit Harold Nicolson's son Nigel's company just a few hundred yards from the enemy. That night he slept with six other officers in the upper room of a battered farmhouse and was given the shock of his life when a rat jumped off his bed in the middle of the night. He felt proud of what he was doing. As he explained to Nan on 20 January, 'It does seem that [al]though I am in civilian clothes and if I were not I would wear no ribbons, I do have some appeal to the chaps.'[62] Later that day he wrote again with news that the group was going to extend its journey to Greece. 'I have been fielding since May 1940,' he wrote, 'and now at last it seems that I have an opportunity of going in to bat ... For Greece is not soldiers' welfare. It is political dynamite.'[63]

While he was in Rome Rob received the first letters Nan had sent him since he left England. They were full of ordinary daily family news and sparkled with Nan's easy, chatty style. It had been bitterly, bitterly cold. Mrs Rowledge in the village was ill. The nanny had taken a couple of days off. Nan worried about whether Rob was taking enough care of his appearance. Their son Richard was up to every trick and naughtiness imaginable. On Monday 22 January Rob penned a very hurried note before going off to the Vatican for an audience with Pope Pius. Dinner at the embassy the night before had been 'an echo of a vanished world – beautiful women, marvellous food, several footmen'. He ended, 'Great haste – but much love. R.'[64]

The next morning the group set off for Greece, flying in two American Expeditor planes, stopping off at Brindisi on the Adriatic. The weather was fine in Rome, but rumours about storms ahead led to some confusion on the tarmac as the group wondered whether to fly, and when they finally decided to take off they ended up in the wrong seats, which meant that Rob was separated from his luggage. Somewhere over the mountains they hit a snowstorm and although the other plane arrived safely, there was no sign of Rob's plane at Brindisi that day or in Greece. Initially there was some hope that the experienced RAF pilot had crash-landed safely somewhere and had not been able to radio through, but that Friday Harold Nicolson picked up the *Evening Standard*, which announced that Rob was missing. 'This knocks me silly,' he wrote. When he arrived at the Commons he found there was an air of gloom and apprehension as Anthony Eden announced that 'the honourable and gallant Member for North Bristol (Captain Bernays) and the hon. Gentleman, the junior Member for Antrim (Mr. D. Campbell), who were visiting our Forces in Italy, are reported missing'.[65] Eden put a brave face on it, hoping that the missing aircraft might yet be found safe, but he gave Harold the distinct impression that there was 'mighty little hope' and he went to bed feeling sore and sad.[66]

Rob's family and friends were devastated. Jean Stratheden wrote to Nan to say that the last time she had seen him, back in September, she had felt him 'even more Rob than ever before, deeper & stronger & happier, & oh dear yes, even funnier!'[67] Churchill rang Nan every night to give her updates and asked if there was anything he could do. 'Well, there is,' she replied. 'Could I have my ATS batman, Winnie Brooks, for a couple of weeks to help with the children?' Within twenty-four hours the redoubtable Winnie was discharged on special instructions of the prime minister – and she stayed with Nan for thirty years.[68] Will Mabane thought that his 'closest political friend … was but at the beginning of his political career' and tried to console Nan with the thought that 'you know of Rob's peculiar quality of courage – or moral courage, and of his determination at all costs to fulfil to the last his duty'.[69]

Eventually, what little hope remained evaporated and on 23 March the Speaker formally announced the deaths of the two MPs. Finally Nan could hold a memorial service at Bristol Cathedral on 20 April, followed by a long-delayed christening for young Edward, at which he was renamed Robert after his father. For years Nan found his name too hard to say and called him Robin. Harold Nicolson, who was godfather to the boys, wrote in his diary that he felt crushed: 'All my best House of Commons friends are now dead – Rob, Ronnie Cartland and Jack Macnamara.'[70]

Epilogue

Parliament Square was so packed on the afternoon of 8 May 1945 that mounted police had to keep back the crowds. Germany had declared its unconditional surrender at 2.41 the previous morning and thousands had gathered to hear Churchill's official declaration of Victory in Europe relayed through loudspeakers and to see the man in person. The government had declared it a national holiday and you could buy red, white and blue material without rations, so there was bunting everywhere. Churchill had also ensured London would not run out of beer and the pubs had extended opening hours. Euphoria and bitter regret made everyone emotional. Strangers kissed one another. Soldiers hugged. Couples draped themselves over the lions in Trafalgar Square. Gone were the blackout curtains and in their place there were vast Union flags.

Nothing was quite normal inside Parliament, either. Thanks to Nazi bombing, the Commons were sitting in the Lords and the Lords were down the other end of the Royal Gallery in the Robing Room. Many MPs and peers were still with their units, but the galleries were full of ambassadors and every seat was taken. The House started as usual with questions, but MPs had to keep them going while they waited for Churchill to make his way from Downing Street after his official broadcast at three o'clock. When they ran out of questions they had nothing to do for a few embarrassed moments, but eventually, 'a little shy – a little flushed', 'smiling but bent', the prime minister appeared behind the makeshift Speaker's chair and 'everyone

rose and cheered and waved handkerchiefs and Order Papers'.[1]
As Churchill started, silence descended on the Chamber and
in Parliament Square. Germany had surrendered. Democracy
had triumphed. The nation could allow herself a moment of
rejoicing, but toil and effort still lay ahead. Japan, with all her
treachery and greed, remained unsubdued. The task still had to
be completed, at home and abroad. He ended with a flourish.
'Advance Britannia! Long live the Cause of Freedom! God Save
the King!' he grunted as he leaned on the despatch box. The
public's cheer of pent-up relief could be heard inside the Palace,
where MPs also cheered – and several wept. Then solemnnity
took hold again as the Speaker, in his full ceremonial robes,
slipped past Churchill and the government's red benches and
led the two Houses out into Central Lobby, past the statues of
Gladstone and Pitt, down the steps to St Stephen's Hall and out
to St Margaret's Church for a service of thanksgiving. It had
rained heavily the night before, but the sunshine was bright,
and Winston blinked as he stepped out through St Stephen's
Porch. Immediately a roar spread through the crowd all the
way up Whitehall to Trafalgar Square as everyone bellowed at
the top of their lungs. It was so loud that Baffy Dugdale could
not hear her own voice and all she could think of as she stood
there in the crowd and saw the MPs file out was the ghosts she
imagined walking beside their old colleagues, especially Victor
and Rob.

Jim Thomas and Harry Crookshank were there, though. In
1951 Churchill would make the two men respectively First
Lord of the Admiralty and Leader of the Commons; and in
1956 they were both made viscounts in the certain knowledge
that they would not be passing on their hereditary titles. Jim
remained utterly discreet until his dying day in 1960, but Harry's
sexuality became more widely known when a much younger
lover, a former captain in the merchant navy called Desmond
Kilvington, moved in with him in 1954 (Harry's mother and
sister both having died). Desmond was selected and promptly
deselected by the Conservative Association in Grimsby in 1959.

Ronnie Tree was present in St Margaret's, too. His marriage was disintegrating under the double pressure of his frequent liaisons with men and an affair with a married American woman working at the Ministry of Information, Marietta Peabody Fitzgerald. They later married and moved to New York, but Marietta constantly fretted about his sexuality and by the 1960s she was having an affair with the sexually ambivalent American diplomat and politician Adlai Stevenson and Ronnie was largely living in Barbados, which had become the latest fashionable resort for queer men.

The service inside St Margaret's was excruciating, with all its thanksgiving to an all-powerful God. Everyone tried to sing the hymns with gusto but, sitting next to Nancy Astor, Harold Nicolson must have found it difficult to sing to the Lord 'with cheerful voice' or 'burst into songs of joy', as the reading from Isaiah told him he should do. It got even worse when the Speaker's chaplain stood in front of two Union flags laid out on the altar and read out the names of the twenty-one MPs who had been killed in action.

Winston sat at the front. He had stronger reasons than most to grieve. He had always admired Ronnie as 'a man of noble spirit, who followed his convictions without thought of personal advancement'.[2] He had known Victor for many years and although their relationship had been through peaks and troughs, he still 'cherished [such] warm feelings of friendship' for him that he had ruled that when the Commons was rebuilt, the names of those MPs who had died in action would be inscribed on its wooden panelling as 'an example to future generations not unworthy of those we have ourselves received from former times'.[3] He had tried his best for Jack, who he thought was 'all that a man sh[oul]d be'.[4] As for Rob Bernays, Winston would probably have agreed with Hugh Molson's tribute in *The Times*, that Rob had believed and proclaimed, 'long before it was popular' that Britain had to rearm to defeat Hitler.[5]

The list over, everyone stood for the final hymn, 'O God, Our Help in Ages Past'. The penultimate verse was especially poignant, 'Time, like an ever-rolling stream/ Bears all its sons away', and it was more than many could manage to sing through to the end, 'They fly, forgotten, as a dream/ Dies at the opening day.' And then the church bells started ringing out for victory.

Harold had tears in his eyes. 'Furtively I wiped them away,' he wrote. '"Men are so emotional," sniffed Nancy Astor, who was sitting next to me. Damn her.'[6]

Notes

ABBREVIATIONS

BB   Robert Boothby, *Recollections of a Rebel*, London, Hutchinson, 1987

BB/RJ   Robert Rhodes James, *Robert Boothby: A Portrait of Churchill's Ally,* London, Viking, 1991

BC   Barbara Cartland, *Polly, My Wonderful Mother,* London, Herbert Jenkins, 1956

BL   British Library

CC   Robert Rhodes James, ed., *Chips, The Diaries of Sir Henry Channon,* London, Weidenfeld & Nicolson, 1967

CH   Stuart Ball, ed., *Parliament and Politics in the Age of Churchill and Attlee: the Headlam Diaries, 1935–1951,* Cambridge, CUP, 1999

CHAR   Churchill College Cambridge, Churchill Archives Centre

HC   House of Commons, *Hansard*

HCD   Bodleian Library, Oxford, Harry Crookshank Diary, 359/217

HL   House of Lords, *Hansard*

HN   Balliol College, Oxford, Harold Nicolson Typescript Diary

HN/NN1   Nigel Nicolson, ed., *Harold Nicolson: Diaries and Letters, 1930–1939,* London, Weidenfeld & Nicolson, 1966

HN/NN2   Nigel Nicolson, ed., *Harold Nicolson: Diaries and Letters, 1939–1945,* London, Weidenfeld & Nicolson, 1967

HN/NN3   Nigel Nicolson, ed., *The Harold Nicolson Diaries and Letters, 1907–1963,* London, Weidenfeld & Nicolson, 2004

HN/Rose   Norman Rose, *Harold Nicolson,* London, Jonathan Cape, 2005

JM   J. R. J. Macnamara, *The Whistle Blows,* London, Eyre & Spottiswoode, 1938

LBN   Benedict Nicolson Archive, GB3010, The Paul Mellon Centre for Studies in British Art, London, UK

OH   John Harvey, *The Diplomatic Diaries of Oliver Harvey, 1937–40,* London, Collins, 1970

RB   Robert Bernays Family Papers

RB/NS   Nick Smart, ed., *The Diaries and Letters of Robert Bernays, 1932–1939,* E. Mellen Press, 1996

RB/SC	Robert Bernays, *Special Correspondent*, Victor Gollancz, London, 1934
RC	Barbara Cartland, *Ronald Cartland*, Hutchinson & Co., London, 1941
RT	Ronald Tree, *When The Moon Was High*, London, Macmillan, 1975
TGA	Tate Gallery Archives
TNA	The National Archives
TNA CAB	Records of the Cabinet
TNA CRIM	Records of the Central Criminal Court
TNA FO	Records of the Foreign Office
TNA KV	Records of the Security Service
TNA MEPO	Records of the Metropolitan Police
TNA WO	Records of the War Office
VC	Eton College, Victor Cazalet Papers
VC/RJ	Rhodes James, *Victor Cazalet: A Portrait*, London, Hamish Hamilton, 1976

PREFACE: THE HIDDEN STORY

1 BB, p. 109.
2 HC, 19 May 1943, vol. 389, col. 1162.

INTRODUCTION: COCKTAILS AND LAUGHTER

1 Edward Carpenter, *The Intermediate Sex*, London, Allen & Unwin, 1908, p. 114.
2 Frank Harris, *Oscar Wilde, His Life and Confessions*, New York, Brentano's, 1916, vol. 1, p. 250.
3 In like fashion, the writer E. F. Benson and the pianist and classical scholar John Ellingham Brooks shared a house on Capri and the Renaissance expert and poet John Addington Symonds moved to Davos, claiming ill-health, and fell in lustful love with a gondolier in Venice, where he was followed by Frederick Rolfe, 'Baron Corvo', who had a similar affair with the 'young, muscular, splendidly strong' Amadeo Amadei, with his 'big black eyes, rosy face, round black head, scented like an angel'.
4 Jean Cocteau, *Le Livre Blanc*, translated as *The White Paper*, by Austryn Wainhouse, Paris, Olympia Press, 1957, p. 1.
5 *The Times*, 3 July 1934, p. 14.
6 Baldwin to A. Chamberlain, 26 October 1924, Austen Chamberlain Papers, University of Birmingham.
7 Cited in G. M. Young, *Stanley Baldwin*, London, 1952, p. 177.
8 CC, p. 152, 21 March 1938.

I EMPIRE ORPHAN

1 *Yorkshire Evening Post*, 23 March 1926, p. 12.

2   *The Times*, 4 March 1926, p. 10.

3   Although known as Paul, his real name was Charles Geddes Clarkson Hyslop.

4   Maggi Hambling telephone interview with the author, 14 March 2018.

5   TNA FO 371/11839, Arthur Lett-Haines to Major Richardson Cox, 27 February 1926.

6   *The Times*, 4 March 1926, p. 10.

7   TGA 8317/1/3/4.

8   TGA 8317/1/3/4.

9   *The Times*, 4 March 1926, p. 10.

10 TNA FO 371/11839, Jack Macnamara to Natalie Orpen, 24 February 1926.

11 TNA FO 371/11839.

12 HC, 4 March 1926, vol. 192, col. 1611.

13 *L'Afrique française*, vol. 36, my translation of 'ne pas regarder de trop près les agissements'.

14 HC, 1 April 1926, vol. 193, col. 2362.

15 *Dundee Courier*, 29 March 1926, p. 5.

16 TNA FO 371/16380.

17 JM, p. 13.

18 JM, p. 13.

19 *Chelmsford Chronicle*, 3 February 1939, p. 7.

20 JM, p. 38. The headmaster was Arthur Tabor.

21 *Chelmsford Chronicle*, 27 January 1939, p. 7.

22 JM, p. 51.

23 *London Gazette*, 4 April 1924.

24 JM, p. 47.

25 JM, p. 45.

26 *Cambridge Daily News*, 3 October 1939, p. 2.

27 Jonathan Gathorne-Hardy, *The Public School Phenomenon*, London, Hodder & Stoughton, 1977, p. 162.

28 William Acton, *The Functions and Disorders of the Reproductive Organs*, London, John Churchill, 1857, p. 38.

29 Gathorne-Hardy, *The Public School Phenomenon*, p. 166.

30 Gathorne-Hardy, *The Public School Phenomenon*, p. 162.

31 Caroline Seebohm, *No Regrets: The Life of Marietta Tree*, New York, Simon & Schuster, 1997, p. 317.

32 JM, pp. 26–7.

33 *Chelmsford Chronicle*, 20 January 1939, p. 7.

34 *News of the World*, 28 March 1926, p. 1.

35 Criminal Law Amendment Act, 48 & 49 Vict. c. 69, s. 11.

36 Vagrancy Act 1824, 5 Geo. IV, c. 83, s. 4.

37 Vagrancy Act 1898, 61 & 62 Vict. c. 39, s.1 (1) (b).

38 HC, 12 November 1912, vol. 43, col. 1856

39 Army Discipline and Regulations Act 1881, 44 & 45 Vict., chapter 58, subsections 18(5) and 16.

40 George Ives, *The Continued Extension of the Criminal Law*, London, privately printed, 1922, p. 8.

41 *Horton v. Mead* (1913), 1 K.B., 157.

42 *Birmingham Daily Gazette*, 9 November 1926, p. 5.

43 *West London Observer*, 3 December 1926, p. 9.

44 *Yorkshire Post*, 20 January 1927, p. 6.

45 The same happened when the police in Eastbourne charged the 62-year-old John Knox-Orde with gross indecency with a 29-year-old hotel porter called James King in 1934. Knox-Orde was mildly famous as an occasional actor of independent means – he appeared as the butler in *For the Love of Mike* in the West End, in *The Case of Lady Camber* at the Theatre Royal in Yarmouth in 1918 and in a few movies in Berlin – and even though many of his neighbours knew nothing of his arrest, he felt the anguish of humiliation deeply. The weekend before he was due to appear in court, he told one neighbour that he was saying goodbye for ever, prompting the strange response, 'Why, are you getting married?' Friends tried to dissuade him from taking his own life and even notified the police, though this could have brought an additional charge of attempted suicide. He gassed himself the night before the trial; King was sent to trial and given six months' hard labour. Likewise, in December 1934 a bank messenger and a taxi-driver tried to drown themselves in the Thames when they were caught in an act of 'grave impropriety' in the latter's taxi.

46 Anne Olivier Bell and Andrew McNeillie, eds., *The Diary of Virginia Woolf*, London, Hogarth Press, 1984, vol. 5, Thursday 30 March 1939, pp. 211–12.

47 Michael Burns, *Turned Towards the Sun*, London, Michael Russell, 2003, pp. 96–7.

48 Michael Bloch, ed., *James Lees-Milne Diaries, 1984–1997*, London, John Murray, 2008, entry for 25 May 1997.

49 Entry for 11 October 1939, LBN/1/1/13, Benedict Nicolson Archive, GB3010, The Paul Mellon Centre for Studies in British Art, London, UK.

2 BRIGHT YOUNG THINGS

1   JM, pp. 65, 67.

2   BC, p. 77.

3   RC, p. 23.

4   BC, p. 127.

5   Robert Graves, *Good-Bye to All That*, London, Jonathan Cape, 1929, p. 66.

6   BC, p. 140.

7   Charterhouse Archives.

8   *Carthusian*, November 1924, p. 710.

9   BC, p. 27.

10 *Carthusian*, March 1925, p. 775.

11 Cambridge University Library, MS JM/I21/7/1.

12 BC, p. 159.

13 *Liverpool Echo*, 7 September 1924, p. 8.

14 *Touch the Stars*, cited in Henry Cloud, *Barbara Cartland, Crusader in Pink*, London, Weidenfeld & Nicolson, 1979, p. 87.

15 John Skeaping, *Drawn From Life*, London, Collins, 1977, p. 86

16   Peter Parker, *Ackerley: The Life of J. R. Ackerley*, London, Constable, 1989, p. 113. J. R. Ackerley, who became influential as literary editor of the BBC's weekly magazine *The Listener*, mistakenly recalls it as being in Old Compton Street. It was used throughout the 1930s as a film set. It marketed itself as 'the restaurant where you are greeted with a smile and a flower'.

17   It moved to Southampton Street in 1927.

18   Michael Luke, *David Tennant: The Gargoyle Years*, London, Weidenfeld & Nicolson, 1991, p. 45.

19   Jocelyn Brooke, *Private View: Four Portraits*, London, J. Barrie, 1954, pp. 1, 88.

20   Ethel Mannin, *Young in the Twenties*, London, Hutchinson, 1971, p. 32.

21   Mark Amery, ed., *The Letters of Evelyn Waugh*, Weidenfeld & Nicolson, p. 505.

22   Luke, *David Tennant: The Gargoyle Years*, p. 24.

23   *Bystander*, 3 May 1933, p. 5.

24   Hugh David, *On Queer Street*, London, HarperCollins, 1997, p. 89.

25   Peter Wildeblood, *Against the Law*, London, Weidenfeld & Nicolson, 1955, p. 37.

26   BC, p. 37.

27   Kenneth Rose, *Oxford Dictionary of National Biography*.

28   *Yorkshire Post*, 30 March 1935, p. 12.

29   Earl of Lytton, *Antony, Viscount Knebworth*, London, Peter Davies, 1935, p. 113.

30   *Ibid.*, p. 205.

31   *Ibid.*, p. 127.

32   RC, p. 37.

33   *Birmingham Daily Gazette*, 28 January 1931, p. 6.

34   Earl of Lytton, *Antony, Viscount Knebworth*, London, Peter Davies, 1935, p. 349.

35   *Ibid.*, p. 343.

36   Interview with the 7th Earl of Portarlington, 21 November 2017.

37   Private interview with the author.

38   *Bystander*, 13 May 1931, p. 11.

39   *Ibid.*, p. 17.

40   *Ibid.*, p. 13. She added that another bachelor 'Sir Michael Duff Assheton-Smith is busy entertaining' and her eye was not far out. Sir Michael did marry, twice, but his first marriage lasted less than a year and the son he and his second wife, Lady Caroline Paget, adopted claimed that his parents were bisexual and had enjoyed a marriage of convenience.

41   *Bystander*, 16 November 1932, p. 17.

42   *Bystander*, 16 November 1932, p. 17 and 23 November 1932, p. 14.

43   *The Times*, 8 January 1937.

44   *Bystander*, 17 February 1937, p. 13.

45   Through Philip Sassoon, Carlow also came to know T. E. Lawrence and was en route to visit him in 1935 when he learned that Lawrence was in Bovington hospital, having come off his motorbike and landed on his head. Carlow stayed with Lawrence for six days while he lay in a coma before dying, and the following year he set up the Corvinus Press with a determination to produce books that were 'beautiful beyond all those yet produced', one of which brought together the two men's tender correspondence. Clearly Carlow had a close affinity with and affection for similarly sexually ambiguous men.

46 BC, p. 41.

47 Rom Landau, *God is My Adventure*, London, Faber & Faber, 1935, p. 5.

48 *Ibid.*, p. 291.

49 *Ibid.*, p. 313.

50 *Argus-Leader*, 6 September 1925, p. 22. The MP was Neil Maclean.

51 RB/NS, p. 79. Winterton was later a notable opponent of homosexual law reform in the 1950s.

3 BERLIN – THE PERVERTS' PARADISE

1 Wyndham Lewis, *Hitler*, London, Chatto & Windus, 1931, p. 21.

2 Christopher Isherwood, *Goodbye to Berlin*, London, Hogarth Press, 1939, p. 191.

3 Christopher Isherwood, *Christopher and his Kind*, London, Vintage, 2012, p. 30.

4 *Ibid.*, p. 30.

5 Stefan Zweig, *The World of Yesterday*, translated by Benjamin W. Huebsch and Helmut Ripperger, London, Cassell, 1943, p. 313.

6 Gerald Hamilton, *Mr Norris and I*, London, Allan Wingate, 1956, p. 129.

7 Isherwood, *Christopher and his Kind*, p. 3.

8 Cited in HN/Rose, p. 82.

9 Nigel Nicolson, ed., *Vita and Harold: The Letters of Vita Sackville-West and Harold Nicolson*, London, Weidenfeld & Nicolson, 1992, p. 60.

10 *Ibid.*, pp. 8, 9.

11 James Lees-Milne, *Harold Nicolson*, London, Chatto & Windus, 1980, vol. 1, p. 160.

12 Diana Souhami, *Mrs Keppel and Her Daughter*, London, HarperCollins, 1996, p. 197.

13 *Ibid.*, p. 148

14 3 November 1927, cited in James Lees-Milne, *Harold Nicolson*, London, Chatto & Windus, 1980, vol. 1, p. 322.

15 7 November 1927, cited in Lees-Milne, *Harold Nicolson*, vol. 1, p. 326.

16 19 December 1927, Lees-Milne, *Harold Nicolson*, vol. 1, p. 327.

17 Robert Sackville-West, *Inheritance: The Story of Knole and the Sackvilles*, London, Bloomsbury, 2010, p. 228.

18 Cited in HN/Rose, p. 82.

19 To Raymond Mortimer, 5 November 1926, cited in HN/Rose, p. 137

20 To Raymond Mortimer, 1 January 1926, cited in HN/Rose, p. 137

21 To Raymond Mortimer, 14 August 1926, cited in HN/Rose, p. 137.

22 Louise DeSalvo and Mitchell A. Leaska, eds., *The Letters of Vita Sackville-West to Virginia Woolf*, London, Macmillan, 1992, p. 324.

23 Dick Richards, *The Wit of Noël Coward*, London, Sphere, 1976, p. 56.

24 Cited in HN/Rose, p. 127.

25 6 October 1928, Lees-Milne, *Harold Nicolson*, vol. 1, p. 352. Campbell-Gray later competed in the individual and team epée events in the controversial Berlin Olympics in 1936.

26   Letter to E. M. Forster, cited in Michael De-la-Noy, *Eddy: The Life of Edward Sackville-West*, London, Arcadia, 1988, p. 117.

27   *Ibid.*

28   19 November 1928, Lees-Milne, *Harold Nicolson*, vol. I, p. 327.

29   Letter to E. M. Forster, cited in De-la-Noy, *Eddy*, p. 117.

30   Lees-Milne, *Harold Nicolson*, vol. I, p. 333.

31   Bowra to Sparrow, 4 July 1928, Sparrow MSS, cited in Leslie Mitchell, *Maurice Bowra: A Life*, Oxford, OUP, 2009, p. 136.

32   Bowra to Sparrow, 6 August 1928, Sparrow MSS, cited in Mitchell, *Bowra*, p. 136.

33   Bowra to Sparrow, 14 September [1929], Sparrow MSS, box 57, cited in Mitchell, *Bowra*, p. 136.

34   Bowra to P. Balfour, 23 August [1930], Huntington Library, Kinross MSS, cited in Mitchell, *Bowra*, p. 136.

35   Cited in Richard Plant, *The Pink Triangle: The Nazi War Against Homosexuals*, Edinburgh, Mainstream, 1987, p. 49.

36   Laurie Marhoefer, *Sex and the Weimar Republic*, Toronto, University of Toronto Press, 2015, p. 151.

37   Eleanor Hancock, *Ernst Röhm, Hitler's SA Chief of Staff*, London, Macmillan, 2008, p. 90.

38   Marhoefer, *Sex and the Weimar Republic*, p. 153.

39   Röhm to Heimsoth, 11 August 1929, in Klotz, *Drei Briefe*, p. 16, cited in Eleanor Hancock, *Ernst Röhm: Hitler's SA Chief of Staff*, London, Palgrave, 2008, p. 89.

40   Sefton Delmer, *Trail Sinister*, London, Secker & Warburg, 1961, pp. 121–2.

41   Robert G. L. Waite, *Vanguard of Nazism*. W. W. Norton and Company, 1969, p. 192.

42   Oswald Mosley, *My Life*, London, Nelson, 1968, p. 243.

43   Archiv FZH, 11C1, Alfred Conn, memoirs, 64, cited in Andrew Wackerfuss, *Stormtrooper Families: Homosexuality and Community in the Early Nazi Movement*, New York, Harrington Park Press, 2015, p. 99.

44   Wyndham Lewis, *Hitler*, London, Chatto & Windus, 1931, p. 12.

45   *Ibid.*, p. 22.

46   *Ibid.*, p. 28.

4   A LUSCIOUS FREEDOM

1   JM, p. 79.

2   JM, p. 82.

3   Peter Parker, *J. R. Ackerley*, London, Constable, 1989, p. 67.

4   JM, p. 96.

5   JM, p. 109.

6   JM, p. 33.

7   *John Bull*, 13 June 1925.

8   Emlyn Williams, *Emlyn: An Early Autobiography, 1927–35*, London, Bodley Head, 1973, pp. 204–5.

9   *Evening Standard*, 14 November 1931, p. 10.

10   W. J. MacQueen-Pope, *Goodbye Piccadilly*, London, Michael Joseph, 1960, p. 320.

11   Williams, *Emlyn*, p. 205.

12   Hall Carpenter Archives, *Walking After Midnight*, London Routledge, 1989, p. 12.

13   Michael Christie, ed., *Derek Jarman's At Your Own Risk: A Saint's Testament*, New York, Overlook Press, 1992, p. 12.

14   Advertisement in *Winning Post Summer Annual*, 1908.

15   Jeffrey Weeks and Kevin Porter, eds., *Between the Acts*, London, Rivers Oram, 1998, p. 130.

16   *Sheffield Independent*, 12 April 1930, p. 1.

17   London Metropolitan Archives LCC MIN 9618.

18   London Metropolitan Archives LCC MIN 9823.

19   Robert Hutton, *Of Those Alone*, London, Sidgwick and Jackson, 1958, p. 53.

20   Donald Mitchell, Philip Reed, eds., *Letters from a Life: Selected Letters and Diaries of Benjamin Britten*, London, Faber & Faber, vol. 1, 3 July 1937, p. 1215.

21   Christie, *Derek Jarman's At Your Own Risk*, p. 12.

22   HN, 16 December 1930.

23   Taylor Croft, *The Cloven Hoof: A Study in Contemporary London Vices*, London, D. Archer, 1932, p. 66.

24   Paul Pry (anon), *For Your Convenience*, London, Routledge, 1937, pp. 9–10.

25   TNA CRIM 1/617.

26   Gerald Heard to Sprott, 4 February 1930, cited in Parker, *Ackerley*, p. 114.

27   Lee Bartlett, ed., *Letters to Christopher*, Black Sparrow Press, 1980, p. 45.

28   'Hyde Park After Dark', *News of the World*, 26 April 1931, p. 5.

29   TNA MEPO 2/8859. The six guardsmen and ex-guardsmen convicted of importuning were given between one and six months with hard labour – William Huggins, Alex Foster, Ronald Large, William Davie, John Redford (twice) and George Harrison.

30   TNA HO 45/24960.

31   TNA MEPO 2/8859.

32   Weeks and Porter, *Between the Acts*, p. 63.

33   TNA CRIM 1/639.

34   *West London Observer*, 24 February 1933, p. 10.

35   *Hartlepool Northern Daily Mail*, 28 February 1933, p. 6.

36   The electoral register has the resident owner as M. Houchin.

5 LEARNING THE HARD WAY

1   John Hope Simpson in Taunton, C. B. Fry in Brighton and Sir Harry Verney in Skipton.

2   Gray was unseated in 1924 after an election petition by his Unionist opponent on the grounds that his agent had falsified his election expenses.

3   Worcester College, Oxford archives.

4   *Rugby Advertiser*, 9 September 1927, p. 7.

5   *Birmingham Daily Gazette*, 13 June 1929.

6   *Ibid.*
7   *Rugby Advertiser*, 17 May 1929, p. 6.
8   RB/SC, p. 17.
9   *Rugby Advertiser*, 18 June 1929, p. 3.
10 *Sun* (Sydney), 14 September 1930, p. 5.
11 *Telegraph* [Brisbane], 27 September 1930, p. 10.
12 *The Australian Star*, 26 June 1900, p. 4
13 *Daily Telegraph*, 12 June 1931.
14 *Sydney Morning Herald*, 25 September 1930, p. 10.
15 *Nambucca and Bellinger News*, 26 September 1930.
16 *Narandera Argus and Riverina Advertiser*, 3 March 1931.
17 RB/SC, p. 50.
18 Cited in Garry Wotherspoon, *Gay Sydney: A History*, Sydney, NewSouth Publishing, 2016, p. 1.
19 RB, MSS Diary, 2 August 1930.
20 RB, MSS Diary, 1 September, 23 and 27 August 1930.
21 RB, MSS Diary, 10 August 1930.
22 RB, MSS Diary, 21 August 1930.
23 HN, 17 January 1937.
24 RB, typescript diary, 13 November 1934.
25 All included in Cambridge University Library Sassoon Papers, MS Add. 9852/9/4.
26 HN, 6 October 1930. The Canadian premier in question was R. B. Bennett, who won a landslide for the Conservatives in August 1930.
27 RB, Jean Stratheden to Nancy Bernays, 8 February 1945.
28 RB, W. James to Nancy Bernays, 2 February 1945.
29 *News Chronicle*, 17 December 1930.
30 RB/SC, pp. 24–5.
31 Paula Byrne, *Mad World: Evelyn Waugh and the Secrets of Brideshead*, London, HarperCollins, 2010, p. 140.
32 National Archives, J 77/2899/9727.
33 Nigel Nicolson, ed., *Vita and Harold: The Letters of Vita Sackville-West and Harold Nicolson*, London, Weidenfeld & Nicolson, 1992, p. 292.
34 RB, typescript diary, 13 May 1933.
35 RB/NS, p. 257.
36 Beaverbrook papers, BBK/H/158.
37 J. P. Wearing, ed., *Bernard Shaw and Nancy Astor*, Toronto, University of Toronto Press, 2005, George Bernard Shaw to Nancy Astor, 15 July 1931, p. 33.
38 RB, typescript diary, 19 February 1935.
39 Adrian Fort, *Nancy: The Story of Lady Astor*, London, Jonathan Cape, 2012, p. 313.

6 THE BACHELOR MPS

1   RB/SC, p. 89.
2   *Western Daily Press*, 28 October 1931, p. 10.
3   RB/SC, p. 97.

4   In 1932 the Liberals under Sir Herbert Samuel resigned over the government's protectionist policies embodied in the Ottawa Accords.

5   HN/NN1, p. 95.

6   HN/NN1, p. 96.

7   VC, MSS Journal, 11 October 1931.

8   *South Wales Daily News*, 23 April 1926. Respectively E. H. G. Roberts, the MP for Flintshire, and Major Sir Harry Barnston, the MP for Eddisbury, who was then fifty-five.

9   VC, MSS journal.

10 VC, MSS journal.

11 VC/RJ, p. 42.

12 VC/RJ, p. 103.

13 *Wiltshire Gazette*, 21 January 1926.

14 *Bath Chronicle*, 9 May 1932.

15 *South Wales Daily News*, 23 April 1926.

16 Thelma Cazalet-Keir, *From the Wings*, London, The Bodley Head, 1967, p. 29.

17 VC, *Journal*, 1 November 1922.

18 *Bystander*, 28 May 1930, p. 5.

19 *Bystander*, 5 July 1933, p. 16.

20 RB, typescript diary, 7 February 1936.

21 A. J. P. Taylor, ed., *Lloyd George: A Diary by Frances Stevenson*, London, Hutchinson, 1971, p. 194.

22 Philpot's long-term lover Vivian Forbes started another commission at the Palace of Westminster, the St Stephen's Hall painting of Sir Thomas More confronting Cardinal Wolsey. So close were the two men that when Philpot died in December 1937, Forbes took his own life immediately after the funeral.

23 John Mack, *A Prince of Our Disorder: The Life of T. E. Lawrence*, Boston, Little, Brown, 1976, p. 425.

24 T. E. Lawrence to Philip Sassoon, 15 May 1929, Houghton Hall Archives, cited in Damian Collins, *Charmed: The Life and Times of Philip Sassoon*, London, William Collins, 2016, p. 196.

25 A. J. P. Taylor, *Lloyd George*, p. 194.

26 VC, MSS Journal, 16 July 1933.

27 BB, p. 77.

28 BB, p. 24.

29 BB, p. 25.

30 Bruce Lockhart was married but was quite au fait with the problems faced by homosexuals. He referred in his diary in 1932 to an attempt to blackmail Prince George for some amorous letters he had sent to a man in Paris.

31 Kenneth Young, ed., *The Diaries of Sir Robert Bruce Lockhart*, London, Macmillan, 1973, vol. 1, p. 226.

32 TNA, KV 2/4097.

33 TNA, KV 2/4097, report 285/27

34 BB, p. 77.

35 James Stuart, *Within the Fringe*, London, Bodley Head, 1967, pp. 145–6.

36 *Sunderland Daily Echo and Shipping Gazette*, 24 April 1933, p. 6.
37 *Bystander*, 3 May 1933, p. 6.
38 *Bystander*, 3 May 1933, p. 5.
39 Anomaly, *The Invert and His Social Adjustment*, London, Bailliere, Tindall & Cox, 1927, pp. 135–6.

7 GERMANY CHANGES

1 HC, 10 November 1931, vol. 259, col. 45.
2 HC, 10 November 1931, vol. 259, col. 51.
3 HC, 10 November 1931, vol. 259, col. 61.
4 *Western Morning News*, 14 April 1931, p. 6.
5 Maurice Gerothwohl, ed., *An Ambassador of Peace: Pages from the Diary of Viscount D'Abernon*, London, Hodder & Stoughton, 1930, p. 139.
6 The association's members held widely divergent political views. Its committee included two Labour MPs, Arthur Greenwood and Major Archibald Church. Greenwood went on to play a key part in forcing Britain to stand up to Hitler, whereas Church openly supported eugenicist policies. In July 1931 he presented a bill 'to enable mental defectives to undergo sterilising operations or sterilising treatment upon their own application, or that of their spouses or parents or guardian'. He said his bill was just a 'first step' enabling a small-scale experiment, but he confidently expected bringing in another bill 'for the compulsory sterilisation of the unfit'.
7 *Western Morning News*, 9 June 1931, p. 7.
8 *Evening Standard*, 22 January 1932.
9 *Evening Standard*, cited in Robert Rhodes James, *Robert Boothby: A Portrait of Churchill's Ally*, London, Viking, 1991, p. 139.
10 BB, p. 107.
11 BB, p. 109.
12 Francis Rose, *Saying Life*, London, Cassell, 1961.
13 *Charleston Daily Mail*, 29 January 1933.
14 *The Times*, 23 August 1932, p. 10.
15 *Ibid.*
16 RB/SC, p. 122.
17 RB/SC, p. 123.
18 RB/SC, p. 135.
19 RB/SC, p. 135.
20 RB/SC, p. 134.
21 RB/SC, p. 128.
22 *Western Daily Press*, 17 December 1932, p. 7.
23 BB, p. 73.
24 RB, typescript diary, 6 June 1933.
25 RB/SC, p. 220.
26 *Ibid.*
27 RB/SC, p. 225.

28 RB/SC, p. 227.

29 RB/SC, p. 221.

30 Wilde went on to lose in the men's doubles finals in 1936 and 1939 and the mixed doubles finals in 1939.

31 VC, MSS Journal, 6 and 27 June 1933.

32 VC, MSS Journal, 4 August 1933.

33 VC, MSS Journal, 15 August 1933.

34 VC, MSS Journal, 4 August 1933. Robert Rhodes James's version omits 'Great fun' and the inverted commas surrounding 'concentration camp'.

35 TGA, 8317/9/1/15.

36 Frances Hodgkins to Arthur Lett Haines, TGA 8317.1.2062.

37 TNA FO 395/493, 2 November 1933.

38 TNA FO 395/493, undated.

39 TNA FO 395/493, undated.

40 TNA FO 395/493, undated.

41 TNA FO 395/493.

42 *Daily Herald*, 8 May 1934, p. 10.

43 TNA FO 395/493, 8 December 1933.

44 TGA 8317.6.1.11.

45 *Yorkshire Post*, 23 December 1933, p. 8.

46 RB/SC, p. 233.

47 RB, typescript diary, 6 June 1933.

48 *Contemporary Review*, November 1933, pp. 521–3.

49 *Western Daily Press*, 15 November 1933, p. 12.

50 *Western Daily Press*, 24 July 1933, p. 5.

51 *Western Daily Press*, 15 November 1933, p. 12.

52 *Western Daily Press*, 23 November 1933, p. 8.

8 THE TURNING POINT

1   *Daily Mail*, 15 January 1924.

2   *Daily Herald*, 17 January 1934.

3   *Birmingham Gazette*, 6 February 1934, p. 8.

4   *Spectator*, 27 April 1934, p. 8.

5   RT, p. 16.

6   *Western Daily Press*, 12 August 1933, p. 7. Since his title was Irish it did not preclude him from standing for the Commons. On 5 November 1961 he took his own life.

7   RT, p. 33.

8   RT, p. 34.

9   Nick Smart, ed., *The Diaries and Letters of Robert Bernays, 1932–1939*, E. Mellen Press, 1996, p. 37.

10 *Ibid.*, pp. 39–40.

11 RT, p. 55.

12 RB/SC, p. 214.

13 *Northampton Mercury*, 10 November 1933, p. 7.

14 Bodleian Library, Ball Papers, 6656. Sir Vernon Kell and Major-General William Thwaites.

15 Robert Rhodes-James, *Memoirs of a Conservative: J.C.C. Davidson's Memoirs and Papers*, London, Weidenfeld & Nicolson, 1969, p. 272.

16 N. J. Crowson, *Fleet Street, Press Barons and Politics: The Journals of Collin Brooks, 1932–1940*, London, Royal Historical Society, 1998, p. 275.

17 Arnold Beichman, 'Hugger-Mugger in Old Queen Street: The Origins of the Conservative Research Department', *Journal of Contemporary History*, vol. 13 (1978), p. 673.

18 Rhodes-James, *Memoirs of a Conservative*, p. 272.

19 E. H. Cookridge, *The Third Man*, London, Barker, 1968, p. 46.

20 Lewis Chester, Stephen Fay, Hugo Young, *The Zinoviev Letter*, Philadelphia, J. B. Lippincott, 1968, p. 162.

21 Ian Colvin, *Vansittart in Office*, London, Victor Gollancz, 1965, p. 191.

22 Cambridge University Library, GB 12 MS.Baldwin, Ball to Baldwin, 1 January 1936.

23 Bodleian Library, Joseph Ball to Neville Chamberlain, 7 May 1934.

24 *Northern Whig*, 27 April 1934, p. 6.

25 *London Gazette*, 5 May 1934. In 1937 the London Regiment was disbanded and the new unit was known as the London Irish Rifles, the Royal Ulster Rifles.

26 *London Gazette*, 27 November 1934.

27 TGA 8317, Lett-Haines Diary, 25 December 1933.

28 TGA 8317, Lett-Haines Diary, 27 April 1934.

29 *The Times*, 14 May 1934, p. 11.

30 *Daily Herald*, 3 May 1934, p. 3.

31 *Daily Herald*, 3 May 1934, p. 3.

32 HC, 10 July 1936, vol. 314, col. 1584.

33 *Dundee Evening Telegraph*, 10 May 1934, p. 7.

34 *Bystander*, 29 May 1934, p. 10.

35 HC, 10 July 1936, vol. 314, col. 1584.

36 *Chelmsford Chronicle*, 14 July 1939, p. 7.

37 RT, p. 55.

38 RB, typescript diary, 19 May 1934.

39 RB/SC, pp. 238–9.

40 *Ibid.*

41 RT, p. 57.

42 RT, p. 59.

43 Cited in Richard Evans, *The Third Reich in Power*, London, Penguin, 2005, p. 32.

44 *Hamburger Tageblatt*, 13 July 1934, cited in Andrew Wackerfuss, *Stormtrooper Families: Homosexuality and Community in the Early Nazi Movement*, New York, Harrington Park Press, 2015, p. 302.

45 Max Gallo, *The Night of the Long Knives*, translated by Lily Emmet, London, Souvenir Press, 1973, p. 264.

46 *The Times*, 3 July 1934, p. 14.

47 *Daily Mail*, 2 July 1934.

48 *Illustrated London News*, 7 July 1934, p. 5

49 RB/NS, p. 146.

50 Frederick Winterbotham, *Secret and Personal*, London, William Kimber, 1969, p. 118.

51 BB/RJ, p. 152.

52 *Hamburger Tageblatt*, 13 July 1934, cited Wackerfuss, p. 302.

53 Translated in Michael Burleigh and Wolfgang Wipperman, *The Racial State: Germany 1933–1945*, Cambridge, CUP, 1991, pp. 192–3.

54 *Ibid.*, pp. 182–3.

55 US Holocaust Memorial Museum website www.ushmm.org, visited 26 March 2018.

56 Interview with Llew Gardner, *Sunday Express*, cited in Dagmar Herzog, ed., *Sexuality and German Fascism*, New York, Berghahn Books, 2005, p. 321.

57 HN, 2 January 1935.

58 RB/SC, p. 248.

59 BB/RJ, p. 152.

9 A MASCULINE ASSEMBLY

1 *Birmingham Daily Gazette*, 23 July 1935, p. 3.

2 *News of the World*, 28 July 1935.

3 *Gloucester Citizen*, 24 July 1935, p. 1.

4 *Sheffield Independent*, 24 July 1935, p. 5.

5 *Daily Mail*, 25 July 1935.

6 *Yorkshire Evening Post*, 24 July 1935, p. 9.

7 TNA WO 209/120, recently opened.

8 So scandalous was Daly's case that another lieutenant colonel, Louis Dominic Daly, who was then based in Gibraltar, successfully sued the *Star* when it incorrectly carried a photograph of him in its report of the court martial and referred to the convicted man as 'Lieutenant-Colonel L. D. Daly'.

9 *Evening World*, 12 November 1935.

10 *Western Daily Press*, 11 November 1935, p. 10.

11 RB/NS, p. 162.

12 RB/NS p. 188.

13 *Birmingham Gazette*, 24 December 1935, p. 4.

14 RB/NS, p. 233.

15 RC, p. 38.

16 Private interview with Robert Bernays.

17 BC, p. 42.

18 Henry Cloud, *Barbara Cartland, Crusader in Pink*, London, Weidenfeld & Nicolson, 1979, p. 71.

19 RC, p. 41.

20 Earl of Lytton, *Antony, Viscount Knebworth*, London, Peter Davies, 1935, p. 316.

21 Tom Moulson, *The Millionaire's Squadron*, Barnsley, Pen & Sword, 2014, p. 28.

22 RC, p. 50.

23 Cloud, *Barbara Cartland*, p. 80.

24 Barbara Cartland, *Polly: My Wonderful Mother*, London, Herbert Jenkins, 1956, p. 134.

25 BC, p. 177.

26 RC, p. 56.

27 RC, p. 63.

28 *Bystander*, 29 May 1934, p. 10.

29 *Chelmsford Chronicle*, 23 November 1934, p. 7.

30 Cited in Matt Houlbrook, *Queer London: Perils and Pleasures in the Sexual Metropolis, 1918–1957*, Chicago, Illinois, University of Chicago Press, 2005, p. 251.

31 *Essex Newsman*, 6 November 1926, p. 1.

32 The chairman of the association referred to this in a tribute to Jack in the *Chelmsford Chronicle*, 5 January 1945, p. 3.

33 *Chelmsford Chronicle*, 23 November 1934, p. 7.

34 HN, 23 August 1935.

35 HN, 14 November 1935.

36 HN/NN1, vol. 1, p. 226.

37 BC, p. 68.

38 HN, 21 November 1935.

39 Richard Law's obituary of Ronald Cartland, *The Times*, 7 January 1941, p. 7.

40 HC, 7 May 1936, vol. 311, col. 1919.

41 JM, p. 142.

42 JM, p. 145.

43 JM, p. 145.

44 Recording as relayed to the author by her grandson, Sam Price.

45 *Gloucester Journal*, 13 June 1936, p. 23.

46 *Bath Chronicle*, 6 October 1934, p. 24, has Canon J. H. Sharp (London) in one room and J. H. Sharp (Stroud) and Mr Macnamara (London) in another.

47 Goronwy Rees, *A Chapter of Accidents*, London, Chatto & Windus, 1971, p. 113.

48 Barrie Penrose and Simon Freeman, *Conspiracy of Silence: The Secret Life of Anthony Blunt*, London, Vintage, 1988, p. 203.

49 Mark Amory, ed., *The Letters of Evelyn Waugh*, London, Weidenfeld & Nicolson, 1980, p. 505.

50 Harold Acton, *Memoirs of an Aesthete*, London, Methuen, 1970, p. 87.

51 James Lees-Milne, *Deep Romantic Chasm: Diaries 1979–81*, London, John Murray, 2000, p. 73.

52 Michael Burns, *Turned Towards the Sun*, London, Michael Russell, 2003, pp. 96–7.

53 DEUTSCH File 89113, vol. 1, p. 250, cited in John Costello and Oleg Tsarev, *Deadly Illusions*, London, Century, 1993, p. 228.

54 Rees, *A Chapter of Accidents*, p. 122.

55 Paul Mellon Centre, Ben Nicolson diary, 25 March 1936.

56 Bodleian Library, Joseph Ball Papers, Crocker to *People*, 27 March 1956.

57 *Ibid.*

58 Edward Henry Cookridge, *The Third Man*, London, Barker, 1968, pp. 46–7.

59 Boris Volodarsky, *Stalin's Agent*, Oxford, OUP, 2014, p. 108.

60 Yuri Modin, *My Five Cambridge Friends*, London, Headline, 1994, p. 93.

61 HC, 18 December 1935, vol. 307, col. 1786.
62 *Ibid.*
63 HC, 18 December 1935, vol. 307, col. 1789.
64 *Nottingham Evening Post*, 21 December 1935, p. 8. Moreover, although nearly every reference to Jack Macnamara in other history books of the period claims he was a member of the Anglo-German Fellowship, his name never appears on any of the available lists.
65 Rees, *A Chapter of Accidents*, pp. 122–3
66 HN, 28 May 1936. My italics.
67 Interview with Sam Price.

IO THE PERSONAL BECOMES POLITICAL

1   HN, 29 November 1935.
2   VC, Cramm to Cazalet, 27 February 1936.
3   VC, Cramm to Cazalet, 4 March 1936.
4   HN, 2 December 1935.
5   Arnold Wilson, 'Walks And Talks', *Nineteenth Century and After*, October 1936, pp. 506–11.
6   JM, p. 209.
7   HCD, 8 March 1936.
8   HC, 9 March 1936, vol. 309, col. 1812.
9   Gerhard L. Weinberg, *Hitler's Foreign Policy, 1933–1939*, New York, Enigma Books, 2010, p. 202.
10 VC, Victor Cazalet Journal, 4–6 March 1936.
11 HN/NN1, p. 254, 23 March 1936.
12 Rufina Philby with Hayden Peake and Mikhail Lyubimov, *The Private Life of Kim Philby*, London, St Ermin's Press, 1999, p. 235.
13 Cited in Boris Volodarsky, *Stalin's Agent: The Life and Times of Alexander Orlov*, Oxford, OUP, 2015, p. 104.
14 JM, pp. 209–10.
15 Office of United States Chief of Counsel for Prosecution of Axis Criminality, *Nazi Conspiracy and Aggression*, Washington: DC, US Government Printing Office, 1946, vol. 4, pp. 624–5.
16 Paul Berben, *Dachau, 1933–45: The Official History*, Norfolk Press, 1975, p. 231.
17 *Ibid.*, p. 233.
18 James McGovern, *Martin Bormann*, London, Barker, 1968, p. 24.
19 JM, p. 209.
20 JM, pp. 209–10.
21 Thomas Kühne, *Belonging and Genocide*, New Haven, Yale University Press, 2010, pp. 67–8.
22 JM, p. 51.
23 *Ibid.*
24 JM, p. 211.

25 John Costello and Oleg Tsarev, *Deadly Illusions: The First Book from the KGB Archives*, London, Century, 1993, p. 229.

26 HC, 10 July 1936, vol. 314, col. 1582–3, my italics.

27 *Action* (the newspaper of the British Union of Fascists), 15 May 1937.

28 *Nelson Leader*, 25 March 1934, p. 13.

29 Churchill College, Cambridge, Bower Papers, 1/5.

30 HC, 10 July 1936, vol. 314, col. 1569.

31 C. G. Grey, 'On Japheth and the Jews', *Aeroplane*, 9 August 1933.

32 HC, 9 March 1933, vol. 275, col. 1351–2.

33 Crawford Greene (Worcester) and Fred Macquisten (Argyll), HC, 24 July 1934, vol. 292, col. 1645.

34 Arthur Bateman (North Camberwell), *Daily Herald*, 28 June 1933.

35 *Blackwood's Edinburgh Magazine*, September 1921.

36 *The Times*, 8 December 1927, p. 8. *Hansard* omits this comment.

37 HN/NN1, p. 76.

38 Ellen Wilkinson, *Peeps at Politicians*, London, P. Allan, 1930, pp. 75–6.

39 HC, 11 April 1933, vol. 276, col. 2361; 25 May 1933, vol. 278, col. 1276; 14 December 1933, vol. 284, col. 541.

40 Cited in Karina Urbach, *Go-Betweens for Hitler*, Oxford, OUP, 2015, p. 242.

41 CC, pp. 23–4, 27 January 1935.

42 CC, p. 120.

43 CC, p. 24.

44 Norman Rose, *The Cliveden Set*, London, Jonathan Cape, 2000, p. 184.

45 HN/NN1, p. 327. Harold harboured his own anti-Jewish views. He referred to Charlie Chaplin as 'a pleasant affable ugly little jew (sic) man' (HN, 26 February 1931), and after the Second World War he wrote in his diary that 'the Jewish capacity for self-destruction is really illimitable … Although I loathe anti-Semitism, I do dislike Jews'. (HN/NN2, p. 469.)

46 Ben Pimlott, ed. *The Political Diary of Hugh Dalton*, London, Jonathan Cape, 1986, p. 226.

47 *News Chronicle*, 21 March 1938.

48 HC, 10 July 1936, vol. 314, col. 1571.

49 HC, 10 July 1936, vol. 314, col. 1629.

50 HN, 10 June 1936.

11 HITLER'S BRITISH FRIENDS

1 University of Southampton, Broadlands Papers, BR81/1.

2 HN, 25 January 1938.

3 *The Times*, 23 March 1936, p. 10.

4 *The Times*, 18 December 1936, p. 10.

5 *The Times*, 8 April 1936, p. 10.

6 *The Times*, 17 April 1936, p. 8.

7 John Marlowe, *Late Victorian: The Life of Sir Arnold Talbot Wilson*, London, Cresset, 1967, p. 20.

8   *English Review,* June 1934.

9   HN, 6 September 1939.

10 V. Khristoforov *et al.,* eds, *Rossiya,* Moscow, 2011, document 129, 31 March 1947.

11 HC, 19 April 1939, vol. 346, col. 357.

12 TNA, KV/3.

13 /www.fourfourtwo.com/features/nazis-tottenham-why-did-swastika-fly-white-hart-lane

14 Karina Urbach, *Go-Betweens for Hitler,* Oxford, OUP, 2015, p. 202.

15 TNA, KV 5/3.

16 TNA, KV 3/71a.

17 CC, 6 August 1936, p. 106.

18 *Ibid.*

19 University of Southampton, Broadlands Papers, BR81/10, Tennant to Mount Temple, September 1935.

20 VC, 3–7 October 1935.

21 *North Wiltshire Herald,* 3 April 1936.

22 CC, p. 74, 3 August 1936.

23 *Hartlepool Northern Daily Mail,* 4 March 1937, p. 4.

24 HC, 10 November 1932, vol. 270, col. 632.

25 HC, 30 July 1934, vol. 292, col. 2339.

26 Bodleian Library, T. E. Lawrence Papers, Sassoon to Lawrence, MS Eng d. 3341 f.1347.

27 HC, 14 March 1933, vol. 275, cols. 1815, 1820.

28 HC, 8 March 1934, vol. 286, col. 2034.

29 HC, 8 March 1934, vol. 286, col. 2030.

30 HC, 8 March 1934, vol. 286, col. 2049.

31 HC, 8 March 1934, vol. 286, col. 2078.

32 HC, 28 November 1934, vol. 295, col. 882.

33 TNA CAB 23/81, 8 April 1934.

34 HC, 19 March 1935, vol. 299, cols. 1015–6.

35 Charles Kingsley, *Alton Locke,* New York, Harper & Brothers, 1850, pp. 67–8.

36 Thomas Mann, banquet speech, translation from www.nobelprize.org.

37 HC, 19 March 1935, vol. 299, col. 1068.

38 Sir Walter Scott, *The Works: The Lay of the Last Minstrel,* Edinburgh, Constable & Co., 1813, vol. 4, p. 274.

39 HC, 17 March 1936, vol. 310, col. 259.

40 HC, 17 March 1936, vol. 310, col. 286.

41 TNA CAB 56/2. My italics.

42 TNA CAB 56/2, 22 January 1937.

43 TNA CAB 56/2, f. 243.

44 HC, 15 March 1937, vol. 321, col. 1684.

45 HC, 15 March 1937, vol. 321, col. 1665.

46 *The Times,* 12 October 1936, p. 8.

47 'The Civil War', *Nineteenth Century and After,* April 1937.

48 *Southend Standard,* 18 March 1937.

49   *The Times*, 3 March 1937.
50   Winston Churchill, *Step by Step*, London, G. P. Putnam's Sons, 1939, p. 51.
51   HN/NN1, 15 July 1937, p. 307.
52   TNA FO 371/20549 f. 187.
53   *The Times*, 3 December 1936, p. 14.
54   HC, 18 December 1936, vol. 318, col. 2831.
55   *The Times*, 29 December 1936, p. 6.
56   *The Times*, 21 June 1937, p. 16
57   *Daily Herald*, 15 December 1936, p. 2.
58   BB, p. 123.

12   GETTING ON

1   RC, p. 133.
2   HC, 17 November 1936, vol. 317, cols. 1645–6.
3   RC, p. 83
4   *The Times*, 4 August 1936.
5   CC, p. 147.
6   Simon Raven, *Shadows on the Grass*, London, Blond & Briggs, 1982, p. 182.
7   Laurence Whistler, *The Laughter and the Urn: The Life of Rex Whistler*, Weidenfeld & Nicolson, London, 1986, p. 200.
8   HC, 10 February 1937, vol. 320, cols. 490–1.
9   HC, 10 February 1937, vol. 320, col. 504.
10   HC, 10 February 1937, vol. 320, col. 533.
11   Bodleian Library, Oxford, Simon Papers, 83 fol. 190.
12   RB/NS, p. 256.
13   RB, letter to Lucy Brereton, 23 December 1936.
14   *Ibid*.
15   RB, letter to Lucy Brereton, 23 and 29 December 1936.
16   RB/NS, p. 292.
17   *Ibid*.
18   *Ibid*.
19   RB/NS, p. 319.
20   HN, 24 December 1933
21   HN, 14 June 1937.
22   RB/NS, p. 317.
23   RB/NS, p. 321.
24   RC, p. 88.
25   HC, 29 November 1937, vol. 329, cols. 1824–5.
26   *Western Daily Press*, 28 February 1938.
27   RC, p. 92.
28   *Birmingham Daily Gazette*, 20 March 1937, p. 7.
29   TNA CRIM 1/903.
30   *Illustrated Police News*, 4 February 1937, p. 8.
31   *Birmingham Daily Gazette*, 22 December 1937.

32   *Birmingham Daily Gazette*, 2 February 1938.
33   HN/NN1, p. 246.
34   HN, 1 November 1937.

13 THE NEW PRIME MINISTER

1   HC, 27 May 1937, vol. 324, col. 425.
2   CC, pp. 134, 148, 150.
3   TNA CAB 127/158, fols. 13–14.
4   Robert Rhodes James, *Anthony Eden*, London, Weidenfeld & Nicolson, 1986, p. 208.
5   Rome, *Serie delle Rappresentanze Diplomatiche*, Londra, 1937, 963/3, Grandi to Ciano, 31 July 1937.
6   BB, p. 126.
7   University of Birmingham, Neville Chamberlain papers 18/1/1009.
8   Robert Self, ed., *The Neville Chamberlain Diary Letters*, vol. 4, Aldershot, Ashgate, 2005, pp. 219–20.
9   *Ibid.*, p. 256.
10   Bodleian Library, Geoffrey Dawson Papers, MS Dawson 79, Dawson to H. G. Daniels, 23 May 1937.
11   Richard Crockett, *Twilight of Truth*, London, Weidenfeld & Nicolson, 1989, p. 10.
12   Brooke was elected MP for Lewisham West in 1938.
13   University of Birmingham, Neville Chamberlain papers, 23 July 1939, 11/1/1108.
14   *Truth*, 28 July 1938.
15   Bodleian Library, Ball Papers, MSS. Eng. c. 6656/40.
16   Rome, Archivio Storico-diplomatico, Ministero degli Affari Esteri, Grandi Papers, Grandi to Ciano, 40/93/2/3, 12 July 1937.
17   OH, p. 61.
18   BL, Correspondence and Papers of Paul Emrys-Evans, BL Add Ms. 89013/2/1/9.
19   University of Birmingham, Chamberlain papers 7/11/31/10, 21 February 1938.
20   *The Times*, 22 February 1938, p. 10.
21   *Manchester Guardian*, 24 February 1938.
22   *Bystander*, 31 January 1934, p. 14.
23   Alistair Horne, *Harold Macmillan*, London, Macmillan, 1990, p. 382.
24   John Vincent, ed., *The Crawford Papers: The Journals of David Lindsay, 27th Earl of Crawford and 10th Earl of Balcarres*, Manchester, MUP, 1984, 2 November 1938.
25   Churchill College, Cambridge, P. J. Grigg to F. A. Grigg, 6 October 1940, PJGG 9/6/9.
26   RT, p. 74.
27   HN/NN1, p. 324.
28   HC, 21 February 1938, vol. 332, col. 100.
29   HN, 21 February 1938.
30   HC, 22 February 1938, vol. 332, col. 209.
31   HC, 22 February 1938, vol. 332, col. 274.
32   *The Times*, 22 February 1938, p. 14.

33 HC, 22 February 1938, vol. 332, col. 278.
34 HC, 22 February 1938, vol. 332, col. 279.
35 HC, 22 February 1938, vol. 332, col. 280.
36 HC, 21 February 1938, vol. 332, col. 142.
37 *Birmingham Daily Gazette*, 5 March 1938, p. 7.
38 Carmarthenshire Archives, Cilcennin Papers, 44.
39 BC, p. 105.
40 RB, cuttings.
41 RB/NS, p. 238.
42 HCD, 22 February 1938.
43 RB/NS, p. 343.
44 HCD, 22 February 1938.
45 OH, p. 98.
46 Robert Bernays (son) interview, 31 August 2018.
47 This account is taken from an extract written by his chauffeur in the Robert Bernays family papers.
48 Robert Rhodes James, *Anthony Eden*, London, Weidenfeld & Nicolson, 1986, p. 201.
49 Robert Rhodes James, *Anthony Eden*, London, Weidenfeld & Nicolson, 1986, p. 201.
50 HC, 21 February 1938, vol. 332, col. 92.
51 John Harvey, *The Diplomatic Diaries of Oliver Harvey, 1937–40*, p. 100.
52 *Bystander*, 9 March 1938, p. 12.

14 THE INSURGENTS

1 CC, p. 150, 11 March 1938.
2 VC, 11, 12 March 1938.
3 HC, 14 March 1938, vol. 333, cols. 47, 52.
4 *Truth*, 23 February 1938, p. 243.
5 *Truth*, 9 February 1938, p. 171.
6 *Truth*, 16 March 1938, p. 347.
7 *Truth*, 5 January 1938, pp. 16–17.
8 *Truth*, 13 April 1938, p. 436.
9 *Truth*, 18 May 1938, p. 658
10 *Truth*, 8 June 1938, p. 766
11 'The Rape of Austria', *Time*, 15 March 1938.
12 *The Times*, 26 February 1938.
13 HC, 14 March 1938, vol. 333, cols. 133–4.
14 *The Times*, 13 May 1936, p. 12.
15 'The Army To-day', *The Nineteenth Century*, September 1937, p. 270.
16 *The London Irish at War*, London, London Irish Rifles Old Comrades' Association, p. 17.
17 Private interview with the author.
18 *The Times*, 17 March 1938, p. 14.

19 HC, 16 February 1938, vol. 331, col. 1879.

20 *Rising Strength,* April 1938, p. 120.

21 *The Times,* 17 March 1938, p. 14.

22 *The Times,* 16 March 1938, p. 10.

23 *The Times,* 21 March 1938, p. 8.

24 *The Times,* 19 March 1938, p. 14.

25 HN/NN1, p. 340.

26 HN/NN1, p. 343.

27 VC/RJ, p. 203. He was right. Lindbergh repeatedly complained about Jewish ownership of the American press, radio and motion-picture industry and that October he received the Order of the German Eagle from Hitler.

28 CC, p. 152, 21 March 1938.

29 Carmarthenshire Archives, Cilcennin Papers, 44.

30 CC, p. 153, 22 March 1938.

31 *Scotsman,* 26 July 1940, p. 4.

32 RB/NS, pp. 347–8.

33 RB/NS, p. 350.

34 VC, Cramm to Cazalet, 4 March 1936.

35 *Bystander,* 8 July 1936, p. 13.

36 *Argus* (Melbourne), 7 December 1937, p. 10.

37 *Courier-Mail* (Brisbane), 15 December 1937, p. 16.

38 *Sydney Morning Herald,* 29 December 1937, p. 10.

39 *Leeds Mercury,* 8 March 1938, p. 1.

40 *Central Queensland Herald,* 19 May 1938, p. 30.

41 VC, Cramm to Cazalet, 4 March 1936.

42 HN/NN3, p. 180.

43 Bracken later persuaded Westminster Council to change the name of the street to Lord North Street after the former prime minister who famously lost America.

44 Carmarthenshire Archives, Cilcennin papers, Ronnie Cartland to J. P. L. Thomas, 22 March 1938.

45 Ben Pimlott, ed., *The Political Diary of Hugh Dalton, 1918–40, 1945–60,* London, Jonathan Cape, 1988, p. 225.

46 Pimlott, *The Political Diary of Hugh Dalton,* p. 226.

47 *Arbroath Herald,* 11 February 1938, p. 3.

48 *Sevenoaks Chronicle and Kentish Advertiser,* 12 August 1938, p. 3.

49 RT, pp. 68–9.

50 HN, 3 August 1938.

51 VC, 13 January 1938.

52 *The Times,* 4 May 1938, p. 10.

53 HC, 29 July 1938, vol. 338, cols. 3355–6.

54 HC, 29 July 1938, vol. 338, col. 3359.

55 *The Times,* 3 September 1938, p. 9.

56 *Belfast News-Letter,* 22 September 1937, p. 11.

57 *Hendon and Finchley Times,* 29 July 1938, p. 20.

58 Anti-Semitism was not limited to thugs. When a by-election was held in
    Cheltenham in June 1937 many people presumed that Daniel Lipson would be
    the official government candidate. He was a former housemaster at Cheltenham
    College and had been elected as the town's mayor as a Liberal who supported
    the National Government. When the sitting MP stood down, Lipson offered
    his services to the Conservative Association and expressly told the local party
    chairman he would take the Conservative whip in Parliament. But a dirty-tricks
    campaign started among Conservative members. It was whispered that he had
    been a conscientious objector in the war and that people would not vote for
    him because he was a Jew. Although he was the only local candidate, the local
    executive refused to interview him and adopted instead a Colonel Tristram
    Harper. Lipson decided to stand anyway, as a Conservative who supported the
    National Government, and after a tumultuous campaign and a recount, he won
    by 339 votes. The people of Cheltenham were clearly less anti-Semitic than the
    local Conservative Association.
59 A. H. M. Ramsay, *The Nameless War*, Britons Publishing Society, 1952, p. 95.
60 HC, 11 November 1937, vol. 328, col. 1836.
61 *Glasgow Herald*, 26 May 1938.
62 HC, 13 December 1938, vol. 342, col. 1808.
63 *Truth*, 21 December 1938, p. 846.
64 Buchan-Hepburn to Dr Knox-Thompson, 27 July 1938, HAIL 1/2, cited in N. J.
    Crowson, *Fleet Street, Press Barons and Politics: The Journals of Collin Brooks, 1932–
    1940*, London, Royal Historical Society, 1998, p. 33.
65 'British Antisemitism was Hitler's Hope', *Wiener Library Bulletin*, XVI, 1,
    1962, p. 17.

15 PEACE WITH DISHONOUR

1   BB/RJ, p. 180.
2   RB, 29 August 1938.
3   RT, p. 84.
4   CC, p. 166, 14 September 1938.
5   CC, p. 166, 15 September 1938.
6   HN, 15 September 1938.
7   HN/NN1, p. 365, 23 September 1938.
8   HN/NN1, p. 367, 26 September 1938.
9   HN/NN1, p. 366, 23 September 1938.
10 CC, p. 167, 17 September 1938.
11 RB/NS, p. 371.
12 HN/NN1, p. 369, 28 September 1938.
13 CC, p. 171, 28 September 1938.
14 HC, 28 September 1938, vol. 339, col. 14.
15 HC, 28 September 1938, vol. 339, cols. 14, 20.
16 HN, 28, 29 September 1938.
17 HC, 28 September 1938, vol. 339, col. 26.

18   CC, p. 171, 28 September 1938.

19   HN/NN1, p. 371, 28 September 1938.

20   RC, p. 112.

21   HN/NN1, 28 September 1938, p. 371.

22   HN/Rose, p. 218.

23   *Daily Mail*, 1 October 1938, p. 5.

24   *The Times*, 1 October 1938.

25   CC, p. 172, 28 September 1938.

26   N. J. Crowson, *Fleet Street, Press Barons and Politics: The Journals of Collin Brooks, 1932–1940*, London, Royal Historical Society, 1998, p. 219.

27   VC, Sara Taylor to Cazalet, 4 November 1938.

28   Rupert Hart-Davis, *Hugh Walpole*, London, Hamish Hamilton, 1952, p. 371.

29   RC, p. 113.

30   HCD, 30 September 1938.

31   RB/NS, p. 372.

32   Robert Self, ed., *The Neville Chamberlain Diary Letters*, vol. 4, Aldershot, Ashgate, 2005, p. 352.

33   Speech delivered 16 December 1938, in Bernays family papers.

34   Self, *The Neville Chamberlain Diary Letters*, pp. 351–2.

35   HC, 5 October 1938, vol. 339, col. 404. This is John Sandeman Allen, MP for Birkenhead West (1935–45), not to be confused with Sir John Sandeman Allen, MP for Liverpool West Derby (1924–35).

36   HC, 5 October 1938, vol. 339, col. 360.

37   HC, 5 October 1938, vol. 339, col. 431.

38   *Birmingham Daily Gazette*, 7 October 1938, p. 6.

39   RC, p. 113.

40   HN/NN3, p. 179.

41   Tree later forgot that he did not resign as a PPS until November.

42   *Daily Mail*, 7 October 1938, p. 8.

43   *Chelmsford Chronicle,* 14 October 1938, p. 9.

44   *Chelmsford Chronicle,* 14 October 1938, p. 9.

45   Self, *The Neville Chamberlain Diary Letters*, pp. 351–2.

46   Hugh Dalton, *The Fateful Years: Memoirs, 1931–1945*, London, Muller, 1957, p. 199.

47   J. Barnes and D. Nicholson, eds., *The Empire at Bay: The Leo Amery Diaries 1929–1945*, London, 1988, p. 528.

48   *Aberdeen Press and Journal*, 17 October 1938, p. 9.

49   OH, p. 213.

50   N. J. Crowson, *Fleet Street, Press Barons and Politics: The Journals of Collin Brooks, 1932–1940*, London, Royal Historical Society, 1998, p. 221.

51   *Daily Mail*, 30 June 1938, p. 8.

52   *Ibid.*

53   *Sketch*, 16 April 1930, p. 41.

54   *Hull Daily Mail*, 16 December 1938, p. 5.

55   RC, p. 115.

56   OH, p. 217.

57   *The Times*, 11 November 1938, p. 14.

58 *Ibid*. Embarrassingly for Goebbels, Rath was well-known to be homosexual.
59 *Essex Chronicle*, 14 October 1938, p. 9.
60 *Chelmsford Chronicle*, 25 November 1938, p. 5.
61 HC, 14 November 1938, vol. 341, col. 621.
62 CC, p. 178.
63 Carmarthenshire Archives, Cilcennin Papers, 34.
64 HC, 1 November 1938, vol. 340, col. 117.
65 *Whitehall News*, 8 December 1938.
66 *Ibid*.
67 *Whitehall News*, 15 December 1938.
68 *Whitehall News*, 5 January 1939.

16 THE 'GLAMOUR BOYS'

1 *Birmingham Mail*, 27 January 1939, p. 12.
2 *Hartlepool Evening Express*, 27 January 1939, p. 4.
3 *Headway in War-time*, League of Nations Union, July 1939.
4 BB, p. 133.
5 Lucy Moorehead, *Freya Stark Letters, vol. 3: The Growth of Danger, 1935–39*, Tisbury, Wiltshire, Compton Russell Ltd., 1976, p. 249.
6 *Liverpool Echo*, 23 March 1939, p. 8.
7 RB/NS, p. 382.
8 RB/NS, p. 385.
9 RB/NS, p. 391.
10 RB/NS, p. 353.
11 RB/NS, p. 382.
12 RB/NS, p. 392.
13 RB/NS, p. 398.
14 *Sketch*, 15 March 1939, p. 13.
15 For a fuller analysis of women's attitudes, see Julie V. Gottlieb, *'Guilty Women', Foreign Policy, and Appeasement in Inter-War Britain*, London, Palgrave Macmillan, 2015.
16 Richard Baxter, *Guilty Women*, London, Quality Press, 1941, pp. 42–3.
17 RB, 17 March 1939.
18 VC, 18 and 20 March 1939.
19 VC, 18 March 1939.
20 *Nottingham Evening Post*, 31 March 1939, p. 6.
21 HN, 20 March 1939.
22 They included Jack Macnamara, Ronnie Cartland, Ronnie Tree, Harold Nicolson, Jim Thomas, Harold Macmillan, Mark Patrick, Paul Emrys-Evans, Anthony Crossley, Sir Derrick Gunston, Admiral Roger Keyes, Commander Bower, Dick Law, Louis Spears and the Churchill set of Bracken and Sandys.
23 J. Barnes and D. Nicholson, eds., *The Empire at Bay: The Leo Amery Diaries 1929–1945*, London, 1988, p. 536.
24 *House of Commons Sessional Papers 1938–9*.

25 HC, 22 March 1938, vol. 333, cols. 1052–3.
26 Chelmsford Conservative Association AGM, 29 March 1938, D/Z 96/4; exec. 6, 27 May 1938, D/Z 96/7.
27 BL Add MS.58247 Eden to Emrys-Evans 15 May 1962 and vice versa.
28 HN/NN1, p. 402.
29 RT, p. 86.
30 BB/RJ, p. 229.
31 HN/NN1, p. 397.
32 BB/RJ, p. 229.
33 *Cambridge Daily News*, 19 April 1939, p. 4.
34 *Yorkshire Post*, 19 May 1939, p. 12.
35 *Western Daily Press*, 5 June 1939, p. 8.
36 Peter Stansky, *Sassoon*, New Haven, Yale University Press, 2003, p. 241.
37 CC, p. 202.
38 *Cambridge Daily News*, 12 July 1939, p. 4.
39 *Scotsman*, 21 July 1939, p. 11.
40 RT, p. 86.
41 RT, p. 87.
42 *People*, 2 July 1939, p. 17.
43 RT, p. 87.
44 HN, 29 May 1939.
45 HN, 8 November 1938.

17 AT WAR WITH GERMANY

1   Under modern Standing Orders only a government minister could table a similar motion and no amendment would be allowed.
2   HN/NN, p. 401.
3   HN/NN, pp. 405, 406.
4   HC, 2 August 1939, vol. 350, col. 2454.
5   The debate is at HC, 2 August 1939, vol. 350, cols. 2425–2525.
6   HC, 2 August 1939, vol. 350, col. 2490.
7   BC, p. 127.
8   BC, p. 129.
9   HN, 2 August 1938.
10 BC, p. 139.
11 HC, 2 August 1939, vol. 350, cols. 2509.
12 *Star*, 31 May 1939.
13 BC, p. 140.
14 *Evening Standard*, 3 August 1939, p. 1.
15 HN, 3 August 1939.
16 *Birmingham Daily Gazette*, 3 August 1939, p. 1.
17 *Birmingham Mail*, 8 August 1939, p. 4.
18 BC, p. 139.
19 Robert Self, ed., *The Neville Chamberlain Diary Letters*, Aldershot, Ashgate, 2005, vol. 4, p. 438.

20 HN/NN, p. 408.
21 Eton College, Cazalet Papers, Bob Boothby to Thelma Cazalet, 17 June 1939.
22 HCD, 2 August 1939.
23 VC/RJ, pp. 215, 216.
24 All quotations from Macnamara in this chapter are from extracts from his diary published in *Emerald*, London Irish Rifles, 1975, pp. 28–9.
25 RC, p. 141.
26 HCD, 24 August 1939.
27 HC, 24 August 1939, vol. 351, cols. 2–10.
28 HC, 24 August 1939, vol. 351, cols. 2–10.
29 RT, p. 89.
30 N.A. Rose, ed., *Baffy: The Diaries of Blanche Dugdale, 1936–1947*, London, Vallentine Mitchell, 1973, p. 140.
31 *Western Daily Press*, 24 June 1939, p. 5.
32 *Leeds Mercury*, 26 June 1939, p. 9.
33 VC, von Cramm to Cazalet, 28 August 1939.
34 *Ballymena Weekly Telegraph*, 26 August 1939, p. 9.
35 *Emerald*, Royal Irish Rifles, 1975, pp. 28–9.
36 Duff Cooper Diaries, p. 274.
37 HN/NN1, p. 417.
38 *Western Daily Press*, 2 September 1939, p. 1.
39 The debate is at HC, 1 September 1939, vol. 351, cols. 125–39.
40 *Emerald*, London Irish Rifles, 1975, p. 29.
41 HC, 1 September 1939, vol. 351, col. 135.
42 Unless otherwise attributed, all Rob Bernays's comments are from his unpublished contemporaneous accounts, which are in the family papers.
43 RB typescript note, undated.
44 HN/NN1, p. 419.
45 All quotations from Rob Bernays in this paragraph are from a typescript account in the family papers.
46 HCD, 2 September 1939.
47 This detail comes from Ben Nicolson's diary in the Paul Mellon Centre.
48 HN/NN1, p. 419.
49 HC, 2 September 1939, vol. 351, col. 282.
50 HC, 2 September 1939, vol. 351, col. 283.
51 HN/NN1, p. 419.
52 *Ibid.*
53 HN, 2 September 1939.
54 *Ibid.*
55 HN/NN1, p. 420.

18 REMOVING THE 'OLD LIMPET'

1 RB typescript note, 3 September 1939.
2 All quotations in this paragraph are from a typescript note in the Bernays family papers.

3   RB, typescript, undated.
4   BB/RJ, p. 232.
5   HN/NN1, p. 422.
6   VC, 6 September 1939.
7   Entry for 10 September 1939, LBN/1/1/15, Benedict Nicolson Archive, GB3010, the Paul Mellon Centre for Studies in British Art, London, UK.
8   HN, 10 September 1939.
9   D. R. Guttery, *The Queen's Own Worcestershire Hussars, 1922–1956*, Stourbridge, Mark & Moody, 1958, p. 7.
10 King's College London, Liddell Hart Papers, 1/151, 15 September 1939.
11 HN, 20 September 1939.
12 RC, p. 142.
13 RC, pp. 145–6.
14 HCD, 2 November 1939.
15 Private interview with the author.
16 RC, p. 144.
17 RC, p. 147.
18 D. R. Guttery, *The Queen's Own Worcestershire Hussars, 1922–1956*, Stourbridge, Mark & Moody, 1958, p. 10.
19 TNA WO 167/581.
20 Guttery, *The Queen's Own Worcestershire Hussars*, p. 10.
21 TNA WO 167/581.
22 RC, p. 148.
23 RC, p. 149.
24 Bodleian Library Oxford, MS. Eng.c.3160, fols. 85–6.
25 TNA WO 167/581.
26 Bodleian Library Oxford, MS. Eng.c.3160, fols. 85–6.
27 RC, p. 154.
28 RC, p. 151.
29 RC, p. 153.
30 RB, Bernays to Nancy Britton, 29 September 1939.
31 RB, 15 March 1940.
32 *Chelmsford Chronicle*, 1 March 1940, p. 3.
33 VC/RJ, p. 218.
34 Entry for 8 September 1939, LBN/1/1/13, Benedict Nicolson Archive, GB3010, the Paul Mellon Centre for Studies in British Art, London, UK.
35 *Ibid.*, 10 October 1939.
36 Brodrick Haldane, *Time Exposure*, London, Arcadia, 1999, p. 82.
37 Jessica Mitford, *Faces of Philip: A Memoir of Philip Toynbee*, New York, Alfred Knopf, 1984, p. 55.
38 Haldane, *Time Exposure*, p. 82.
39 Jessica Mitford, *Faces of Philip: A Memoir of Philip Toynbee*, New York, Alfred Knopf, 1984, p. 40.
40 *Ibid.*
41 Cited in Emma Vickers, *Queen and Country*, Manchester, MUP, 1988, p. 77. It was named in homage to Jean Cocteau's favourite queer hangout in Paris.

42 *Ibid.*

43 Stephen Bourne, *Fighting Proud*, London, L. B. Tauris, 2018, p. 49.

44 *Bystander*, 20 March 1940, p. 3.

45 Cited in Matthew Sweet, *The West End Front: The Wartime Secrets of London's Grand Hotels*, London, Faber & Faber, 2011, pp. 190–1.

46 VC, 6 September 1939.

47 VC, 11 October 1939.

48 VC, 21 December 1939.

49 VC/RJ, p. 219.

50 VC, 27 November 1939.

51 Robert Self, ed., *The Neville Chamberlain Diary Letters*, Aldershot, Ashgate, 2005, vol. 4, p. 433, 20 December 1939.

52 John Vincent, ed., *The Crawford Papers*, Manchester, MUP, 1984, p. 601.

53 David Dilks, ed., *The Diaries of Sir Alexander Cadogan*, London, Putnam, 1972, p. 242.

54 Brian Bond, ed., *Chief of Staff: The Diaries of Lieutenant-General Sir Henry Pownall*, London, Leo Cooper, 1972, vol. 1, p. 203.

55 *Truth*, 7 July 1939.

56 *Truth*, 8 September 1939, p. 291.

57 *Truth*, 15 September 1939, p. 307.

58 HN, 12 December 1939.

59 VC/RJ, pp. 222–3.

60 HN, 7 January 1940.

61 CCC, Vansittart Papers, II/32, 'Report on Truth', p. 42.

62 *Truth*, 12 January 1940, p. 29.

63 'Belisha Once More', *Truth*, 19 January 1940.

64 *Free Press*, February 1940.

65 CC, p. 243.

66 HC, 8 May 1940, vol. 360, col. 1264.

67 VC, 7 and 8 May 1940.

68 HC, 8 May 1940, vol. 360, col. 1266.

69 Robert Rhodes-James wrote in his biography of Victor (pp. 226–7) that he 'very reluctantly voted for the Government', but the division lists show that Victor abstained and the only Cazalet to vote that day – with Chamberlain – was his sister Thelma.

70 *Daily Herald*, 9 May 1940, p. 1.

71 RT, p. 114.

72 VC, 7 and 8 May 1940.

73 VC, 9 May 1940.

74 BB/RJ, p. 241.

75 Hugh Dalton, *Fateful Years*, London, Frederick Muller, 1957, p. 308.

76 Charles Lysaght, *Brendan Bracken*, London, Allen Lane, 1979, p. 160.

77 Dalton, *Fateful Years*, p. 308.

78 HC, 9 May 1940, vol. 360, col. 1438.

19 THE STAND AT CASSEL

1   TNA WO 167/581 53 Tank.
2   RC, p. 156.
3   Bodleian Library Oxford, MS. Eng.c.3160.
4   Wild's Report, p. 258.
5   TNA CAB 106/292, p. 74.
6   Melville Thomas Report, cited in Hugh Sebag-Montefiore, *Dunkirk*, London, Penguin, 2015, p. 259.
7   Bridgeman Report, p. 261.
8   TNA CAB 106/292, p. 74.
9   Maurice Gilmore's report, p. 44, cited in Sebag-Montefiore, *Dunkirk*, p. 271.
10 TNA CAB 106/292, p. 80.
11 Winston Churchill, *Their Finest Hour*, London, Cassell, 1949, p. 73.
12 Tom Carmichael's 'Active Service Diary 1940', p. 80, cited in Sebag-Montefiore, *Dunkirk*, p. 368.
13 TNA WO 167/400
14 RC, p. 157.
15 TNA CAB 106/292, p. 101.
16 TNA WO 167/400.
17 Imperial War Museum, Documents 2303, Brigadier Somerset Papers, Diary.
18 *Daily Telegraph*, 19 February 1948.
19 TNA CAB 106/292, p. 103.
20 TNA WO 167/581 53 Tank.
21 Imperial War Museum, Documents 2303, Brigadier Somerset Papers, Diary.
22 *Ibid.*
23 RC, p. 146.
24 BC, p. 216.
25 RC, p. 155.
26 https://www.bbc.co.uk/history/ww2peopleswar/stories/68/a2349768.shtml
27 RC, p. 158.
28 BC, p. 223.
29 King's College London, Liddell Hart Papers, 1/151, 8 August 1942.
30 *Daily Telegraph*, 19 February 1948.
31 *The Times*, 7 January 1941, p. 7.

20 ITCHING FOR ACTION

1   Bodleian, Ball Papers, MS. Eng. C. 6652.f.44–8.
2   The authors were Michael Foot MP, Frank Owen and Peter Howard, respectively Labour, Liberal and Conservative journalists, all three of whom worked for Lord Beaverbrook's newspapers. W. H. Smith refused to sell the book.
3   VC, 5 August 1940.
4   *Emerald*, London Irish Rifles, 1975, pp. 28–9.
5   *The London Irish at War*, London, London Irish Rifles Old Comrades' Association, p. 22.

6   He was killed aged twenty-six on 3 March 1944 on the beach at Anzio.

7   *Chelmsford Chronicle*, 5 January 1945, p. 2. The paper says they were on the white cliffs at Dover, but the LIR War Diary WO 166/4435 cites the Dungeness road.

8   *Daily Telegraph*, 2 June 1941, p. 3.

9   *Hull Daily Mail*, 4 September 1941, p. 6.

10   *The Times*, 5 September 1941, p. 2.

11   *Eastbourne Herald*, 6 September 1941, p. 6.

12   *Liverpool Daily Post*, 6 September 1941, p. 1.

13   HC, 24 February 1942, vol. 378, cols. 103.

14   CHAR 20/97B/125, 16 October 1942.

15   Ismay thought of Jack as a 'tame lunatic' and had received a secret memorandum from the War Office saying that although Jack was 'admitted to be a good trainer of troops, the R.A.F. Regiment would be only too glad to dispense with his services'. Moreover, Ismay told Churchill that as a substantive lieutenant colonel and a temporary colonel, Jack was too senior to lead a battalion but not equipped to command a brigade.

16   CHAR 20/97B/135, 2 December 1942.

17   CHAR 20/97B/136, 17 December 1942.

18   Lambeth Palace Library, William Temple Papers, vol. 17, f.4.

19   CHAR 20/97B/141, 29 June 1943.

20   CHAR 20/97B/144, 3 August 1943.

21   TNA CAB 120/809.

22   *Chelmsford Chronicle*, 6 October 1944, p. 1.

23   Michael Davie, ed., *The Diaries of Evelyn Waugh*, London, Weidenfeld & Nicolson, 1976, p. 605.

24   William Deakin, Elisabeth Barker and Jonathan Chadwick, eds., *British Political and Military Strategy in Central, Eastern and Southern Europe in 1944*, London, Macmillan, 1998, p. 114.

25   *Chelmsford Chronicle*, 24 November 1944, p. 1.

26   *Ibid.*

27   King's College London, Davy Papers, unpublished memoir.

28   WO 170/1432 LIR 1944.

29   *The London Irish at War*, London Irish Rifles Old Comrades' Association, p. 19.

30   CHAR 20/198B/139.

31   *Sunday Mirror*, 31 December 1944, p. 1.

32   *Chelmsford Chronicle*, 5 January 1945, p. 2.

33   *Chelmsford Chronicle*, 5 January 1945, p. 3.

34   VC, 5 July 1940.

35   VC, 9 July 1940.

36   VC/RJ, p. 262.

37   VC, 1 October 1940.

38   VC/RJ, p. 280.

39   *New York Times*, 17 April 1941.

40   HC, 19 May 1943, vol. 389, col. 1157.

41   HC, 19 May 1943, vol. 389, col. 1159.

42 VC/RJ, p. 286.
43 *Gibraltar Magazine*, July 2009, p. 79.
44 Curiously, Whiteley, the MP for Buckingham, left the majority of his estate to the playwright and scriptwriter John Antrobus.
45 Surrey History Centre, Ref. 2332/Box 32/4.
46 *Wisconsin Jewish Chronicle*, 23 July 1943, p. 1.
47 *The Times*, 6 July 1943, p. 2.
48 *Belfast Telegraph*, 5 July 1943, p. 3.
49 HC, 3 July 1941, vol. 372, col. 1547.
50 RB, Bernays to Nancy Britton, 5 July 1941.
51 RB, Bernays to Nancy Britton, 30 March (no year, but probably 1941).
52 RB, Bernays to Nancy Britton, 26 August 1941.
53 RB, Bernays to Nancy, 18 December (no year, but probably 1940).
54 RB, Bernays to Nancy Britton, 18 March, no year, before September 1941.
55 RB, Bernays to Nancy Britton, 19 February 1942.
56 *Western Daily Press*, 27 April 1942, p. 3.
57 RB, 1 November 1943.
58 RB, 1 September 1943.
59 RB, 20 December 1944.
60 RB, 2 January 1945.
61 RB, 8 January 1945.
62 RB, 20 January 1945.
63 RB, 20 January 1945.
64 RB, 22 January 1945.
65 HC, 26 January 1945, vol. 407, col. 1143.
66 HN/NN3, p. 308.
67 RB, Jean Stratheden to Nancy, 8 February 1945.
68 Interview with Robert Bernays.
69 RB, Will Mabane to Nancy, 5 February 1945.
70 HN/NN3, p. 308.

EPILOGUE

1 CC, p. 406.
2 RC, p. 15.
3 HC, 6 July 1943, vol. 390, col. 1947.
4 CHAR 20/198B/139.
5 *The Times*, 29 March 1945, p. 7.
6 HN/NN3, p. 458.

Bibliography

Primary sources

Balliol College, Oxford, Harold Nicolson typescript diary
Birmingham University, Neville Chamberlain Papers
Bodleian Library, Oxford
   –Geoffrey Dawson Papers
   –Harry Crookshank Manuscript Diary
   –Sybil Colefax Papers
   –Sir Joseph Ball Papers
British Library, Paul Vychan Emrys-Evans Papers
Cambridge University Library, Sassoon Papers
Carmarthenshire County Records, Jim Thomas, Lord Cilcennin papers
Charterhouse School Archives
Churchill Archives Centre, University of Cambridge
   –Chartwell Papers
   –Hailsham Papers
Eton College Library, Victor Cazalet Papers
King's College London
   –George Mark Oswald Davy Papers
   –Ian Hamilton Papers
   –Basil Liddell Hart Papers
   –Louis Edward Spears Papers
   –Hastings Ismay Papers
Lambeth Palace Library
Robert Bernays Family Papers
Royal Irish Rifles Regimental Museum
Sharp family photographs, papers and recordings
Southampton University, Lord Mount Temple Papers
Tate Gallery Archive
The National Archives
Worcester College Oxford, Archives

Newspapers and journals

Aberdeen Press and Journal
Arbroath Herald
Argus (Melbourne)
Ballymena Weekly Telegraph
Bath Chronicle and Weekly Gazette
Belfast News-Letter
Belfast Telegraph
Birmingham Daily Gazette
Birmingham Daily Post
Blackshirt
Blackwood's Edinburgh Magazine
Bystander
Cambridge Daily News
Central Queensland Herald
Charleston Daily Mail
Chelmsford Chronicle
Chester Chronicle
Chesterfield Herald
Contemporary Review
Cornishman
Courier-Mail (Brisbane)
Croydon Advertiser
Daily Express
Daily Herald
Daily Mail
Daily Telegraph
Derby Daily Telegraph
Derbyshire Times
Dudley Evening Telegraph
Dundee Evening Telegraph
Eastbourne Herald
Edinburgh Evening News
Emerald
Essex Newsman
Evening News
Gloucester Citizen
Gloucester Journal
Gloucestershire Echo
Hamburger Tageblatt
Hartlepool Northern Daily Mail
Hendon and Finchley Times

BIBLIOGRAPHY

Hull Daily Mail
Illustrated London News
Illustrated Police News
John Bull
Lancashire Evening Post
Leeds Mercury
Lincolnshire Echo
Liverpool Daily Post
Liverpool Echo
London Gazette
Manchester Guardian
Market Harborough Advertiser
Nambucca and Bellinger News
National Review
Nelson Leader
New York Times
News Chronicle
News of the World
Nineteenth Century and After
North Wiltshire Herald
Northants Evening Telegraph
Nottingham Evening Post
Nottingham Journal
People
Portsmouth Evening News
Rugby Advertiser
Scotsman
Sheffield Independent
South Wales Daily News
Southend Standard
Sunderland Daily Echo and Shipping Gazette
Sydney Morning Herald
The Times
Time
Truth
Wells Journal
West London Observer
Western Daily Press
Western Gazette
Western Morning News
Wisconsin Jewish Chronicle
Wiltshire Gazette
Yorkshire Evening Post
Yorkshire Post and Leeds Intelligencer

Books and articles

Aberconway, Christabel, *A Wiser Woman? A Book of Memories*, London, Hutchinson, 1966

Ackerley, J. R., *My Father and Myself*, London, Bodley Head, 1968

Acton, Harold, *Memoirs of an Aesthete*, London, Methuen, 1970

Acton, William, *The Functions and Disorders of the Reproductive Organs*, London, John Churchill, 1857

Adamthwaite, Anthony, 'The British Government and the Media, 1937–1938', *Journal of Contemporary History*, vol. 18, April 1983

Aldington, Richard, *Death of a Hero*, London, Chatto & Windus, 1929

Amory, Mark, ed., *The Letters of Evelyn Waugh*, London, Weidenfeld & Nicolson, 1980

Andrew, Christopher and Mitrokhin, Vasili, *The Mitrokhin Archive: The KGB in Europe and the West*, London, Allen Lane, 1999

Anomaly, *The Invert and His Social Adjustment*, London, Bailliere, Tindall & Cox, 1927

Atcherley, Tony and Carey, Mark, *Hitler's Gay Traitor: The Story of Ernst Röhm*, Trafford Publishing, 2007

Ball, Stuart, ed., *Parliament and Politics in the Age of Churchill and Attlee: The Headlam Diaries, 1935–1951*, Cambridge, CUP, 1999

Barnes, J. and Nicholson, D., eds., *The Empire at Bay: The Leo Amery Diaries 1929–1945*, London, Hutchinson, 1988

Bartlett, Lee, ed., *Letters to Christopher*, London, Black Sparrow Press, 1980

Beaton, Cecil, *Diaries: 1922–39: The Wandering Years*, London, Weidenfeld & Nicolson, 1961

Beaumont, Rex B., *Me, Myself and I*, Mullingar, privately published, 1973

Beck, Gad, *An Underground Life: Memoirs of a Gay Jew in Nazi Berlin*, Madison, Wisconsin, University of Wisconsin Press, 1999

Beichman, Arnold, 'Hugger-Mugger in Old Queen Street', *Journal of Contemporary History*, vol. 13, 1978

Benschoff, Harry M., *Monsters in the Closet*, Manchester, MUP, 1997

Bernays, Robert, *Naked Fakir*, London, Victor Gollancz, 1931

—, *Special Correspondent*, London, Victor Gollancz, 1934

Bessel, Richard, *Political Violence and the Rise of Nazism*, London, Yale University Press, 1984

Blunden, Edmund, *Undertones of War*, London, R. Cobden-Sanderson, 1929

Bolitho, Gordon, *The Other Germany*, London, Lovat Dickson, 1934

Bolitho, Hector, *Combat Report*, London, B. T. Batsford, 1943

Bond, Brian, ed., *Chief of Staff: The Diaries of Lieutenant-General Sir Henry Pownall*, London, Leo Cooper, 1972

Boothby, Robert, *Recollections of a Rebel*, London, Hutchinson, 1987

Bourne, Stephen, *Fighting Proud*, London, L. B. Tauris, 2018

Bouverie, Tim, *Appeasing Hitler*, London, Bodley Head, 2019

Boyd, Julia, *Travellers in the Third Reich*, London, Elliott & Thompson, 2017

Brooke, Jocelyn, *Private View*, London, J. Barrie, 1954

Buckle, Richard, ed., *Self Portrait with Friends: The Selected Diaries of Cecil Beaton 1926–1974*, London, Weidenfeld & Nicolson, 1979

Bullock, Malcolm, *Austria, 1918–1938: A Study in Failure*, London, Macmillan, 1939

Burleigh, Michael and Wipperman, Wolfgang, *The Racial State: Germany 1933–1945*, Cambridge, CUP, 1991

Burns, Michael, *Turned Towards the Sun*, London, Michael Russell, 2003

Byrne, Paula, *Mad World: Evelyn Waugh and the Secrets of Brideshead*, London, HarperCollins, 2010

Campbell, Bruce, *The SA Generals and the Rise of Nazism*, Lexington, University Press of Kentucky, 1998

Cartland, Barbara, *Polly: My Wonderful Mother*, London, Herbert Jenkins, 1956

—, *Ronald Cartland*, London, National Book Association, 1945

Cazalet, Victor, *With Sikorsky to Russia*, London, Curwen Press, 1942

Cazalet-Keir, Thelma, *From the Wings*, London, Bodley Head, 1969

Christie, Michael, ed., *Derek Jarman's At Your Own Risk: A Saint's Testament*, New York, Overlook Press, 1992

Churchill, Winston, *Their Finest Hour*, London, Cassell, 1949

Cloud, Henry, *Barbara Cartland: Crusader in Pink*, London, Weidenfeld & Nicolson, 1979

Cockett, Richard, 'Ball, Chamberlain and Truth', *Historical Journal*, vol. 33, 1990

Collins, Damian, *Charmed Life: The Phenomenal World of Philip Sassoon*, London, William Collins, 2016

Cookridge, Edward Henry, *The Third Man*, London, Barker, 1968

Copp, Bruce, *Out of the Firing Line ... Into the Foyer*, London, History Press, 2015

Costello, John and Tsarev, Oleg, *Deadly Illusions*, London, Century, 1993

Coward, Noël, *Future Indefinite*, London, Heinemann, 1954

Creed, Jack, *Mars & Venus*, Studley, Warwickshire, Brewin Books, 2000

Croall, Jonathan, *John Gielgud*, London, Methuen, 2011

Crockett, Richard, *Twilight of Truth*, London, Weidenfeld & Nicolson, 1989

Croft, Taylor, *The Cloven Hoof: A Study in Contemporary London Vices*, London, D. Archer, 1932

Crowson, N. J., ed., *Fleet Street Press Barons and Politics: The Journals of Collin Brooks*, Cambridge, CUP, 1998

Dalton, Derek, 'Genealogy of the Australian Homocriminal Subject: a study of two explanatory models of deviance', *Griffith Law Review*, vol. 16, no. 1, 2007, pp. 83–106

Dalton, Hugh, *Fateful Years*, London, Frederick Muller, 1957

David, Hugh, *On Queer Street*, London, HarperCollins, 1997

Davie, Michael, ed., *The Diaries of Evelyn Waugh*, London, Weidenfeld & Nicolson, 1976

Deakin, William, Barker, Elisabeth and Chadwick, Jonathan, eds., *British Political and Military Strategy in Central, Eastern and Southern Europe in 1944*, London, Macmillan, 1998

De-la-Noy, Michael, *Eddy: The Life of Edward Sackville-West*, London, Arcadia, 1988

Delmer, Sefton, *Trail Sinister*, London, Secker & Warburg, 1961

DeSalvo, Louise and Leaska, Mitchell A., eds., *The Letters of Vita Sackville-West to Virginia Woolf*, London, Macmillan, 1992

Dilks, David, ed., *The Diaries of Sir Alexander Cadogan*, London, Putnam, 1972

Feinberg, David B., *Gay American Autobiography*, Madison, Wisconsin, University of Wisconsin Press, 2009

Fischer, Conan, *Stormtroopers*, London, George Allen & Unwin, 1983

Fort, Adrian, *Nancy: The Story of Lady Astor*, London, Jonathan Cape, 2012

French, R., *Gays Between the Broadsheets: Australian Media References to Homosexuality, 1948–1980*, Darlinghurst, NSW, Gay History Project, 1986

Gallo, Max, *The Night of the Long Knives*, London, Souvenir Press, 1973

Gathorne-Hardy, Jonathan, *The Public School Phenomenon*, London, Hodder & Stoughton, 1977

Gerothwohl, Maurice, ed., *An Ambassador of Peace: Pages from the Diary of Viscount D'Abernon*, London, Hodder & Stoughton, 1930

Gottlieb, Julie V., *'Guilty Women', Foreign Policy, and Appeasement in Inter-War Britain*, London, Palgrave Macmillan, 2015

Griffiths, Richard, *Fellow Travellers of the Right: British Enthusiasts for Nazi Germany 1933–39*, Oxford, OUP, 1983

—, *Patriotism Perverted: Captain Ramsay, the Right Club and British Anti-Semitism*, London, Faber & Faber, 2015

Guttery, D. R., *The Queen's Own Worcestershire Hussars, 1922–1956*, Stourbridge, Mark & Moody, 1958

Hancock, Eleanor, *Ernst Röhm, Hitler's SA Chief of Staff*, London, Macmillan, 2008

Harris, Frank, *Oscar Wilde: His Life and Confessions*, New York, Brentano's, 1916

Hart-Davis, Rupert, *Hugh Walpole*, London, Hamilton, 1952

Harvey, John, ed., *Diplomatic diaries of Oliver Harvey, 1937–1940*, London, Collins, 1970

Heger, Heinz, *The Men With the Pink Triangle: The True Life-and-Death Story of Homosexuals in the Nazi Death Camps*, Alyson Books, 1994

Herzog, Dagmar, ed., *Sexuality and German Fascism*, New York, Berghahn Books, 2005

Hirschfeld, C., 'The Tenacity of a Tradition: Truth and the Jews 1877–1957', *Patterns of Prejudice*, vol. 28, 1994, pp. 67–85

Hoare, Philip, *Noël Coward*, London, Sinclair-Stevenson, 1995

Houlbrook, Matt, *Queer London: Perils and Pleasures in the Sexual Metropolis*, Chicago, Illinois, University of Chicago Press, 2005

—, 'The man with the powder puff in interwar London', *Historical Journal*, 50 (1), 2007, pp. 145–71

Hutton, Robert, *Of Those Alone*, London, Sidgwick & Jackson, 1958

Isherwood, Christopher, *Christopher and his Kind*, London, Vintage, 2012

Ives, George, *The Continued Extension of the Criminal Law*, London, privately printed, 1922

Kershaw, Ian, *Making Friends with Hitler*, London, Penguin, 2004

Kessler, Charles, ed., *Berlin in Lights: The Diaries of Count Harry Kessler, 1918–1937*, New York, Grove Press, 2001

Kingsley, Charles, *Alton Locke*, New York, Harper & Brothers, 1850

Kushmer, Tony, *The Persistence of Prejudice*, Manchester University Press, 1989

Landau, Rom, *God is My Adventure*, London, Faber & Faber, 1935

Lees-Milne, James, *Harold Nicolson*, Chatto & Windus, 1980, 2 vols

—, *Deep Romantic Chasm: Diaries 1979–81*, London, John Murray, 2000

Lewis, Jeremy, *Cyril Connolly: A Life*, London, Jonathan Cape, 1997

Lewis, Wyndham, *Hitler*, London, Chatto & Windus, 1931

Liddell Hart, Basil, *The Real War, 1914–1918*, London, Faber & Faber, 1930

Lownie, Andrew, *Stalin's Englishman: The Lives of Guy Burgess*, London, Hodder & Stoughton, 2015

Luke, Michael, *David Tennant: The Gargoyle Years*, London, Weidenfeld & Nicolson, 1991

Lysaght, Charles, *Brendan Bracken*, London, Allen Lane, 1979

Lytton, Earl of, *Antony, Viscount Knebworth*, London, Peter Davies, 1935

Mack, John, *A Prince of Our Disorder: The Life of T. E. Lawrence*, Boston, Little, Brown, 1976

Macnamara, J. R. J., *The Whistle Blows*, London, Eyre & Spottiswoode, 1938

MacQueen-Pope, W. J., *Goodbye Piccadilly*, London, Michael Joseph, 1960

Mannin, Ethel, *Young in the Twenties*, London, Hutchinson, 1971

Marhoefer, Laurie, *Sex and the Weimar Republic*, Toronto, University of Toronto Press, 2015

Marlowe, John, *Late Victorian: The Life of Sir Arnold Talbot Wilson*, London, Cresset Press, 1967

Mitchell, Donald and Reed, Philip, eds., *Letters from a Life: Selected Letters and Diaries of Benjamin Britten*, London, Faber & Faber, 2012

Mitchell, Leslie, *Maurice Bowra: A Life*, Oxford, OUP, 2009

Mitford, Jessica, *Faces of Philip: A Memoir of Philip Toynbee*, New York, Alfred Knopf, 1984

Modin, Yuri, *My Five Cambridge Friends*, London, Headline, 1994

Moseley, Sydney, *The Night Haunts of London*, London, Stanley Paul & Co., 1920

Mosley, Oswald, *My Life*, London, Nelson, 1968

Moulson, Tom, *The Millionaire's Squadron*, Barnsley, Pen & Sword, 2014

Mulvah, Jane, *Madresfield: One Home, One Family, One Thousand Years*, London, Doubleday, 2008

Nichols, Beverley, *The Sweet and Twenties*, London, Weidenfeld & Nicolson, 1958

Nicolson, Nigel, ed., *Harold Nicolson: Diaries and Letters, 1930–1939*, London, Weidenfeld & Nicolson, 1966

—, ed., *Harold Nicolson: Diaries and Letters, 1939–1945*, London, Weidenfeld & Nicolson, 1967

—, ed., *Vita and Harold: The Letters of Vita Sackville-West and Harold Nicolson*, London, Weidenfeld & Nicolson, 1992

—, ed., *The Harold Nicolson Diaries and Letters, 1907–1963*, London, Weidenfeld & Nicolson, 2004

Paillole, Paul, *Notre Espion Chez Hitler*, Paris, Laffont, 1985

Parker, Peter, *J. R. Ackerley*, London, Constable, 1989

Patrick, James and Mark, *India from a Back Bench*, London, Methuen, 1934

Penrose, Barrie and Freeman, Simon, *Conspiracy of Silence: The Secret Life of Anthony Blunt*, London, Vintage, 1988

Pimlott, Ben, ed., *The Political Diary of Hugh Dalton*, 1918–40, 1945–60, London, Jonathan Cape, 1988

Porter, Kevin and Weeks, Jeffrey, eds., *Between the Acts*, London, Routledge, 1991

Pryce-Jones, David, ed. *Cyril Connolly's Journal and Memoir*, London, Collins, 1983

Raven, Simon, *Shadows on the Grass*, London, Blond & Briggs, 1982

Read, Anthony and Fisher, David, *Colonel Z: The Life and Times of a Master Spy*, London, Hodder & Stoughton, 1984

Rees, Goronwy, *A Chapter of Accidents*, London, Chatto & Windus, 1972

Rhodes James, Robert, ed., *'Chips': The Diaries of Sir Henry Channon*, London, Weidenfeld & Nicolson, 1967

—, *Victor Cazalet: A Portrait*, London, Hamish Hamilton, 1976

—, *Anthony Eden*, London, Weidenfeld & Nicolson, 1986

—, *Robert Boothby: A Portrait of Churchill's Ally*, London, Viking, 1991

Rose, Francis, *Saying Life*, London, Cassell, 1961

Rose, Norman, ed., *Baffy: The Diaries of Blanche Dugdale, 1936–1947*, London, Vallentine Mitchell, 1973

—, *The Cliveden Set*, London, Jonathan Cape, 2000

—, *Harold Nicolson*, London, Jonathan Cape, 2005

Sackville-West, Robert, *Inheritance: The Story of Knole and the Sackvilles*, London, Bloomsbury, 2010

Sebag-Montefiore, Hugh, *Dunkirk*, London, Penguin, 2015

Seebohm, Caroline, *No Regrets: The Life of Marietta Tree*, New York, Simon & Schuster, 1997

Seel, Pierre, *I, Pierre Seel, Deported Homosexual: A Memoir of Nazi Terror*, trans. Joachim Neugroschel, Philadelphia, Basic Books, 1995

Self, Robert, ed., *The Neville Chamberlain Diary Letters*, Aldershot, Ashgate, 2005, 4 vols

Sherriff, R. C., *No Leading Lady: An Autobiography*, London, Victor Gollancz, 1968

Siemens, Daniel, *Stormtroopers: A New History of Hitler's Brownshirts*, Yale University Press, 2017

Skeaping, John, *Drawn From Life*, London, Collins, 1977

Smart, Nick, ed., *The Diaries and Letters of Robert Bernays, 1932–1939*, Lampeter, E. Mellen Press, 1996

Souhami, Diana, *Mrs Keppel and Her Daughter*, London, HarperCollins, 1996

St Clair, Hugh, *A Lesson in Art & Life: The Colourful World of Cedric Morris & Arthur Lett-Haines*, Pimpernel Press, 2019

Stansky, Peter, *Sassoon*, New Haven, Yale University Press, 2003

Stehlin, Paul, *Témoinage pour l'histoire*, Paris, Robert Laffont, 1964

Storer, R.V., *Sex in Modern Life*, Melbourne, James Little & Sons, 1933

Stuart, James, *Within the Fringe*, London, Bodley Head, 1967

Tree, Ronald, *When the Moon was High*, London, Macmillan, 1975

BIBLIOGRAPHY

Trythall, A. J., 'The Downfall of Leslie Hore-Belisha', *Journal of Contemporary History*, 16.3, 1981

Urbach, Karina, *Go-Betweens for Hitler*, Oxford, OUP, 2015

Vickers, Emma, *Queen and Country*, Manchester, MUP, 1988

Vincent, John, ed., *The Crawford Papers*, Manchester, MUP, 1984

Volodarsky, Boris, *Stalin's Agent: The Life and Death of Alexander Orlov*, Oxford, OUP, 2015

Wackerfuss, Andrew, *Stormtrooper Families, Homosexuality and Community in the Early Nazi Movement*, New York, Harrington Park Press, 2015

Waite, Robert G. L., *Vanguard of Nazism*, New York, W. W. Norton and Company, 1969

Walker, Christopher, *Oliver Baldwin: A Life of Dissent*, London, Arcadia, 2003

Webster, Nesta, *Germany and England*, London, Boswell Printing, 1938

Weeks, Jeffrey and Porter, Kevin, eds., *Between the Acts*, London, Rivers Oram, 1998

Weeks, Jeffrey, *Coming Out: Homosexual Politics in Britain from the Nineteenth Century to the Present*, London, Quartet Books, 1977

Wheen, Francis, *Tom Driberg: His Life and Indiscretions*, London, Chatto & Windus, 1990

Whisnant, Clayton J., *Queer Identities and Politics in Germany: A History, 1880–1945*, New York, Harrington Park Press, 2016

Whistler, Laurence, *The Laughter and the Urn: The Life of Rex Whistler*, Weidenfeld & Nicolson, London, 1986

Wildeblood, Peter, *Against the Law*, London, Weidenfeld & Nicolson, 1955

Wilkinson, Ellen, *Peeps at Politicians*, London, Philip Allan, 1930

Williams, Emlyn, *Emlyn: An Early Autobiography, 1927–35*, London, Bodley Head, 1973

Winterbotham, F. W., *Secret and Personal*, William Kimber, London, 1969

Woodhouse, Adrian, *Angus McBean: Face-Maker*, London, Alma Books, 2006

Woolf, Cecil, ed., *The Venice Letters*, London, Cecil & Amelia Woolf, 1974

Wotherspoon, Garry, *Gay Sydney: A History*, Sydney, University of New South Wales Press, 2016

Young, Edward, ed., *The Robert Bruce Lockhart Diaries, 1915–1938*, Macmillan, 1973

Young, G. M., *Stanley Baldwin*, London, Rupert Hart-Davis, 1952

Zinovieff, Sofka, *The Mad Boy, Lord Berners, My Grandmother and Me*, London, Jonathan Cape, 2014

Acknowledgements

This book has been a long time in the making, not least because I originally presumed that shame would have consigned the private lives of these men to oblivion. Times have changed, however, and many families have been happy to talk to me about their ancestors, especially the Bernays, Macnamara, Sharp and Nicolson families. In addition, other people's diaries that have been published, either after 1967 or posthumously, have thrown up a great deal of hitherto little-noticed information. I am conscious that without this forthright honesty, this book could never have been written, so I am grateful. I am equally grateful to my agent, Jim Gill, and the whole team at United Agents, who have seen this book through several iterations. The team at Bloomsbury, most especially my editor Alexis Kirschbaum, and Bill Swainson, have provided much of the polish the original lacked; thanks also to Jasmine Horsey, Kate Quarry, Sarah Ruddick, David Mann, Hannah Paget, Anna Massardi and Amy Wong.

Paul, Patrick and Edith Macnamara helped me with information about Jack Macnamara. Sam Price and the Dunlop family showed me their family album, including photos of Jack Macnamara and their ancestor Herbert Sharp in Germany, and shared Herbert's daughter Katherine's reminiscences. Robert Bernays and his brother Richard allowed me exceptional access to their father's papers, including large bundles of his speeches and personal letters to their mother, Nan. Rebecca and Vanessa Nicolson helped me track down further material relating to their grandfather, Harold.

The following all provided additional invaluable assistance: Andrew Lownie; Anne Gibbins and Ben Wegg-Prosser; Michael Bloch; the Earl of Courtown; General Stamford Cartwright of the Worcestershire Yeomanry; Bill Wiggin MP and Mrs Maggie Heath; Robert Hutton; Captain Nigel Wilkinson; Geordie Greig; Eloise Tyson and John Barrett at the All England Lawn Tennis Club; Charlotte Brunskill of the Paul Mellon Centre for Studies in British Art; Catherine Smith at Charterhouse; Julie Barkhuizen at Rossall School; Heather Edwards-Hedley at Haileybury; Emma Goodrum at Worcester College, Oxford; Richard O'Sullivan of the London Irish Rifles Association; Dr Lucy Gwynn at Eton College; the Earl of Portarlington, Maggi Hambling; Philip Howard of Naworth Castle; Mark Bills of Gainsborough House; Henry Cobbold of Knebworth House; and Dr Derek Dalton of Flinders University. I am indebted to the always-helpful archivists and librarians at Tate, Lambeth Palace, the Bodleian, Cambridge University, Balliol College, Oxford, King's College London, the Universities of Birmingham and Southampton and the House of Commons.

Above all, I am grateful to the people of the Rhondda, who have repeatedly elected me as their MP. Despite the stereotypes of Welsh mining communities, I have always felt proud that when a young railway porter from the Rhondda called Thomas was charged with importuning in London in 1925 – the only evidence of his crime provided being the lady's powder puff in his pocket – his local Labour MP, the Baptist deacon and former miner Will John, stood witness for his character in court, and after Thomas served three months in prison his mother reported that he was soon back at his old work and had 'the complete confidence of all his superiors'. I too have depended on the generous forbearance of the people of the Rhondda – and I am immensely grateful.

Index

and Eden resignation,
218, 220, 222–3
and Muirhead
suicide, 311–12
and Nazi Germany, 155,
208–9, 223
and outbreak of war,
309–17, 323, 325
and Philip Sassoon,
202–4, 209
politics, 35–7, 44,
153–60, 165, 210
and recess
debate, 285–92
sexuality, 44–8
and Special Areas
debate, 201–2
war service and death,
329–41, 362, 365
Cartwright, General
Stamford, 311
Castle Stewart, Earl
(Arthur Stuart), 131
Cavendish, Diana, 102
Cavendish, Dorothy, 102
Cawson, Colonel G., 124
Cazalet, Edward, 97
Cazalet, Mollie, 356
Cazalet, Peter, 318
Cazalet, Thelma, 97,
109, 290–1
Cazalet, Victor, 7, 10–11,
94–9, 101, 109–10,
131, 157, 165, 215
and appeasement era,
229, 235–6, 242, 256,
274, 290–1, 293–4
and British anti-
Semitism, 243, 247,
353–4, 356
conversion to Christian
Science, 98
and Gottfried von
Cramm, 167–8, 179,
237–9, 293–4

and Guy Burgess,
161, 163
and Nazi Germany,
121–3, 128, 168–72,
186
and outbreak of war,
309, 315, 317–21,
323–7
politics, 96–7, 122, 153
sexuality, 97–8
and Spanish Civil War,
193–4
and Thelma's wedding,
290–1
war service and death,
344, 351–6, 365
Chamberlain, Austen, 8,
17–18, 214–15
Chamberlain, Ida, 217, 290
Chamberlain, Joseph, 214
Chamberlain, Neville,
9–10, 134–5, 158–9
and appeasement,
229–31, 236, 239–41,
249–66, 269, 274–8,
283–93, 296–303
attends Thelma
Cazalet's wedding,
291
becomes prime
minister, 211, 213–28
campaign against
Hore-Belisha, 322–3
downfall and
resignation, 324–7
'friend of Hitler',
287, 289
love of fishing, 271, 291
and outbreak of war,
303, 307–8, 310,
315–16, 321–7
retirement and
death, 343–4
and Special Areas
debate, 201–2

and womanhood, 273
Champain, Francis, 29–30
Chanel, Coco, 191
Channon, Henry 'Chips',
9–10, 45, 57, 122, 177,
185–6, 194, 202, 213,
227, 229, 236, 243,
252–6, 258, 265, 279,
324, 326
Channon, Honor, 122
Chappell, Billy, 76
Charterhouse School,
34–6, 330
Cheevers, Harold, 257
Chhatarpur, Maharajah
of, 64
Chotzner, Alfred, 133,
135, 137–8
Churchill, Clementine,
272
Churchill, Randolph,
20, 272
Churchill, Winston, 3,
9–11, 99, 101, 116,
123, 125, 153, 159,
178, 203
and appeasement era,
234, 236, 240, 255,
258–60, 262–3, 265,
277, 280, 284, 286, 288,
293, 297, 299, 302
becomes prime
minister, 327,
329, 345
and Eden resignation,
222, 226–7
and end of war, 363–5
and Kinross
by-election, 265
and outbreak of war,
308, 315, 317, 323–4
and rearmament,
188, 365
and Spanish Civil
War, 194

A Note on the Author

Chris Bryant has been the Member of Parliament for Rhondda since 2001. He was Deputy Leader of the House of Commons and Minister for Europe in the last Labour government, and has been Shadow Secretary of State for Culture, Media and Sport and Shadow Leader of the House of Commons. The author of six previous books, he has written regularly for the *Guardian* and the *Independent*, and has appeared on every major TV and radio news and current affairs programme. He was the first gay MP to celebrate his civil partnership in the Palace of Westminster.

A Note on the Type

The text of this book is set in Bembo, which was first used in 1495 by the Venetian printer Aldus Manutius for Cardinal Bembo's *De Aetna*. The original types were cut for Manutius by Francesco Griffo. Bembo was one of the types used by Claude Garamond (1480–1561) as a model for his Romain de l'Université, and so it was a forerunner of what became the standard European type for the following two centuries. Its modern form follows the original types and was designed for Monotype in 1929.